Marriages of
SURRY COUNTY, NORTH CAROLINA

1779–1868

Marriages of
SURRY COUNTY, NORTH CAROLINA

1779–1868

Compiled by
BRENT H. HOLCOMB

Indexed by Gary Parks

CLEARFIELD

Reprinted for
Clearfield Company, Inc. by
Genealogical Publishing Co., Inc.
Baltimore, Maryland
1993, 1998, 2001

Copyright © 1982
Genealogical Publishing Co., Inc.
Baltimore, Maryland
All Rights Reserved
Library of Congress Catalogue Card Number 81-86328
International Standard Book Number 0-8063-0975-X
Made in the United States of America

INTRODUCTION

THIS VOLUME contains abstracts of all marriage bonds extant for Surry County, North Carolina. Although Surry County was formed in 1771 from Rowan County, no bonds are extant before 1779. The bonds are listed here in alphabetical order by groom, with brides and bondsmen indexed. Most of these bonds are in the North Carolina Archives, Raleigh, North Carolina. However, about 120 bonds and licenses were found in recent years still in the Surry County Court House, Dobson, North Carolina, where they remain. The designation *(C. H.)* after an entry indicates that that bond or license is one remaining in the courthouse, in the office of the Register of Deeds.

Marriage bonds are the only public records of marriage prior to 1851. The marriage bond law was enacted in 1741 and remained in force until 1868. In 1851 the clerk of the county court was required to keep a register of marriages performed by license (issued with the bond). The bonds alone are not proof that a marriage took place, only that a marriage was intended. Marriages could also be performed after publication of banns, and therefore no bond, license, or other public record of the marriage was kept.

BRENT H. HOLCOMB, C. A. L. S.
Columbia, South Carolina

SURRY COUNTY MARRIAGES, 1779-1868

Absher, Samuel J. & Polly Wilson, 31 Oct 1850; Samuel Jones, bm. (C. H.).

Acree, Abner & Sarah Tucker, 22 Oct 1809; Marmaduke Kimbrough, Richbell Mott, bm.

Adams, Abraham & Keturah Swach, 10 March 1790; Jeremiah West, bm.

Adams, Bird, son of Samuel and Nancy Adams, & Mary Donathan, daughter of Larkin & Vincey Donathan, 9 Feb 1868; m by P. Worth, J. P., 9 Feb 1868.

Adams, Daniel & Elizabeth Harris, 20 Apr 1796; Thomas Cummins, Abraham Adams, bm.

Adams, Gabrial & Franky Ann Swaim, 12 Apr 1851; m 13 Apr 1851 by John A. Davis.

Adams, George & Lizebeth Thornton, 25 Feb 1806; Daniel North, bm; Jno Williams, wit.

Adams, George & Lydia Parker, 31 Dec 1818; William Vestal, bm.

Adams, George & Lovey Cannon, 5 Oct 1822; Branch Holcomb, bm; John Wright, wit.

Adams, George & Sally Todd, 29 July 1837; John Zachary, bm; W. D. Somers(?), wit.

Adams, Harvy J. & Sarah Hutchans, 21 Apr 1847; Winston Brown, bm; John Martin, J. P., wit.

Adams, Jacob & _____, 15 July 1795; Thomas Cummins, bm; J. Williams, wit.

Adams, James & Rachal Gester, 15 Dec 1817; John Fleming, bm.

Adams, Jesse & Rebekah Parker, 6 Aug 1822; John Adams, bm.

Adams, Joel Sandford, son of Firman & Sendarilla Adams, & Martha Rebecca Hurt, daughter of Joel & Dicy Hurt, 28 Sept 1868; m 3 Oct 1868 by Rev. W. J. Combs.

Adams, John & Mary Phillips, 27 May 1811; George Adams, bm.

Adams, John & Sarah Hutchens, 19 Aug 1822; Jas. Adams, bm.

Adams, John A. & Eliza E. McGuffin, 12 Sept 1865; R. F. McGuffin, bm; S. A. Freeman, wit; m 12 Sept 1865 by J. H. Lewellin.

SURRY COUNTY MARRIAGES, 1779-1868

Adams, Johnathan & Nancy Morefield, 5 Dec 1829; Martin Canting (?), bm; John Wright, wit.

Adams, Jonathan Junr & Rachael Brown, 28 Sept 1817; William Brown, bm.

Adams, Joshua & Jane Lowe, 31 Aug 1867; John C. Lowe, bm; A. Simmons, wit; m 31 Aug 1867 by G. A. Lowe, J. P.

Adams, Thomas J., son of John A. and Sally A. Adams, & Francis Jones, daughter of James and Sally Jones, 9 Jan 1867; m 11 Jan 1867 at Sary Jones, by Joseph Aresom(?), J. P.

Adams, Thomas Wade, son of Ceasor Womack and Cinda Adams, & Marinda Agurs Adams, daughter of Henry Wilkerson and Rhoda Adams, persons of color, 21 Dec 1867; m 22 Dec 1867 by Elder Henry Steele.

Adams, William & Ann Hutson, 19 Oct 1865; Jno M. Cloud, bm; H. C. Hampton, wit.

Adams, Zachary & Francis Fletcher, 27 Jan 1845; John Fleming, bm; F. K. Armstrong, wit.

Adkins, Alfred & Sarah Ring, 1 March 1849; William Ashburn, bm; H. C. Hampton, wit.

Adkins, Alfred & Miss Salena J. Fowler, 3 Nov 1855; Little Adkins, bm; T. V. Hamlin, wit; m 4 Nov 1855 by J. Copeland, J. P.

Adkins, Barlett & Susan Aubury, 17 Feb 1849; Ambrous J. Loftis, bm; A. Dunnagan, wit.

Adkins, Isaac & Elizabeth Williamson, 7 Apr 1844; Isham Doss, bm; Elisha Banner, wit.

Adkins, Ruel & Miss Sarah Wall, 18 Aug 1853; James A. Wall, bm.

Adkins, Samuel & Kasander Dick, 28 Nov 1867; m 28 Nov 1867 by J. A. Bingman, J. P.

Adkins, Thomas & Elizabeth Pike, 21 June 1844; Blewman Hagmon, bm; Elisha Banner, wit.

Agee, James & Sarah Sams, 2 Feb 1866; Pinkney Wilkes, bm; m 2 Feb 1866 by G. A. Lowe, J. P.

Airs, Clevlin & Anna Allen, 3 Dec 1847; Joshua Nester, bm; A. Dunnagan, wit.

Aker, Andrew T. & Malinda Arnold, 28 July 1849; Anderson Arnold, bm.

Aker, John & Margaret Arnold, 24 July 1849; Anderson Arnold, bm; A. Dunnagan, wit.

Akers, Calvin & Sarah Montgomery, 14 Feb 1854; Milton Montgomery, bm; m 14 Feb 1854 by A. Simmons, J. P.

Akers, David & Mariah Roop, 16 Jan 1848; Jas. H. Unthank, bm.

Akers, William & Elizabeth Alltiser, 6 Jan 1853; Crockett Roop, bm.

SURRY COUNTY MARRIAGES, 1779-1868

Alberty, Frederick & Elizabeth Roper, 29 March 1788; Peter Murphy, bm; Robt Williams, wit.

Alberty, Federick & Matilda Harison, 20 May 1828; Martin Smith, bm.

Alberty, Lemuel B. & Lucinda White, 20 Jan 1864; m 22 Jan 1864 by D. H. Cooper, J. P.

Alberty, Nathan & Rebecca Bray, 15 March 1832; James L. Bray, bm.

Alderman, Eli M. & Elizabeth Alexander, 10 April 1861; m 10 April 1865 by G. A. McCraw, J. P.

Aldridge, Henry & Lydia Johnson, 14 March 1827; William Cary, bm; John Wright, wit.

Aldridge, Henry & Nancy Morrison, 3 Jan 1828; Joseph Aldridge Junr, by Henry Hamrick, bm.

Aldridge, Joseph & Ruth Masemore, 23 Dec 1818; John Mony, bm; Jas. Parks, wit.

Algood, Peter & Polly Brown, 11 May 1811; John Sharmer, bm; J. Wright, wit.

Allen, Anderson & Ann Mariah Stricklin, 4 Jan 1864; F. Booker, bm; m 4 Jan 1864 by Wm. Golden, J. P.

Allen, Daniel & Elizabeth Ramsay, 20 Dec 1785; William Allen, bm.

Allen, Jackson & Masse A. Coleman, 11 June 1853; Mason W. Keller, bm; m 11 June 1853 by A. Simmons, J. P.

Allen, John & Malinda Head, 25 Sept 1831; John Marler, bm; G. Poindexter, wit.

Allen, Martin & Elizabeth Money, 13 Oct 1827; Isaac Mony, bm; John Wright, wit.

Allen, Reuben & Elizabeth Hendrick, 29 Dec 1795; James Ellis, bm.

Allen, Richard & Sally Johnson, 8 April 1805; Charles Johnson, bm.

Allen, Richard & Sarah Hampton, 27 Feb 1813; Henry Hampton, bm; Obadiah Martin, wit.

Allen, Samuel & Nancy M. E. Jones, 22 July 1858; William Allen, bm; E. Barnes, wit.

Allen, Thos & Nancy Pruett, 26 Jan 1812; Charles Johnston, bm.

Allen, Thomas & Betsey Myrs, 28 May 1826; William Harrod, bm; J. Unthank, wit.

Allen, Wm. & Lucinda Ayres, 26 May 1823; Archibald Burnett, bm.

Allen, William & Mary R. Brown, 29 Jan 1867; John Allen, bm; H. C. Hampton, wit; m 30 Jan 1867 by Miles Foy.

SURRY COUNTY MARRIAGES, 1779-1868

Allgood, Henry & Polly Asheby, 9 Dec 1816; John Hutchins (son of John), Balas Hutchins, bm.

Allgood, Henry & Elizabeth Shores, 24 Feb 1827; Royal Allgood, bm; N. L. Williams, wit.

Allgood, Jesse & Jinaty Shugart, 8 Nov 1846; Edward Iredell Reece, bm; John Martin, J. P., wit.

Allgood, Presley & Elizabeth Clarke, 6 Dec 1809; Robt Clark, bm.

Allgood, Royal & Mary Pilcher, 2 April 1814; Thomas Norman, bm.

Allin, Nathan & Winneford Ride, 22 Dec 1784; Silvanus _____, bm.

Allison, John & Marthy W. Leak, 24 July 1831; Thos. J. Riley, bm; W. W. Earley, wit.

Allred, Settle T. & Eliza J. Betton, 2 March 1848; James R. Filmer, bm.

Altiser, Joseph & Melvina Dulany, 15 June 1856; Edmonson Altiser, bm; A. Simmons, wit.

Alltizer, J. W. & Minty Sumpter, 22 March 1860; J. Alltizer, bm; Wm. M. Hicks, J. P., wit; m 22 March 1860 by W. M. Hicks, J. P.

Aldridge, Drewry & Sarah Brandle, 14 Dec 1819; John Holcomb, bm; Jas. Parks, wit.

Alva, Wisey & Patsey Hicks, 27 _____ 1829; Henry Samuel, bm.

Alveson, Elijah & Nancy Cook, 2 Feb 1816; Valentine Cook, bm.

Alvey, Lenard & Coartny Creekmoor, 18 Jan 1827; Thomas Creekmore, bm; Polly Wright, wit.

Alvey, Wisdom & Ruth Hicks, 3 Feb 1836; William Perdue, bm.

Alvy, Wm & Matilda Bryan, 5 Dec 1845; Wm Seagraves(?), bm.

Ambern, Samuel & Nancy Hicks, 27 April 1826; John Hicks, bm.

Anderson, George & Lucindy Dunkin, 15 May 1817; Micajah Hix, bm; Jas. Parks, wit.

Anderson, George & Isbell Crumpler, 31 May 1827; Samuel Gordon, bm.

Anderson, Nathan & Sarah Burch, 3 Nov 1807; James Fitzgerald, bm.

Anderson, Robert & Lizzey Jarvis(?), 8 April 1792; Jabez Jarvis Junr, bm; W. Meredith, wit.

Andrew, Richmond & Mary Pellet, 15 March 1811; Richd Wilbourn, bm; Obadiah Martin, wit.

Andrew, John & Fanney Dannel, 21 Dec 1804; Joseph Andrews, bm.

Angel, Cornelius & Rachael Fleming, 14 Nov 1849; Barnet C. Myers, William Jester, bm.

SURRY COUNTY MARRIAGES, 1779-1868

Angel, Henry & Lucinda Evans, 20 Jan 1847; Anderson Dunagan, bm.

Angel, James S. & Huldah Jane Hinshaw, 25 Dec 1850; Cornelius Angel, bm. (C. H.).

Angel, John J. & Keziah Davis, 12 July 1835; Lemuel J. Davis, bm; F. K. Armstrong, wit.

Angel, Nicholas & Rebeckah Taylor, 23 Aug 1821; Edmon Taylor, bm. (C. H.).

Anthony, David & Nancy Austin, 3 Nov 1835; David Day, bm.

Anthony, Henry G., son of S. F. & Serena Anthony, & Nancy E. Roberts, daughter of S. W. and Malinda Roberts, 27 Nov 1867; m 28 Nov 1867 by Joseph Ansom, J. P.

Anthony, John & Mary Whitlock, 26 Feb 1799; John Elsbery, bm.

Anthony, Thomas F. & _____, 13 July 183-; Wm. C. Martin, bm; F. K. Armstrong, wit.

Archer, Geo. & Elizabeth Davis, 5 Oct 1833; Wm. Archer, bm.

Argabright, John & Susanna Harriss, 5 Nov 1850; Floyd Shell, bm.

Arman, Thos & Charity Dowlin, 29 Jan 1790; John McBride, bm; Robt Williams, wit.

Armfield, Marcus D. & Ruth A. Prather, 23 June 1857; m 23 June 1857 by Alson Gray.

Armstrong, Andrew & Pricilla Cook, 5 Jan 1831; Evan Davis, bm; L. M. Armstrong, wit.

Armstrong, James & Loye Oley(?), 3 Jan 1817; William Armstrong, bm.

Armstrong, James & Elizabeth Swaim, 7 June 1818; James Chappel Sr., bm; Jas. Parks, wit.

Armstrong, L. M. & Jane Jessop, 16 Aug 1831; Evan Davis, bm; F. K. Armstrong, wit.

Armstrong, William & Mildred Senter, 29 Aug 1787; William Burress, bm; Hugh Armstrong, wit.

Armstrong, William & Betsy Blaylock, 4 June 1825; Thomas Chatman, bm; N. L. Williams, wit.

Arnold, George & Nancy Aker, 17 Jan 1853; Thomas R. Dunford, bm; A. Simmons, wit.

Arnold, Jacob & Milley Longins, 9 Oct 1807; James Longins, bm; J. Wright, wit.

Arnold, James & Margaret Bagby, 16 March 1813; Wm. Martin, bm; Obadiah Martin, wit.

Arnold, James & Keziah Monfield, 2 Aug 1845; Jacob Arnold, bm; F. C. Hauser, wit.

Arnold, John & Phebe Moorefield, 28 Dec 1816; Jas. Chappel Jr., bm; Jas. Parks, wit.

SURRY COUNTY MARRIAGES, 1779-1868

Arnold, Joseph & Nancy East, 1 Sept 1827; Hughes East, bm; S.W. Lowers, wit.

Arnold, Thos & Bedda Moorfield, 7 Oct 1817; Joseph Brenninger, bm; Jas. Parks, wit.

Arvin, Jamason & Nancy Thornton, 24 Jan 1802; Wm. Thornton, bm.

Asbell, John & Elizabeth Coyle, 31 Jan 1788; Joseph Davis, bm.

Ashborn, William & Mary Jane Flinchin, 16 Dec 1857; m 17 Dec 1857 by Joel Denny, J. P.

Ashbourn, William & Susanna Ring, 27 April 1822; Thomas Ring, bm.

Ashburn, C. H. & Mary E. Davis, 6 Nov 1865; B. F. Wood, bm; H. C. Hampton, wit; m 12 Nov 1865 by J. N. Barker, Minister of the Gospel.

Ashburn, Denson & Saluda Key, 28 Aug 1816; John Anderson Key, bm; Susanna M. Williams, wit.

Ashburn, Denson & Peggey Ring, 5 Oct 1844; John R. Strange, bm; H. C. Hampton, wit.

Ashburn, Denson A. & Lucinda E. Shore, 10 Oct 1859; Thomas Ashburn, bm.

Ashburn, Denson D. & Elizabeth Copeland, 2 July 1866; m 5 July 1866 by M. G. Harbour, J. P.

Ashburn, James W. & Martha A. Flenchum, 6 Jan 1866; John Denny, bm; H. C. Hampton, wit.

Ashburn, Jefferson & Mitty Ashburn, 18 Nov 1847; Andrew J. Fulk, bm; W. W. Wolff, wit.

Ashburn, John & Martha _____, 15 May 1845; Martin Ashburn, bm; W. W. Wolff, wit.

Ashburn, John S(?), & Tennessee Key, 11 June 1864; Jefferson Ashburn, bm; m 17 June 1864 by Lacy Snow, J. P.

Ashburn, Martin & Mary Ashburn, 28 March 1847; John Ashburn, bm; W. W. Wolff, wit.

Ashburn, Thomas & Delpha R. Shores, 30 Oct 1859; J. W. Ashburn, bm.

Ashburn, William & Nancy Ring, 17 Sept 1843.

Ashburn, William & Mahala Jones, 12 May 1868; m 14 May 1868 by A. Whitaker, J. P.

Ashburn, William W. & Anna P. Atkerson, 13 May 1863; M. G. Harbour, bm; m ___ June 1868 by Jas. H. Lewellin.

Ashby, Alexander & Levin Grose, 19 Feb 1821; William Brown, bm.

Ashby, David & Elizabeth Welch, 12 June 1823; Thomas D. Kelly, bm.

Ashby, James & Mary Burton, 23 Dec 1838; Joseph Richardson, bm.

SURRY COUNTY MARRIAGES, 1779-1868

Ashby, James & Jennett Woodruff, 18 Dec 1829; Daniel Hunt, bm; John Wright, wit.

Ashby, John & Rebecca Woodruff, 1 Nov 1825; Micajah Woodruff, bm; Winston Somers, wit.

Ashby, Samuel & Rachael Groce, 4 Sept 1819; Anthony Bates, bm.

Ashby, Travis & Rebekah Groce, 30 Sept 1815; Isaac Brewbaker, bm.

Ashley, Howel & Patty Blackman, 2 April 1806; Adam Bunagan(?), bm.

Ashworth, Mark A. & Malinda Nunn, 28 July 1858; William M. Nunn, bm; m 28 July 1858 by E. Banner, J. P.

Assman, Christian H. & Honor Wishon, 27 March 1838; Bryant Jarvis, bm.

Aston, Pinkny & Jane Edwards, 5 July 1862; A. G. Cozort, bm.

Athor, Joseph & Martha T. Grant, 16 Oct 1832; J. G. Pettit, bm; Jno P. Clingman, wit.

Atkins, D. W. & Mary White, 14 Dec 1865; Thos M. Snow, bm; J. E. Reeves, wit; m 14 Dec 1865 by R. F. McGuffin, J. P.

Atkins, Hausey & Hannah Love, 14 May 1852; Bartlet Atkins, bm. (C. H.).

Atkins, James P. & Nancy E. Chanler, 6 Nov 1856; Robt J. Harris, bm; m 6 Nov 1865 by A. Simmons, J. P.

Atkins, Jeremiah & Emsly Simpson, 25 Nov 1862; Sandy Sawyer, bm; m 26 Nov 1862 by Wm. T. Lewis, J. P.

Atkins, Lewis & M--- Welmoth, 10 Jan 1838; Algius Cave, bm.

Atkins, Robert & Caty Greenwood, 10 Oct 1808; Bartley Greenwood, bm; Tho. A. Word, wit.

Atwood, James & Peggy McCollom, 12 Nov 1810; Branch Holcomb, bm; J. Wright, wit.

Atwood, Jesse & Sarah Waddle, 14 May 1816; John Atwood, bm; J. Williams, Junr., wit.

Auberry, Elijah & Polly Burris, 31 March 1825; Clawell P. Shipp, bm; Jon. Unthank, wit.

Auberry, Wm. & Mandy Low, m 22 Sept 1867 by B. J. D---, J. P.

Auldridge, William R. & Nancy Basier, 2 Feb 1851; Jesse M. Casey, bm.

Austain, Robert & Jane Dails, 16 Feb 1846; Stephen Johnson, bm.

Austell, Isaac & Cloe Holcomb, 15 Feb 1831; Phillip Holcomb, bm.

Austill, Isaac Jr. & Temperance Sisk, 24 March 1835; Majer Austinn Jr., bm; F. Hampton, wit.

Austell, James & Hethina Sisk, 7 April 1820; Abram Carter, bm;

SURRY COUNTY MARRIAGES, 1779-1868

Austill, Mager Jr. & Mary B. Maser(?), 16 Oct 1836; Thomas W. Carter, bm; F. Hampton, wit.

Austill, Moses & Elizabeth Elmore, 1 Dec 1831; Benedick Cassleman(?), bm; Polly Wright, wit.

Austin, James & Martha J. Allen, 22 Oct 1860; m 22 Oct 1860 by Elisha Bannen, J. P.

Axsom, Andrew & Elizabeth Welding, 29 June 1830; David Reavis, bm; E. Rutledge, wit.

Axsom, Martin & Susannah Lundy, 3 May 1826; George H. Kimbrough, bm.

Axsom, Saml J. & Phebe Nicholson, 19 Dec 1857; Joseph Axsom, bm; T. V. Hamlin, wit.

Axum, Israel P. & Jennella Nicholson, 21 Dec 1849; Martin Axsom, bm; F. K. Armstrong, wit.

Axum, Samuel & Winny Matthews, 16 Dec 1828; William May, bm; E. Rutledge, wit.

Ayers, Alexander & Susanna Williams, 10 March 1833; Stephen H. Lyon, bm.

Ayers, Elbonan & Lucinda Foderal, 7 Feb 1855; Enoch Ring, bm; M. A. York, wit; m 8 Feb 1855 by Joel Denny, J. P.

Ayres, Green & Elizabeth P. Smith, 19 June 1851; Allen Demsy, bm.

Ayres, Joshua & Elizabeth Gwyn, 17 Nov 1853; James J. Ayres, bm; m 17 Nov 1853 by A. Simmons, J. P.

Ayers, William & Tabitha Johnson, 23 June 1795; William Johnson, bm.

Ayres, Joel & Patcy Whitaker, 18 Jan 1849; Abraham Whitaker, bm.

Ayres, Uriah & Letty A. M. J. McMillan, 23 Sept 1852; James Gwynn, bm.

Ayres, William A. & Julina Crager, 29 Sept 1853; John C. Ayres, bm; m 29 Sept 1853 by A. Simmons, J. P.

Ayres, William R. & Katharine Philips, 6 Jan 1853; Joshua Ayres, bm.

Baber, Samuel & Sally Whitaker, 8 Dec 1856; F. J. Manom(?), bm.

Badgett, Abraham & Mickey Holser, 13 Dec 1810; Ransom Badgett, bm; J. Williams Jun., wit.

Badgett, Burrel, son of James & Elizabeth Badgett, & Martha Pilson, daughter of M. & Rebecca Pilson, 13 Jan 1868; m 16 Feb 1868 by Nathan Alberty.

Badgett, Burrell & Lucy Forkner, 19 Jan 1814; Ransom Badgett, bm.

Badgett, James & Elizabeth Copeland, 4 Oct 1845; Albert White, bm; H. C. Hampton, wit.

SURRY COUNTY MARRIAGES, 1779-1868

Badgett, Presley & Elizabeth Moris(?), 24 Nov 1845; William Jarvis, bm; F. K. Armstrong, wit.

Bagby, Abner & Lucinda Whittimer, 9 July 1836; John S. Phillips, bm; F. Hampton, wit.

Bagby, William & Sarah Woodruff, 7 Nov 1809; John Bagby, bm; Obadiah Martin, wit.

Baggarly, John & Eliza Johnson, 11 April 1826; John Johnson, bm; John Wright, wit.

Baily, Henry & Sarah Bohannon, 15 Dec 1847; Wm Reese, Martin Reese, bm.

Bailey, James & Martha J. Clendinen, 29 Dec 1855; Anderson Atkins, bm.

Bailey, Mathew & Polley Wallis, 19 Oct 1803; Benjamin Sharks, bm.

Baily, Burrill & Francis Tator, 11 March 1847; William Parrish, bm.

Baily, John & Jane Person, 3 April 1811; John Andrew, bm; Obadiah Martin, wit.

Baity, David & Mary Joiner, 23 Sept 1826; Henry R. Allgood, bm; N. L. Williams, wit.

Baity, John & Catharine Danner, 17 Sept 1836; Andrew Cranfield, bm.

Baity, John & Sally Hoot--, 13 Nov 1830; Isom Baity, bm; E. Rutledge, wit.

Baity, Pleasant & Harriet _____, 27 Jan 1830; Jos. Clanton, bm; E. Rutledge, wit.

Baity, Ransom & Mary Jenkins, 5 March 1829; Wm. Baity Junr., bm.

Baker, A. C. & Margaret Poindexter, 30 Dec 1849; M. H. Baker, bm; R. C. Poindexter, wit.

Baker, Benjamin & Martha Ann Merphey, 25 Oct 1855; John Winley Fulk, bm.

Baker, David & Elizabeth Huchins, 24 Feb 1860.

Baker, Geo. & Priscilla Christopher, 31 July 1833; Wm. D. Somers, bm.

Baker, Isaac Mc. & Martha A. Bagnal, 9 Dec 1847; Allen Denny, bm.

Baker, John & Catharine Winscott, 13 Dec 1785; Abraham Winscott, bm.

Baker, Lewis, son of John and Polly Baker, & Virginia Mager, daughter of Pleasant Walton, 3 Jan 1868; m 5 Jan 1868 by A. Whitaker, J. P.

Baker, Martin H. & Sarah Poindexter, 12 Nov 1844; Riley F. Petree, bm.

SURRY COUNTY MARRIAGES, 1779-1868

Baker, Nicholas & Lucy Lawrence, 20 June 1791; Richard Laurence, bm.

Baker, William & Polly Reed, 7 March 1837; James Moore, bm.

Baker, William & Nancy Ballore, 24 June 1847; Wm. Martin, bm; John Martin, J. P., wit.

Baldwin, David & Parthania Hall, 2 Oct 1833; Benjamin Taylor, bm.

Balentine, James & Lucinda Edwards, 23 Dec 1834; Joel Ashworth, bm; Jas. Tucker, wit.

Balis, Asa & Susanna Fletcher, 2 Aug 1817; John Lockhart, bm.

Baley, John & Nancy Stonstreet, 10 Aug 1811; Elisha Stonestreet, bm.

Ball, Daniel E. & Elizabeth Southard, 6 Jan 1864; Wiley Willey, bm.

Ball, Henderson & Margaret Luper(?), 28 March 1836; Thomas Holcomb, bm.

Ball, Isom & Charity Swaim, 30 Dec 1835; William J. Chappel, bm.

Ball, John & Nancy Chamberlin (no date).

Ball, John & Lucy Gentry, 10 Oct 1831; Nicholas Ball, bm; John Wright, wit.

Ball, John & Sarah McDaniel, 8 Feb 1866; John Day, bm; D. A. Eldredge, wit.

Ball, Vinson & Sarry Greene, 20 Oct 1828; James J. Spier, bm.

Ball, William & Sally Smith, 23 Sept 1864; Vincent Ball, bm.

Banister, Henderson & Sarah Evens (no date).

Banister, Henderson & Polly Combs, 13 Feb 1811; Wm. Combs, bm.

Banner, A. E. & Elizabeth Martin, 6 Feb 1837; Stephen Haynes, bm.

Banner, C. L. & Charity R. Prather, 4 June 1860; W. R. Hollinsworth, bm; W. M. Hicks, J. P.

Banner, Elisha & Susan R. Billing, 6 July 1853; C. L. Banner, bm; M. R. Randleman, wit.

Banner, Henry, son of James and Lucinda Banner, & Caroline Bunker, daughter of Milly Bunker, m 8 March 1868 by C. L. Banner, J. P.

Banner, Isaac, a freedman and formerly a slave belonging to Elisha Banner, and Mahalia, a free woman formerly a slave belonging to ____ Burge, acknowledge that they had been legally married and lived together for many years, 28 Aug 1866.

Barber, Levi & Nesley Lawson, 20 Feb 1819; Hickman Isbell, bm.

SURRY COUNTY MARRIAGES, 1779-1868

Barchan, John & Sytha Jones, 18 Sept 1819; Silas Jones, bm.

Barker, Daniel & Susannah Norman(?), 17 April 1852.

Barker, Gideon & Mary Munker, 6 Dec 1837; James Gallion, bm.

Barker, Green B. & Margaret Gorden, 19 May 1829; Wm. Striclin, bm.

Barker, Harasha & Veleria Taylor, 9 Oct 1839; Colby C. Gordon, bm.

Barker, Horatio & Lucinda Taylor, 11 May 1851; Wm. Terry, bm.

Barker, Horatio & Margaret Griffith, 11 Sept 1819; John Simmons, bm.

Barker, James & Elizabeth Barnes, 8 May 1867; m 8 May 1867 by Wm B---, J. P.

Barker, Jerimiah & Susannah Gallian, 5 Feb 1816; Young Gallian, bm.

Barker, Jessee & Rebeca Brinkley, 31 Dec 1859; C. L. Banner, bm; Will Hicks, J. P., wit.

Barker, Leander & Lewezy Collins, 2 March 1847; Gideon Barker, bm; Jo. Phillips, wit.

Barker, Martin V. & Rebecca Hickman, 1 Feb 1862; Benjamin F. Kidd, bm.

Barker, Squire & Malinda Edwards, 12 April 1846; Iredell A. McGee, bm; E. Banner, wit.

Barker, Thomas & Phoebe Chandler, 23 Aug 1820; Thos. A. Word, bm.

Barker, Thomas J. & Sarah Smith, 28 Dec 1865; G. W. Hiatt, bm.

Barker, Thornton & Sary Ann Barker, 13 May 1845; Squire Barker, bm.

Barker, Thornton & Lucretia Creech, 5 April 1851; Alford Zachary, bm.

Barkley, Edward & Sarah Mosser, 9 Nov 1783; Adam Binkly, bm.

Barkley, Rehel & Elisabeth Creed, 24 Sept 1865.

Barlow, John & Johanna Kinneck, 17 Dec 1822; Peter Mock, bm.

Barna, Saml & Mattilda Bray, 4 Feb 1827; Winston Somers, bm; Seth Hickerson, wit.

Barnard, James & Anne Walker, 24 Oct 1809; Christopher Barnard, bm.

Barnett, William & Isabela Carnahan, 10 Nov 1851; Samuel Freman, bm.

Barnard, Christopher & Liddy Brown, 28 Jan 1806.

Barnott, John & Elizabeth Hutchins, 14 April 1801.

SURRY COUNTY MARRIAGES, 1779-1868

Barr, John W. & Martha Kittle, 15 Oct 1851; C. E. Culler, bm; D. C. Wolff, wit; m 15 Oct 1851 by W. W. Wolff, J. P.

Bartley, Eliga & Prudence Branoch, 22 Jan 1844; Sandford Munius (?), bm.

Bartly, James & Mary Dickens, 7 Oct 1844; Calaway Golwyn, bm.

Bass, Aaron & Barbara Normon, 29 March 1812; Isaac Bass, bm.

Bass, Aaron & Malinda Wooton, 26 Sept 1822; Thompson Johnson, bm; Wiley Thornton, wit.

Bass, Isaac & Hannah Freeman, 29 June 1802.

Bass, Nelson & Nancy Keziah, 19 May 1811.

Bass, William & Elin Bullen, 4 Jan 1851; Henry Denton, bm; H. C. Hampton, wit.

Bass, Wright & Peggy Gorges(?), 18 Dec 1822; John Gorges, bm; Seth Hickerson, wit.

Bates, Anthony & Catharine Ashley, 2 Jan 1812; George Bates, James Gough, bm.

Bates, William & Elizabeth Moore, 7 Dec 1784; John Curry, bm.

Bates, William & Martha J. McBride, 26 April 1851.

Baley, Isom & Nancy Ploughman, 11 March 1827; William Shores, bm.

Bawl, James & Elizabeth Gilley, 7 March 1828; Benjamin Hinshaw, bm; Wm. Somers, wit.

Bayes, Raleigh & Rebecca Cavaness, 11 Nov 1852; John Payne, bm.

Bayse, Raleigh & Frances Snow, 22 Jan 1834; Benjamin Snow, bm.

Bayse, Raleigh & Elizabeth Lane, 26 Feb 1855; Joab Caviness, bm; m 26 Feb 1855 by A. Simmons, J. P.

Beaber, William & Lydia Airs, 28 March 1815; Leonard Airs, bm.

Beall, Cranbury A. & Margaret Gentry, 11 June 1836; Uriah J. Douthit, bm.

Beall, Robert & Elizabeth Johnson, 7 Nov 1835; J. Uriah Douthit, bm.

Beaman, Thomas W. & Rebecca A. Lewis, 26 Dec 1819(?); John Haynes, bm.

Beamer, Adam J. & Mary Golding, 28 March 1867; W. H. Beamer, bm; m 11 Sept 1867 by F. Booker, J. P.

Beamer, Frost & Mary Cunningham, 24 June 1839; West Freeman, bm.

Beamer, Jacob & Rachel Cunningham, 4 Feb 1838; Munistree Golding, bm; S. H. Jones, wit.

Beamer, W. H. & Lucy P. Hatcher, 19 Jan 1867.

SURRY COUNTY MARRIAGES, 1779-1868

Beasley, Jonathan & Hannah Beasley, 6 Feb 1846; Allen Bengman, bm.

Beasley, Shadrack & Martha Harris, 28 Jan 1821; Jordan Hall, bm.

Beason, Richard & Polly Banister, 30 July 1822; William Marion, bm; W. Thornton, wit.

Beaty, John & Jane Beason, 10 Dec 1801.

Beaty, John & Mary Barnett, ___ Feb 1835; G. Denny, bm.

Beavour, William & Nancy Moody, 6 Nov 1799.

Beazley, William & Mary Ann Fare, 29 March 1786; Barnabas Fair, bm; Richd Goode, wit.

Beck, Samuel & Mary Wells, 10 Oct 1801.

Bedsoul, Elisha & Mary Williams, 25 Aug 1867; Wm. Hodge, bm.

Bedsoul, Peter & Malinda Baker, 15 Oct 1846; James Snow, bm.

Beeman, James & Rachael Allin, 21 March 1793; Edward Clanton, bm.

Beeman, James & Nancy Moore, 8 April 1794; John Moore, bm.

Beeman, Thomas & Sarah Brown, 30 June 1808; Joshua Brown, bm.

Beeson, Alexander & Nancy Dobbins, 20 March 1845; Wilson Holyfield, bm; H. C. Hampton, wit.

Beeson, Edward & Sarah Johnson, 5 March 1827; Isaac Beeson, bm; Polly Wright, wit.

Beeson, Joseph & Mary Macy, 27 Oct 1804.

Beeson, Joseph & Elizebeth Johnson, 6 March 1802.

Beeson, Richard & Frances Key, 13 July 1811; Achilles Key, bm.

Bell, Andrew K. & Lucy S. Morstall, 2 Dec 1825; John Sanders, bm.

Bell, John R. & Syntha M. Saunders, 28 Oct 1853; Henry T. Manges, bm; m 28 Oct 1853 by A. Simmons, J. P.

Bells, John, son of Gustave, & Elizabeth Williams, 3 April 1813; Daniel Bells Jun., bm.

Bellin, Burrel & Thursy Hill, 25 Jan 1867; m 26 Jan 1867 by W. M. Hicks, J. P.

Belton, Francis M. & Charity E. Briggs, 5 July 1863; J. W. Jackson, bm; m 9 July 1863 by A. Simmons, J. P.

Belton, James & Susannah Forker, 28 Aug 1847; Seth Alred, bm.

Belton, James & Leatha Belton, 23 Oct 1859; Philip Douthit(?), bm; m 23 Oct 1859 by E. Banner, J. P.

Belton, John B. & Lucinda E. Nichols, 17 May 1856.

SURRY COUNTY MARRIAGES, 1779-1868

Belton, William & Eliza J. Leatherage, 22 May 1854; Alfred Leatherage, bm.

Belvin, James & Mary York, 3 Feb 1814; Littleton Isbell, bm.

Benbow, Evan & Elizabeth Hair(?), 22 Feb 1847; Isaac A. Grant, bm.

Benehnoll, John & Susannah McGuire, 30 Aug 1816; Thomas Jacks, bm; Jas. Parks, wit.

Benge, Elisha & Nancy E. Combs, 15 Feb 1846; Henry Stokes, bm; Josiah Cowles Jr., wit.

Benge, Micajah M. & Polly Creekmore, 9 April 1823; James Hicks, bm; John Wright, wit.

Benge, Obediah & Elizabeth Ware, 4 Aug 1787; Michael Bacom, bm.

Benge, Thomas & _____, (no date), Thomas Vestell, bm.

Benge, Thomas & Nancy Bowl, 19 Jan 1826; Thomas Carter, bm; W. Somers, wit.

Benge, William & Mary Sammons, 27 Jan 1847; William Pettyjohn, bm.

Benham, B. B. & Eliza Ann Cowles, 31 March 1835; J. F. Dowthit, bm.

Bennet, James & Louvina Boyles, 3 Aug 1858; John Boyles, bm; E. Banner, wit.

Bennett, Henderson & Sally Whittington, 21 Feb 1857.

Bennett, Moses & Fanny D. Willard, 23 Jan 1847; William W. Myers, bm.

Benson, John & Lucinda J. Scott, 16 Aug 1853; Shadrack F. Scott, bm; W. M. Freeman, J. P., wit.

Benton, Absolem & Sally Hodges, 28 Feb 1829; Thomas Hickman, bm; H. D. Armstrong, wit.

Bercham, John & Sally Campbell, 15 Oct 1836; John Crouse, bm.

Bernard, Germain & Miss Juliette Gillam, 24 Sept 1845; Louis M. Gillam, bm.

Berriman, Charles & Nancy Tate, 13 Nov 1787; Battaling Bryan, bm.

Berton, William H. & Amanda F. Stone, m 11 Aug 1862 by A. Simmons, J. P.

Bevel, George & Martha Stalmon, 10 Dec 1850; Amos Ireland, bm.

Beval, John & Jane Edwards, 29 Jan 1863; C. C. Golden, bm.

Bevil, John N. & Martha M. Johnson, 14 Feb 1865; m 14 Feb 1865 by G. A. McCraw, J. P.

Bevill, G. H. & Susan Crowel, 3 April 1845; Martin Sparger, bm.

Bevins, John & Mary Wall, 6 Dec 1851; Gabriel Hiatt, bm.

SURRY COUNTY MARRIAGES, 1779-1868

Billings, Pearce & Nancy Everton, 28 Oct 1818; James Everton, bm.

Billings, Robert H. & Mary Collings, 13 Feb 1858; Elisha Collings, bm; m 16 Feb 1858 by J. Gray, J. P.

Billetor, James & Nancy Colley, 27 Sept 1819; David Riding, bm.

Bills, Daniel & Rachel Summers, 3 Oct 1812; Daniel Davis, bm; Susanna M. Williams, wit.

Bills, Daniel & Patse Jarvis, _____ 1805.

Bills, Daniel Junr. & Polly Ketchum, 31 Dec 1813; Edwin Chaffin, bm.

Bills, Thomas & Mary Collins, 11 Feb 1813; Gersham Bills, bm.

Bingham, Stephen N. & Synthey Pritchard, 20 Dec 1817; William Ilis, bm.

Bingman, James A. & Mary A. Sparger, 11 April 1849; Bennett Creech, bm.

Bingman, Leonard H. & Lethy Jessop, 2 April 1845; Samuel Walker, bm.

Binkley, Fridrik & Elizabeth Tull, 18 March 1786; Heinrich Doll (Nicholas Tull), bm.

Brinkly, George & Catharine Chinn, 17 Nov 1826; Nicholas Dull, bm.

Binkley, Henry & Mary Sims, 14 Sept 1819; Fredrick Tanner Junr, bm.

Binkley, Jacob & Rosanna Gross, 16 Nov 1822; Henry Long, bm.

Binkley, John & Sally Mock, 5 Aug 1816.

Binkley, John & Elizabeth Hudson, 24 Sept 1817; George Hudson, bm.

Bishop, Abel & Polly James, 11 Aug 1821; Archibal McPeak, bm.

Bishop, Jacob C. & Lucy Cox, 15 Dec 1858; Br--- Cox, bm.

Black, Fredrick & _____ (no date), Michael Wily, bm.

Black, George & Nancy Beck, 26 Dec 1808.

Black, Jacob & Delight Jinkins, 30 Oct 1822; Vallentine Jenkings, bm.

Black, John & Caty Etcherson, 7 March 1823; Peter Reehtor, bm.

Black, John & Susan Calton, 27 Nov 1855; John H. Crawford, bm.

Blackburn, Emberry & Katharine Collins, 23 Dec 1847; Daniel Shore, bm.

Blackburn, J. C., son of Hulch Blackburn & Bethursa Covington, & Nancy Kinner Praetor, daughter of J. W. Huchmand & Nancy Bald, m 10 Sept 1868 by C. M. Miller, Minister of the M. E. Church, South.

SURRY COUNTY MARRIAGES, 1779-1868

Blackley, Wiley & Keedy Robertson, 15 Nov 1834; Harden Mays, bm.

Blacks, Fredericks & _____ (no date), Johannes Mock, bm.

Blackwell, Stephen & Sarah Arnold, 24 May 1849; S. S. Arnold, bm.

Blackwood, Robert N. & Susan Stanley, 2 May 1848; John M. Edwards, bm.

Blair, William & Charity Sheppard, 30 Aug 1808; Jeremiah King, bm.

Blakly, James R., son of Sempl & Jane Blakely, & Eastor Baker, daughter of Wm & Mary Baker, m 22 Oct 1868 by M. G. Harbour, J. P.

Blansett, Pleasant & Nancy Matrey, 14 June 1837; Vernon Surratt, bm.

Blear, George & Elizebeth Turner, 13 Oct 1801.

Bledsoe, Arthur & Sally McCollam, 5 July 1856; T. V. Hamlin, bm; m 6 July 1856 by W. D. Rutledge, J. P.

Bledsoe, Arthur & Mary Standley, 1 March 1826; Jesse Standley, bm; Winston Somers, wit.

Bledsoe, C. C. & Ann V. Bray, 5 Dec 1865; m 5 Dec 1865 by R. F. McGuffin, J. P.

Bledsoe, J. W. & Katharine Barker, 20 Feb 1845; Henderson Ellis, bm.

Bledsoe, James & Lucy Perry, 28 April 1849; Jonathan H. Bledsoe, bm.

Bledsoe, Johnathan & Lucy An Jenkins, 5 Feb 1856.

Bledsoe, Jonathan H. & Lucinda Oliver, 14 Feb 1833; William Gates, bm.

Bledsoe, Lewis & Mary Marsh, 7 Sept 1813; Isaac Bledsoe, bm.

Bledsoe, T. B., son of Gillie Bledsoe, & Mahala Bray, daughter of S. Poindexter & Matilda Poindexter, 6 June 1868; m 7 June 1868 by R. T. Pilson, J. P.

Bledsoe, Wiley & Betsey Campbell, 15 Feb 1820; John Campbell, bm.

Blume, Lewis & Martha Bynum (no date); Francis Stauber, bm.

Bobet, Charles & Sally Defrier, 29 Dec 1825; William Hodges, bm.

Bobbitt, Calvin R. & Matilda J. Whitaker, 29 Jan 1857; Thomas D. Davis, bm.

Bobbet, Charles & Lucinda Redsaul, 8 Nov 1863; C. C. Golden, bm; m 8 Nov 1863 by Wm. Golden, J. P.

Bobet, Greenbery, & Nancy J. Brint, 19 Oct 1862; Wm. Spencer, bm; m __ Oct 1862 by Wm. Golden, J. P.

SURRY COUNTY MARRIAGES, 1779-1868

Bodenhamer, Jacob A. & Eliza Ann Badgett, 9 Aug 1849; Jacob B. Bodenhamer, bm.

Bohannon, John & Sarah Cassaday, 19 Nov 1786; John Williams, bm.

Bohannon, John & Rebekah Carlton, 10 Oct 1823; William Vestal, bm.

Bohannon, Neal and Ann Headly, _____ 1805.

Bohannon, Neal & Dinah Marshall, 8 March 1830; Saml Weatherman, bm.

Bohannon, Simon & Edy Greer, 29 Sept 1829; James Cartwright, bm.

Bohannon, Wm. B. & Gracy Cordel, 5 Feb 1847; Thos S. Kelly, bm.

Bolen, William B. & Rebecca Marris, 1 Nov 1849; Abner Dean, bm.

Boles, William & Eliza Melvin, 24 May 1848; D. C. Wolff, bm; W. W. Wolff, wit.

Bolejack, Samuel & Milly Doss, 28 Jan 1823; L. D. Kelly, bm.

Boleyjack, Alfred M. & Nancy Ann Whitaker, 7 Oct 1846; Saml H. Boleyjack, bm.

Boling, Alfred & Jane Sutliff, 29 Oct 1827; Frances Vest, bm.

Boling, George & Patsey Hall, 11 March 1827; Michael Shepwash, bm.

Bolisheck, John & Mary Forrest, 11 Aug 1786; James Forrest, bm.

Bolt, Andrew J. & Sarah Marshall, 14 April 1851; Reuben McPeak, bm.

Bolt, Hiram & Lucresy Harris, 21 March 1819; Eli Cook, bm.

Boman, Gilbert & Ruth Duncan, 23 Sept 1852; Isham Boman, bm.

Boman, Isham & Melind Boman, 4 March 1847; Rice Duncan, bm.

Boman, James & Jane Whitteker, 13 Feb 1864; Isham Cox, bm.

Boman, Pleasant & Mary Morris, 20 Aug 1837; Peter Boman, bm.

Boman, Rawley & Peniny Boman, 1 Dec 1859; Joel Mankin, bm.

Boman, William & Tildy Dinkin, 21 July 1847; William Lawson, bm.

Bond, Abel & Sarah Ann Sisemore, 26 March 1844; Stephen Davis, bm. (C. H.).

Bone, James Jr. & Levicy Whitaker, 11 Nov 1847; James Bone, bm.

Bone, Joseph & _____; Benjamin Holmes, bm. (no date).

Bone, Nathan & Rhody Hutchens, 16 April 1850; Jesse Adams, bm. (C. H.).

Bonns, Jacob & Catharine Fesius, 25 March 1791.

Booker, F. & Nancy Jane Axsom, 4 Sept 1865.

SURRY COUNTY MARRIAGES, 1779-1868

Booker, Forester & Elizabeth Fleming, 10 May 1848; Charles Whitlock, bm.

Booker, Henry C. & Sarah Bryan, 28 Sept 1846; Mordecai Fleming, bm.

Boon, Benjamin & Margarett A. Fisher, 27 April 1855; Joseph Loving, bm; m 27 April 1855 by A. Simmons, J. P.

Booth, Hugh & Mary Greggory, 31 May 1821; Evan Davis, bm.

Booth, William C. & Sally Ann Fulks, 18 Nov 1845; Thomas S. Fulks, bm.

Boothe, Jesse L. & Elmirah Whittaker, 10 April 1850; Andrew Burge, bm. (C. H.).

Booze, John & Martha Baldin, 22 Nov 1855; William Cook, bm; m 22 Nov 1855 by Wm. Gillam, J. P.

Bourn, Thornton & Lydia Anderson, 11 Feb 1826; Jacob Eddleman, Michael Shipwash, bm.

Bovender, Jacob & Lilly Hill, 7 Dec 1830; Bennet Doss, bm.

Bovender, John & Rachel Brown, 19 Feb 1815; Thomas Vestal, bm.

Bovender, John & Arabell Ferington, 2 Feb 1847; Hugh Brown, bm; John Martin, wit.

Bovender, Squire & Nancy Sturad, 2 May 1852; C. L. Banner, bm.

Bowden, Jesse & Lidia Williams, 6 Feb 1808; Ebenezer Eaton, bm.

Bowdin, William & Frances Hampton, 27 April 1833; Enoch Johnson, bm; Jas Tucker, wit.

Bowen, Andrew & Sarah Padget, 12 March 1822; Clayton Benhoy, bm.

Bowles, Abraham & Elizabeth Jackson, 15 Aug 1827; Jehu Jervis, bm.

Bowles, James & Milly Bray, 1 Oct 1827; John Jervis, bm.

Bowles, James & Lucinda Freeman, 4 Nov 1854; Jas. T. Edmonds, bm; m 4 Nov 1854 by D. M. McGee, J. P.

Bowles, John & Lusindy Copeland, 3 Oct 1853; Melren M. Copeland, bm; m 25 Dec 1853 by H. C. Brey, J. P. (John Bowles, son of James, on certificate).

Bowles, William Jur. & Sally Stanly, 9 April 1846; Chalwell V. Butcher, bm.

Bowling, Joseph H. & Mary Jane Pharis, __ Dec 1865.

Bowles, William & Alcy Rainwater, 1 Feb 1822; James Fitzgerald, bm.

Bowman, Aaron & Mary Bowman, 2 June 1835; Greensville Willis, bm.

Bowman, Alfred P. & Mary Ann Knighten, 26 March 1846; Suttle T. Allred, bm.

SURRY COUNTY MARRIAGES, 1779-1868

Bowman, Archibald & Mary Watkins, 13 Aug 1846; James Brim, bm; J. Hollinsworth, wit.

Bowman, Byram & Rebecca Dilard, 3 Feb 1848; Daniel Epperson, bm.

Bowman, Ewell & Martha J. Lighton, 15 July 1852; H. V. Allred, bm.

Bowman, Julks & Jeddida Nighin, 10 April 1851; Wm Bowman, bm.

Bowman, Harrison & Elizabeth Cox, 3 March 1850; Martin Cox, bm. (C. H.).

Bowman, Isaac H. & Celia E. Bowman, 27 Dec 1865; Jefferson McBride, bm.

Bowman, Samuel, son of Oliver & Louisa Bowman, & Elizabeth Dickens, daughter of Jesse & Julie Dickens, 31 Dec 1868.

Bowman, Thornton & Judith Sawyers, 4 Jan 1827; Martin Sawyers, bm.

Bowmon, Andrew & Mary Ann Cloud, 30 Nov 1847; Thos D. Ashworth, bm.

Bowmon, John H. & Fanny Normon, 16 Oct 1822; Archabel Bowmon, bm.

Bowmon, William & Mary Jackson, 28 June 1849; Clon Bowmon, bm.

Bowyer, Adam & _____, 13 May 1794.

Bowyer, John & Olley Wadkins, 25 April 1798; "Stokes County".

Boyd, Hugh & May Dudly, 22 Aug 1829; Thompson Robert, bm.

Boyd, John & Massy Hariet Haynes, 8 July 1858; Andrew Hexter, bm.

Boyer, Joseph & Barbara Petree, 26 March 1801; John Boyer of Stokes County, bm.

Boyes, Stephen & Nancy McCraw, 21 Aug 1832; William Davis, bm.

Boyles, Alexander & Temperance Johnson, 28 June 1844; Wm Boyles, bm.

Boyles, Alexander & Elizabeth Edwards, 18 Dec 1855; John W. Culler, bm.

Boyles, John H. & Sarah Needham, 7 Nov 1858; John Weyniss, bm; m 9 Nov 1858 by J. H. Caudle.

Boyles, Solomon C., son of Alexander and Nancy Boyles, & Mary E. Hill, daughter of Joel and Emily Hill, m 12 April 1868 by James Needham, M. G.

Boze, Harrison, son of Jane Smith, & Martha Hill, daughter of Hillika Hill, 15 March 1868.

Braben, John & Lucy Johnson, 20 Dec 1812.

Bracker, Isaac & Lucrecy Walker, 2 Oct 1823; Micajah Hicks, bm. (C. H.).

SURRY COUNTY MARRIAGES, 1779-1868

Bradberry, John & Mary Farmer, 28 July 1856; Samuel J. Roop, bm.

Bradly, James & Milly Brown, 29 Oct 1810.

Brady, B. B., son of Isaac & Elizabeth Brady, and Mary Johnson, daughter of Hiram and Lydia Johnson, 9 Aug 1869.

Brandle, Daniel & Margaret Vestal, 15 Sept 1837; John Wright, bm.

Brandle, William & Nancy Callaway, 16 Oct 1827; Christopher Weatherman, bm.

Brandon, George C. & Pillar Hutchins, 1 July 1815; Richard Sellevan, bm.

Branick, Wilson & Lucinda Low, 14 Jan 1834; William Hodges, bm.

Brannock, John & Catharine Maize, 29 March 1855; Samuel Smith, bm; m 29 March 1855 by John Ramey, J. P.

Branon, Wm & Fanny Haines, 19 Oct 1830; Wm. Gentry, bm.

Branon, Wm. H. & Julia M. King, 5 March 1850; J. L. Fulk, bm.

Branscom, Edmond & Ruth Fleming, 6 June 1854; Reuben Branscom, bm; m 6 June 1854 by A. Simmons, J. P.

Branson, Daniel & Elizabeth Hutchins, 11 Sept 1831; Enoch Hutchins, bm.

Branson, Stuard & Eliza Eaton, 9 Feb 1854; James L. M----, bm.

Branum, Jones M. & Olla Gibbs, 26 Jan 1851; Hugh Brown, bm; John Martin, J. P., wit.

Brassfield, Jonathan & Rebeca Gorden, 11 Oct 1830; Charles Combs, bm.

Braswell, Boardvine & Elizebeth Lawson, 4 Jan 1820; Martin D. Word, bm.

Bratton, Hubbard & Mary Slate, 12 April 1862; John Waller, bm; m 12 April 1862 by A. Simmons, J. P.

Bratton, Rufus M. & Mary A. Nixson, 25 March 1855; Michael Smith, bm.

Bray, Alison & Miss Ruth York, 7 April 1857; Nathaniel Stoltz, bm; m 8 April 1857 by C. Canter, J. P.

Bray, Artha & Mary Whitaker, 14 Feb 1821; David Bray Jr., bm.

Bray, Calvin & Mary Reed, 4 Dec 1860; Lebanan Bray, bm; D. M. Cooper, wit.

Bray, David & Sarah Bledsoe, 18 Aug 1845; John Bowles, bm.

Bray, David Jr. & Nelly Whealoss, 27 Sept 1803; James Fitzgerald, bm.

Bray, E. W. & Nancy Reed, 3 Sept 1863; D. M. Cooper, bm; m 3 Sept 1863 at the house of Elizabeth Reed by John Jones.

SURRY COUNTY MARRIAGES, 1779-1868

Bray, Edward W. & Miss Martha E. Albartz, 16 May 1857; Thomas D. Davis, bm; m 17 May 1857 by W. D. Rutledge, J. P.

Bray, Hanan & Polly Snow, 11 April 1836; B. F. Bray, bm.

Bray, Henry & Sarah Sparks, 14 May 1803; Stephen Mankem, bm.

Bray, Henry C. & Martha Poindexter, 27 Jan 1834; J. K. Underwood, bm.

Bray, James L. & Susan Davis, 20 Oct 1828; Ambrose Jems, bm.

Bray, Joel & Talitha Hill, 23 May 1820; Hanon Bray, bm.

Bray, John A. & Nancy Walker, 11 Oct 1830; John Walker, bm.

Bray, Joseph & Elizabeth Lindsay, 11 May 1820; John Williams, bm.

Bray, Lebanan & Martha Smith, 25 Dec 1833; David Bray, bm.

Bray, Lewis W. & Clarice Roberts, 31 Aug 1844; George Butcher, bm.

Bray, Milton & Mary Draughon, 23 June 1832; Joel Bray, bm.

Bray, Nathan & Judith Horn, 17 Jan 1799; David Bray, bm; W. Meredith, wit.

Bray, Oliver & Polly Butcher, 4 March 1847; Chatwell V. Butcher, bm.

Bray, Reuben & Rebecca Laffoon, 28 Dec 1826; Samuel Burns, bm.

Bray, Richard & Polly Mcguire, 17 Oct 1808.

Bray, William A. & Martha M. Poindexter, 16 Dec 1856; T. V. Hamlin, bm.

Brazier, William & Sarah Horn, 21 May 1803; Samson Keen, bm.

Breedin, James L. & Lucinda Massie, 16 July 1852; James Owen, bm.

Breeding, William W. & Rebecca Fugate, 10 Nov 1854; Jesse H. Fugate, bm; m 10 Nov 1854 by A. Simmons, J. P.

Brendle, Danl & _____ (no date); John Weatherman, bm.

Brendle, Jas. F. & Sintha C. Culbert, 17 Jan 1867; Joel S. Adams, bm; m 20 Jan 1867 by N. H. Gwyn(?), J. P.

Brendle, John Fletcher, son of George and Mary Brendle & Lucinda York, daughter of Adam and Mary York, m 20 Oct 1868 by R. W. Pegram.

Brenne, William & JaneAshby, 16 Oct 1819; Anthony Bates, bm; Robt Williams, wit.

Brewer, Asa & Darkas Williams, 24 Oct 1807.

Brewer, Jesse & Christina Lamb, 24 Oct 1807.

Brewer, William & Mary J. Thompson, 10 Jan 1826; William Marsh, bm.

SURRY COUNTY MARRIAGES, 1779-1868

Brickle, J. Bryan & Frankey Harrison, 29 Jan 1823; Joshua Reece, bm.

Bridgefarmer, Martin & Mary Sheak, 4 Feb 1786; Samuel Mosley Ju., bm.

Bridgeman, Isaac & Polly Sneed, 7 Aug 1818; John Amos McGehee, bm; Will Thornton Jun., wit.

Bridgeman, Matthew & Fanny Chandler, 24 Feb 1813; Robert Ferguson, bm.

Briggs, William & Rebecah Baler, 4 March 1823; Robert Hill, bm.

Brim, Archaberry & Miss Nancy Lewis, 13 Nov 1854; m 16 Nov 1854 by Wright Johnson, minister.

Brim, Hamon & Susana Marshall, 6 Sept 1837; John Hicks, Jun, bm.

Brince, Daniel & Mahaly Jentry, 9 Feb 1855; J. B. Eldridge, bm.

Brindel, Henry & Leah Vestal, 14 Feb 1839; James Starbuck, bm.

Brindle, John & Mary Starr, 16 April 1789; Jacob Bonn, bm.

Brindle, Mathew & Levuna Edwards, 13 Jan 1864; J. L. Gillaspie, bm.

Brindle, Richard & Hulda Atkins, 15 Jan 1846; Ambrose J. Loftess, bm.

Brinninger, Joseph & Talitha Fitzgerald, 16 April 1818; Leroy Holcomb, bm.

Brinegar, Jacob & Nancy Fraiser, 19 March 1800.

Brinkley, James E. & Jane Wood, 5 June 1864; J. J. Medkiff, bm; m by John Jones "at my house" 12 June 1864.

Brinkley, Robert R. & Francis Hite, 19 Jan 1839; Abraham Reece (Fuller), bm.

Brinkley, Robert W. & Clarecy J. Badgett, 2 Sept 1866; B. W. Badgett, bm.

Brinkley, Robert W., son of Robert W. and Frances Brinkley, & Frances Perkins, daughter of Isaac and Nancy Perkins, m 12 March 1868 by James Needham, M. G.

Brinkley, Thomas & Pheba Dracon, 26 Dec 1836; Charles Brinkley, bm.

Brinkley, Jeremiah & Rebecca Lovell, 30 Aug 1831; Thos P. Lovell, bm.

Brison, James & Mulvina Breeden, 18 Feb 1855; S. D. Critz, bm; m 18 Feb 1855 by A. Simmons, J. P.

Brittain, John & Lucy Martin, 8 Aug 1846; Ephraim L. Humby, bm.

Brittain, William & _____, 15 March 1802; William Wright, bm.

Brock, Benjamin & Rebekah Kimbrough, 15 April 1826; Richard C. Puryear, bm.

SURRY COUNTY MARRIAGES, 1779-1868

Brogden, Sion & Rebekah Smith, 25 Oct 1818; Benjamin Kelly, bm.

Brogdon, William & Betsy Gentry, 2 Nov 1818; Alfred Brogdon, bm.

Brooks, P. L. W. & Sarah Ballard, 23 Jan 1811; William Forkner, bm.

Brooks, Samuel & Sarah Swain, 3 Jan 1814; Isaac Patterson, bm.

Brooks, Thomas & Jane Beck, 13 Sept 1797; James Beck, bm.

Brothers, Nathaniel & Jane Huey, 12 March 1787; Thomas Huey, bm.

Browder, B. M. & S. A. McCraw, 1 March 1859; G. H. Stovall, bm.

Brown, Adam & Nancy Steelman, 19 Dec 1833; Jno Waggoner, bm.

Brown, Alfred & Elizabeth Adams, 20 Oct 1839; William Brown, bm.

Brown, Archabil & Clary Wishon, 3 April 1824; James Liggon, bm.

Brown, Barnett & Chestiny Fry, 25 March 1862; J. S. Snow, bm; m 27 March 1862 by L. J. Stanley, J. P.

Brown, Benjamin & Mary Dixon, 21 Dec 1810; William Dixon, bm.

Brown, Crosby M. & Catharine E. Fulk, 10 Nov 1866; William N. Brown, bm.

Brown, Daniel & Ellender Bond, 30 Nov 1820; William Phillips, bm.

Brown, Ephraim & Mary York, 1 April 1821; Jacob Brown, bm.

Brown, Esquier & _____, 20 Sept 1844; William Hunter, bm; Joshua Patterson, wit.

Brown, George & Rachel Fellon, 30 Dec 1788; Samuel Gentry, bm; Robt Williams, wit.

Brown, Hugh & Sally Brown, 9 Feb 1847; Jackson Bond, bm.

Brown, Isaac & Amy Stow, 20 Jan 1848; Wm Douglass, bm.

Brown, Isaac T. & Rebecca Day, 8 April 1834; Elisha Musick, bm.

Brown, Jacob & Abigal Hadly, 17 Oct 1814; Moses Brown, bm.

Brown, Jacob & Elizth. Caloway, 22 Aug 1837; Wm. Callaway, bm.

Brown, James & Penelope Hitson, 29 Dec 1791; John Steelman, bm; Robt Williams, wit.

Brown, James & Cattron Shugart, 1 Jan 1798.

Brown, James & Sally Russel, 6 Oct 1817; Joseph Brown, bm; Susanna M. Williams, wit.

Brown, James & Merinda Garriss, 7 May 1838; Landsley Gregory, bm.

Brown, James & Elizabeth Collins, 7 Sept 1865.

Brown, Jefferson & Lydia Brown, 19 Oct 1835; Matthew C. Healan, bm; John E. Roberts, wit.

SURRY COUNTY MARRIAGES, 1779-1868

Brown, Jesse & Jean Cleark, 5 June 1795; Robert Cleark, bm.

Brown, Jesse & _____, 14 Aug 1797.

Brown, Jesse & Conna Lain, 5 Nov 1799.

Brown, Jesse & _____, ----- 180-; Jeremiah Marsh, bm; Jesse Lester, wit.

Brown, Jesse & Matilda Jennings, 20 Jan 1825; Jesse Reece, bm.

Brown, Jesse & Lucinda Jane Evans, 15 June 1844; Aaron A. Crissman, bm.

Brown, Jesse & Patsey Pendry, 22 Aug 1835; William Brown, bm.

Brown, Joel & Lucy Bevinder, 18 Jan 1821; Jonathan North, bm.

Brown, Joel & Elizabeth Waggoner, 12 Jan 1836; Moses Waggoner, bm.

Brown, John & Sarah Brown, 5 Jan 1803.

Brown, John & Betsey Fry, 5 Aug 1813; John Horn, bm.

Brown, John & Bashebe Mullis, 8 April 1816; Elijah Salmon, bm; Susanna M. Williams, wit.

Brown, John & Lovy Massack, 14 July 1820; Henry Brown, bm.

Brown, John & Polly Kell, 12 Nov 1820; Thomas Hinshaw Junr, bm.

Brown, John & Luista Niblorn(?), 4 Dec 1844; Henry Robinson, bm.

Brown, John & Polly Bowles, 14 Oct 1845; Miner Marsh, bm.

Brown, John O. & Adaline Puckett, 25 April 1848; James McKinston, bm.

Brown, Jonathan & Ellina Gibbs, 6 Sept 1818; William Brown, bm.

Brown, Joseph & Grace Coddle (no date).

Brown Joshaway & Patssey Dinkins, 3 Apr 1800.

Brown, Josiah & Polly Johnson, 1 June 1825; Benjamin Matthews, bm; Lewis Williams, wit.

Brown, Josias & Anna Pigg, 20 Sept 1784; Thomas Coker, bm.

Brown, Lewis & Cintha Willard, 14 Feb 1844; William B. Gibbs, bm.

Brown, Minetious & Martha J. Kernes, 16 April 1853; William Maxwell, bm; m 16 April 1853 by A. Simmons, J. P.

Brown, Moses & Elizebeth Hadley, _____ 1806.

Brown, Moses & Hannah Carter, 28 Dec 1797.

Brown, Randolph & Serren Wright, 11 Feb 1784; Loughley Flynn, bm; John Thos Longine, wit.

Brown, Randolph & Phebee Powell, 4 June 1794.

SURRY COUNTY MARRIAGES, 1779-1868

Brown, Richard & Hannah Morris, 23 Aug 1812; George Adams, bm.

Brown, Samuel & Patience Deaver, 24 July 1819; Edward Cornell, bm.

Brown, Solomon & Lydia Adams, 1 Jan 1813; George Adams, bm.

Brown, Tho. & Elizabeth Lunsford, 26 July 1834; Hiram Lunsford, bm.

Brown, Thos. & Nancy Waters, 29 March 1792.

Brown, Thomas & Rachael Flemings, 8 Oct 1809; George Adams, bm.

Brown, Thomas & Mary Head, 18 Aug 1816; Absalom Matthews, bm.

Brown, Thomas & Sally Benge, 3 Dec 1827; Joseph Nix, bm.

Brown, Thomas A. & Susanna Kinny, 24 April 1823; Isaac Brown, bm.

Brown, Thommus & Ann Fraley, 7 Sept 1799.

Brown, William & Sarah Hagard, 10 July 1797.

Brown, Wm & Nancy Hutchins, 8 April 1830; Harrison Daniel, bm.

Brown, William & Nancy Whitaker, 29 March 1838; William Bullen, bm.

Brown, William & Mary P. Worden, 26 Oct 1850; E. C. Brown, bm. (C. H.).

Brown, William J. & Marthy Key, 22 Feb 1856; m 24 Feb 1856 by R. S. Reeves, J. P.

Brown, William W. & Sally Draper, 11 July 1832; Abraham R. Stow, bm.

Brown, Winston & Sarah Adams, 8 Feb 1848; George Hobson, bm.

Browning, David & Polly Miller, 23 Oct 1805.

Brubaker, Isaac & Betsy Diam, 5 April 1825; Asa Vestal, bm.

Brubaker, Jacob & Cynthia Hall, 27 Feb 1833; Moses Rich, bm; L. G. Pettit, wit.

Bruce, Charles & Ann Gray, 4 Dec 1782; John Bruce, bm.

Bruce, John D. & Suzanner Douling (no date).

Bruce, William & Ruth Webster, 8 Nov 1845; Robert Sears, bm; Joshua Patterson, wit.

Bruner, Tandy A. & Sarah C. Hill, 7 Aug 1862; Martin Hyatt, bm.

Bruthers, Absalom & Keziah Keen, 26 Aug 1793; William Brewer, bm.

Bryan, G. & Lucy Roberts, 19 March 1865; William H. Davis, bm; m 19 March 1865 by A. Simmons, J. P.

Bryan, Hugh & Jinney Patterson, 26 Dec 1837; Charles Bryan, bm.

SURRY COUNTY MARRIAGES, 1779-1868

Bryan, Jesse & Eliza. Baliss, 22 May 1797.

Bryan, John & Elizabeth Hinkle, 14 Sept 1797.

Bryan, John & Nancy Thompson, 22 Dec 1826; John R. Moody, bm.

Bryan, Jonathan & Elizabeth Howard, 27 May 1794; Jesse Bryan, bm.

Bryan, William & Charlotte Woodruff, 1 Nov 1830; Thomas F. Prather, bm.

Bryant, Aed & Frances Balwin, 31 Dec 1866; Watson Marshall, bm; m 2 Jan 1867 by M. A. Hall, J. P.

Bryant, Charles & Ann Adams, 7 July 1812; Jonathan York, bm.

Bryant, Charles & Jemima(?) Patterson, 2 Feb 1845; W. J. Chappel, bm.

Bryant, George H. & Martha A. Walters, 15 May 1867; m 19 May 1867 by Solomon Long, Min.

Bryant, Madison & Pauline Jane Tayler, 3 Dec 1859; Sandy Cook, bm.

Bryant, Moses & Margaret Adams, 1 Dec 1834; Moses Adams, bm.

Bryant, Samuel & Nancy Hanks, 17 Oct 1866; D. Cain, bm; m 7 Oct 1866 by W. Golding, J. P.

Buchanan, Cornelius & Emily Johnson, 17 Sept 1821; David Buchanan, bm.

Buckley, Alexander & Lucy Cave, 15 Nov 1818; Miley Cave, bm.

Buckley, Hawsey & Polly Perkins, 5 June 1814; James Roberts, bm; Susanna M. Williams, wit.

Buckley, Jackson & Anne Williams, 26 Dec 1821; Isaac Bently, bm. (C. H.).

Buckner, John & Sarah Tucker, 6 Feb 1836; James F. Tucker, bm; M. W. Early, wit.

Buffalo, James & Elmina Boyse, 23 July 1830; E. Bingham, bm; R. M. Wright, wit.

Bullen, Charles & Eleanor Holyfield, 11 Feb 1835; Bird Wood, bm.

Bullen, Edmon & Martha Snow, 31 Jan 1855; K. H. Bray, bm; T. V. Hamlin, wit; m 31 Jan 1855 by John Hamlin, J. P.

Bullen, George & Delila Coe, 19 June 1863; S. W. Snow, bm; m 21 June 1863 by S. W. Snow, J. P.

Bullen, Jesse & Lucinda Hutson, 3 March 1855; Jefferson Doss, bm; M. A. York, wit; m 4 March 1855 by J. Copeland, J. P.

Bullen, William & Sally Holyfield, 7 Feb 1831; A. Mickle(?), bm.

Bullin, Alexander M. & Rachael Colomer, 26 May 1845; James W. Langly, bm.

SURRY COUNTY MARRIAGES, 1779-1868

Bullen, Jackson & Peggy Williamson, 19 Jan 1819; Jesse Johnson, bm.

Bullen, James & Polly Sturcly, 20 May 1856; Ruben Cure, bm; J. H. Dobson, wit.

Bullen, John & Patsy Edwards, 18 April 1851; Joseph Edwards, bm; D. C. Wolff, wit.

Bullen, James & Susan Laffoon, 18 Nov 1858; Jos. Gordon, bm; T. F. Anthony, wit.

Bunch, William H. & Eliza Sporgur, 6 Sept 1836; Joseph M. Richardson, bm.

Bundy, William J. & Caroline Greenwood, 8 Jan 1852; William R. Greenwood, bm.

Bunting, Henry & Sarah Hudspeth, 2 Oct 1845; John Hampton, bm; Calvin J. Cowles, wit.

Burch, Isaac & Sarah Wellborn, 11 Dec 1846; George W. Brown, bm.

Burch, James & Mary Spargen, 24 Jan 1821; John Tanner, bm.

Burch, Joel & Maryan Brown, 15 Aug 1821; Samuel Callaway, bm.

Burch, John & Betsey York, 27 Dec 1814; John Roberts, bm.

Burch, John & Levicy Boys, 17 Oct 1823; John P. Boys, bm.

Burch, William & Elizabeth Wacther(?), 31 March 1812; George Burch, bm.

Burch, William & Martha Davis, 17 March 1845; Saml P. Jones, bm.

Burch, William & Mary Ann Gates, 26 Nov 1860; Albert Gates, bm; m 26 Nov 1860 by L. J. Norman, J. P.

Burchem, Levi D. & Carey Jentry, 13 March 1856; m 16 March 1856 by Reuben Sparks, D. D.

Burcham, William & Sarah Dobbins, 24 Feb 1831; John Crouse, bm.

Burcham, George & Huldy Dorne, 13 Sept 1865.

Burcham, John & Mahala Smith, 31 Aug 1837; Bartholomew Smith, bm.

Burchet, Jackson & Lucinda Money, 10 Aug 1859; Jos. Soyars, bm.

Burchet, Jackson & Catharine Southard, 29 Aug 1867; m 1 Sept 1867 by J. E. Turner, J. P.

Burchett, Eli & Creely Hodges, 13 Jan 1845; P. B. Moody, bm.

Burgess, John H. & _____, 25 Oct 1858; W. L. Minter, bm.

Burgis, Edward T. & Nancy P. Windsor, 30 Dec 1850; R. R. Windsor, bm.

Burgiss, William & Elizabeth Day, 22 March 18__; Thomas B. Wright, bm; John Wright, wit.

Burk, Elihu & Mary Hineman, 21 Feb 1785.

27

SURRY COUNTY MARRIAGES, 1779-1868

Burk, William H. & Allmiria C. W. Handley, 7 Nov 1844; William P. Kerin, bm.

Burnett, George W. & Virginia Scott, 14 Oct 1863; Samuel D. Critz, bm; m 14 Oct 1863 by A. Simmons, J. P.

Burnett, Granville & Rutha Duggans, 23 Sept 1855; R. S. Coleman, bm; m 23 Sept 1855 by A. Simmons, J. P.

Burnett, William & Cordilla Reynolds, 30 June 1864; John Robertson, bm; m 30 June 1864 by A. Simmons, J. P.

Burns, Henry & Sarah Myers, 24 Jan 1851; Jesse W. Nichols,bm.

Burns, William & Hulda Spence, 14 Sept 1845; David Collier, bm.

Burrass, Henry & Sophia Smith, 22 Feb 1836; Frederick Rinehart, bm.

Burriss, Jonathan & Polly Mays, 8 Dec 1835; Hardin Mays, bm.

Burrus, Miley & Jean Hadly(?), 21 Dec 1837; Wm. Auberry, bm.

Burroughs, C. F. & Mary F. Cundiff, 7 Jan 1862; A. B. Cundiff, bm.

Burrus, George & Mira Pell, 8 May 1808; Thos Burrus, bm.

Burrus, John R. & Achsoh Whitaker, 26 March 1846; John M. Edwards, bm.

Burrus, L. H. & Polly Riggans, 2 Sept 1863.

Burus, Emory & Christeny Cunningham, 9 May 1867; m 9 May 1867 by T. S. Lawson, M. G.

Burton, Henry & Elizabeth Smith, 24 Oct 1789.

Burton, William & Tildalita Whitacre, 1 July 1834; John Martin Jr., bm.

Burton, William H. & Amanda F. Stone, 11 Aug 1862; Harmon Roop, bm.

Butcher, Chatwell & Franky Norton, 8 Aug 1844; James P. Childress, bm. (C. H.).

Butcher, Chatwell V. & Mary Venable, 29 Dec 1850; Joseph Dobson, bm. (C. H.).

Butcher, George & Lucinda Snow, 12 March 1844; Lewis W. Bray, bm.

Butcher, Henry & Nancy Coe, 3 Feb 1824; William Stanley, bm.

Butcher, Jackson & _____, 16 July 1863; Wilie Southerland, bm.

Butcher, James & Elizabeth Melton, 16 Aug 1856; Reubin Cave, bm; T. V. Hamlin, wit; m 21 Aug 1856 by Lacy Snow, J. P.

Butcher, John & Sythia Summers, 20 Oct 1812; William Mickle,bm.

Butcher, Nicholas & Nancy Golding, 8 Dec 1849; Reubin Golding, bm.

SURRY COUNTY MARRIAGES, 1779-1868

Butcher, L. Q. C. & Elizabeth A. Whitlock, 22 Nov 1837; Yancy Brown, bm.

Butner, Christian & Anna Poff, 26 March 1819; Andrew Fults, bm.

Butner, Edward S. & Mary Ann Wolffe, 8 Feb 1847; Jesse Briggs, bm.

Butner, Thomas & Mary Morgan, 23 Jan 1821; Andrew Fultz, bm.

Butner, Thomas & Rebecca B. Brindle, 12 Feb 1826; Iredell Jackson, bm; Seth Hickerson, wit.

Buxton, Richard N. T. & Jane Nicks, 27 Aug 1849; William Buxton, bm; James L. Nesbitt, wit.

Bynum, H. W. & Mary P. Speas, 27 May 1850; Francis W. Hall, bm. (G. H.).

Cadle, Demsy & Mary Atkins, 3 Oct 1821; Robert Atkins, bm.

Cain, Benjamin & Rebeckah Stanfield, 27 Dec 1790; William Steelman, bm.

Cain, Daniel & Elizabeth Hutchins, 21 Dec 1789; William Steelman, bm. (C. H.).

Cain, Daniel & Mande Crofford, 8 March 1862; Richard Snow, bm; m 8 March 1862 by William Golden, J. P.

Cain, Henderson & Marthy E. Cook, 28 Jan 1858; Edward F. Cook, bm; m 28 Jan 1858 by J. Gray, J. P.

Cain, John & Nancy Whitworth Tucker, 9 March 1784; Thos Whitworth, bm; Robt Lanier, wit.

Cain, John & Sarah Simmons, 10 Jan 1827; Andrew Cain, bm.

Cain, Solomon & Mary Taylor, 20 April 1816; Richard Stuthard, bm.

Cain, William & Nancy Trimber, 19 Nov 1844; Churchwell J. Lundy, bm.

Caldwell, Granville H. & Loucetta Prim, 15 Sept 1853; Jacob Hagy, bm.

Call, Adam & Elizabeth Starr, 17 Dec 1785; Evan Ellis Junr., bm.

Call, Isaac & Elizabeth Slater, 10 March 1816; John Thompson, bm.

Callaway, Daniel C. & Mary Brown, 28 Nov 1836; Wm. D. Sommers, bm.

Callaway, Free & Hannah Walker, 18 Oct 1803; Robert Walker, bm.

Callaway, Isaac & Catharine Foote, 4 Sept 1823; James Harris, bm.

Callaway, James A. & Nancy F. Snow, 9 Nov 1852; James Jones, bm.

Callaway, James R. & Mary Thompson, 11 Feb 1851; Samuel Callaway, bm.

Callaway, William & Ann Brindle, 20 June 1834; Wm Brindle, bm; A. C. Duvall, wit.

Calloway, William Jr. & Sarah Waggoner, 14 April 1846; John Davis Jr., bm.

Callihon, Mark & Jeslin Burns, 7 Jan 1833; Silas Riggs, bm.

Caloway, Jas. & Sarah Gross, 23 Oct 1834; William Brunnel, bm.

Calton, Amasa & Lidia Lawder, 27 July 1817; Wm. Calton, bm.

Calton, Lewis A. & Rody Hardie, 25 Feb 1848; Robt Hendricks, bm.

Cambell, Adam & Disa Denny, 15 Oct 1808; Samuel Cart(?), bm; Thomas Wright, wit.

Cambell, Mattw & Sarah Shelton, 10 Dec 1789; Abijah Elmore, bm.

Campbell, Anderson & Jinsey Johnson, 24 Jan 1832; Wm Demsy, bm.

Campbell, David & Nancy Gargus, 31 Aug 1815; Joel Gargus, bm; Lewis Williams, wit.

Campbell, Thomas & Seania Odle, 8 Dec 1860; m 9 Dec 1860 by J. Gray, J. P.

Campbell, William & _____, _____ 1795; Johannes Hauser(?), bm.

Campbell, William & Nancy Kellion, 5 Jan 1823; Aaron Collins, bm.

Canada, Drury & Sarah Waggoner, 2 Dec 1844.

Canada, Marshal & Josaphene Rains, 30 Nov 1854; Stephen F. Moore, bm; m 30 Nov 1854 by A. Simmons, J. P.

Canada, William & Rachel Thompson, 15 May 1819; George Duglass, bm.

Canady, Larkin & Elizabeth Ricks(?), 24 March 1817; David Riggs, bm.

Canter, Allen & _____, 12 July 1833; Benjamin Taylor, bm.

Canter, Erasmus & Matilda Key, 28 Nov 1837; John M. Marion, bm.

Canter, Thomas & Rebecker Hoges, 20 Jan 1801; James Hoges, bm.

Canter, William S. & Elizabeth Key, 5 Oct 1867; m 7 Oct 1867 "at my house" John Jones.

Carbey, Wm. & Asslady Cook, 27 May 1803; Stadge Cook, bm; Oby. Martin, wit.

Carico, Sims & Elizabeth Bishop, 25 April 1852; Richard Bishop, bm; J. Phillips, wit.

Caringer, David & Rebecer Mure, 22 July 1805; G. D. Holcomb, bm.

Carlan, Daniel & Sarah Megehee, 20 March 1838; Leander H. Dobson, bm.

SURRY COUNTY MARRIAGES, 1779-1868

Calton, Eligy & Elizabeth Wooten, 7 March 1836; Moses Calton, bm; Robt C. Duvall, wit.

Carlton, Elijah & Nancey Long, 31 Oct 1836; Nathan Price, bm.

Carlton, George & Rachael Rutledge, 10 June 1814; Joel Carlton, bm.

Carlton, John & Letuice Morefield, 16 Feb 1816; William Carlton, bm.

Carlton, Lindsey & Racheal Carter, 29 Sept 1818; George Carlton, bm; Will Thornton Jun, wit.

Carlton, Lindsey Jr. & Polly Rutledge, 7 March 1822; Jonathan Hinshaw, bm.

Carlton, Micajah & Mary Taylor, 1 May 1810; Joel Carlton, bm.

Carlton, William & Elizabeth Weaver, 8 July 1819; John Carlton, bm.

Carlton, William & Lizzie Smith, 8 May 1849; Bennet Smith, bm.

Carmical, John & Mary J. Ranes, 26 Sept 1850; James Haly, bm. (C. H.).

Carmical, Richard & Polly Graves, 26 June 1812; Archibald Carmical, bm.

Carmichael, John & Rachel Morten, 14 Sept 1817; Larkin Strong, bm.

Carmichal, Archibald Junr. & Martha Pennington, 2 Aug 1824; Richd. Carmichael, bm.

Carnaf, Joseph, son of Moses and Margarett Carnaf, and Sarah J. Crage, daughter of William and Nancy Crage, m 30 June 1868 by A. Simmons, J. P.

Carnahan, Robert & Jane Raasse, 22 Feb 1851; Wyatt Parker, bm.

Carpenter, Benjamin & Mary Ann Howlet, 19 Dec 1865; J. A. Hall, bm. (C. H.).

Carpenter, Phillip & Sally Ann Glastown, 18 May 1853; John Smith, bm.

Carrico, Stephen & Jane Brison, 4 Jan 1844; Andrew Faddis, bm.

Carrient, Bryant & Julia Ann Merkle, 1 Nov 1838; John Dobbins, bm.

Carson, Caleb & Delila Jessop, 9 Sept 1818; John Starbuck, bm.

Carson, Jacob & Alsa Jackson, 9 Aug 1811; Absalom Sumner, bm.

Carson, James & Elizabeth Douglass, 13 Jan 1792; Thomas Carson, bm.

Carter, Abel & Rhody Turner, 5 March 1793; Elias Turner, bm.

Carter, Abraham & Emboset Smith, 16 Nov 1866; m 16 Nov 1866 by Murlin Spargee, J. P.

SURRY COUNTY MARRIAGES, 1779-1868

Carter, Benjamin & Rebecca Marshall, 21 Oct 1831; Saml Marshall, bm.

Carter, Charles H. & Marget Addleman, 18 Dec 1826; Jesse E. Chinn, bm.

Carter, Clemmin & Honner Loagin, 2 June 1807; Nimrod Elliott, bm.

Carter, Don or Robert Cole & Elizabeth Badgett, 12 March 1801; J. Shepperd, bm; (filed under DonCarlos).

Carter, Edward & Sarah Hutchins, 1 Feb 1818; Solomon Carter, bm.

Carter, Gran B. & Elizabeth Spurlin, 8 Sept 1837; Thos. F. Anthony, bm.

Carter, Isaac & Sarah Hurt, 28 Aug 1829; Edward Carter, bm.

Carter, Isaack & Jean Brown, 4 Dec 1797; Joseph Carter, bm.

Carter, J. & Gemima L. Williams, 25 Dec 1865; m 27 Dec 1865 by D. A. Eldridge, J. P.

Carter, James & Rhoda Poenix, 23 Sept 1833; Daniel Arnold, bm.

Carter, Joab & Rutha Davis, 27 March 1844; William Whiticher, bm; T. C. Hauser, wit.

Carter, John & Nancy Williams, 6 Dec 1808; Isaac Williams, bm.

Carter, Joseph W. & Abigail Reynolds, 21 Dec 1844; Spencer Hadley, bm.

Carter, Joshua & Sarah Pinright, 29 March 1821; Wm. Macker, bm.

Carter, Melton & Elizabeth Jacks, 2 May 1824; Wilson Leeke, bm.

Carter, Samuel & Sally Holebrooks, _____ 18--; John Carter, bm.

Carter, Samuel H. & Nancy Jones, 16 June 1867; J. S. Adams, bm; m 16 June 1867 by J. K. Rose, Baptist minister.

Carter, Thomas & Marium Cartright, 6 Feb 1821; Joshua Carter, bm; Susanna M. Williams, wit.

Carter, Wm. & Elizabeth Allen, 24 Dec 1833; Daniel Arnold, bm.

Carter, William M. & Ann R. Burchan, 17 Aug 1866; G. M. Burchan, bm.

Cartwright, James & Polly Carlton, 15 Oct 1822; Moses Carlton, bm.

Carver, Michal & Elezebeth Chanler, 21 July 1804; George Chandler, bm.

Casey, Jesse M. & Margaret Windsor, 3 April 1847; Riley Windsor, bm.

Casey, W. R. & Adalade McDaniel, 6 Feb 1864; W. T. McDaniel, bm; m 11 Feb 1864 by W. F. Adams, Baptist minister.

Cash, Lewis & Mary Cook, 15 Aug 1850; John Dickerson, James F. Johnson, bm.

SURRY COUNTY MARRIAGES, 1779-1868

Cassturis, Bundick & Anne Elmer, 13 May 1817; Isaac Austill, bm.

Casterus, John & Patience Martin, 19 Aug 1806; William Money, bm.

Cast, Elisha & Preshus Johnson, 18 Nov 1787; Joseph Johnson, 18 Nov 1787; Joseph Johnson, bm.

Cast, Robert & Lucy Riley, 16 Feb 1790; Ninian Riley, bm; S. Wood, bm.

Cast, Samuel & Letty Taylor, 31 Oct 1808; John Myers, bm.

Cartephens, Peter & Polly Collins, 3 Oct 1817; Thomas Minish, bm.

Castious, Martin & Susan Durham, 28 Dec 1828; Jacob Waggener, bm.

Cate, James & Nancy Jones, 12 Sept 1809; Benjamin Potter, Elijah Thompson, bm; Chas Taliaferro, bm.

Cathy, George & Jane Hill, 17 May 1862; Samuel D. Critz, bm.

Caudle, Aaron & Melinda Grover, 21 Nov 1826; Moses Caudle, bm.

Caudle, Aquila J. & Penlina Campbell, 9 Nov 1854; John Black, bm; m 9 Nov 1854 by A. Simmons, J. P.

Caudle, Jackson & Abigail Adams, 20 Feb 1850; James Caudle, bm. (C. H.).

Caudle, James & Elizabeth Adams, 20 July 1823; Jas. Adams, bm.

Caudle, James & Mary Yarbrough, 22 Jan 1849; Jackson Caudle, bm.

Caudle, John & Emeline Caudle, 15 June 1833; Thos. F. Daniel, bm.

Caudle, John J. & Mary Laffoon, 24 May 1849; Reuben H. Bray, bm.

Caudle, Moses & Sintha Chapple, 20 July 1828; Martin Castephens, bm.

Caudle, Sampson & Patience Bohannon, 27 Dec 1849; N. B. Dozier, bm.

Caudle, William & Nancy Brown, 22 March 1826; James Caudle, bm.

Cave, Algius & Mary A. Burrus, 14 Sept 1864; George M. Jarvis, bm; m 15 Sept 1864 by T. J. Lawson.

Cave, Algius & Dorcas Cunningham, 1 Dec 1823; consent from William Cunningham, 29 Nov 1823 for "my infant daughter Dorcas".

Cave, Algius & Elizabeth Aimfield, 30 July 1819; John Taliaferro, bm.

Cave, Galin & Susanna Easley, 5 Jan 1828; Algius Cave, bm.

Cave, Henry & Matilda Busby, 14 April 1849; William Cave, bm.

Cave, John & Jane Talbott, 1 June 1819; James McCraw, bm.

SURRY COUNTY MARRIAGES, 1779-1868

Cave, John & Eathy White, 7 July 1862; T. V. Hamlin, bm; m 10 July 1862 by L. J. Norman, J. P.

Cave, Reubin & Adaline Mitchel, 20 Jan 1859; D. K. Davis, bm.

Cave, Thomas & Elizabeth Bemer, 30 April 1825; Galen Cave, bm.

Caviness, Jackson & Sally McCraw, 26 Oct 1859; George W. McCraw, bm.

Caveniss, John & Susan Mills, 5 Jan 1860; m 5 Jan 1860 by G. A. McCraw, J. P.

Ceasor, Jesse, son of Fanney Ceasor & Sarah Nelson, m 8 March 1868 by J. A. Bingman, J. P.

Celton, George & Mary Shearmour, 27 May 1797; James Cassada, bm.

Chaffin, Edwin & Deborah Bills, 17 Nov 1809; Matthew M. Hughes, bm.

Chaffin, Standley & Elizabeth McGlamery, 10 July 1812; Peter Clingman, bm.

Chamberlain, Martin & _____, 21 Nov 1850; Pinkney Lindsey, bm.

Chamberlain, Thomas N. & Caroline Whitlock, 20 Dec 1849; John B. Johnson, bm.

Chamblin, William & Sally Gentry, 21 Dec 1828; John Ball, bm.

Chamberlain, William & Rebecca Stutman, 26 March 1851; Anderson E. Swinny, bm.

Chandlez, Joseph, son of Campbell and Nancy Chamblez, & Hattie E. Pratt, daughter of Madison and Elizabeth Pratt, m 8 Nov 1868 by J. Shanb, J. P.

Chandlar, Joseph & Anny Jessop, 12 Jan 1813; Thomas Barker, bm.

Chandler, David & Celia Gorden, 6 Sept 1852; Wm. Jones, bm; m 6 Sept 1852 by William Hill, J. P.

Chandler, James & Mary Barker, 16 May 1846; Iredell A. McGee, bm.

Chandler, P. T. & Aby Ives, 9 Feb 1863; W. W. Wolff, bm.

Chandler, William & Nancy Cain, 21 July 1813; David Cane (Cain), bm.

Chandler, William & Susanah Cretchfield, 2 Aug 1858; Isaac Chandler, bm.

Chandler, Wm. H. & Jane Montgomery, 22 Sept 1865; J. Y. Reynolds, bm.

Chandler, Wilson & Eliza Denny, 1 Dec 1866; Riley Warden, bm.

Chaney, Josea & Sarah Golden, 11 Feb 1817; Gius Cave, bm.

Chanler, Clanton & Sally Forkner, 17 Jan 1819; Evan Davis, bm.

SURRY COUNTY MARRIAGES, 1779-1868

Chapel, Joshua & Sarah Carter, 15 Nov 1826; Dempsy Joiner, bm.

Chappel, Wm. J. & Mary Swaim, 23 Jan 1836; Phillip Holcomb, bm.

Chappell, Anderson & Sophia Arnold, 3 May 1849; James Farr---, bm.

Chapman, Thomas & Sally Hill, 20 Jan 1820; Elias Turner, bm.

Chappel, Elisha & Sally Tolbert, 26 Dec 1807; Amos Chappel, bm.

Chappel, Harrison & Susanah Money, 31 Aug 1835; Jas. Chappel, bm.

Chappel, James & Ruth Foster, 6 Sept 1816; Ambrose Chappel, bm.

Chappel, James & Sally Smith, 13 May 1812; Ambrose Chappel, bm.

Chappel, Moses & Kessiah C. Swaim, 7 April 1851; Joel Brooks, bm.

Chappel, Sherrel & Mahala Groad, 30 Aug 1823; John Swaim, bm. (C. H.).

Chappel, William & Ann Vestal, 20 Jan 1830; James Chappel, bm.

Chappel, Alexander & Luisa Ayres, 18 Jan 1844; Luke Thompson, bm.

Chappell, William A. & Mary Ann Gentry, 18 March 1847; Hezekiah F. Freeman, bm.

Charles, Oliver & Elizabeth Heath, 14 May 1788; Wm Heath, bm; Robt Williams, wit.

Chatham, Alexander & M. E. Gwyn, 26 Sept 1862; J. O. Chatham, bm; m 28 Sept 1862 by W. H. Bobbitt at Elkin, N. C.

Cheek, Albert of Davy County, & Mrs. Elizabeth C. Gillim of Surry County, m 25 Dec 1855 by Rev. John M. Gwin.

Cheek, Samuel & Nancy Elrode, 22 March 1802; Jacob Elrode, bm.

Cheek, William & Rhoda Money, 1 March 1819; John Cheek, bm.

Cheeks, John & Mary Elmore, 6 Sept 1809; Mathew Sparks, bm.

Childress, Joseph & Elizabeth Pinkley, 10 Aug 1787; John Brinkley, bm.

Chilton, John B. & Mary Daniely, 29 April 1867; Daniel T. Peel, bm.

Chilton, Raleigh & Mary McKinny, 28 Jan 1828; Martin Smith, bm.

Chilton, Rolly & Olive McKinny, 5 Dec 1850; A. Fitzgerald, bm.

Chinalt, Samuel & Cealy Ann Andrews, 28 Feb 1856; Randolph Chinalt, bm. (C. H.).

Chinnall, James & Mary Andrew, 16 Jan 1853; Michel Harrold, bm; m 16 Jan 1853 by A. Dunnagan, J. P.

Cheshur, John C. & Martha J. Devenport, 8 April 1855; Saml Cheshur, bm; m 9 April 1855 by John Jones "at my house".

Childers, Ausburn & Sarough Sfarger, 22 Jan 1848; J. A. Bingman, bm.

Childress, Hastin & Matilda M'craw, 27 Jan 1816; Samuel Rogers, bm; Susanna M. Williams, wit.

Childress, Benjamin & Ann Susan Franklin, 30 Dec 1835; Anthony Collins, bm.

Childress, James & Nancy Butcher, 16 Jan 1833; John H. Dobson, bm.

Childress, Jonathan & Rebecca Wood, 15 June 1834; Belson B. Benhan, bm.

Childress, T. W. & Susa J. Axum, 11 Aug 1866; F. A. Axsom, bm; m 12 Aug 1866 by Joseph Axsom, J. P.

Childress, William & Polly Campbell, 13 Oct 1837; D. Jervis, bm.

Childers, Wm & Sarah White, 11 Sept 1856; Wm. White, bm; m 11 Sept 1856 by J. E. Stanly, J. P.

Childress, William E. & Huldah Smith, 20 Oct 1866; Zion Smith, bm; m 21 Nov 1866 by S. W. Roberts, J. P.

Chilton, Ira W. & Martha A. Jessup, 27 Sept 1858; William H. Jessup, bm.

Chilton, James A. & Sarah Ann Pell, 21 Dec 1866; m 31 Dec 1866 by M. A. Hall, J. P.

Chilton, James W., son of Armstead & Tobitha Chilton, & Rebecca W., daughter of Thomas and Nancy Bryant, m 30 July 1868 by James Needham, M. G.

Chilton, Stephen V. & Adaline Perking, 29 July 1833; Jones Taylor, bm.

Chinn, James & Sally Williams, 3 Nov 1821; Jason Williams, bm.

Chinn, Jesse & Sarah Ridings, 20 April 1819; Isaac Ridings, bm.

Chinn, Rauleigh & Elezebeth Gough, 18 Oct 1806; Robert Freemon, bm.

Chipman, Joshua, son of Thos Chipman, and Laura Young, daughter of Solomon and Eda Young, m 28 Jan 1872 by James Wells, J. P. (C. H.).

Chipman, Thomas C. & Clarisa Day, 20 Feb 1862; Michael Sprinckle, bm; m 20 Feb 1862 by Joel Hurt, J. P.

Churcher, Thomas & Elizabeth Gunnel, 11 March 1859; Jeremiah Gibson, bm.

Clanton, Benjamin (son of Thomas) and Susannah Allgood, 21 Jan 1822; Hugh Thompson, bm.

Clanton, Charles & Mary Wiles, 26 Jan 1801; Luke Wiles, bm.

Clanton, Edward & Rachel More, 15 Nov 1797; Saml Clanton, bm.

Clanton, James & Polly Atwood, 14 Aug 1829; Jo. Steelman, bm.

SURRY COUNTY MARRIAGES, 1779-1868

Clanton, James & Betsy Joiner, 24 June 1820; Philip Wishon, bm.

Clanton, Thomas & Sarah Moore, 21 March 1793; Edward Clanton, bm.

Clark, Henry & Nancy Southrin, 11 Sept 1860; m 11 Sept 1860 by E. Banner, J. P.

Clark, J. F. & Leticia Fugate, 2 Dec 1860; m 2 Dec 1860 by E. Banner, J. P.

Clark, R. M. & Miss Rhody Ann Tipton, 14 Sept 1866; m 14 Sept 1866 by William Rawley, L. D. of the Methodist Church.

Clark, Samuel & Lucinda Arner, 26 June 1846; Abraham Short, bm.

Clark, Thomas & Roda Dunigan, 3 Feb 1814; Caleb Jessup, bm.

Clark, William & Tamsa Pruet, 29 Sept 1860; m 29 Sept 1860 by E. Banner, J. P.

Clarke, John S. & Sarah F. King, 26 March 1851; Jesse M. Canny, bm.

Clarke, Robert & Alse Howell, 30 Oct 1786; Zepheniah Dowden, bm.

Clansel, Richard B. & Miss Jane R. Mozby, 20 Dec 1828; Richard C. Puryear, bm.

Clay, George L. & Eliza J. Widdle, 2 July 1857; Jacob S. Helms, bm; m 2 July 1857 by A. Simmons, J. P.

Clayton, Britton & Lewsy Bailey, 13 Nov 1787; Charles Clayton, bm.

Clayton, M. C. & Sally McKinney, 25 Feb 1866; W. R. Martin, bm; J. E. Reeves, wit.

Clemmens, Joseph & Synthia Ghoff, 21 July 1827; Thomas J. Word, bm.

Clemmons, Alfred & Susan Shelton, 27 Jan 1855; Andrew Burge, bm; m 27 Jan 1855 by A. Simmons, J. P.

Clingman, Alexr. B. & Anna M. Clingman, 8 Sept 1829; Wm. C. Mosby, bm.

Clingman, Jacob & Jane Poindexter, 10 Aug 1811; Ormon Kimbrough, bm.

Clingman, John P. & Camilla S. Cash, 21 Dec 1847; Leon H. Cash, bm.

Clone, James L. & Delila Willis, 12 Sept 1854; Greensvill Willis, bm; m 12 Sept 1854 by R. Marshall, J. P.

Cloud, William H. & Sarah E. Slusher, 16 Sept 1866; m by A. Simmons, J. P.

Co, John L. & Mary McCollum, 17 Feb 1821; Nathaniel McCollum, bm.

Coal, Archibald H. & Nancy Ann Smith, 30 Oct 1865; Edward D. Ray, bm. (C. H.).

SURRY COUNTY MARRIAGES, 1779-1868

Cobb, Benjamin & Violetta Morris, 6 Oct 1790; Chesley Cobb, bm.

Coblar, Green & Tabitha Simmons, 18 May 1858; J. M. Owens, bm; m by A. J. Cassell.

Cock, Enoch & Nancy J. Ayres, 19 Nov 1852; Mark A. Smith, bm. (C. H.).

Cock, Jackson & Mary Philips, 7 March 1851; Anderson Philips, bm.

Cockerham, C. C. & Fanny N. Bryant, 20 Nov 1862; J. E. Reeves, bm; m 23 Nov 1862 by Jno. J. Ninnickle, J. P.

Cockerham, D. S. & P. M. Jones, 3 May 1858.

Cockerham, P. C. & M. C. Hamby, 27 Dec 1866; S. A. Waugh, bm.

Cockerham, Daniel & Sarah Jones, 16 Oct 1808; John Shugart, bm.

Cockerham, David & Nancy P. Reese, 9 Jan 1849; Henderson Ellis, bm.

Cockerham, Daniel C. & Lucinda Reece, 26 Aug 1831; William W. Edwards, bm.

Cockerham, Hewey & Nancy Fulk, 29 Dec 1831; Wm. Auberry, bm.

Cockerham, Hughes & Huldah Snow, 4 Oct 1851; William Cockerham Jr., bm; m 14 Oct 1851 by J. E. Stanly, J. P.

Cockerham, John & Polly Doudge, 21 Nov 1833; John Reece, bm.

Cockerham, Joseph & Mary Marshall, 2 March 1830; Wm. Cockerham, bm.

Cockerham, Joseph & Miss Julian Thompson, 27 March 1854; Henry M. Freeman, bm; m 27 March 1857 by Rev. Geo. Douglas.

Cockerham, Joseph & Emiline Greenwood, 12 Nov 1867.

Cockerham, M. F. & Thirsa Kannedy, 2 Aug 1849; Williams Cockerham, bm.

Cockerham, Pleasant & Tennessee Kannedy, 10 Nov 1846; Pleasant R. Cockerham, bm.

Cockerham, Pleasant R. & Polly Thompson, 18 Jan 1848; S. W. Cockerham, bm.

Cockerham, S. W. & Jane Jones, 28 Dec 1854; P. L. Cockerham, bm; m 28 Dec 1854 by D. R. Cockerham, J. P.

Cockerham, Samuel & Rutha Smith, 11 Jan 1868; m by F. J. Dick, J. P.

Cockerham, Williams & Sally Cockerham, 12 Nov 1856; William Cockerham, bm. (C. H.).

Cockerham, William & Nancy E. Willey, 2 May 1867; D. J. Cockerham, bm.

Cocklereece, Daniel & Martha Mosley, 2 Dec 1856; Bennet Creed, bm; W. M. Freeman, J. P., wit; m 3 Dec 1856 by W. M. Freeman.

SURRY COUNTY MARRIAGES, 1779-1868

Cocklereece, John & Mary Midkiff, 16 Nov 1858; Charles Poor, bm.

Cokelreece, Julius & Martha A. Sopshire, 28 Oct 1861.

Cockram, John & Elizabeth Jones, 5 March 1811; James Jackson, bm.

Cockram, William & Bershaba Masting(?), 23 Nov 1801; Grove Cook, bm.

Coderus, Columbus & Elizabeth Richardson, 23 Dec 1849; A. Simmons, bm.

Coe, Dudly & Lucy Ann Hutson, 25 July 1862; J. L. Gillaspie, bm; m 25 July 1862 by L. J. Norman, J. P.

Coe, Giles & Sarah Lovill, 13 Dec 1816; Isaac Garret (Jarratt), bm.

Coe, Haston, son of William & Rachel Coe, & Sarah Stantz, daughter of Garret & Mima J. Stantz, m 15 March 1868 by R. T. Pilson, J. P.

Coe, Jackson & Julia Stanly, 2 Oct 1855; T. V. Hamlin, bm.

Coe, Person & Lucy Butcher, 18 March 1845; Andrew Jackson Coe, bm.

Coe, Samuel Hampton & Manervy J. Harris, 17 Feb 1867; Chamliss Coe, bm; m 18 Feb 1867 by S. W. Snow, J. P.

Coe, William & Rachel Holyfield, 27 June 1845; A. J. Coe, bm.

Coe, William Jr. & Elizabeth Baker, 10 Aug 1848; Leander H. Burrus, bm.

Coggeshall, Gayer & Lettuce Worth, 11 Oct 1816; William Petty, bm.

Cogins, John & Sarah Whelus, 10 Dec 1798; James Durham, bm.

Coker, Joseph & Mary Brown, 28 April 1800; Jse. Brown, bm.

Cole, Robert or Don Carter & Elizabeth Badgett, 21 March 1801; J. Shepperd, bm. (filed under DonCarlos).

Cole, William & Jestena Forkner, 31 Dec 1850; James W. Jackson, bm. (C. H.).

Coley, James & _____, 15 Oct 1839; Hezekiah Smith, bm.

Collins, Anthony & Elliet L. Runion, 6 July 1853; William Collins, bm; m 6 July 1853 by A. Simmons, J. P.

Collins, A. R. & Sarah Jane Hutson, 1 Nov 1857; K. H. Bray, bm; m 1 Nov 1857 by H. M. Waugh, J. P.

Collins, Calvin & Rebecca Dingler, 16 Feb 1848; Henry Cheek, bm; Josiah Cowles Jr., wit.

Collins, Alex S. & Matildia Low, 10 Sept 1865; m by B. J. Dickens, J. P.

Collins, H. W. & Mary Hardy, 23 Dec 1860; T. V. Hamlin, bm; m 27 Dec 1860 by L. J. Stanley, J. P.

Collins, Hiram & Phebe Tucker, 8 Jan 1828; William Masters, bm.

Collins, Jackson & Rebeca McKinney, 5 March 1849; David Wood, bm.

Collins, Jackson & Milly Boman, 20 April 1854; Martin Childress, bm; m 20 April 1854 by R. Marshall, J. P.

Collins, Jacob & Emily Maab, 15 April 1854; James Doss, bm; m 15 April 1854 by A. Simmons, J. P.

Collins, James & Cristeena Johnson, 2 Oct 1867; m 3 Oct 1867 by A. Brim, J. P.

Collins, John & Patsey Hammons, 27 Feb 1819; Wm. C. Dobson, bm.

Collins, John & Susanna Elmore, 9 March 1829; Josiah Cowles, bm.

Collins, John & Chesteena Oddre, 15 Nov 1849; Jackson Collins, bm.

Collins, Joseph & Dillaney Smallwood, 13 Sept 1818; Joseph Hickmon, bm.

Collins, Levi & Grace M. Swaim, 6 April 1835; Braxton Ray, bm.

Collins, Levi & Rhoda Money, 9 July 1849; John S. Holcomb, bm.

Collins, Levi & Christiana Dollarhide, 2 Nov 1865; W. H. Collins, bm; m 2 Nov 1865 by G. A. Lowe, J. P.

Collins, Lewis & Polly Spencer, 17 Nov 1823; Richard Snow, bm.

Collins, Obadiah & Elizabeth Vanhoy, 26 Feb 1830; Clayton Vanhoy, bm.

Collins, Sidney & Franky Johnson, 11 Nov 1838; Josiah Cowles, bm.

Collins, William K. & Catharine Hough, 20 March 1852; m 25 March 1852 by T. V. Hamlin, J. P.

Colvard, Benjamin & Elizabeth Hunter, 28 May 1832; Thomas Calvert, bm.

Colvard, Benjamin & Nancy Durret, 6 Aug 1833; William Harding, bm.

Colvard, Henry & Salley Scokey, 20 Aug 1837; Isaac P. Stow, bm.

Colvard, Thomas & Rebekah Thornton, 16 Dec 1810; John Colvard, Benjamin Colvard, bm.

Colvin, Thomas & Celia Cresom, 24 May 1825; James H. Lynch, bm.

Combs, Charles & Abigal Reavis, 28 Dec 1819; Wiley Brassfield, bm.

Combs, J. F. & Lucinda Stantliff, 23 Feb 1867; Fred Hawks, bm; m 23 Feb 1867 by W. Golding, J. P.

Combs, John W. & Matilda J. Burres, 30 Sept 1867; m 3 Oct 1867 by Rev. William J. Combs.

SURRY COUNTY MARRIAGES, 1779-1868

Combs, Sinklar & Sarah Kerney, 17 Sept 1849; Henry Hawks, bm.

Combs, Stephen & Sally Hudson, 9 Feb 1819; Thomas Duglass, bm.

Combs, Thomas & Adaline Hiatt, 6 June 1852; James J. Ayres, bm.

Comer, Archabald & Amelia Winsor, 19 Jan 1844; John Holcomb, bm.

Comer, James Q. & Lucinda Johnson, 27 June 1850; W. R. Johnson, bm.

Conley, James T. & Sarah J. Kingsbury, 11 Oct 1860; m 30 Oct 1860 by Isaac Avent, P. C. of Surry Co., N. C. Conference of Methodist E. Church, South.

Connoly, Russel & Martha Cozort, 10 Feb 1857; P. M. Nicks, bm.

Conner, Danl & Cary McLemore, 6 July 1795; Wright McLemore, bm.

Conrad, A. E. & Pamelia A. Shore, 24 Feb 1851; A. P. Poindexter, bm; R. C. Poindexter, wit.

Conrad, John & Elizabeth Miller, 26 Dec 1803; John Miller, bm.

Conrad, John C. & Edny Brown, 6 Jan 1861; m 6 Jan 1861 by W. W. Wolff, J. P.

Conrad, John Joseph & Keziah Harding, 25 Feb 1827; F. Thomas Conrad, bm.

Cooke, Abell & Justin Simmons, 29 Nov 1831; B. D. Gardner, bm.

Cook, Alfred & Rebeca Simmons, 9 March 1865; Lewis C. Taylor, bm; m 12 March 1865 by M. A. Hall, J. P.

Cook, Ambrose & Alcy Bell, 17 Jan 1829; Evans Cook, bm.

Cook, Anderson & Nancy Booker, m 24 May 1853 by A. Simmons, J. P.; W. H. Davis, bm.

Cook, Eli & Elizey Jessup, m 1 May 1855 by J. Gray, J. P.

Cook, Evans & Suckey Murphey, 11 Aug 1826; John Philips, Jacob Eddleman, Jacob Eddleman, bm.

Cook, Harus & Mary Simms, 9 April 1837; John Shores, bm.

Cook, Henry & Susanna Johnson, 10 Oct 1828; Axum Halleman, bm.

Cook, Isaac & Mary Heath, 16 Dec 1859; William Fullin, bm.

Cook, Isham & Malinda Warden, 2 Aug 1832; Andrew Cain, bm.

Cook, Isham T. & Lucretia E. Lowe, 19 Nov 1867; m 28 Nov 1867 by Alex: Moran.

Cook, James & Eliza Vest, 24 May 1838; John S. Hadley, bm.

Cook, James W. & Juliann McCollum, 23 Dec 1858; E. P. Shelton, bm.

Cook, Jefferson & Elizabeth Jacks, 14 Nov 1835; John Brittain, bm; Robt C. Powall, wit.

Cook, John & Sarah Pope, 8 July 1813; Valentine Holderfield, bm.

SURRY COUNTY MARRIAGES, 1779-1868

Cook, John & Edith Jessop, 8 June 1814; James Cook, bm.

Cook, John & Courtney Bulty, 4 Dec 1832; Allen Sisk, bm.

Cook, John & Prescilla Jessup (no date); Caleb Jessop, bm.

Cook, John T. & Martha C. Simmons, 18 Dec 1866; m 30 Dec 1866 by M. A. Hall, J. P.

Cook, Newel & Rebecca Jessup, 23 Oct 1856; John H. Lowe, bm.

Cook, Peyton & Mary Cook, 13 Nov _____; Z. Riggs, bm.

Cook, Philip & Jenny Meredith, 20 Dec 1790; John Critchfield, bm.

Cook, Samuel & Belsa Hendrick, 17 Jan 1803; David Cook, bm.

Cook, Sandy & Mary Katharine Heymore, 30 April 1864; Lewis Taylor, bm.

Cook, Sanford & Nancy F. Jessup, 10 Jan 1868; Oliver Stanliff, bm.

Cook, Stage & Mary Shores, 4 May 1799; William Holleman of Stokes Co., bm.

Cook, Valentine & Amey Wooten, 26 Aug 1808; Alex. Cook, bm.

Cook, Val. & Amia Whotan, 27 Aug 1808; Byrd Combs, bm.

Cook, William & Phebery Norman, 16 June 1823; Danel Norman, bm.

Cook, William & Patsey Benge, 29 Nov 1833; Lewis Mock, bm.

Cook, William & Eliza. Denton, (no date); James Merrit, bm; Robt Lanier, wit.

Cook, William A. & Nancy Dunford, 28 Feb 1852; E. G. Carter, bm.

Cook, William M. & Susan J. Cook, 19 Aug 1864; Andrew H. Jackson, bm.

Cooper, Charles W. & Katharine A. Anderson, 5 Nov 1851; John B. Absher, bm.

Cooper, David M. & Mary Cassman, 25 Aug 1845; Thomas F. Hampton, bm.

Cooper, John & Frances Taylor, 3 April 1822; William Hiett Senr, bm. (C. H.).

Cooper, John & Paulina Philips, 12 Nov 1846; Wm. A. Whitaker, bm.

Cooper, Martin & Betsey Cordel, 23 Dec 1810; James Brown, bm.

Cooper, William & Nancy Terry, 12 Feb 1850; Davidson Akers, bm. (C. H.).

Copeland, Garrett & Nancy McKinney, 5 Feb 1816; Richard E. Reves, bm.

Copeland, Isaac & Miss Elizabeth Harris, 27 Jan 1855; D. M. McGee, bm; m 28 Jan 1855 by D. M. McGee, J. P.

SURRY COUNTY MARRIAGES, 1779-1868

Copeland, Isaac & Elizabeth Winfrey, 23 July 1833; Edward M. Dobson, bm.

Copeland, Isham & Erica Draper, 26 Sept 1851; Isham Venable, bm; m 26 Sept 1851 by D. M. McGee, J. P.

Copeland, James L. & Sarah A. Copeland, 29 Aug 1853; King H. Bray, bm; m 30 Aug 1853 by T. V. Hamlin, J. P.

Copeland, Jesse & Elizabeth Forkner, 1 Nov 1826; Winston Somers, bm.

Copeland, Jesse & Elizabeth Creed, 14 Oct 1846; James L. Copeland, bm.

Copeland, John & Cynthia Scruggs, 21 Nov 1804; William Copeland, bm.

Copeland, Melvin W. & _____, 24 Oct 1854; Edward Bullen, bm.

Copeland, Samuel & Margret Linvell, 12 Jan 1822; Ephraim Desern, bm.

Cordell, John & Susan Tilley, 19 Sept 1860; C. H. Harris, bm; m 25 Sept 1860 by Rev. William J. Combs.

Corder, Enoch & Catherine Bledsoe, 7 Feb 1858; A. R. Collins, bm; m 7 Feb 1858 at the house of Thomas Corder, Surry Co., by John Jones.

Corder, William & Frances Lawson, 20 Oct 1815; Ransom Dudly, bm.

Corbin, William & Elizabeth Jones, 29 Nov 1838; Daniel S. Jones, bm.

Cornelius, Greenberry & Hanah Cimmons, 17 Aug 1811; Samuel Jessop, bm.

Cornelius, James & Lucy Forkner, 22 Jan 1818; James Forkner, bm.

Cornelius, John H. & Sarah L. Cundiff, 18 Feb 1866; M. Jessup, bm.

Cornelius, Robert & Mary Holaman, 18 April 1811; Samuel Stewart, bm; Wm. Thornton, wit.

Cornell, James & Mary Sullivan, 11 Sept 1798; Samuel James, bm.

Cornell, James & Mary Paul, 7 Nov 1820; Thomas Paul, bm.

Cornell, John & Ann Burd, 21 Aug 1804; Jesse King, bm.

Cornett, George B. & Lidy J. Adams, 17 March 1846; Harvy J. Adams, bm; John Martin, J. P., wit.

Cornwell, Henry & Hannah Critele(?), 8 June 1808; John Consolvy, bm.

Cornwell, Marion & Mary Hall, 13 Oct 1862; R. W. Wright, bm; m 14 Oct 1862 by S. W. Roberts, J. P.

Cotten, Caleb & Nancy Meredith, 16 Nov 1801; Thos. C. Burch, bm; W. Meredith, wit.

SURRY COUNTY MARRIAGES, 1779-1868

Couch, O. L. & Ruthy A. Prather, 23 Oct 1855; m 28 Oct 1855 by D. M. Davis, Methodist minister.

Covey, Reason & Jane Simkins, 20 Feb 1853; Russell Roope, bm; m 20 Feb 1853 by A. Simmons, J. P.

Covington, Thomas & Rebecca Sailes, 12 April 1854; Mason W. Keller, bm; m 12 April 1854 by A. Simmons, J. P.

Cowles, Calvin J. & Temperance M. Duvall, 18 Sept 1844; Jno Banner, bm.

Cox, Ambrus & Elizabeth Sumter, 16 March 1854; Anderson Philips, bm; m 16 March 1854 by A. Simmons, J. P.

Cox, Andrew J. & Christena Dalton, 8 Oct 1865; Ballwod P. Cox, bm; m 8 Oct 1865 by R. F. McGuffin, J. P.

Cox, Bedford B. & Mary S. Thompson, 9 Sept 1867; m 10 Sept 1867 by J. N. Barker, Parson.

Cox, Elias & Silva Williams, 15 Dec 1844; Ely Williams, bm.

Cox, Henry & Prudence Simmons, 29 Aug 1820; John Cook, bm; Tho. A. Word, wit.

Cox, Isham & Catharine Care, (no date); John Martin, bm; Jo. Winston, wit.

Cox, Isham & Martha Holt, 17 Jan 1866; J. M. Cox, bm.

Cox, J. M. & Martha Perkins, 11 Sept 1855; H. Denny, bm; m 16 Sept 1855 by William Hill, J. P.

Cox, John H. & Jane George, 15 Sept 1855; m 16 Sept 1855 by William Hill, J. P.

Cox, Loven & Nancy Philips, 20 Nov 1847; Anderson Philips, bm.

Cox, Mahlon & Catherine Mackey, 28 Feb 1813; Robert Mackie, bm.

Cox, Solomon & Julyatha Cox, 27 Nov 1784; Samuel Brown, bm.

Cox, Washington & Faitha Haymore, 22 Dec 1853; Bluman Haymore, bm; m 22 Dec 1853 by Wm. Haymore, J. P.

Cox, Wilcher & Caroline Franklin, 1 Feb 1855; Harvey Denney, bm.

Cox, William T. & Martha A. Satterfield, 20 Sept 1858; Elisha Barnes, bm; m 20 Sept 1858 by Jesse Roberts, M. G.

Cozort, William C. & Polly Haines, 2 Aug 1828; David Holcomb, bm.

Craft, Nathan & Mary Padgett, 1 Dec 1827; Jacob C. Padgett, bm.

Craft, Nathan & Margaret Tucker, 3 June 1835; Josiah Cowles, bm; Robt C. Duvall, wit.

Craft, Thomas & Summervill Hudson, 17 Sept 1823; Nicholas Miller, bm.

Craft, Wiley & Augathee Sparks, 28 Jan 1812; Allen Sisk, bm.

Crafton, Williamson & Martha P. Draper, 20 July 1848; Drury D. Tiller, bm.

Craig, Alexander & Milley White, 6 Nov 1789; Allen Chapman, bm.

Craige, Robert & Jemimah Bray, 6 March 1825; Moses Bray, bm.

Cranfield, Isaac & Polly Jindkins, 25 Nov 1838; Henry Jinkins, bm.

Cranfill, John & Rebecca Brown, 15 March 1828; John Garner, bm.

Crause, John & Nancy Burcham, 20 July 1825; Landon Armstrong, bm.

Crawford, John & _____, 5 March 1867; Santifr Smith, bm.

Crawford, John H. & Julia A. Caudle, 27 Nov 1855; John Black, bm; m 27 Nov 1855 by A. Simmons, J. P.

Crawford, Thomas & Unica Evans, 4 July 1807; Jacob Eastrap, bm; consent from William Grayham for his daughter Unica Evans, 4 July 1807.

Crawley, Samuel & Elizabeth Morris, 3 Dec 1788; Nathaniel Morris, bm.

Creasy, Walter S. & Edith E. Sparger, 29 Oct 1867; Allen J. Sparger, bm; m 25 April 1868 by R. T. N. Stephenson.

Creasy, James D. & Caroline Smith, 7 Feb 1866; m 8 Feb 1866 by William _____.

Creed, Anderson & Martha A. Durham, 13 Oct 1867; m 13 Oct 1867 by C. L. Banner, J. P.

Creed, Bartlett & Sarah Philips, 8 Jan 1787; Joseph Philips, bm.

Creed, Bennett & Marthy Dunagin, 7 Sept 1832; Samuel Moore, bm.

Creed, Colby & Rebecca Moore, 13 March 1809; Bennet Creed, bm.

Creed, Edward, son of Bennet & Mary Creed, & Mary Rainey, daughter of Joseph & Matilda Rainey, m 3 March 1868 by Thos. J. Law, M. G.

Creed, E. M. & Mary Holder, 24 Feb 1853; Richard Hill, bm; m 24 Feb 1853 by Martin P---, J. P.

Creed, Enoch & Elizabeth Stone, 20 Jan 1840; Colly C. Gorden, bm.

Creed, Enoch & Margaret Coudle, 17 Feb 1844; Benjamin Scott, bm.

Creed, George W. & Lydia Laffoon, 15 June 1849; Warren Galaspie, bm; m 17 June 1847 by William Laffoon, J. P.

Creed, John & Sarah Ann Durham, 25 Dec 1866; Enoch Creed, bm.

Creed, King & Sally Hodges, 30 Sept 1845; Lazes Creed, bm.

Creed, Lazarus & Winny Nichols, 20 Dec 1838; Robert Moore, bm.

SURRY COUNTY MARRIAGES, 1779-1868

Creed, Meshack & Susanna McDaniel, 4 Jan 1831; Hickman Isbell, bm.

Creson, Abram & Mary Lewis, 13 Aug 1788; Jo. Williams, bm; Jno Goode, wit.

Cresor, Charles & Elizabeth Rosh, 1 Aug 1830; Charles H. Center, bm.

Creson, George & Unius Hadley, 7 July 1817; Thomas Kelly, bm.

Creson, Joshaway & Mary Young, 16 March 1807; Abraham Creson, bm.

Creson, Joshua & Rebekah Hardin, 27 June 1814; Abraham Creson, bm.

Creson, Joshua C. & Mary Rash, 8 June 1847; Charles A. Joyner, bm.

Creson, William & Mary Bowen, 26 May 1812; Thos. D. Kelly, bm.

Creekmore, Nicholas & Elizabeth Hinshaw, 13 March 1828; Caleb Creekmore, bm; Polly Wright, wit.

Crickmore, William & Susan Edmons, 29 Dec 1828; Nicolas Creekmore, bm; Polly Wright, wit.

Crigger, Micael & Sophena Williams, 5 June 1854; L. A. McCollum, bm; m 5 June 1854 by A. Simmons, J. P.

Crisley, George W. & Elcy M. Farmer, 28 June 1854; m 28 June 1854 by A. Simmons, J. P.

Crisley, Samuel & Seany Wheler, 21 Jan 1855; G. H. Booker, bm; m 21 Jan 1855 by A. Simmons, J. P.

Crismon, A. J. & Francis Hicks, 30 Aug 1854; Ellis Smith, bm; Wm. Haymore, wit; m 30 Aug 1854 by Wm. Haymore, J. P.

Cristy, Joseph & Hannah Mullis, 20 March 1822; Thomas Forcum, bm; Polly Wright, wit.

Critchfield, Amos & Lydda Cooms, 27 Aug 1783; James Jones Jr., bm.

Critchfield, Ira & Mary Reece, 22 Oct 1830; Joel Reece, bm.

Critchfield, Jesse & Mary Ann Mankins, 27 March 1849; Joseph S. Greenwood, bm.

Critchfield, Palmer & Rebecca Mallet, 13 Aug 1783; Michael Hend----, bm.

Critchfield, Richard & Nancy Bowles, 9 March 1863; D. M. Cooper, bm; m 9 March 1863 by L. J. Stanly, J. P.

Critchfield, Richard & Sarah Franklin, 6 Nov 1822; Abraham Reece, bm.

Crocket, Ephraim D. & Seluda Ellison, 25 June 1833; Jackson Carter, bm.

Crockett, Ephraim D. & Mary M. Boyd, 12 Nov 1855; John Bowden, bm.

SURRY COUNTY MARRIAGES, 1779-1868

Crockett, Robert M. & America J. Corchern, 2 Dec 1852; J. B. Dosson, bm.

Croford, John & Dolly Ann Bowman, 3 March 1867; m 3 March 1867 by Murlin Sparger, J. P.

Crook, Sampson W. & Senca Low, 26 Nov 1836; John Richerson, bm.

Crotts, John & Maria B. Easter, 9 July 1846; Lewis Forkner, bm.

Crouse, Edwin & Lucy Gorden, 22 July 1866; m by Joel Denny, J.P.

Crouse, Henry & Henrietta Shoup, 20 Aug 1836; Edward F. Lovill, bm.

Crouse, Shuble B., son of John and Nancy Crouse, & Nancy Crouse, daughter of Henry and Henrietta Crouse, 4 Feb 1868; m 14 Feb 1868 by Joel Denny, J. P.

Crow, Hiram & Margaret Norman, m 30 Dec 1858 by Reuben Sparks, D. L.

Crowder, Madison & Frances Bratton, 2 Aug 1856; Stephen Bell, bm.

Crumel, John & Elizabeth Evans, 5 April 1838; Emanuel Alspaugh, bm.

Crumel, William & Rebecca Wright, 5 June 1831; Thos York, bm.

Crumpler, Thomas & Miss Esther Swann, 14 Sept 1856; John M. Nicholson, bm.

Crumpler, Thomas & Elizabeth J. Parks, 9 May 1831; Richard H. Parks, bm.

Crumply, Eli & Rossey Davis, 19 Aug 1839; Iredell Davis, bm.

Culler, A. A. & Mary Booze, 4 March 1861; m 4 March 1861 by J. A. Lovill, J. P.

Culler, Alexander & Rebecca Howlit, 12 Sept 1854; William H. Savage, bm.

Culler, Constantine & Martha E. Scott, 18 Oct 1858; L. W. Hauser, bm; m 21 Oct 1858 by Sam Scott, J. P.

Culler, John W. & Margaret Marshall, 9 Oct 1850; Francis J. Marion, bm. (C. H.).

Cumbo, George & Catharine Cummings, 9 May 1832; Thomas Wood, bm.

Cummings, Alphius, son of Isaac & Naomi Cummings, & Louisa E. Williamson, daughter of William and Ruth Williamson, m 29 March 1868 by J. E. Turner, J. Peace.

Cummings, George W. & Elizabeth C. Young, 23 Oct 1856; Cicero Williams, bm.

Cummings, J. W. & Mary E. Tate, 26 Dec 1865; Wm. H. Calloway, bm; m 28 Dec 1865 by R. F. McGuffin, J. P.

Cummins, Jno & Penelope Clutton, 27 June 1831; Joseph Fulk, bm.

Cummins, Moses & Margaret Morgan, 17 March 1792; Edmund Adams, bm.

SURRY COUNTY MARRIAGES, 1779-1868

Cummins, Moses & Sally Bowden, 24 Feb 1821; Marmaduke Kimbrough, bm.

Cummins, Thomas & Nancy Philips, 22 July 1792; Edmund Adams, bm.

Cundiff, J. T. & Malinda Harmon, m 10 Feb 1867 by Martin Sparger, J. Peace.

Cunningham, Abraham & Nancy Groce, 23 June 1819; George Steelmon, bm.

Cunningham, John & Elizabeth Pinion, 7 May 1819; Jacob Donathan, bm.

Cunningham, John & Mary Groce, 24 Nov 1819; George Steelman, bm.

Cunningham, Nicholas F. & Christina Chrissman, 17 Jan 1854; A. T. Crissman, bm.

Cunningham, Richard & Elizabeth Franklin, 18 Feb 1833; Nicholas Freeman, bm.

Cunningham, Wm. F. & Nancy Moody, 7 Sept 1864; J. E. Reeves, Pleasant Hodges, bm; m 7 Sept 1864 by Geo. A. Jervis, J.P.

Curby, Jesse & Sarah Muncus, 24 May 1820; Henry Muncus, bm.

Curd, James & Abigal Stewart, 12 July 1786; John Lynch, bm; Robt Williams, wit.

Cuthrell, James & Nancy James, m 10 April 1851 by David W. Doub.

Dagg, Peter & Nancy Jinkins, 5 Aug 1793; Moses Cummins, bm.

Dalton, Jonathan & Sally Bird, 11 May 1813; Nathl. Lash, of Stokes Co., bm.

Daniel, A. J. & Levina Escue, 22 Feb 1844; E. Banner, bm.

Daniel, Thomas & Ann Reece, 14 Sept 1823; Edward Reece, bm.

Danily, Isaac & Martha Woten, 10 Oct 1813; Hanan Bray, bm.

Danley, Newton, son of William & Sarah Danley, and Stacy Draughn, daughter of William and Nancy Draughn, m __ Dec 1867 by Solomon Long.

Danly, Thomas J. & Mahala Johnson, 20 Dec 1855; Henry Johnson, bm; m 23 Dec 1855 by J. W. Flippen, J. P.

Danner, Adam & Susannah G. Liggon, 21 Feb 1818; Sterling Gregory, bm.

Dannar, John & Sarah Gregory, 5 June 1817; Sterling Gregory, bm.

Danner, Samuel & Margaret Batey, 29 Aug 1829; B. J. _____, bm.

Dannely, William & Sarah Bryant, 8 Sept 1835; Richd Beeson, bm.

Darnall, Augustin & Sally Sisk, 1 Dec 1855.

Dause, Dennis & Elizabeth Vestal, 24 Feb 1824; Joseph Bringar, bm.

SURRY COUNTY MARRIAGES, 1779-1868

Daughhety, Samuel & Mary Adkins, 18 Jan 1785; Timothy Coe, bm.

Davenport, J. T., son of A. and Rebecca Davenport & C. H. Blackwood, daughter of N. H. and Mary Blackwood, m 23 Nov 1868 by D. C. Stinson.

Davies, Gabriel & Barbara Long, 17 Aug 1787; Thomas Clanton, Edward Clanton, bm.

Davis, Adison & Eliza Worth, 11 March 1848; N. H. Blackwood, bm.

Davis, Anderson & Mary Ann Chipwash, 9 June 1849; Benjamin J. Hutchins, bm.

Davis, Andrew J. & Norah Alleman, 29 March 1838; Sterling Taylor, bm.

Davis, Caleb & Lydia Bartlett, 4 Jan 1814; Thomas Coe, bm.

Davis, Charles & Bridgett Hadly, 24 Feb 1816; John Hickmon, bm.

Davis, Daniel & Polly Tull, 29 Dec 1811.

Davis, Daniel & Elizabeth Cockerham, 8 Dec 1818; Daniel Bills (son of Gersham), bm.

Davis, Darias & Jestin Stoneman, 13 Dec 1855.

Davis, David B. & Crissy Peel, 23 March 1835; Ralph Barton, bm.

Davis, Drury K. & Miss Jane Snow, 29 April 1854; Samuel Jones (Min), bm; m by Wilson Laffoon.

Davis, Haston & Margaret Moore, 18 March 1849; J. Martain Davis, bm.

Davis, Elijah & Susannah Taylor, 27 Nov 1828; Edmund Wooton, bm.

Davis, Evan & Rebecah Marshal, 29 March 1818; Jona. Unthank, bm.

Davis, Evan & Hannah Gardner, 4 Nov 1831; H. D. Armstrong, bm.

Davis, Ezra & Ellenor Hadly, 26 July 1819; Jacob Davis, bm.

Davis, George & Nancy Shinn, 13 Oct 1829; Asa Lewis, bm.

Davis, Henry & Sela Carter, 26 July 1802; James Carter, bm.

Davis, Hewly C. & Mahala Edwards, m 7 Oct 1855 by B. F. Scott, J. P.

Davis, Hugh & Sally Hoppis, 30 March 1815; Charles Steelman, son of George, & Edward Hoppis, bm.

Davis, Iredell & Martha A. Fleming, 15 July 1839; W. P. Tucker, bm.

Davis, Isaac & Prisciler Newton, 22 Jan 1846; Timothy Joiner, bm.

Davis, Jacob & _____, ---- 180-; Chas. Taliaferro, bm; Betsey Taliaferro, wit.

Davis, Jacob & Lucy Rose, (no date).

49

Davis, James & Elizabeth Veneable, 26 May 1821; Bracer Linvell, bm.

Davis, James & Carney Gorgiss, 23 Aug 1835; George Davis, bm.

Davis, James & Jane Reece, 26 Sept 1846; Jno Davis, bm.

Davis, James W. & Edna J. Smith, 28 Nov 1854; Ice Snow, bm; m by Jesse Roberts.

Davis, James W. & Mary E. Turner, 20 Aug 1862; Joseph Loyd, bm; m 20 Aug 1862 by James H. Lewellin, Minister.

Davis, Jeremiah & Sally Adams, 3 April 1856.

Davis, Jesse & Elizabeth Jackson, 12 July 1832; Blewmon Haymore, bm.

Davis, Joel & Jane Martin, 5 Jan 1817; Joel Carlton, bm.

Davis, John & Rachael Scaggs, 22 Nov 1784; Henry Scaggs, bm.

Davis, Jno & Elizabeth Jervis, 23 May 1810.

Davis, John & Nancy Davis, 27 Jan 1811; Jas. McCraw, bm.

Davis, John Junr & Catharine Shugart, 2 Nov 1822; Daniel Davis, bm.

Davis, John & Jane Lovell, 29 Dec 1818; James Lovell, bm.

Davis, John W. & Amanda Meskeep, 8 July 1848; David M. Gibson, bm.

Davis, Jonathan & Patience Kerzy, 5 Feb 1809; John Seagroves, bm.

Davis, Jonathan & Rachel Fleming, 13 Nov 1833; Joel Hutchens, bm.

Davis, Jonathan & Mary Cunningham, 10 Nov 1839; Drury Hodges, bm.

Davis, Jonathan & Jane Taylor, 9 Nov 1859; William Parker, bm.

Davis, Jonathan & Rebecca Ann Fulks, 8 April 1867; Jesse G. Jervis, bm; m 11 April 1867 by S. J. Lawson, M. G.

Davis, Joseph & Catharine Farmer (no date); Jacob Davis, bm.

Davis, Joseph & Rebeca Cob, 2 April 1833; Wm. A. Stewart, bm.

Davis, Joseph S. & Emily Eastwood, 26 Nov 1852; John H. Crawford, bm.

Davis, Lemuel J. & Axa Vestal, 22 Oct 1837; James Reece, bm.

Davis, Luckel & Jershia Mosley, 1 Sept 1797.

Davis, Morris & Sarah McCane, 1 April 1812; David McCane, bm; Gardner J. Grant, wit.

Davis, Reece & Patsey Childers, 18 Aug 1823; Colwel P. Shipp, bm.

SURRY COUNTY MARRIAGES, 1779-1868

Davis, Richard M. & Martha H. Fulks, 25 June 1853; Harden Hawks, bm; m 30 June 1853 by Martin Pyne, J. P.

Davis, Robert & Bechella Ridings, 25 Dec 1826; Francis Vest, bm.

Davis, Saml & _____, 4 Sept 1803; L. Davis, Jno Kelly, bm.

Davis, Sandy, son of Patrick & Susan Davis, & Mary McKinney, m 26 Dec 1868 by Thomas School, J. P.

Davis, Simon & Abbey Freeman, 27 Aug 1813; John Davis, bm.

Davis, Thomas & Elizabeth Hutchins, 29 March 1813; George Adams, bm.

Davis, Thomas & Betsey Golding, 27 Oct 1819; Eli Cook, bm.

Davis, Thomas & Nancy Kelly, 3 Aug 1822; Robert Carson, bm.

Davis, Thomas & Elizabeth D. Veach, 14 May 1831; Absolem T. Kerr, bm.

Davis, Thomas & Emily Koger, 28 Oct 1866; m 28 Oct 1866 by A. Simmons, J. P.

Davis, Thomas D. & Hannah Smith, 7 Jan 1860.

Davis, Tolaver & Penelope Davis, 27 July 1786; Pouncey Michel, bm.

Davis, Uriah & Rebecky Emily Hugent, 25 Aug 1855.

Davis, Warren & Matilda Thorp, 7 Feb 1850; Alford Zachary, bm. (C. H.).

Davis, William & Ann Hutchens, 20 Jan 1810; Robert Bartley, bm.

Davis, William & Rebeca Somes, 8 Sept 1816; Edward Hoppers, bm.

Davis, William & Pheby Isbell, 22 Feb 1817; Hickmon Isbell, bm.

Davis, Wm & Nancy Winfrey, 15 Sept 1838; Nathan Bond, bm.

Davis, William & Margaret Ann Bohanon, 30 March 1847; Wm. H. Speer, bm.

Davis, William E. & Arbella Hill, 22 Dec 1853; Hardin E. Davis, bm; m 23 Dec 1853 by James Needham.

Davis, William H. & Mary Jane Simmons, 22 Aug 1860.

Davis, Wm. R. & M. Jane Tate, 14 Jan 1868; James M. Snow, bm; m 16 Jan 1868 by Richard J. Pilson, J. P.

Day, David & Lucy Windsor, 31 Jan 1835; William W. Windsor, bm.

Day, Elliott & Melinda Elmore, 15 Dec 1831; Moses Austill, bm; Polly Wright, wit.

Day, James & _____, (no date); Namrod Elliott, bm.

Day, John & Priscilla Swaim, 3 March 1830; David Day, bm.

Day, John A. & Phebe E. Woodruff, 22 Jan 1867; Sinclair J. McMickle, bm; m 22 Jan 1867 by Joel Hurt, J. P.

SURRY COUNTY MARRIAGES, 1779-1868

Day, Samuel & Jincey Padgett, 12 April 1836; Daniel Arnold, bm.

Day, Triplet & Elizabeth Swaim, 29 Feb 1844; Ephraim L. Hamby, bm.

Day, Warren & Rachael Swaim, 5 Aug 1835; John Day, bm.

Day, William & Nancy Triplett, 8 Jan 1810; James Day, bm.

Dean, Alfred W., son of James D. & Esther Dean, and Margaret M. Gwynn, daughter of Franklin & Martha Gwynn, m 27 Dec 1868 by W. H. Beamer.

Dean, Calvin R. & Charity L. C. Moser, 6 March 1861.

Dean, Lorenzo D. & Mary Walk, 23 Dec 1854; Henry H. Dean, bm; m 23 Dec 1854 by A. Simmons, J. P.

Deatherage, Achillis & Betsey Taliafero, _____, 180-; Chs. Taliaferro, bm.

Deatherge, James A. & Ruth J. Sweptin, 11 Jan 1862; James Bullin, bm; m 16 Jan 1862 by Wm. R. Bray, J. P.

Deatheridge, John & Eleanor Childress, 11 Jan 1833; William Shelton, bm.

Deavenport, Elisha & Elizabeth Minten, 4 Dec 1821; Welcum Garrett, bm. (C. H.).

Detherage, Robert & Mariah C. Hall, 16 Nov 1846; J. A. Bingman, bm.

Deatherge, William & Sally Jackson, 17 July 1834; J. M. Richardson, bm.

Deboard, John & Emily Somers, 18 May 1831; James Sprinkle, bm.

Deboard, John & Martha Edwards, 13 Jan 1795.

Debord, George & Lydia Debord, 8 Nov 1803; Ben Debord, bm.

Decamp, John & Rirlina Dunkin, 29 May 1848; Allen Denny, bm.

Defrees, David & Nansey Low, 15 Aug 1808; Moses Harvill, bm.

Dehaven, Isaac W. & Chestenia Stockner, 14 Aug 1862; James Leftwick, bm; m 14 Aug 1862 by Wm. R. Bray, J. P.

Denney, Jason & Caroline Windsor, 7 July 1849; William H. Windsor, bm.

Denny, Jourdan & Martha Burcham, 8 May 1818; Josiah Vandepool, bm.

Denney, William & Elizabeth Hoffman, 9 Oct 1833; Jno. P. Douthit, bm.

Dennis, George C. & Phebe E. Peters, 1 Oct 1855; James H. Bonham, bm; m 1 Oct 1855 by A. Simmons, J. P.

Denny, Achillas M. & Louisa E. Ashburn, 1 Oct 1867.

Denny, Azariah & Betsy Stone, 23 Oct 1810; Charles Herrin, bm.

SURRY COUNTY MARRIAGES, 1779-1868

Denny, C. B. & A. E. Gorden, 12 Dec 1866; John Denny, bm.

Denny, Edmond & Sarah Johnson, 25 Jan 1821; Josiah Cowles, bm.

Denny, Elbert & Lucy A. Madison, 9 Feb 1847; East Mosely, bm; John Madison, bm. (two bonds).

Denny, Eli & Margaret H. Doak, 22 Jan 1850.

Denny, Gabriel, son of Joel and Nancy Denny, & Sarah Delphina B. Stone, daughter of Francis R. and Sarah C. Stone, m 14 June 1868 at the residence of Francis R. Stone in Surry Co., by John Jones.

Denny, George & Elizabeth Wells, 9 March 1823; Edmond Denny, bm.

Denny, Harvey & Rebecca Fulk, 5 Jan 1838; Lendry Key, bm.

Denny, Jessy & Poley Crouse, 27 March 1820; Allin Sisk, bm. (C. H.).

Denny, Joel & Nancy B. Jones, 31 Dec 1838; John Jones, bm.

Denny, John & Elizabeth Edgington, 9 Nov 1804.

Denny, John & Laura Stolts, 1 March 1867; Gabriel Denny, bm; m 28 March 1867 by John Jones at the house of Daniel Stults.

Denny, Jorden & Polly Gibson, 14 March 1832; E. Vanderpool, bm.

Denny, Martin & Peggy Wilkerson, 9 April 1816; Stephen Wood, Jun., bm.

Denny, Samuel & Elizabeth Wooten, 10 Feb 1793; Nathan Meeks, bm.

Denny, Stephen & Elizabeth Windsor, 15 Jan 1820; Aquilla Windsor, bm.

Denny, Stephen & Susan Wishon, 23 May 1845; John Ball, bm.

Denny, Willam & Nancy Fulk, 5 Nov 1813; Jacob Fulk, bm.

Denson, Thomas & Martha Doss, persons of color, 16 Feb 1867; Henry Adams, bm.

Denton, Jerry & Jane Loftice, 26 Jan 1850; Allgias Dunnagan, bm.

Desern, Elijah & Sarah Harrison, 23 March 1814; William Merrion, bm.

Desern, Elijah & Nancy Campbell, 1 July 1813; Ephraim Desern, bm.

Desern, Reuben & Phebe Farington, 24 Jan 1829; William Coe, bm.

Devenport, Absalom & Rebecca Nichols, 5 May 1845; David Reed, bm.

Devenport, John and Sarah Elder, 22 Dec 1795.

Desern, Elijah & Anna Jackson, 22 May 1832; M. Morison(?), bm.

Dezern, Ephraim & Catherine Gibbens, 17 Nov 1846; John Moore, bm.

53

SURRY COUNTY MARRIAGES, 1779-1868

Dezern, Jesse & Nancy Brown, 15 June 1828; Jacob Donathan, bm.

Dial, Daniel & Roddy Martin, 27 March 1828; Jones Dial, bm.

Dial, James & Martha Martin, 7 Aug 1827; Jesse Flemming, bm.

Dial, Shadrach & Susanah Read, 18 March 1803; Jesse Bryan, bm.

Dick, Thomas M. & Elizabeth Jones, 21 June 1849; Samuel Jones, bm.

Dicken, Albert & Jincy Johnson, 18 March 1854; Herron Gaigean, bm; m 18 March 1854 by John Ramey, J. P.

Dicken, Julius & Betsey Gallion, 11 Feb 1818; Young Gallion, bm.

Dicken, Benjamin & Luvisy Bean, 22 Jan 1853; Ambrose Dicken, bm; m by Wm Hodges, J. P.

Dicken, Samuel & Amy Hodges, 27 Oct 1850; Thomas Nation, bm. (C. H.).

Dicken, Thomas & Susan Hodges, 30 Nov 1853; Jackson Low, bm.

Dickens, Daniel & Leacy Jane Johnson, 21 Nov 1849; Preston Hodges, bm.

Dickens, Ephraim & Syannah Philips, 1 Feb 1847; Ransom Dickens, bm.

Dickens, Etheldred & Elizabeth Crook, 10 March 1827; Hardin P. Franklin, bm.

Dickens, Jonathan & Mary Hurst, 21 Aug 1838; John Jackson, bm.

Dickens, Thomas & Milly Maberry, 10 July 1857; Reuben Dickens, bm; m 10 July 1857 by A. Dunnagan, J. P.

Dickerson, James & Catherine Logan, 17 Aug 1832; William Bowen (?), bm.

Dickerson, James & Sarah Stow, 8 Oct 1845; Sheriden S. Arnold, bm.

Dickerson, Stephen & Margarett Pratt, 17 Sept 1817; Elisha Pratt, bm.

Dickerson, William & Sally Caudle, 17 July 1817; Thos Brown, bm.

Dickerson, William & Peggy Hickman, 17 Aug 1826; Jesse Brown, bm.

Dickson, David & Becky Steelman, 27 Dec 1826; Knesel Vestal, bm.

Dickson, John & Mary Skidmore, 5 Oct 1806; Benjamin Brown, bm.

Dickson, William & Easter Rilly, 7 April 1821; John Skidmore, bm.

Dickson, William & Lezebeth Brown, 21 Dec 1802; David Welch, bm.

Dillard, Isaac & Judith Lindsey, 11 Jan 1808.

SURRY COUNTY MARRIAGES, 1779-1868

Dillard, Jno & Frances Miller, 8 June 1807.

Dillion, John & Martha Evans, 24 Aug 1838; Andrew Evans, bm.

Dingler, Samuel D. & Mary Noling, 7 Oct 1826; James Gadberry, bm.

Dinkins, Franklin & Mehaly Hutchins, 7 Jan 1846; Cary Warden, bm.

Dinkins, Chapman & Lidy Bovender, 9 April 1846; John Gregory, bm.

Dinkins, John & Viney Keaten, 10 Oct 1815; Daniel Pilcher, bm.

Dinkins, John & Martha C. Joyner, 3 April 1833; Saml Spilman, bm.

Dinkins, John H. & Elisebeth Adams, 6 March 1845; Hugh Brown, bm.

Dinkins, Samuel & Rachel Joyner, 8 Jan 1831; Sabird Dinkins, bm.

Dinkins, William & Betsy Russell, 12 Aug 1820; Talbert Russell, bm.

Dinsmore, James & Tabitha Johnson, 4 Jan 1819; Thomas Stanley, bm.

Dishons, Newton & Mary Buckley, 9 July 1848; Logan D. Roberts, bm.

Dixon, Abraham & Martha Joyner, 18 July 1829; M. Hudspeth, bm.

Dixon, Henry S. & Elizabeth Jane Williams, 17 Dec 1846; Richard S. Philips, bm.

Dixon, John & Elizabeth Hill, 4 Sept 1827; Alexander D. Kelly, bm.

Dixson, James & Sary Langeley, 10 June 1832; Jacob Brewbaker, bm.

Dobbins, Abraham & Catherine Baker, 22 Nov 1818; Thomas H. Reece, bm.

Dobbins, Jacob & Sarah Speer, 24 April 1808.

Dobbins, Jacob Jun. & Jane Carter, 19 April 1825; Zechariah Reece, bm.

Dobbins, Joel & Sarah Carter, 11 March 1839; William Reece, bm.

Dobbins, John & Elizabeth Cavender, 6 Oct 1831; Abraham Dobbins, bm.

Dobbins, Joshua & Nancy Farmer, 11 Dec 1814; Simon Marshal, bm.

Dobbins, Joshua & Susanna Burcham, 10 May 1831; Abraham Reece, bm.

Dobbins, Nathan & Vestal Calloway, 30 Sept 1847; William A. Gennings, bm.

SURRY COUNTY MARRIAGES, 1779-1868

Dobbins, Pleasant & Elizabeth Carter, 14 Aug 1837; Wilson Reece, bm.

Dobbins, Thos & Delina Noling, 11 Aug 1812; James Callaway, bm.

Dobbins, William & Rebeca Burcham, 19 Nov 1836; Abner Fuller, bm.

Dodson, Alexander & Elizabeth Roberts, 21 Jan 1823; John McGilvary, bm.

Dobson, Dandy & Lucinda Dobson (colored), 13 Aug 1867; Dandy is the son of Sucky Dobson, his father unknown, Lucinda is the daughter of Charles Bowles, her mothers name was Lucinda, formerly the property of J. H. Dobson, P. Worth, J. P.

Dobson, Joseph & Sally Jane Hamlin, 22 Feb 1853; Jno M. Cloud, bm; m 22 Feb 1853 by A. Roby, minister.

Dockery, Saml & Eatha M. Gates, 29 Oct 1860; Rich. Martin, bm; m 30 Oct 1860 by Lacy Snow, J. P.

Dodge, James R. & Susan Williams, 24 May 1826; A. H. Sherbert, bm.

Dodson, Elias & Sally Gelaspie, 15 Dec 1863; J. H. Mosley, bm; m 15 Dec 1863 by D. A. Eldredge, J. P.

Dodson, Reuben & Agness Whitlock, 10 Feb 1780.

Dol, David & _____, 13 April 1783.

Dolehide, Andrew & Nancy Johnson, 26 Jan 1867; Squire Johnson, bm.

Dolehide, Samuel & Mary Shelton, 14 July 1859; Wm. F. Shelton, bm.

Doll, Abraham & Margaret Smith, 4 Dec 1804; John Hoihst, bm.

Doll, Daniel & Polly Purdan, 6 March 1804; Fridrik Binkley, bm.

Doll, Frederick & Alha Elrode, 3 Feb 1789; John Elrode, bm; Robt Williams, wit.

Dollehide, Samuel & Polly Johnson, 11 Jan 1826; Jonathan Taylor, bm.

Dolton, William & Mariah Dolton, 12 March 1838; Thomas Hall, bm.

Donothan, Benjamin & Reany Mitchell, 16 Jan 1837; Jesse Reeves, bm.

Donathan, Jacob & Parthenia Donathan, 29 Aug 1865; Wm Mooney, bm; m 30 Aug 1865 by _____.

Donathan, Larken & Viney Holyfield, 4 Feb 1840; Wm. D. Somers, bm.

Donathan, Lewis H. & Julia Chesher, persons of doubtful color, 24 Aug 1867.

Donnell, Morrison & Evalina H. Wall, 14 Dec 1833; John B. Edmondson, bm.

SURRY COUNTY MARRIAGES, 1779-1868

Donnelly, Thos & Mary Smith, 15 Dec 1791.

Doran, Michael & Welthy Taylor, 4 Feb 1863; James R. Fulford, bm; m 4 Feb 1863 by A. Simmons, J. P.

Dornall, Bryson & Harriett Hough, 5 Jan 1838; Orvis Bartlett, bm.

Doss, Gabriel & Frances Greenwood, freed people, 28 Dec 1866; William Norman, bm; m 28 Dec 1863 by A. Simmons, J. P.

Doss, Henry & Caroline Aakins, 22 Oct 1835; Michael Idell, bm.

Doss, James & Fanny Waff, 15 April 1854; Jacob Collins, bm; m 15 April 1854 by A. Simmons, J. P.

Doss, John P. & Nancy E. Logan, 31 March 1847; Richard S. Phillips, bm.

Doss, Martin & Susan Allgood, 23 Jan 1853; R. H. Allgood, bm; m 23 Jan 1853 by W. W. Wolff, J. P.

Doss, Ruell & Amy Bray, 14 Aug 1857; Litell Adkin, bm; m 16 Aug 1857 by J. J. Norman, J. P.

Doss, Thomas Jefferson & Elizabeth Holyfield, 16 May 1845; William Bullen, bm.

Doss, William & Sarah Philips, 10 Oct 1811; William Phillips, bm.

Doss, William & Barbara Bates, 25 July 1818; Fredrick Dannor (Tannor), bm.

Doss, William & Sabra Wood, 19 April 1847; William Bullen, bm.

Dotson, Eliza & Gemima Frances Holensworth, 2 Nov 1844; James Snow, bm.

Dotson, Lazarus & Celia M. Katt, 17 July 1849; John Hagans, bm.

Doudge, Peter & Mary Ann Edmons, 19 March 1832; Simon Reece, bm.

Dougherty, William A. & Sarah A. Dennis, 12 Oct 1852; Crockett Roop, bm. (C. H.).

Douglass, Abraham & Clanpa Rutledge, 13 Feb 1852; William W. Rutledge, bm.

Douglas, Anday & Rebeca Poindexter, 26 Oct 1833; James Flinn, bm.

Douglas, Thos & Martha Martin, 19 April 1789.

Douglas, Thomas & Jane McGlemery, 2 July 1832; E. M. Dobson, bm.

Douglass, Fortuneberry & Jane Hutchens, 23 Aug 1834; William Harding, bm.

Douglass, Thomas & Sally Harris, 4 April 1844; Harrison Thompson, bm.

Douglass, William & Phebe Kennedy, 18 Nov 1824; Thomas Douglass, bm.

57

Douthit, Jacob & Polly Moreland, 26 Nov 1808; Jeremiah Moreland, bm.

Douthit, James & Susannah Howard, 8 Sept 1802; Wm. Howard, bm.

Dowel, John & Mary Jones, 7 Jan 1857; Ambrose M. Johnson, bm; m 1 Jan 1857 by A. Simmons, J. P.

Dowel, Peter & Margaret Martin, 13 Feb 1810; Joel Reese, bm.

Dowel, William & Judith Colbert, 7 March 1844; Lewis F. Madison, bm.

Downaly, Samuel & Anna Cook, 5 April 1786; Peter Downaly, bm.

Downes, Edward & Mariam Jinnings, 27 Feb 1805; George Hunt, bm.

Downey, William & Louisa Davis, 3 Nov 1803; David Cook, bm.

Draper, Alexander & Sarah Coe, 5 Aug 1847; Wm. Coe, bm.

Draper, Alexander & Sarah Coe, 31 Dec 1829; Shadrach Morris, bm.

Draper, Byrd & Sally York, 26 Feb 1825; George Draper, bm.

Draughn, Elias & Elender Reed, 19 Feb 1845; Isaac Wooton, bm.

Draughn, James D. & Sarah F. Creed, 22 Dec 1866; Enoch Creed, bm.

Draughn, John & Hannah Marion, 3 Aug 1837; Robt. R. Brinkley, bm.

Draughn, Martin & Huldah F. Walker, 4 April 1867.

Draughn, Michal & Nancy J. Walker, 25 July 1866; Martin Draughn, bm.

Draughn, William & Emsetta Mchone, 29 July 1858; R. D. R. Moss, bm; m 29 July 1858 by A. Simmons, J. P.

Dudley, Charles & Nancy Money(?), 3 Jan 1846; Samuel Shore, bm.

Dudley, Charles S. & Miss Hariett A. Jinia, 30 Dec 1854; Saml L. Gilmer, bm.

Dudley, Ransom & Jency Lyon, 26 April 1818; John Davis, bm.

Dudley, William & Polly Deatherage, 12 Feb 1820; Jonathan Roberts, bm.

Duglass, William & Rutha Eddleman, 13 Oct 1826; Thomas Duglass, bm.

Dull, William & Sarah Shelton, 30 Jan 1847; S. C. James, bm.

Dunnagan, James & Elizabeth Bowles, 9 Jan 1832; H. C. Bray, bm.

Duncan, John R. & Susan Roberts, 10 July 1854; John R. Patterson, bm.

Duncan, Lewis & Sarah Smith, 30 Aug 1820; Branch Tucker, bm.

Duncan, Rice & Cetture Bowman, 12 Nov 1846; William Bowman, bm.

SURRY COUNTY MARRIAGES, 1779-1868

Dunford, F. M. & Rebeca A. Dearman, 24 Aug 1865; John L. Parris, bm. (C. H.).

Dunigan, Henry & Sarah Richardson, 7 Jan 1863; L. B. Jones, bm; m 8 Jan 1863 by Nathan York, Baptist minister.

Dunigan, Stephen & E. M. Holyfield, 3 Jan 1866; H. D. Stanly, bm; m 4 Jan 1866 by Isaac Davis, minister.

Duning, Noah & Elizabeth Senter, 31 Dec 1850; Azel Williams, bm.

Dunkin, John H. & Katharine Willson, 15 Dec 1850; Francis Collins, bm. (C. H.).

Dunn, Hiram & Nelly Day, 15 Feb 1835; Major Austill, bm.

Dunnagan, Absalom & _____, (no date); Martin Armstrong, bm.

Dunnagan, Anderson & Margaret Jane Prather, 18 May 1848; J. R. Gilmer, bm.

Dunn, Riley & Martha P. Forkner, 19 May 1856.

Dunnagan, James & Nancy Rowark, 8 Dec 1817; Conway Stone, bm; Harden P. Franklin, wit.

Dunnagan, Windham & _____, 180-; John Dunnagan, bm.

Durham, Armstead J. & Hannah Sutfin, 24 Oct 1858; C. L. Bolt, bm.

Durham, James & Elizabeth Summers, 21 Dec 1808; John Parker, bm.

Durham, Micajah & Nancy Sawyers, 15 Feb 1819; Wm Durham, bm.

Durham, Moses & Mary J. Penright, 5 Feb 1850; William Durham, bm.

Durham, William & Rhoda Sawyers, 24 Oct 1815; John Money, bm.

Durham, William & Nancy Penright, 30 Aug 1846; William Holcomb, bm.

Dyre, Joel & Anny Moser, 2 April 1832; F. P. West(?), bm.

Dyson, Wm. C. & Mary Turner, 10 Oct 1833; Geo. Blair, bm.

Eades, Wm. H. & Lucinda Draughon, 1 June 1861; m 4 June 1861 by L. A. Key, J. P.

Earhart, James F. & Phebe Ann Baldwin, 10 April 1853; Denison B. Baldwin, bm; m 10 April 1853 by A. Simmons, J. P.

Earley, Miller W. & America Cox, 16 June 1836; H. P. Franklin, bm.

Early, Sion & Sally Haines, 28 Feb 1816; Micajah Reeves, bm.

Early, C. S. & Lucy Golden, 9 Jan 1834; John Cave, bm.

Early, Joseph & Catey Deatherage, 17 Feb 1785; John Deatherage, bm.

Early Stephen J. & Rebecah Cunningham, 2 Aug 1813; John Snow, bm.

SURRY COUNTY MARRIAGES, 1779-1868

Easley, William & Sarah Smith, 2 Feb 1792; Mallory Smith, bm.

East, Hughs & Rosena Hodge, 10 Aug 1827; Pleasant Venable, bm.

East, John & Mary Burch, 11 Oct 1801; James London, bm.

East, John & Elizabeth Tilley, 18 June 1849; William East, bm.

East, Joseph C. & Jestin Pell, 3 Aug 1814; John East, bm.

Easter, David & Elizabeth Nooncastel, 5 Dec 1848; Michael Nooncastle, bm.

Easter, Levi & Eliza Ann Lenard, 28 March 1854; Michel Ester, bm; m 2 April 1854 by Eld. Hugh Jones.

Easter, Lewis & Catharine Carter, 12 Nov 1848; Michael Nooncaster, bm.

Easter, Michael & Elizabeth Noonkester, 25 Feb 1853; Daniel Easter, bm.

Easter, Robert S. & Huldah A. McCollom, 14 Aug 1866; Jesse Kidd, bm; m 15 Aug 1866 by H. Laffoon, J. P.

Eaton, Calvin & Mary E. J. Strange, 26 Dec 1851; James W. Lawson, bm.

Eaton, H. M. & Mary E. King, 25 Aug 1860; D. Y. Gorden, bm; m 26 Aug 1861 by W. W. Wolff, J. P.

Eaton, J. E. & July F. Fulk, 2 Sept 1863; T. E. Mickey, bm.

Eaton, Peter & Sarah Smith, __ June 1814; Samuel Smith, Junr., bm.

Eaton, Peter & Abitha Harbin, 20 Oct 1807; Jesse Bowden, bm.

Eddlwman, Jacob & Ruth Cain, 9 Sept 1791; Mathias Steelman, bm.

Eddleman, John & Betsy Phillips, 13 Jan 1823; William Douglass, bm.

Edgington, Thomas & Polly Osburn, 26 Aug 1816; James Talbert, bm.

Edlemon, John & Alse Burns, 4 Sept 1786; Peter Edlemon, bm.

Edlemon, Peter & Rachael Elrode, 8 Nov 1784; Robert Elrode, bm.

Edmond, McGowan & Miss Sally Ann Doss, 29 Aug 1855; Litle Adkins, bm.

Edmonds, Isham & Lucy Ann Hawkins, 30 March 1837; Edmund Parker, bm.

Edmonds, Isaac & Charlotte Venable, 16 Feb 1853; H. C. Bray, bm.

Edmonds, James Tyre & Miss Rebecca Johnson, 23 Nov 1856; Iredell Freeman, bm.

Edmonds, John Henry, son of Isham & Lucy A. Edmonds, and Louisa Bowles, daughter of James and Amelia Bowles, m 20 Aug 1868 by John Jones, at the house of sd. Amelia Bowles.

SURRY COUNTY MARRIAGES, 1779-1868

Edmonds, Samuel L., son of Isham & Charlotte Edmonds, & Martha Wood, daughter of Andrew and Lucinda Wood, m 13 Dec 1868 at the house of Andrew Woods, by John Jones.

Edmondson, John S. & Sarah Winningham, 2 Feb 1834; Jno. P. Clingman, bm.

Edmonson, Jno. B. & Sarah Balyjack, 23 June 1837; John C. Dobson, bm.

Edwards, Alexander M. & Malinda J. Melton, 21 Jan 1855; Granville H. Booker, bm; m 21 Jan 1855 by A. Simmons, J. P.

Edwards, Ansel & Nancy Blesing, 16 Sept 1851; Thomas Morrison Deck, bm.

Edwards, Daniel & Lockey Bullen, 14 July 1844; Joseph Edwards, bm.

Edwards, Ebenezer & Lidia Dunagan, 29 May 1848; Logan D. Roberts, bm.

Edwards, Enoch & Rebeckah Moore, 20 Aug 1837; Hance H. Reney, bm.

Edwards, Enock & Hester Ramsey, 1 Jan 1793; Elijah Marlow, bm.

Edwards, William Henry & Elizabeth Edwards, 20 Dec 1862; John Bevel, bm; m 20 Dec 1863 by Wm. Golden, J. P.

Edwards, James & Sarah McCollum, 27 Jan 1808; William Johnson, bm.

Edwards, James & Paulina Johnson, 21 Nov 1844; William Lewis, bm.

Edwards, Jesse M. & Elizabeth Johnson, 15 May 1851; Andrew Burge, bm.

Edwards, John & Nancy Frances Hodges, 17 Dec 1848; William Dickens, bm.

Edwards, John & Katharine Poor, 3 Aug 1851; Walter Akin, bm.

Edwards, John T. & Malinda Payne, 7 Sept 1867; William A. Johnson, bm; m 8 Sept 1867 on the premises of Forrester Booker, the father of female WM Carling, mother of female Elizabeth Carling, the parents of the male not known; F. Booker, J. P.

Edwards, Joseph & Equilly Lawson, 26 June 1844; William Edwards, bm.

Edwards, Levi & Jane Edwards, 22 April 1855; Richard Edwards, bm; m 22 April 1855 by A. Simmons, J. P.

Edwards, Madison & Rodah Tipton, 15 Nov 1849; Asa S. Payne, bm.

Edwards, Richard A. & Sarah Goard, 4 Nov 1855; Anslum Phibbs, bm; m 4 Nov 1855 by A. Simmons, J. P.

Edwards, Stokes & Elisabeth Couch, 26 July 1865; H. M. Waugh, bm; m 26 July 1865 by Jno F. Mitchell(?).

Edwards, Wm & Patsy Johnson, 1 Nov 1820; Willeby Miller, bm.

SURRY COUNTY MARRIAGES, 1779-1868

Edwards, Wm & Keziah Jones, 15 Nov 1820; Etheldred Edwards, bm.

Edwards, William & Sally Haynes, 24 Feb 1848; Stephen Haynes, bm; Wm. M. Nance, wit.

Edwards, Wm A. & Obeda Coe, 14 Feb 1865; m 14 Feb 1865 by G. A. McCraw, J. P.

Edwards, William W. & Martha Dejournett, 7 Oct 1834; William C. Deyournett, bm.

Elder, Peter & Sarah Savage, 10 April 1804; Kendal Savage, bm.

Elder, William & Mary Devenport, 5 Jan 1800; Thomas Robinson, bm.

Eldridge, Daniel & Maryann McMickle, 7 Aug 1854; John B. Eldridge, bm; D. R. Cockerham, J. P., wit.

Elison, Tirus & Nancy Stone, 31 March 1820; Ephraim Stone, bm.

Elliott, John & Mary Lynch, 10 Oct 1810; William Cook, bm.

Elliott, Martin & Elizabeth M. Long, 26 March 1856; Michael S. Poff, bm.

Elliott, Washington & Polly Pinix, 25 Feb 1805; Jed Long, bm.

Ellis, Daniel & Sally Butcher, 29 Sept 1844; Anderson Dunnagan, bm.

Ellis, Henderson & Mary Venable, 31 Dec 1845; Nicholas Brickell, bm.

Ellis, Henderson & Miss Alcy Gentry, 5 May 1855; Williamson E. Haymore, bm; m 6 May 1855 by John Hamlin, J. P.

Ellis, John & Elizabeth Smith, 18 Feb 1836; Edward M. Dobson, bm.

Ellis, Thomas & Sally Morten, 9 July 1836; John Martin, bm.

Ellis, William B. & Mary Taylor, 24 Feb 1836; Thomas B. Roberts, bm.

Ellis, Winston & Sarah Butcher, 16 Nov 1844; Chatwell Butcher, bm.

Elrod, Adam & _____, 21 Feb 1785; Adam Elrod, bm; Robert Williams, wit.

Elrode, Abraham & Margery Stenton, 10 Nov 1788; Christopher Stenton, bm.

Elrode, Jeremiah & Mary Null, 19 Sept 1785; Peter Elrode, bm.

Elrode, John & Sarah Riddle, 11 Jan 1786; John Winscott, bm.

Elrode, Joseph, of Rowan County, & Rosa Bearrod, 4 Jan 1811; Christopher Elrode of Rowan Co., bm.

Elsbery, John & Permealia Husbands, 26 Feb 1799; John Anthony, bm.

Ennis, Anderson & Polly Goin, 23 Sept 1827; William East, bm.

SURRY COUNTY MARRIAGES, 1779-1868

Eperson, John H. & Elisabeth Reng, 4 Feb 1868; Wiley Reng, bm; m 4 Feb 1868 by Marquis L. Wood, minister.

Erwin, John P. & Fanny S. Williams, 13 June 1815; Lewis Williams, bm.

Estep, Abraham & Hannah Humphreys, 11 Jan 1798; Stephen Ho---, bm.

Estep, Isaac & Ruth Moore, 8 Feb 1794; George Moore, bm.

Estep, Jacob & Ruth Crokit, 4 March 1799; Samuel Crocket, bm.

Etcherson, Sellers & Betsy Riley, 28 Dec 1822; John Kare, bm.

Eton, John & Elizabeth Marsh, 1 Sept 1794; Ezekiel Marsh, bm.

Evans, Barnet & Elizabeth Bowles, 3 Nov 1847; William Bowles, bm.

Evans, Daniel & Ann Flynt, 22 Sept 1788; Thomas Flynt, bm.

Evans, Elias & Nancy Marion, 5 Oct 1839; Wm. Holderfield, bm.

Evans, Jacob & Elizabeth J. Whitaker, 8 June 1867; Pleasant Evans, bm; m 9 June 1867 by A. Whitaker, J. P.

Evans, John & Low McAnally, 5 Oct 1786; John Winston, bm; Chas. McAnally, wit.

Evans, John & Nancy Caudle, 20 March 1826; Moses Caudle, bm.

Evans, Plesant & Elizabeth Fulk, 15 Nov 1844; Isaac Whitaker Jr., bm.

Evans, Richard & Lucinda Smith, 30 Jan 1828; William Smith, bm.

Evans, Stephen & Peggy Foster, 13 Dec 1829; John Evans, bm.

Evans, Thomas & Elizabeth Poindexter, 14 July 1787; William Poindexter, Henry Pattillo, bm.

Evans, Thomas & Mary Sparger, 31 Dec 1853; Samuel Forkner, bm; m by Jesse Roberts.

Evans, Tyson & Elizabeth L. Nicholson, 8 Sept 1866; Wm Holyfield Jr., bm; m 13 Sept 1866 by N. Alberty.

Evans, William & Eveline Marion, 18 Jan 1845; Isaac Whitaker Jr., bm.

Evens, Alexander & Rebekah Wooton, 9 Oct 1809; Isaac Whitaker, bm.

Evens, Wm & Francis Jones, 2 Dec 1849; John Evens, bm.

Everage, William & Mary K. Padgett, 25 May 1846; Sollomon Everage, bm.

Eversal, Isaac & Roxanna Woolford, 3 April 1853; John Southers, bm.

Evins, Thomas & Sally Smith, 17 May 1833; Thos H. Poindexter, bm; B. B. Barham, wit.

SURRY COUNTY MARRIAGES, 1779-1868

Ezell, Anderson & Willy Richardson, 16 Sept 1850; H. V. Allred, bm. (C. H.).

Ezell, Samuel & Rachael Pain, 19 Dec 1818; Lewis Pain, bm.

Faircloth, Jacob & Eliza Cartwright, 26 March 1828; Solomon Vestal, bm.

Faircloth, William & Dice Hendricks, 1 March 1817; Michael Fender, bm.

Fallin, Wm. L. & Lettie M. Flincham, 19 May 1866; Daniel T. Peel, bm.

Fare, Barnabas & Clary Jackson, 7 Sept 1824; Thomas Apperson, bm.

Fare, Pleasant & Elizabeth Mackie, 18 Sept 1849; A. P. Poindexter, bm.

Fargeson, John & Martha Scott, 13 Feb 1791; Philip Howard, Joseph Carter, bm.

Fargisson, Robert & Elizabeth Coe, 6 March 1791; John Stewart, bm.

Farguson, Stephen & Mary Moore, 30 Dec 1788; Jno Bowles, bm.

Fariss, Archabald & Elizabeth Hill, 30 Dec 1846; R. Hill, bm; Wm. M. Nance, wit.

Farmer, Enoch & Febe Vestal, 27 April 1806; Robert Finney, bm.

Farmer, John J. & Clarinda Massy, 10 April 1862; J. M. Owen, bm; m 10 April 1862 by Elisha Banner, J. P.

Farmer, John W. & Nancy Corrico, m 5 Feb 1852 by B. F. Scott, J. P. (C. H.).

Farmer, Levi & Margrett Smith, 12 Nov 1812; Gershom Bills, bm.

Farr, Barnabas & Elizabeth Waggoner, 19 Sept 1785; Peter Elrode, bm.

Farras, William J. & Julia Ann Cox, 2 March 1863; m 2 March 1863 by E. Banner, J. P.

Farrington, Wm. S. & Kittcarn Haynes, 2 Oct 1831; John Dunvender(?), bm.

Farriss, Coleman L. & Sarah J. Ashby, m 13 Nov 1855 by W. E. Davis, marriage wit. by Robert Hill, C. D. Hill.

Farriss, John H. & Stacy Gorden, 22 Nov 1844; Edmund Denny, bm.

Falkner, Thomas A. & Susan Furrow, 30 Jan 1867; Samuel D. Critz, bm; m 30 Jan 1867 by A. Simmons, J. P.

Faulkner, William & Caroline Word, 1 June 1816; Thomas A. Word, bm.

Feaggins, Henry S. & Mary Francis, 20 Aug 1845; Joseph Hill, bm.

Felps, Joshua & Sarah Kempler, 24 Feb 1851; Theodore Felps, bm.

SURRY COUNTY MARRIAGES, 1779-1868

Felton, Ameriah & Agnes Gentry, 29 Sept 1788; John Allen, bm.

Felton, Job & Elizabeth Speer, 15 Sept 1786; Robert Ayres, bm.

Felts, Eliza & Nancy Talbert, 30 May 1835; James Jones, bm.

Felts, Harrison & Sarah Tolbert, 23 March 1837; Hiram Felts, bm.

Felts, Hiram & Milly Talbert, 21 June 1838; Elza Felts, bm.

Fetlz, Jerdin & Nancy Payne, 24 March 1855; m 24 March 1855 by B. F. Scott, J. P.

Felts, Jinkins R. & Sally Jones, 22 July 1831; James Jones, bm.

Felts, William & Jane Owen, 21 Feb 1867; Zachariah Payne, bm; m 21 Feb 1867 by Wm. Golden, J. P.

Fender, Andrew & Sally Bass, 7 Oct 1811; Simon Grouce(?), bm.

Fields, Stephen & Sally Thompson, 14 Aug 1827; James Fields, bm.

Fields, James & Eleth. Thompson, 24 Aug 1817; Squire Harris, bm.

Fields, Jeremiah & Martha Davis, 27 Jan 1817; James McCraw, bm.

Finch, Millington & Betsey Harvel, 19 Jan 1807; Jesse Patterson, bm.

Finney, Robert & _____, 180-; Joseph Finney, bm; Jesse Lester, wit.

Finny, Jason & Margaret Bullard, 24 Jan 1849; Leroy Holcomb, bm.

Finny, Phillip & Mary Mathews, 9 Jan 1845; Ephraim L. Hamby, bm.

Fipps, Joel & Sarah Edwards, 8 Jan 1853; Bartlett Atkins, bm.

Fisher, Levi & Nancy Dodson, 14 May 1844; Augustin Stone, bm.

Fisher, Richard & Nancy Childers, 4 Jan 1819; Mathew Childers, bm.

Fitzgerald, Asa & Nancy W. Foster, 23 Dec 1831; John Vawter, bm.

Fitzgerald, Francis & Jemima Webb, 18 Oct 1833; Archibald M. Kerr, bm.

Fitzgerald, James & Mary Lester, 24 Aug 1807; Thomas A. Word, bm.

Fitzgerald, Thomas & Lydia Crissmon, 2 Jan 1838; E. Cranor, bm.

Flemons, Jesse & Margret Adams, 8 June 1802; George Adams, bm.

Fleming, Asa & Mary E. Rodwell, 22 March 1851; Edward C. Hinshaw, bm; m 27 March 1851 by R. R. Davis, J. P.

Fleming, Columbus & Emily Keller, 9 Dec 1856; John Fleming, bm; m 9 Dec 1856 by A. Simmons, J. P.

Fleming, Isaac & Eliza J. Barry, 23 March 1846; Simon Reece, bm.

SURRY COUNTY MARRIAGES, 1779-1868

Fleming, Job & Elizabeth Angel, 26 Sept 1848; Lewis Gadberry, bm.

Fleming, Job & Martha Baugh, 8 Feb 1835; James Adams, bm.

Fleming, John & Ruth Whitlock, 30 Nov 1822; John Spurgeon, bm.

Fleming, John & Azeneth Vestal, 17 Jan 1848; Lamuel Fleming, bm.

Fleming, Lemuel & Elizabeth Jane Allen, 23 Jan 1845; Lewis Gadberry, bm.

Fleming, Sampson & Patsey Nance, 20 Nov 1816; William Hutchens, bm.

Fleming, Sampson & Joanna Tull, 9 Sept 1837; Uriah Fleming, bm.

Fleming, Samuel M. & Eliza Ann Marshall, 27 Dec 1860; m by E. Barren, J. P.

Fleming, Uriah & Milly Vanderpool, 21 Oct 1825; Riley Brown, bm.

Flemming, Job & Betsy Jester, 20 Oct 1808; William Brown, bm.

Flemming, William Henry & Eliza Ann Bays, 17 Jan 1846; Andrew Bowman, bm.

Flemmins, John & Mary Perkins, 9 March 1807; William Brown, bm.

Fletcher, Abraham & Elizabeth Elrode, 5 Sept 1802; James Fletcher, bm.

Fletcher, Azariah & Mary Moore, 6 May 1837; John Baker or John Moore, bm.

Fletcher, James & Maryann Jones, 22 Dec 1819; Philip Phillips, bm.

Fletcher, James M. & Elizabeth Davis, 24 Aug 1846; Wm Spillman, bm.

Fletcher, John & Rachel Denny, 28 Oct 1814; Henry Fulk, bm.

Fletcher, Joseph & Lidia Snow, 27 Sept 1802; Frostin Snow, bm.

Fletcher, Robert & _____, 18--; J. M. Fletcher, bm.

Flin, James & Fanney Martin, 15 Jan 1796; James Holcomb, bm.

Flin, James & Katherine Prim, 28 Dec 1834; Burrell Parnel, bm.

Flincham, James E. & Lucinda Ashburn, m 17 Dec 1847 by Joel Denny, J. P.

Flincham, John W. R. & Sarah Peel, 11 Feb 1862; Wilson Fulk, bm.

Flincham, William M. & Arilla Fulk, 22 Feb 1863; Aaron Fulk, bm; m 27 Feb 1863 by John Jones at the house of Widow Fulk.

Flinn, Burwell & Matildy Roberts, 1 Jan 1847; Benjamin Pettit, bm.

Flinn, George & Eleanor Prather, 27 Sept 1779; Lauflin Flinn, bm.

SURRY COUNTY MARRIAGES, 1779-1868

Flinn, Lauflin & Elizabeth Wright, 27 Sept 1779; George Flinn, bm.

Flippin, John & Mahala Jessop, 1 Feb 1821; A. Jessop, bm; Evan Davis, wit.

Flippin, Joseph & Miss Rosana J. Reynolds, 20 March 1857; Milton Flippin, bm.

Flippin, Milton & Francis M. Watton (Walton?), 15 Nov 1859; John C. Dobson, bm.

Flyn, George & Frances Johnson, 29 Nov 1829; Elijah Deazen, bm.

Flyn, Thomas & Jane Forrester, 3 Dec 1808; Ransom Badgett, bm.

Flyn, William & Cyntha Hall, 31 Jan 1839; James Matthews, bm.

Flynn, Hezekiah & Mary Elliott, 23 Feb 1789; George Flynn, bm; Robt Williams, wit.

Flynn, James & Elizabeth Speer, 1 March 1816; Oswell Philips, bm.

Flynn, John & Mary Speer, 10 May 1820; Jesse Fleming, bm.

Flynn, John & Rebecca Stinson, 6 Sept 1823; James Melton, bm.

Folger, M. Y. & Elizabeth Gray, 22 Oct 1851; D. D. Tellar, bm; m 25 Oct 1851 by D. M. McGee, J. P.

Folger, Milton Young (Dr.) & Elizabeth Gray, 17 March 1851; D. D. Tellar,bm; m 17 March 1851 by N. H. Blackwood, J. P.

Foote, Henry & Marry Wright, 16 Feb 1821; William Foote, bm.

Foote, William C. & Harriet Vestal, 23 Aug 1850; Christian Royal, bm.

Forbis, Joseph & Mary Bryant, 13 Sept 1791; Jesse Bryan, Robt Williams, bm.

Forcum, Thomas & Betsy Denny, 6 April 1822; James Rutledge, bm.

Ford, S. A. & Miss Eunice Folger, 3 Jan 1861; m by F. H. Jones, 3 Jan 1861.

Ford, William & Rebekah Williams, 27 March 1813; John Turner, bm.

Foren, William & Tobitha Talley, 3 July 1844; Calvin Johnson, bm.

Foreman, Jno & Hetty ---, 14 March 1801; James Steelman, bm.

Forkner, Dalton & Mary Freeman, 20 Feb 1855; Samuel Forkner, bm; m 26 Feb 1855 by D. M. Cooper, J. P.

Forkner, Daniel P. & Rebecca Midkiff, 23 Dec 1847; John A. Summers, bm.

Forkner, Elijah & Betsey Strawn, 10 June 1821; Jackson Tromel (?), bm.

Forkner, Hugh & Polly Creed, 26 July 1828; Clinton Chandler,bm.

SURRY COUNTY MARRIAGES, 1779-1868

Forkner, Hugh & Rachael Thorp, 28 Aug 1828; H. D. Armstrong, bm.

Forkner, Isaac & Sarrah Ellez, 11 Sept 1813; Ransom Dudley, bm.

Forkner, Jefferson & Eliza Parker, 5 Dec 1835; Daniel Riggs, bm.

Forkner, Jesse & Mary Bedsaul, 21 March 1850; Thomas M. Thorp, bm. (C. H.).

Forkner, John & Letha Richards, 13 Oct 1833; John King, bm.

Forkner, Joseph & Rebeckah Hickman, 18 May 1817; Thos. Forkner, bm.

Forkner, Laurence & Jesten Golden, 22 May 1826; John McGilvary, bm.

Forkner, Lewis & Elizabeth Eaton, 8 Dec 1830; West Mosely, bm.

Forkner, Samuel & Betsey Bryson, 11 Jan 1817; Thomas D. Kelly, bm.

Forkner, Smmuel & Sarah Annefield, 17 June 1856.

Forkner, Thomas & Elizabeth Simmons, 7 Feb 1826; John Davis, bm.

Forkner, Thomas & Elizabeth Tilly, 28 April 1845; J. C. Davis, bm.

Forkum, Allen & Lydia Ward, 1 Jan 1808; Edward Selvey, bm.

Forkum, Peter & Margrett Huffhines, 3 Nov 1814; Thomas Colvard, bm.

Forman, Harvy J. & Elizabeth Ann Marshall, 1 Sept 1862; Samuel D. Critz, bm; m 1 Sept 1862 by A. Simmons, J. P.

Forrest, Baraham & Lucy Jane Slate, 12 Nov 1846; Isaac James Slate, bm.

Forrest, Fielding & Elizabeth Bruce, 9 Nov 1787; James Forrest, Robert Bruce, bm.

Forrest, John & Sarah Cooper, 28 Oct 1787; William Cooper, bm.

Fortner, Samuel & Milley Johnson, 23 Dec 1867; m 24 Dec 1867 by Thos. L. Lawson, M. G.

Foster, Elijah & Polley Everage, 24 April 1820; Hillary M. Foster, bm.

Foster, Henry G. & Sarah Joiner, 31 Jan 1821; Thomas W. Poindexter, bm.

Foster, Henry G. & Charity Akers, 27 Oct 1828; William A. Robey, bm.

Foster, Russell A. & Jane Lewis, 26 Aug 1851; Anthony Lewis, bm; A. Simmons, wit.

Foster, Weldon & Silpha Brickhouse, 29 Dec 1823; William Spilmon, Junr., bm.

SURRY COUNTY MARRIAGES, 1779-1868

Fowler, Charles & Miss Rachel E. Fulk, 19 March 1855; Alfred Atkins, bm; m 20 May 1855 by J. Whitaker, J. P.

Fowler, Wesley & Mehala Peel, 21 Sept 1858; Thomas Peel, bm.

Fowler, William & Asanett Chandler, 10 Aug 1858; Jackson Glassgow, bm.

Fox, Jacob & Rachel Carnston, 19 May 1823; George Watters, bm.

Frday, Ephraim & Nancy Defreese, 7 Aug 1810; Edward Cornell, John Renagar, bm.

France, Haman & Mary Clark, 24 May 1785; James Dickerson, Haman Critz, bm.

Franklin, Gideon & Sally Bowles, 19 Feb 1825; Jesse Standly, bm.

Franklin, Gideon E. & Ann Hughes, 26 March 1832; Francis P. Clingham, bm.

Franklin, Hardin & Nancy Gentry, 24 Jan 1818; John Jarvis, bm.

Franklin, Hardin P. & Martha E. Franklin, 5 May 1837; Jesse D. Franklin, bm.

Franklin, James K. & Lydia Melton, 31 Aug 1866; J. J. Jenkins, bm.

Franklin, Jesse & Elizabeth Gentry, 18 Oct 1817; Joseph Gentry, bm.

Franklin, Jesse & Sarah Grogan, 9 Aug 1866; William Stuart, bm; married 9 Aug 1866 by J. T. Johnson, J. P. (couple are persons of color).

Franklin, John & Polly Jarvis, 30 Dec 1816; Stephen Jarvis, bm.

Franklin, M. & Milley Edwards, 2 July 1802; Joel Riggs, bm.

Franklin, Shearwood & Meeky Greenwood, 3 Sept 1830; Lot Wilmoth(?), bm.

Franklin, Taliaferro & Nancy Early, 13 March 1826; Newel Jackson, bm.

Franklin, Wylee & Polley Taliaferro, 20 Dec 1826; Dickerson Taliaferro, bm. (C. H.).

Frasuer, George & Elizabeth Roton, 17 Aug 1813; Thomas Whitlock, bm.

Frasier, Caleb & Rachel Haines, 3 Aug 18--; Isam Owens, bm.

Frazier, William & Polly Caudel, 29 July 1816; Robert Mackey, bm; Mathw. M. Hughes, wit.

Frasier, James & Polly Dowel, 28 April 1803; Thomas Whitlock, bm.

Freeman, Elisha & Polly Kellehan, 19 March 1830; Timothy Peel, bm.

Freeman, Foster & Nancy Freeman, 17 Aug 1809; Jeremiah King, bm.

SURRY COUNTY MARRIAGES, 1779-1868

Freeman, George & _____, 14 Oct 1867; Thomas Jones, bm; T. W. Prather, J. P., wit.

Freeman, Iredell & Nancy Edmons, 30 Nov 1836; Crawford Wall, bm.

Freeman, James O. & Martha Brown, 7 Sept 1865.

Freeman, John & Mary Spence, 1 April 1819; Simon Marshill, bm.

Freeman, John & Elizabeth Isbell, 9 Aug 1796; Joshua Freeman, bm.

Freeman, Menoah & Nancy Brown, 1 Jan 1790; Thomas Childress, John Brown, bm.

Freeman, Robt & Susanah Gunston, 14 Nov 1805; Mos. Adams, bm.

Freeman, Saml A. & Susan E. Waugh, 26 Jan 1864; A. Dunnagan, bm; m 26 Jan 1864 by Jas. H. Lewellin, Min. Gos.

Freeman, Samuel P. & Sally Norman, 14 Jan 1845; Henry M. Freeman, bm.

Freeman, Tyre & Elizabeth Stoe, 8 March 1808; Joshua Freeman, bm.

Freeman, William & Sabey Henley, m 21 June 1869 by Thomas Schauf, J. P.

Freeman, Hawkins & Mary Cave, 28 Dec 1852; m 28 Dec 1852 by Geo. A. Jervis, J. P.

Freeman, Samuel & Margaret Carnahan, 10 Nov 1851; William Barnett, bm.

Freman, Henry M. & Salina C. Bodenhamer, 13 July 1854; Charles W. Hiatt, bm; m 13 July 1854 by H. M. Waugh, J. P.

Fretwill, John & Lear Jentree, 24 March 1801; John Poindexter, bm.

Friend, Joseph & Elon Mattison, 2 May 1803; Henry McDaniel, bm.

Frost, Ebenezer & Nancy Clary, 21 April 1822; Thos Donaldson, bm.

Frost, John Jr. & Rebecka York, 2 Sept 1832; John H. Hurt, bm.

Frost, John & Martha Hale, 3 June 1852; George Harman, bm.

Frost, Stephen & Martha A. Bedson, 29 Aug 1854; James M. Leonard, bm; m 29 Aug 1854 by A. Simmons, J. P.

Fugate, Jesse & Lucinda Tipton, 10 Nov 1854; Wm. W. Breeding, bm; m 10 Nov 1854 by A. Simmons, J. P.

Fulford, Franklin & Sharlott Fry, 20 Feb 1851; Stephen Smythers, bm.

Fulford, Josiah & Sally Warner, 5 July 1850; Jordan Austin, bm. (C. H.).

Fulk, Adam & Elizabeth Carmichael, 17 July 1820; Richard Cormikel, bm.

SURRY COUNTY MARRIAGES, 1779-1868

Fulk, Andrew J. & Julia Stone, 18 July 1850; Wm. R. Lovill, bm.

Fulk, Augustin & Emily Key, 2 April 1852; Augustin Key, bm.

Fulk, Brison & Emily Stone, 1 Oct 1846; Jacob L. Fulk, bm.

Fulk, George & Nancy Gouff, 18 Feb 1852; Rowly Fulk, bm.

Fulk, Henry & Caler King, 20 July 1813; Jacob Fulk, bm.

Fulk, Joel & Polly Stone, 12 Feb 1844; Jacob L. Fulk, bm.

Fulk, John & Rebecca Smith, 1 March 1825; Peter Graves, bm.

Fulk, Joseph & Drucilla Ashbourn, 9 Aug 1822; James York, bm.

Fulk, Solomon & Susan Brassfield, 24 Aug 1828; Jacob L. Fulk, bm.

Fulk, Thomas & Pamela Harrison, 4 March 1832; J. L. Fulk, bm.

Fulk, Wilson & Mary Flippin, 13 Oct 1849; Joseph W. Flipping, bm.

Fulks, James & Mary Ann Tuttle, 13 March 1847; Wm. W. McCraw, bm.

Fulks, James C. & Matilda J. Moore, 2 Dec 1851; William R. Hurst, bm.

Fulks, John R. & Elizabeth M. Davis, 12 May 1861; Jesse P. Jervis, bm; m 22 May 1862 by George A. Jervis, J. P.

Fulks, Samuel L. & Elizabeth Robinson, 12 Dec 1835; Joseph Cockerham, bm.

Fulks, Thomas S. & Polly Cockerham, 29 Dec 1831; Hugh Cockerum, bm.

Fulks, Thomas S. of Caroll Co., Va., & Franky Hodges, 8 July 1855; A. B. C. Jervis, bm.

Fulks, Thomas S. & Rosy Cain, 10 Nov 1862; C. C. Golden, bm; m 10 Nov 1863 by Wm. Golden, J. P.

Fuller, Abner & Polly Stow, 30 Aug 1837; Lewis Gadberry, bm.

Fuller, Gideon & Amee Sollomon, 15 Jan 1811; John Britton, bm.

Fuller, Thomas & Sarah Masters, 25 Aug 1812; William Holloway, bm.

Fulton, Baraby, son of Joel and Jane Fulton, & Sary Talor, daughter of Robert & Jane Talor, m 22 Dec 1868 by J. A. Bingman, J. P.

Fulton, Winston & Mary Hollinsworth, 24 Feb 1847; Stephen Johnson, bm.

Fultz, Henry & Polly Dial, 13 Jan 1824; Jacob Pfoff, bm.

Galaspee, John B. & _____, 23 Aug 1823; Terry Dunagan, bm.

SURRY COUNTY MARRIAGES, 1779-1868

Galaspie, Riley J., son of Ellick & Elizabeth Galaspie, & Mahaly J. Creed, daughter of Buri and Rachel Creed, m 24 Jan 1869 by James Needham, M. G.

Galaspy, Alexander & Betsey Dunnigan, 9 March 1814; Wm. Dunnagan, bm.

Galespy, Elijah & Sarah Laffoon, 15 July 1820; Tirey Galaspy, bm.

Galaspy, Thomas J. & Martha Jane Patterson, 26 Oct 1849; Jesse W. Galaspy, bm.

Galaspy, Tyre R. & Sarah McCarter, 5 Aug 1812; Anthony Foster, bm.

Galaspy, Tyre P. & Polly Riggs, 16 March 1816; Elijah Galaspy, bm.

Galaspy, Wilson & Elizabeth Mosely, 28 July 1834; Theophilus Mosely, bm.

Galimore, Stanly & Nancy McCraw, 13 July 1858; Charles Caroll, bm.

Galispie, Jesse W. & Susan York, 10 April 1857; Algias Dunegan, bm; m 12 April 1857 by C. Thompson, J. P.

Gallaspie, J. L. & Rouney Cintha Powers, 30 April 1862; Joseph Gordan, bm; m 8 May 1862 by L. J. Norman, J. P.

Gallean, William & Nancy Rector, 26 Feb 1827; Julius Dickings, bm.

Gallemore, John & Hannah Gaines, 13 June 1813; Thos. J. Word, bm.

Gallimore, Wilson & Frances Primm, 15 Aug 1852; Columbus Coatney, bm; m 15 Aug 1852 by A. Simmons, J. P.

Gallian, James & Elizabeth Munkus, 21 Jan 1833; Samuel Gallian Jr., bm.

Gallian, John & Polly Norman, 24 Dec 1822; Jesse Holder, bm.

Gallion, Shadrack & Mahaly Rector, 8 Nov 1822; Young Gallion, bm.

Gallreath, Bartrom & Cinthia Honaker, 30 Jan 1834; Reuben Cloud, bm.

Galyer, Ephraim & Rody Thompson, 20 Nov 1856; Byrd Snow, bm; m 20 Nov 1856 by W. M. Freeman.

Gallyer, Tolaver & Martha Lowe, m 24 July 1866 by F. J. Dickens, J. P.

Galoway, Jack & Allis Moore, 25 Nov 1866; m 25 Nov 1866 by Murlin Spargue, J. P.

Galyan, Samuel & Elizabeth Thorp, 10 Nov 1831; Elijah Raney, bm.

Galyear, Calaway & Elizabeth Hawks, 9 Feb 1846; Robert Hawks, bm.

SURRY COUNTY MARRIAGES, 1779-1868

Galyean, William & Mary Low, 10 Sept 1853; Kerby Low, bm; John Ramsy, J. P., wit; m by Wm. Hodges, J. P.

Galyearn, Bennett & Martha J. Nicks, 3 Feb 1853.

Galyer, Byrum & Cealy Low, 21 May 1851; Jacob Low, bm.

Galyer, Henderson & Tellitha Hodges, 20 Feb 1853; Samuel Smith, bm; m 27 Feb 1853 by Jo. Philips, J. P.

Galyer, Jonathan & Catherine Allen, 21 April 1859; Andrew Galyer, bm.

Galyer, Shadrick & Ruth Low, 21 Feb 1848; Julius Dickens, bm.

Galyon, Byrum & Rebecah Smith, 26 Aug 1852; m by Wm. Hodges, J. P.

Gammon, Thomas & Sarah Clarke, 13 June 1837; Gabriel H. Forkner, bm.

Gammons, Wm. & Matilda Gregory, 29 Jan 1835; Wm. D. Somers, Joseph Howard Junr., bm.

Gardner, Brian D. & Paline Perkins, 26 Jan 1833; G. C. Crouse, bm.

Gargus, Joel & Elizabeth Zachary, 21 July 1819; Russel Shugart, bm.

Gargus, Joel & Rebekah McCollum, 7 Oct 1813; David Zachary, bm.

Gargus, John & Elizabeth Bass, 9 Dec 1816; Joel Gargus, Andrew McCollum, bm.

Garnand, George & Elizabeth Smith, 16 Nov 1833; Spragg Wincter, bm.

Garner, Archibald & Lydia Cranfill, 22 Dec 1846; Wm Weatherman, bm.

Garner, Arge & Jemimah Davis, 19 July 1785; Tolaver Davis, bm.

Garner, Jacob & Mary Hoots, 29 Dec 1797; Adam Miller, bm.

Garner, Saml & Margret Lash, 7 Sept 1801; Peter Mock, bm.

Garner, Vincent & Susannah Howard, 21 March 1793; Martin Bridgefarmer, bm.

Garner, Wm & Evea Call, 29 Dec 1789; Danl Call of Rowan, bm; William Wright, bm.

Garrett, Isom & Polly Puckit, 25 April 1814; Lewis Garrett, bm.

Garrett, Joshua & Polly Cox, 3 Jan 1814; Wm Lyon, bm.

Garrett, Lewis & Maryan Johnson, 14 May 1807; Saml Sparks, bm.

Gates, William & Etta M. White, 6 April 1823; John White, bm.

Gates, William & Miss Eliza Barker, 25 Jan 1856; Albert Gates, bm.

SURRY COUNTY MARRIAGES, 1779-1868

Gates, William B. & Zilpah Ingrum, 28 May 1849; W. A. Prather, bm.

Geare, Thomas F. & Aranna Carry, 17 July 1846; Jeremiah Ward, bm.

Gentle, John & Eliza. Keen, 14 Jan 1800; William Brazier, bm.

Gentry, Alford & Margaret Murphy, 17 Nov 1851; Calvin Jentry, bm; m 20 Nov 1851 by John C. Thompson.

Gentry, Allin & Sallay Brittain, 24 March 1822; David Buckhannon, bm.

Gentry, Allen P. & Mary Gentry, 2 March 1800; Shadrach Holcomb, bm.

Gentry, Allen of Wilks County, & Lucindy Wilbourn, 3 Jan 1831; Robert Wilbourn, bm.

Gentry, Allen & Mehala Suthard, 21 Nov 1847; Geo. A. Jervis, bm.

Gentry, Calvin & Polly Hodges, 1 Oct 1845; Jesse Davis, bm.

Gentry, Elisha & Smith Denney, 2 Feb 1811; Abraham Badgett, bm.

Gentry, Gardner & Susannah Weatherman, 1 Feb 1830; Shadrach Gentry, bm.

Gentry, J. F. & Rhody Thompson, 9 Dec 1858; J. W. Woodruff, bm.

Gentry, James S. & Miss Sarrah Hodges, 12 Nov 1853; C. L. Banner, bm; m 13 Nov 1853 by Geo. A. Jervis, J. P.

Gentry, James & Rebecca M. Fulks, 30 Nov 1855; m 12 Dec 1855 by B. F. Scott, J. P.

Gentry, Joseph & Mary Hodges, 28 July 1816; James Robertson, bm.

Gentry, Joseph & Sally C. Faulks, 1 Nov 1860; Archalous Vaughn, bm.

Gentry, M. B. & Susan Hodges, 4 Feb 1863; Barnet Payne, bm; m 9 Feb 1863 by T. J. Lawson.

Gentry, Michael B. & Sarah Burrus, 13 Nov 1811; James Jervis, bm.

Gentry, Pleasant & Lucy Alred, 28 July 1804; George Hudspeth, bm.

Gentry, R. H. & Levina Collans, 22 Dec 1867; m 24 Dec 1867 by B. J. Dickens, J. P.

Gentry, Robert & Nancy Hodge, 21 Sept 1820; George A. Jervis, bm.

Gentry, Samuel & Sarah Brock, 24 May 1787; Robert Hooker, bm.

Gentry, Shadrac & Milinda Messick, 2 Feb 1847; Lawson G. Penix, bm.

Gentry, Shadrach & Polly Jacks, 14 Oct 1810; William Vanhoy, bm.

SURRY COUNTY MARRIAGES, 1779-1868

Gentry, Wiley, son of Calvin & Polly Gentry, & Catharine Lyon, 17 Dec 1870; m 25 Dec 1870 by G. W. Thompson, J. P.

Gentry, William & Betsey Day, 13 April 1809; Robert Ashley, bm.

Gentry, Wm & Lucy Myres, 1 Dec 1830; Jeremiah Francis, bm.

Gentry, William M. & Martha E. Nickson, 9 Oct 1847; Giles N. Harris, bm.

Gentry, William W. & Cyntha Haines, 27 July 1830; Wm. Dickerson, bm.

George, Franklin & Jemima Eldridge, 24 July 1855; J. B. Eldridge, bm.

George, John & Elizebeth Jinnins, 1 Feb 1807; Partrick Hutchins, bm.

George, Samuel J. & Eliza J. Mires, 12 Dec 1852; John Morefield, bm.

Gibbins, Elbert & Sally Hill, 28 Sept 1850; Henry Moore, bm. (C. H.).

Gibbs, John & Sarah Norman, 18 Jan 1844; William B. Gibbs, bm.

Gibbs, John C. & Mary Ann Jester, 18 Dec 1839; Jefferson Brown, bm.

Gibbs, Peter & Anny Brown, 27 April 1811; Thomas Vestal, bm.

Gibbs, William & Ailsey Woodson, 17 Feb 1844; Wilie J. Spence, bm.

Gibson, Joseph & Mary A. M. Henley, 8 March 1863; Ewel Smith, bm; m 8 March 1863 by A. Simmons, J. P.

Gibson, Minyard & Rachel Waller, 7 Feb 1813; Henry Davis, bm.

Gillaspie, Warren & Jane Riggs, 26 Feb 1866; A. H. Freeman, bm; S. S. Freeman, wit.

Gilliam, J. W. & Judey Minish, 9 Oct 1864; m 16 Oct 1864 by W. H. Pardue.

Gilly, Peter & Edy Morris, 9 Oct 1828; James Morrison, bm.

Gilman, Michael & Mary Hine, 15 Oct 1844; John Midkiff, bm.

Gilmer, Samuel L. & Matilda C. Moore, 3 July 1855; m by W. W. Mebane, 3 July 1855 at the house of Samuel Moore.

Gilmer, William & Phillis Hollingsworth, freed people, m 27 Sept 1866 by A. Simmons, J. P.

Gilmore, William & Frances Beazley, 25 Feb 1860; m by C. L. Banner, J. P.

Gilpin, Richamond & Elenor Stonestreet, 15 Jan 1811; Elisha Stonestreet, bm.

Gilpin, William & Alsey Foster, 8 Jan 1814; Elias Turner, bm.

Ginnings, John & Alesey Bills, 25 Dec 1806; John Bills, bm.

SURRY COUNTY MARRIAGES, 1779-1868

Gittens, John & Mary Boyde, 14 Aug 1788; Roger Girdins, bm.

Glaspie, James & Martha J. Laffoon, m 15 May 1856 by Wm. Haymore, J. P.

Glass, James & Martha Reeves, 15 May 1850; D. C. Wolff, bm. (C. H.).

Glen, Jeremiah & Mary Hauser, 4 Jan 1834; Henry Mouter, bm.

Glen, Squire S. & Dorotha A. Pettit, 29 March 1825; Tyre Glen, bm.

Glen, Thompson & Martha Hudspeath, 16 Aug 1788; John Thos. Longine, bm.

Goade, Andrew & _____, 8 July 1849; Wm. Mabury, bm.

Goen, James & Elizabeth Beasley, 25 Nov 1846; Eli Crouk, bm.

Goen, David & Nancy Harris, 9 Nov 1820; Thomas Going, bm.

Goin, Dudly & Tobitha Ker, 28 Sept 1816; Martin Mathias, bm.

Goin, Morgan & Kerry Love, 24 Sept 1828; Peter Norman, bm.

Goin, Morgan & Sally Beasley, 5 April 1862; William Gilmer, bm; m 8 April 1862 by J. Gray, J. P.

Going, Albert, son of William & Rebecka Going, & Elizabeth Johnson, daughter of William Johnson; m 29 Oct 1868 by Thomas Schoule, J. P.

Going, Frederick & Nancy Caims, 10 Dec 1818; William Going, bm.

Going, Fuel & Sintha Hain, 12 April 1848; John Kimbell, bm.

Going, George W. & Mary E. Clark, 21 Feb 1862; J. A. Whittington, bm; m 21 Feb 1862 by A. Dunnagan, J. P.

Going, Perrin & Nancy Lawson, 14 Jan 1861; m 14 Jan 1861 by Wm. R. Bray, J. P.

Going, William & Rebeca Jones, 10 Dec 1850; Granville McKinney, bm. (C. H.).

Going, William H. & Mary Kimble, 10 Jan 1854; Allgius Dunnagan, bm; m by Wright Johnson, 25 Jan 1853.

Going, Wm. P. & Laura Davis, m 1 Nov 1866 by B. J. Dickens, J.P.

Golden, Thomas & Charlotte Felts, 12 March 1850; Andrew Christman, bm. (C. H.).

Golden, William & Jane Fets, 17 Aug 1843; John A. Jones, bm.

Golden, William & Mary Snow, 9 Jan 1854; William Golden, bm.

Golding, Wm & Nancy Snow, 26 Jan 1833; Simpson Snow, bm.

Golding, Abner & Deborah Wright, 21 July 1849.

Golding, James & Jane Snow, 5 Dec 1835; Calvin Snow, bm.

Golding, John & Matildy Snow, 22 Jan 1835; Georg Burres, bm.

SURRY COUNTY MARRIAGES, 1779-1868

Golding, Reubin & Nancy Butcher, 9 Oct 1849; Nicholas Butcher, bm.

Golding, Richard & Charlott Cave, 2 Jan 1817; Elias Cave, bm.

Golding, Semcer & Ellen Bray, 7 March 1849; Nicholas Butcher, bm.

Golding, Thomas & Ayzina Butcher, 30 Nov 1848; Nicholas Butcher, bm.

Gonnel, James & Clary Eads, 19 Oct 1831; Elisha Norten, bm.

Good, Tyree W. & Julia Ann Crumpton, 5 March 1851; Shadrach Collier, bm.

Gooden, John & Margaret Carter, 7 Nov 1837; James Dean, bm.

Goodman, Essick, son of Harry and Nancy Hampton, and Caroline Adams, daughter of Peter Carter, m 30 Jan 1869 by J. A. Bingman, J. P.

Gordan, Colley C. & Lucinda E. Buckley, 19 Dec 1846; William Rawley, bm.

Gorden, David & Nancy Cruse, 30 May 1814; Iredel Armstrong, bm.

Gorden, Frank, son of Robert Armstrong & Charlotte Gorden, & Ellise Davis, daughter of John and Patcy Davis, persons of color, m 20 Dec 1867 by Joel Denny, J. P.

Gorden, Harden & Lucy West, 21 Aug 1827; Iredel Armstrong, bm.

Gorden, J. D. & Martha Ann Eatens, 18 Oct 1856; Samuel P. Gorden, bm; m 19 Oct 1856 by T. H. Gorden, J. P.

Gorden, W. M. & Emily J. Hill, 11 Dec 1854; Robert Hall, bm; m 11 Dec 1854 by E. Banner, J. P.

Gorden, William C. & Nancy Davis, 20 Feb 1837; Samuel N. Gorden, bm.

Gordon, Charls & _____, _____ 180-; Thomas Jol(?), bm.

Gordon, James M. & Nancy Slayton, 14 Nov 1846; Joseph Slayton, bm.

Gordon, Jonathan D. & Elizabeth Bullin, 29 Jan 1864; William Land, bm.

Gordon, Joseph & Maryann Bodenhamer, 5 May 1855; John C. Laffoon, bm; m 10 May 1855 by Wilson Laffoon, J. P.

Gordon, Joseph & Mary McKinney, 3 Sept 1860; Jas. S. Snow, bm; m 4 Sept 1860 by L. J. Norman, J. P.

Gordon, Joseph & Elizabeth J. Laffoon, 11 Nov 1863; William G. Laffoon, bm; m 12 Nov 1863 by Jas. Lazar, J. P.

Gordon, Seth C. & Lamira Talbert, 28 Dec 1848; Lewis F. Madison, bm.

Goss, Jackson & Fanny Jacks, 11 Aug 1847; Henry Bunting, bm.

Gross, Kincehn & Ruth Norman, 3 April 1844; Elijah Norman, bm.

77

Gough, Thomas & Rachael Williams, 7 Nov 1813; Travis Ashley, Henry Skidmore, bm.

Gough, John E. & Sarah Mackie, 25 Dec 1844; James Sheek(?), bm.

Gough, Samuel & Rachael Steelmon, 2 Nov 1815; Jesse Chinn, bm.

Gowen, Allen & Martha Beasly, 28 Nov 1834; Anderson Ennis, bm.

Gowen, Isaac & Nancy Graham, 28 Sept 1820; John Taylor, bm.

Gowen, Seabard & Sally Reynolds, 27 March 1818; Nathaniel Reynolds, bm.

Gowings, William P. & Lavina J. Davis, 1 Nov 1866; F. V. Banner, bm.

Goyn, Ambris & Molise J. Dunkin, 18 July 1866.

Goyne, Sanders & Hanah Raynales, 28 Jan 1851; Hugh Hicks, bm.

Grace, Abell & Sarah Cole, 22 Jan 1794.

Grace, Allen & _____, 1 Jan 1787.

Grace, Daniel & Rachael Billator, 1 April 1785; George Grace, bm.

Grace, Worker & Elizabeth Poindexter, 9 Jan 1804.

Graham, Levi & Mary Redpath, 21 April 1861.

Grant, Robertson & Sarah Turner, 13 March 1830; Thomas Chapman, bm.

Graves, James & Sarah Watkins, 13 June 1809; Charles Latham, bm.

Graves, Peter & Sarah Merion, 21 Dec 1809; Daniel Merion, bm.

Graves, Peter & Sarah Carmical, 15 May 1811; Peter Graves Senr., bm.

Grace, John & Susannah Truit, 14 Jan 1793; John Truit, bm.

Gray, Benjamin & Hannah Astill, 19 March 1812; Benjamin Gray, bm.

Gray, Iredel J. & Elizabeth J. Love, 24 Dec 1860.

Gray, James W. & Susan Dethrage, 24 July 1849; Mathew M. Dethrage, bm.

Gray, Joseph & Mary Kelly, 30 Jan 1832; Charles Russell, bm.

Gray, Rouzee P. & E---- Mitchell, 16 Sept 1834; Zachariah Montgomery, bm.

Gray, Terrel & Nancy Armstrong, 9 March 1844; William Gilliam, bm.

Gray, William B. & Mary Morefield, 8 April 1820; Annenias Gray, bm; (C. H.).

Gray, Willis & Tellunday(?) Johnson, 15 Sept 1845; Meredeth Armstrong, bm.

SURRY COUNTY MARRIAGES, 1779-1868

Grean, Wilborn & Sarah Haulcomb, 29 Feb 1804.

Green James & Polly Jacks, 10 Oct 1826; William Vannoy, bm.

Green, John & Nancy Shores, 23 March 1832; George W. Brown, bm.

Green, John S., son of James S. and Ann Green, and Evaline Hill, daughter of Joel and Emily Hill, m 17 March 1868 by James Needham, M. G.

Green, Richard & Charity Jacks, 4 March 1804; Isaac Minick, bm.

Green, William & Elizabeth Swiney, 2 Oct 1786; Johnson Whitaker, bm.

Greenwood, Bartley & _____, 5 Sept 1801; George Shugert, bm.

Greenwood, Bartley & Nancy Cody, 18 July 1806; Amos London Junr., bm.

Greenwood, George W. & Elizabeth Reece, 27 Sept 1838; James Starbuck, bm.

Greenwood, James & Sally Spencer, 19 Aug 1811.

Greenwood, James & Lydia Reece, 1 Aug 1844; Gideon McMickle, bm.

Greenwood, John & _____; Bartley Greenwood, bm. (no date).

Greenwood, John R., son of James & Lidy Greenwood & Nannie A. Armsfield, daughter of Isaac and Mary Armfield, m 24 Dec 1868 by Thomas Schaub, J. P.

Greenwood, Joseph S. & Elizabeth A. Scritchfield, 29 Oct 1844; Gideon J. McMickle, bm.

Greenwood, Thomas & Lydia Moore, 2 June 1806; Martin Armstrong, bm.

Greenwood, Thomas & Malinda E. Burch, 9 Nov 1847; Isaac Burch, bm.

Greenwood, William & Lucinda Burch, 1 Aug 1836; Thomas C. Greenwood, bm.

Greer, Charles & Martha Newton, 9 Sept 1820; William Carter, Jr., bm.

Gregory, Abraham R. & Sarah Pruett, 28 March 1829; James H. Clanton, bm.

Gregory, Ambrose J. & Polly P. Davis, 24 March 1818; Thomas Davis, bm.

Gregory, Gabriel & Jane McGathy, 4 Oct 1818; James McCraw, bm.

Gregory, John & Martha Hall, 3 Sept 1844; Frederick Hutchins, bm.

Gregory, Sterling & Sarah Donnar, 5 June 1817; John Danner (Tanner), bm.

Grey, Ananias & Polly Alston, 29 Dec 1814; Benjamin Grey, bm.

SURRY COUNTY MARRIAGES, 1779-1868

Griffey, Benjamine & Salley Bonds, 17 May 1787; Thomas Ball, bm.

Griffey, Daniel & Liza Griffey, 3 Jan 1817; Jesse Brown, bm.

Griffin, Archabel & Hannah Hutchins, 10 April 1845; Calvin Hutchins, bm.

Griffin, Balden & Betsy Key(s), 27 July 1821; Micajah Reeves, bm.

Griffin, John & Cyntha Colvert, 9 Nov 1797.

Griffin, Lott & Meekey Honey, 29 July 1809; Abraham Badgett, bm.

Griffith, Benjamin & Rebeca Dick, 28 March 1854; Sumrel Forkner, bm; m by Jesse Roberts.

Griffith, Daniel & Levicy Barker, 28 Jan 1825; Jesse Brown, bm.

Griffith, James & Polly Slator, 8 Aug 1820; John Thornton, bm.

Griffith, John & Polly Rawls, 22 Sept 1819; Robert Poor, bm.

Griffith, John & Elizabeth Marsh, 25 Dec 1851; John Brown, bm; m 26 Dec 1851 by J. H. Dobson, J. P.

Griffith, John W. & Melinda Creasey, 16 June 1863; John H. Creasey, bm; m 17 June 1863 by J. Gray, J. P.

Griffith, Meshack T. & Lucy Jane Worden, 30 Aug 1860.

Griffith, Samuel & Polly Poor, 26 Dec 1819; Horatio Barker, bm.

Griffith, Samuel & _____, 4 Nov 1820; Horatio Barker, bm.

Griffith, Samuel Abraham & Mahaly J. Franklin, 29 Jan 1860; Elijah Moore, bm.

Griffith, William & Charity Childress, 28 Dec 1854.

Grimes, Jabez & Sarah Riddle, 4 May 1811; George Kinneck, bm.

Groce, Abraham & Sarah Miller, 7 Jan 1806; John Brinkley, bm.

Groce, Abraham & Eliza Lee, 9 June 1844; Alva Hutchens, bm.

Groce, Alexr. & Martha C. Harville, 4 Nov 1833; Daniel Speer, bm.

Groce, Edward & Elisabeth Childress, 8 Nov 1821; Thomas Moreland, bm.

Groce, Henry & Tabitha Rigsby, 29 July 1806; John Brinkley, bm.

Groce, Isaac & Polly Gough, 17 Oct 1812; Isaiah Humphreys, bm.

Groce, Jacob & Mary Rinager, 20 Nov 1797.

Groce, John & Mary Ann Rinegar, 18 March 1845; Samuel Hammons, bm.

Groce, Moses & Sarah Holcomb, 3 Jan 1829; Martin Castiphens, bm.

SURRY COUNTY MARRIAGES, 1779-1868

Groce, Peter & Catron Tomson, 26 Jan 1802; Jacob Shouss, bm.

Groce, Simon & Dorinda M. Pryor, 16 Jan 1844; Wiley Long, bm.

Grogg, Henry & Elliott Stone, 1 Jan 1855; John W. Newman, bm; m by A. Simmons, J. P.

Groos, John & Lizebeth Groos, 23 Nov 1802; John Shown, bm.

Grosclose, Solomon & Eliza J. Fisher, 31 March 1850; John W. Blizzard, bm. (C. H.).

Gross, Daniel & Elizabeth Gross, 24 May 1837; Daniel Wagoner, bm.

Gross, Jacob & Ailsey Harris, 12 Nov 1833; George Gross, bm.

Gross, James & Nancy Day, 30 Sept 1844; Simon Gross, bm.

Gross, Sandy & Alminda Chesher, 31 July 1867; Riley Warden, bm.

Grover, John & Polly Wilkins, 14 June 1828; Jacob Grover, bm.

Grub, Jesse & Rebecca Cox, 22 June 1863; James Gibbins, bm; m 23 June 1863 by James Needham.

Guins, Levi & Dency Daniel, 10 Sept 1820; John Guinn, bm.

Guine, Arthur & Polly Harris, 7 June 1816; Robt. Harris, bm.

Gunnel, James & Jane Puckett, 23 May 1844; Henry Young, bm.

Gunter, George F. M. & Ruth Bray, 13 Feb 1866; Wm. B. Simpson, bm; m 15 Feb 1866 by L. A. Key, J. P.

Gunter, John N. & Malinda F. Smith, 17 Nov 1853; Hugh C. Meredith, bm; m 17 Nov 1853 by A. Simmons, J. P.

Gwin, John & Nancy Poor, 27 Aug 1827; Solomon Odell, bm.

Gwyn, Franklin & Martha Childers, 23 Jan 1845; James Sparger, bm.

Gwyn, James F. & Frances E. Blair, 24 July 1865.

Gwyn, Richard Jr. & Elizabeth M. Hunt, 20 April 1820; John P. Parks, bm.

Gwynn, Aaron & Mariah J. Ayres, 5 June 1853; Joshua Ayres, bm; m 5 June 1853 by A. Simmons, J. P.

Haawks, Henry & Mary Combs, 20 Dec 1845; Nathan Hawks, bm.

Hadley, John S. & _____, 30 Dec 1839; Hiram Lovil, bm.

Hadly, Simon & Mary Spenser, 9 Jan 1786; John Martain, bm.

Hadly, Spenser & Carroline Wilson, 22 Sept 1828; George Raynolds, bm.

Hageman, Joseph & Elizabeth Speer, 14 April 1796; Strangeman Hutchens, bm.

Hagy, Jacob & Nancy Landreth, 3 March 1854; Tazwell Hagy, bm; m by A. Simmons, J. P.

SURRY COUNTY MARRIAGES, 1779-1868

Hagy, Tazwell & Polly A. Winesit, 3 March 1854; Jacob Hagy, bm; m by A. Simmons, J. P.

Haight, Benjamin F. & Jane Dyerle, 13 Oct 1856; William Windel, bm; m by A. Simmons, J. P.

Haighst, Daniel & Rebekah Cumming, 25 Jan 1811.

Hail, Francis & Priscilla Lamb, 15 Jan 1808; James Fitzgerald, Thomas Longine, Thomas C. Burch, Jesse Johnson, John East, bm.

Hail, Vinson & Lusa Spine, 14 Jan 1803; Ezekiel Kendrick, bm.

Haines, Alexander & Elizabeth(?) Plowman, 13 Oct 1831; Christopher Weatherman, bm.

Haines, Evan & Charity Enyart, 19 March 1788.

Haines, Jonathan & Polly King, 16 May 1816; William Hutchens, bm.

Haines, Jonathan & Mary McKinney, 27 Sept 1837; Eli Crumply, bm.

Haines, Nathan & _____, 10 Feb 1796; Jonthn. Haines, bm.

Haines, Nathaniel & Elizabeth Howard, 2 Aug 1837; Wm. R. Lovill, bm.

Hair, Andrew J. & Margaret Welmouth, 29 Aug 1845; James H. Wilburn, bm.

Haixl, Frederick & Mary Shambling, 10 Dec 1799; Friedrich Binkly, bm.

Haixl, George & Prudence Forkum, 26 Aug 1817; Peter Forkum Junr., bm.

Haixt, Jacob & Polly Cumming, 2 Sept 1818; Henry Baugh, bm.

Halcomb, John & Fanny Britten, 20 May 1806; Chrestin Weatherman, bm.

Halcomb, John, son of Cloe, & Fanny Holcomb, 10 March 1847; Braxton Ray, bm.

Hall, A. C. & L. E. Briggs, 3 Oct 1862; D. B. Haymore, bm.

Hall, Elliott & Nelly Morrison, 26 July 1830; Meredith Parkes, bm.

Hall, George & Mary Myrs, _____ 185-; Hamilton Wills, bm.

Hall, Henry C. & Susan Montgomery, 12 Jan 1868; James H. Sparger, bm; m 12 Jan 1868 by M. Sparger, J. P.

Hall, Henry J. & Lucinda Williamson, 22 Oct 1853.

Hall, Jacob & Polly Martin, 17 Dec 1819; William Kittle, bm.

Hall, John & Nancy Karr, 18 July 1822; Josiah Brown, bm.

Hall, Lewis & Polly Scott, 1 July 1810; Jesse Johnson, bm.

SURRY COUNTY MARRIAGES, 1779-1868

Hall, Martin & Amy Trulove, 3 Nov 1832; Hugh Martin, bm.

Hall, Martin & Mildred Ann Barksdale, 28 Dec 1839; Absalum Kerr Junr., bm.

Hall, Mady A. & Easter Joyce Sparger, 18 Nov 1847; J. A. Bingman, bm.

Hall, Miles C. & Rebeca Inman, 22 Dec 1851; James P. Haymore, bm; m 23 Dec 1851 by William Maymore, J. P.

Hall, Thomas & Sarah Guinn, 3 July 1858; Thomas B. Hicks, bm.

Hall, Thomas Junr. & Rebekah Kerr, 18 May 1811; James Brown, bm.

Hall, William M. & Mary J. Samuel, 22 July 1856; m 30 July by Wm. Haymore, J. P.

Hall, William M. & Nancy E. Linville, 18 April 1859; William H. Haymore, bm.

Halliman, Thomas & Nancy Moreland, 30 May 1803.

Ham, Jordain & Columbia McMilion, 18 July 1848; Wm. Bowman, bm.

Hamby, A. C. & Bettie Kennedy, 12 Nov 1867; m by A. H. Kapp, J. P.

Hamby, Gabriel & Nancy Horn, 13 Feb 1809; Jeremiah King, bm.

Hamil, James & _____, ----- 180-; William _____, bm.

Hamlin, Thomas & Sarah Jane Askew, 13 Nov 1844; Job Worth, bm.

Hamlin, William & Mary Vestell, 12 Dec 1819; James Fitzgerald, bm.

Hammock, John & Siller Johnson, freed people, 28 March 1867; John T. Johnson, bm; m 28 March 1867 by J. T. Johnson, J.P.

Hammons, James & Milley Nelson, 30 June 1822; Thomas Wright, bm.

Hammons, James & Susanna Patterson, 26 Nov 1822; Josiah Brown, bm.

Hammons, William & Eve Collins, 30 Dec 1813; James Kyle, bm.

Hamons, Samuel & Celey Eddelman, 2 Jan 1832; William L. Petterson(?), bm.

Hampton, John & Elizabeth Wilson, 19 June 1830; Willis Wilson, bm.

Hampton, Samuel & Theney Bostick, 19 Aug 1785; Richd. Goode, bm.

Hamrick, John & Phebe Morrison, 20 Dec 1806; George Hamrick, bm.

Hancks, Joshua & Ruth Bryan, 16 Aug 1784; George Martin, bm.

Hanes, Ellis & Naoma Mackie, 19 Jan 1850; S. A. Hough, bm.

SURRY COUNTY MARRIAGES, 1779-1868

Hanes, Harbirt & Delilah Brittain, 31 Jan 1804; Wiley Dickson, bm.

Hanes, John & Rebecca Shinn, 23 Sept 1835; Lewis Cash, bm.

Hanes, John & Mary E. Hanes, 10 Dec 1850; Alfred W. Martin, bm.

Hanes, S. F., son of Harrison & Rebecca Hanes, & Annette A. Wolfe, daughter of H. N. & Rachal Wolfe, 1 Dec 1868.

Hanes, Thomas & Nancy Ball, 6 Aug 1837; Willis Hayes, bm.

Hanes, Wm. M. & Mary M. Armstrong, 20 Oct 1848; James C. Armstrong, bm.

Hanes, William & Mary Boyd, 30 June 1853; Litle Hanes, bm; m by A. Simmons, J. P.

Hanks, George W. & Elizabeth Morris, m 4 Jan 1852 by Martin Pyne, J. P. (C. H.).

Hanks, Henry & Beeney Felts, 3 Nov 1849; Enoch Hanks, bm.

Hanks, Jacob & Polly Richardson, 13 Nov 1832; John Richardson, bm.

Hanks, Martin & Jane Hedgeens, 6 Sept 1863; Henry H. Dean, bm; m 6 Sept 1863 by Wm. Golden, J. P.

Hanks, Thomas & _____ Moore, 1 Jan 1819; Edward Moore, bm.

Hanks, Thompson & Lucy C. Roberts, 21 Aug 1856; Edward Hanks, bm; m 21 Aug 1856 by A. Simmons, J. P.

Hanks, William & _____, _____ 180-; Jos. Finney, bm; Chas Taliaferro, wit.

Hanks, William & Sally Powel Edwards, 17 June 1849; Enoch Hanks, bm.

Hanks, Wm & Elizabeth Lain, 8 Nov 1863; Joshua Felts, bm; m 8 Nov 1863 by Wm. Golden, J. P.

Harbin, Cion & Elizabeth Jones, 23 June 1812; Benjamin Stonestreet, bm.

Harbour, Adonijah & Charlotte Dolton, 3 April 1791; Wm. London, bm.

Harbour, Thomas & Jane Dolton, 12 Feb 1793; Adonijah Harbour, bm.

Hardee, John & Celia J. Ring, 26 Feb 1867; m 28 Feb 1867 by J. A. Whitaker, J. P.

Hardin, Rany & Rebecker Paterson, 7 Sept 1803; John Williams, bm.

Hardin, Tom & Elizebeth Cove, 14 Dec 1801.

Hardin, Toms. & Rurza Cook, 25 Dec 1803; John Williams, bm.

Hardy, Allen & Eliza Beasly, 7 March 1844; Thomas K. Beasly, bm.

SURRY COUNTY MARRIAGES, 1779-1868

Hardy, Henry & Winaford Gibbons, 22 April 1800; Joshaway Brown, bm.

Hardy, Henry J. & Jestin Jennings, 17 Sept 1854; Andrew J. Hardy, bm; m 17 Sept 1854 by A. Simmons, J. P.

Hardy, Isham & Sarah Slate, 31 Oct 1852; m by A. Simmons, J. P.

Hardy, John H. & Derinda Stanly, 2 Oct 1865; James M. Collins, bm. (C. H.).

Hardy, John S. & Elizabeth Gregory, 18 Jan 1839; D. M. McGee, bm.

Hardy, Thomas & Sally Carson, 23 March 1837.

Hargrove, Howell & Mary Denton, 7 Dec 1785; William Hughlett, bm.

Hargrove, James & Rebecah Warren, 11 July 1818; William Waram (?), bm.

Harmon, James & Elizabeth Bernet, 1 March 1845; Jackson Briant (Barnet), bm.

Harmon, Wilson & Elizabeth Richerson, 29 Dec 1834; George Bowers, bm.

Harold, Moses P. & Frances Holder, 23 Feb 1836; David M. Holder, bm.

Harp, John & Catharine Shores, 7 July 1834; Daniel Arnold, bm.

Harp, Wiley & Mary Penix, 20 March 1813; Lewis Harp, bm.

Harp, William & Sally Lindley, 8 Sept 1822; J. Cowles, bm.

Harrill, William & Mary Francis, 23 Feb 1850; John H. Jackson, bm. (C. H.).

Harris, Alpheus & Pamala E. Howard, 13 April 1837; Robert Sprouse, bm.

Harris, Archebald & Keturah Mosley, 17 Sept 1808; M. D. Kimbrough, bm.

Harris, Benjamin & Margarett England, 12 Oct 1784; Aaron England, bm.

Harris, Benjamin & Cathrine Beasly, 2 Aug 1823; Shadrach Beasley, bm.

Harris, C. H. & Nancy Cordell, 1 Oct 1860; John C. Cordel, bm; m 25 Sept 1860 by Rev. William Combs.

Harris, Chompten T. & Nancy Mock, 18 Nov 1826; Enoch Salmons, bm.

Harris, Daniel & Nancy Ford, 14 Nov 1852; Turner Harris, bm. (C. H.).

Harris, Ephraim & Peggy Foot, 17 Nov 1814; John Foot, bm.

Harris, Ephraim D. & Mary M. Clements, 24 May 1836; Jesse A. Waugh, bm.

SURRY COUNTY MARRIAGES, 1779-1868

Harris, Esquire & Sallie Wilmoath, 23 Dec 1865; James Tilley, bm; m 24 Dec 1865 by Henry N. Wolfe, J. P.

Harris, Harrison & Caroline Greenwood, m 16 Sept 1867 by Rev. William J. Combs.

Harris, Jacob & Charlotte Stewart, 14 Jan 1837; Stephen Haynes, bm.

Harris, James & Milly Foot, 9 Dec 1813; Ephraim D. Harris, bm.

Harris, James M. & Nancy Cordal, 11 Nov 1867.

Harris, James W. & Sally A. Cordal, 7 Dec 1866; William Richardson, bm.

Harris, Jesse T. & Mildred E. Carnaham, 13 Nov 1856; Ballard P. Hurst, bm; m 13 Nov 1856 by A. Simmons, J. P.

Harris, Joel & Sarah Norman, 17 Dec 1833; Lewis Harris, bm.

Harris, John & Judith Shelton, 16 Jan 1827; Thomas M. Shaw, bm.

Harris, John & Hannah Lowden, 25 Dec 1833; Elza Walsh, bm.

Harris, John & Elizabeth Davis, 19 June 1844; Solomon Doss, bm.

Harris, John Verdel & Jane Young, 24 Dec 1864; P. C. Cockerham, bm; m 25 Dec 1864 by A. Eldridge, J. P.

Harris, L. L. & Ann M. Captevens, 27 May 1865; W. H. Wolff, bm.

Harris, Lewis T. & Mildred R. Naylor, 10 Dec 1833; Thomas B. Naylor, bm.

Harris, Martin, son of Charles & Chane Harris, & Eliza Tickle, daughter of Henry and Frances Tickle, m 8 Nov 1868 by John Jones, at the house of Henry Tickles.

Harris, Newel & Elizabeth Tuttle, 13 Sept 1847; Settle T. Allred, bm.

Harris, Robert J. & Jane Fleming, 9 Aug 1853; E. G. Carter, bm; m 5 Sept 1853 by A. Simmons, J. P.

Harris, Silas & _____ Franklin, 7 Dec 1801; Walter Franklin, bm.

Harris, Thomas & Mary E. Phillips, 14 Feb 1855; m 7 March 1855 by A. Probtz, J. P.

Harris, Thomas N. & Sicily Scott, 4 Jan 1859; Gideon L. Hodges, bm.

Harris, William & Elizabeth Grooce, 24 Jan 1832; David Joyner, bm.

Harris, William & Caroline Poe, 23 Dec 1852; Cicero Williams, bm; m 23 Dec 1852 by _____, J. P.

Harris, William H. & Elvina Davis, 31 July 1839; B. T. Wall, bm.

Harrison, Armstead, & Mary Ann Danly, 17 Feb 1849; D. D. Tiller, bm.

SURRY COUNTY MARRIAGES, 1779-1886

Harrison, James & Ruth Howell, 23 July 1813; Jonathan Howell, Thomas Gough, bm.

Harrison, James & Rebeca Carrison, 26 April 1866; Richard Lundy, bm.

Harrison, Joel & Jane Taylor, 14 Oct 1830; B. Wooten, bm.

Harrison, Joel & Martha Davis, 28 March 1850; Columbus Thompson, bm.

Harrison, Joel, son of Joseph and Maryann Harrison, and Mary Bryant, daughter of Thomas and Ruthy Bryant, m __ Jan 1868 by James Needham, M. G.

Harrison, John & Julina Barker, 2 Feb 1867.

Harrison, Litle & Katharine Ford, 26 Sept 1863; John D. Creed, bm; m 28 Sept 1863 by Geo. A. Jervis, J. P.

Harrison, Nathl & Jemimah Stewart, 22 May 1797.

Harrison, William & Susanah Herrin, 28 June 1803; Nelson Jackson, bm.

Harrison, William & Delpha Forrester, 25 Sept 1821; William Whitaker, bm.

Harrison, Wm & Nancy Yerbs(?), 28 Dec 1866; Richard Shinault, bm.

Harrold, Elijah & Catharine Scott, 15 March 1838; Newel Eaton, bm.

Harrold, Franklin & Elizabeth Eads, 6 April 1848; Thomas E. Harrold, bm.

Hart, David & Hannah Dufriest, 9 March 1801; James Fitzgerald, bm.

Hartgrove, William & Nancy Poindexter, 10 Aug 1839; J. J. Poindexter, bm.

Harvey, Thomas & Sucky Smith, 27 July 1802; John Moss, bm.

Harvill, John & Charlotte Elliott, 5 Jan 1795; John Allen, bm.

Harvill, Moses & Levina Williams, 7 Dec 17 1807; Abiram Carter, bm.

Hatcher, Charles F. & Nancey Pettet, 4 Oct 1833; Frances Pettet, bm.

Hatcher, Jerimiah & Janan McDonald, 3 Feb 1827; Isaac Copland, bm.

Hatcher, Uriah & Martha Roberson, 2 Oct 1865; Thomas H. Lamkin, bm; m 2 Oct 1865 by Jos. H. Lewellin.

Hatley, John & Elizabeth Stone, 12 Oct 1815; Elijah Stone, bm.

Hauser, Egbert & Mary A. Melvin, 27 March 1861; m by W. W. Wolff, J. _.

Hauser, H. B. & V. M. Kerby, 11 Feb 1866; D. J. Cockerham, bm.

SURRY COUNTY MARRIAGES, 1779-1868

Hauser, Jacob & Sarah McBride, 22 Nov _____; Henry Sater, bm.

Hauser, John & Cristena Pinkley, 1 Aug 1809; Peter Pinkley, bm.

Hauser, John & Elizabeth C. Poindexter, 18 Oct 1829; John G. Pettit, bm.

Hauser, Joseph & Katharine Stroope, 6 April 1786; Adam Elrode, bm. (filed under Houzar).

Hauser, Joseph M. & Mary Ward, 7 March 1814; John Stonestreet, bm.

Hauser, Thomas & Polly Moreland, 2 May 1820; George Hudson, bm.

Hauser, Thomas & Martha Griffith, 13 Nov 1849; M. C. Norman, bm.

Hawkins, Robert & Polly Graves, 4 Aug 1806; Martin Armstrong, bm.

Hawkins, William & Catharine Steelman, 7 Jan 1837; Samuel Cain, bm.

Hawks, Abraham & Beauty Briant, 3 April 1834; Robert Hawks, bm.

Hawks, Dalton & Sary Payne, 10 Aug 1848; Jackson Payne, bm.

Hawks, Harden & _____, 31 Oct 1836; Payton Talley, bm.

Hawks, Hugh & Suffina Williams, 3 April 1855.

Hawks, J. T. & Elizabeth Hawks, 17 March 1864.

Hawks, Loranzy Dow & Malviny Hawks, 9 July 1848; Wm. Golden, bm.

Hawks, Martin & Martha J. Comer, 3 Feb 1856; m by B. F. Scott, J. P.

Hawks, Richard & Gincy Johnson, 16 Aug 1855; m by B. F. Scott, J. P.

Hawlley, John & Emily McDonnel, 20 Oct 1856; William H. Pillar, bm; m 20 Oct 1856 by A. Simmons, J. P.

Hayes, Charles & Polly Cope, 8 Dec 1819; John Longworth, bm.

Hayes, William & Ann Cunningham, 15 Aug 1820; Joseph Ramey Junr., bm.

Haymore, Albert & Lamy Cherkman, 1 April 1862; Joseph Williams, bm; m 3 April 1862 by Wm. R. Bray, J. P.

Haymore, Britten & Polly Taylor, 28 Jan 1823; Thomas Barker, bm.

Haymore, D. B. & Lucyann Redman, 22 Dec 1863; Sandy Cook, bm; m 24 Dec 1863 by M. A. Hall, J. P.

Haymore, H. W. & Elizabeth Beasley, 25 June 1863; Daniel Haymore, bm; m 26 June 1853 by William Haynes, J. P.

Haymore, Hastlan & Sarah Marion, 14 April 1863; D. M. Cooper, bm; m 16 April 1863 by M. A. Hall, J. P.

Haymore, Jarmon & Jane Pitmon, 2 Jan 1830; Blewmon Haymore, bm.

SURRY COUNTY MARRIAGES, 1779-1868

Haymore, John J. & Elizabeth Jane Inman, 5 Jan 1847; Mady A. Hall, bm.

Haymore, William D. & Keziah Ann Hall, 2 Oct 1849; Columbus Thompson, bm.

Haymore, Williamson E. & Elizabeth Venable, 21 Oct 1851; Columbus Thompson, bm; m 30 Oct 1851 by William Haymore, J. P.

Haynes, Archable & Matilda Combs, 9 Jan 1868; Edward J. Gwyn, bm; m 9 Jan 1868 by Murlin Sparger, J. P.

Haynes, Caleb H. & Margret Davis, 23 March 1857; m 6 May 1857 by E. Banner, J. P.

Haynes, James & Frances Cox, 7 Oct 1846; Wm. H. Moore, bm.

Haynes, John & Matilda Combs, 6 Feb 1856; Lemuel Gwyn, bm; m 6 Feb 1856 by A. Simmons, J. P.

Haynes, Joseph & Susan L. Johnson, 12 May 1850; Philip W. Johnson, bm. (C. H.).

Haynes, S. M. & Sinthy Goyn, 22 Dec 1867; Samuel Haynes, bm; m 22 Dec 1867 by Murlin Sparger, J. P.

Haynes, Samuel & Margaret Johnson, 13 Dec 1849; William Edwards, bm.

Hazelwood, Hiram G. & Nancy J. McGee, 14 Sept 1865; Lemuel McGee, bm.

Head, Abraham & Elizabeth Brown, 2 May 1801.

Head, Anthony & Nancy Johnson, 2 Aug 1824; Stephen Shelton, bm.

Head, Benjamin & Fanny Speer, 13 Jan 1816; William Pettitt, bm.

Head, Daniel & Lydia Cordle, 12 Feb 1845; William Adams, bm.

Head, George & Ellender Cory, 10 May 1800.

Head, Isaac & Jane Dial, 5 Jan 1821; Nathaniel Norman, bm.

Head, James & Catherine Groce, 31 Aug 1818; Thomas Brown, bm.

Head, John & Dinah Fargusson, 30 Sept 1808; Isaiah Stewart, bm.

Head, John & Anny Shelton, 21 April 1823; Stephen Shelton, bm.

Head, John A. & Jane Taylor, 13 Nov 1850; Isaac Hutchins, bm. (C. H.).

Head, Joseph & Polly Dial, 8 March 1819; Matthew Taylor, bm.

Head, Josiah C. & Sarah Taylor, 22 Dec 1849; John Norman, bm.

Head, William & Sarah Currey, 16 April 1791; David Poindexter, bm.

Heath, John & Elizabeth Fulk, 6 April 1864; Caleb D. Hill, bm; m 9 April 1864 by James Needham, M. G.

Hedgecock, John L. & Elizabeth Edwards, 30 Jan 1857; Jas. L. Copeland, bm; m 30 Jan 1867 by D. M. McGee, J. P.

SURRY COUNTY MARRIAGES, 1779-1868

Hedge, Grayson & Ferabee Grimes, 3 Oct 1847; S. D. Moore, bm.

Helms, Madison & Mary A. Serman, 27 June 1858; Claborn Lawson, bm.

Helper, Tyson & Martha Brinkley, 2 Oct 1865.

Hemmons, James & Elisabeth K. McBride, 1 Nov 1864; Edward McBride, bm; m 6 Nov 1864 by J. Gray, J. P.

Hemmons, William C. & Jincy Taylor, 12 May 1858; James W. Hemmons, bm.

Hemrick, Henry & Amelia Tucker, 16 Oct 1830; Hamel Money, bm.

Hemrick, John & Mary Buckhanon, 17 July 1830; Henry Hemrick, bm.

Hemrick, Levi & Susanna Howel, 9 Feb 1838; Sidney Collins, bm.

Henderson, Jackson Brown & Louisa Caroline Mimsk, 8 Nov 1856; m 9 Nov 1856 by J. N. Burkem, parson.

Henderson, Pleasant & Sarah Martin, 27 Jan 1786; Thomas Henderson, William Meredith, bm.

Hendrick, Benjamin & Nancy S. Waff, 4 Dec 1853; William Hines, bm; m 4 Dec 1853 by A. Simmons, J. P.

Hendricks, George & Sally Jefferson, 25 May 1846; Lewis Cash, bm.

Hendricks, John & Lidey Garner, 2 May 1825; John Garner, bm.

Hendricks, Joseph & Polly West, 6 Jan 1827; Frederick Hendricks, bm.

Hendrix, Henry & Ann Ross, 14 Nov 1837; James Langly, bm.

Henly, Josiah & David Midkiff (sic), 10 Jan 1840; David Midkiff, bm.

Henning, Adam & Anne Webster, 17 March 1832; Henry Shoen, bm.

Henric, William & Martha Olvy, 7 March 1835; Henry Money, bm.

Herndon, Jesse & Nancy Shelton, 27 Nov 1828; James Taylor, bm.

Herndon, Robert & Sally Pikes, 8 March 1838; Daniel Shenall, bm.

Herring, Delany & Jensey Fletcher, 11 Feb 1799.

Herring, Harden & Elizabeth Dudley, 3 Nov 1828; William Gorden, bm.

Herring, Henry H. & Sarah Mildred Johnson, 17 Aug 1865; Wm. Haymore, bm; m 20 Aug 1865 at the house of William John Lows, by John Jones.

Hervy, James & Ollive Bryson, 5 Aug 1814; John Bryson, bm.

Hester, Jeremiah W. & Rebecker Smith, 6 Dec 1853; m 6 Dec 1853 by D. M. Cooper, J. P.; C. L. Banner, bm.

SURRY COUNTY MARRIAGES, 1779-1868

Hester, Stephen & Elizabeth Watson, 24 Sept 1798.

Hiatt, Jacob & Arminda Berker, 6 March 1845; Iredell A. Venable, bm.

Hiatt, James M. & Louisa A. Walton, 23 March 1867; Harrison Patterson, bm; in 31 March 1867 by A. Whitaker, J. P.

Hiatt, John & Mary Boyd, 2 May 1855; James L. McMillion, bm; m 2 May 1855 by A. Simmons, J. P.

Hiatt, Jno. M. & Eliza M. Holyfield, 27 Dec 1864; Alfred Adkins, bm; m 27 Dec 1864 by John Jones at the dweling of Alfred Atkins.

Hiatt, Jonathan & Frances Taylor, 20 Dec 1854; Daniel Haymore, bm; m 21 Dec 1854 by Wm. Haymore, J. P.

Hiatt, Nathan & Nancy McMillion, 16 May 1848; Ephraim Hiatt, bm.

Hiatt, Nathan & Ruthia Brinkley, 6 Nov 1859; Jesse L. Barker, bm; m 6 Nov 1859 by E. Banner, J. P.

Hiatt, Wesley, son of Martin Hiatt, and Elizabeth B. Atkerson, daughter of Johnson & Elizabeth H. Atkinson, m 9 Feb 1868 by Jas. H. Lewellin.

Hiatt, William & Elizabeth Boyd, 11 May 1862; James Boyd, bm; certificate says William McMilon and Elizabeth Boyd, m 11 May 1862 by Wm. R. Bray, J. P.

Hiatt, William & Sally Dunigan, 21 Dec 1817; Saml Simmons, bm.

Hiatte, George W., son of Adaline Hiatte, and Julina Childres, daughter of Robert & Masse Childres, m 3 Aug 1868 by Marquis L. Wood, minister.

Hickman, Joseph & Mary Brown, 8 Jan 1805; Wm. Brown, bm.

Hickmon, Jefferson & Mahala Taylor, 18 Dec 1855; Caleb D. Hill, bm; m 20 Dec 1858 by William Hill, J. P.

Hickmon, John & Dinah Davis, 29 Oct 1810; Robert Bartlett, bm.

Hickman, Jefferson & Mary Needham, 23 Dec 1845; John Midkiff, bm.

Hickmon, Thomas & Hannah Adams, 7 Jan 1835; Gideon E. McKinney, bm.

Hickmon, Thomas & Sarah Isbell, 19 Aug 1817; Richard Isbell, bm.

Hickman, Wm. H. & Gemima Creed, 28 Sept 1831; Watson Holyfield, bm.

Hickmon, Edwin & Betsey Isbell, 4 Aug 1823; Hickman Isbell, bm.

Hicks, Geo. W., son of Wm. H. & Sarah Hicks, & Lydia Hodges, daughter of John and Malissa Hodges, m 20 Dec 1868 by M. H. Armsfield, J. P.

Hicks, Henry S. & Adaline Gentry, 30 Nov 1837; Shadrac Gentry, bm.

SURRY COUNTY MARRIAGES, 1779-1868

Hicks, J. F. & Sarah A. Bray, 18 May 1852; Andrew Burge, bm.

Hicks, James & Elizabeth Davis, 16 Oct 1799.

Hicks, John & Martha Harison, 11 May 1846; J. Hollinsworth, bm.

Hicks, Joshua F. & E. E. Combs, 22 May 1865; Churchwell Combs, bm.

Hicks, Martin & Margaret Jinnings, 5 Oct 1858; Canaan Ogle, bm.

Hicks, Marvill & Patsey Brewbaker, 18 June 1814; Jas. A. Thornton, bm.

Hicks, Samuel & Lucy James, 14 Oct 1809; James Hicks, bm.

Hicks, Thomas B. & Mildred O. Zackery, 29 March 1859; m 29 March 1859.

Hicks, William & Polly Moss, 28 May 1802; Thomas Wright, bm.

Hicks, Wm. & Ann Davis, 31 Dec 1799; Samuel Hicks, bm.

Hiett, Calep & Patsy Roberts, 3 Dec 1815; Ransom Dudley, bm.

Hiett, Edmond & Rebeca Taylor, 25 Feb 1851; Drury McGee, bm; m 25 Feb 1851 by Wm. Haymore, J. P.

Hiett, G. W. & Mariah C. Taylor, 30 Aug 1867; Samuel D. Critz, bm; m 1 Sept 1867 by M. A. Hall, J. P.

Hiett, Jesse & Julia Taylor, 20 March 1818; Samuel Simmons, bm.

Hiett, Moses & Patsey Donelly, 9 May 1811; Matthew Kincanor, bm.

Hiett, William & Mary Taylor, 15 Oct 1845; Daniel Taylor, bm.

Higgins, Hiram and Martha Thompson, 6 Jan 1868; m by A. H. Kapp, J. P.

Hight, John C. & Charlotte J. Wood, 21 Oct 1863; Elisha Banner, bm; m 21 Oct 1864 by E. Banner, J. P.

Hill, Benjamin & Mary Standfield, 15 Oct 1808.

Hill, Benjamin & Milly Horton, 12 March 1865; William H. Davis, bm; m 12 March 1865 by A. Simmons, J. P.

Hill, Charles & Elizabeth Briggs, 16 March 1849; Jacob Crouse, bm.

Hill, Clement & Betsey Brown, 8 Aug 1813; James Brown, bm.

Hill, Clemont & Ann Raughton, 16 Dec 1826; Thomas Minish, bm.

Hill, David & Catharine Moore, 5 May 1864; m 5 May 1864 by W. M. Hicks, J. P.

Hill, Harison & Sarah Ann Stewart, 23 March 1865; Jenrel Hill, bm; m 23 March 1864 by J. R. Patterson, J. P.

Hill, James S. & Mary L. Banner, 28 May 1860; m by J. W. Avent, Methodist minister.

SURRY COUNTY MARRIAGES, 1779-1868

Hill, Joel & Emily Davis, 3 Feb 1836; Leonard Davis, bm.

Hill, John & Elizabeth Douglass, 25 Dec 1794; Solomon S. Yerrell, bm.

Hill, John & Dizzy Gibson, 2 July 1791; John Gibson, bm.

Hill, John & Nancy Simmons, 28 March 1848; Wm. Mathews, bm.

Hill, Joseph & Mary Ann Lovins, 6 Nov 1846; Elisha Banner, bm.

Hill, Joseph & Margarett Seaser, 28 Sept 1862; Samuel D. Critz, bm; m 28 Sept 1862 by A. Simmons, J. P.

Hill, Joshua & Fanny Seasar, 15 Jan 1854; Allen Denny, bm; m 15 Jan 1854 by A. Dunnagan, J. P.

Hill, Noah & Lucretia Hill, 20 Oct 1840.

Hill, Richard & Sarah Bray, 5 Sept 1814; Edwd. Beeson, bm.

Hill, Richard & Priscilla Peel, 1 Sept 1820; Joseph Fagg, bm.

Hill, Riley & Mary Seaser, 19 Feb 1864; Peter Seaser, bm; m 21 Feb 1864 by A. Simmons, J. P.

Hill, Robert & Mary A. Jones, 17 Jan 1864; John H. Hill, bm; m 24 Jan 1864 by James Needham, M. G.

Hill, Thomas & Sarah Hill, 13 Oct 1839; James Jarvis, bm.

Hill, William & Demaris Colvard, 4 Nov 1804.

Hill, William & Delila Hanks, 13 March 1830; C. S. Easley, bm.

Hill, William & Dasha Whitaker, 8 March 1842.

Hill, William & Nancy A. Whittington, 25 Jan 1859; John H. Boyles, bm.

Hill, William & Saluda Patterson, 1 March 1867; Gabriel Denny, bm; m 3 March 1867 by J. A. Whitaker, J. P.

Hill, Zepheniah & Susan Hauser, 26 July 1831; Moses Ritchy, bm.

Hilsabeck, Henry & Alsey Childress, 17 July 1792; Jacob Helsabeck, bm.

Hilsaback, Henery & Crisy Martain, 1 Nov 1800.

Hilton, Abraham & Rebecker Vestall, 30 Oct 1801.

Hilton, Allen & _____ Davis, 28 Nov 1821; Niel Vestal, bm.

Hines, Robert & Susan Forkner, 18 Nov 1833; Madison D. Carter, bm.

Hinsdale, Henry & Sally Gowin, 4 Nov 1864; m 16 Nov 1864 by Julius Terrill.

Hinshaw, Benjamin & Sarah Vestal, 10 Nov 1812; Jonathan Hinshaw, bm.

Hinshaw, Benjamin & Rebecka Patterson, 4 March 1826; Simon H. Martin, bm.

SURRY COUNTY MARRIAGES, 1779-1868

Hinshaw, Benjamin Junr. & Ruth Carter, 9 Oct 1814; Benjamin Hinshaw, bm.

Hinshaw, Eli & Phebe Vestal, 20 March 1816; Peter Dowel, bm.

Hinshaw, James C. & Elizbeth Reece, 29 Oct 1836; Wilson Reece, bm.

Hinshaw, John & Hannah Carter, 1 June 1823; Benjamin Hinshaw, bm.

Hinshaw, Thomas & _____, 11 Feb 1794; David Vestal, bm.

Hinshaw, William & Jane Hamm, 5 March 1795; "Wm Johnson son of Martha to pay a Dollar so says Moses Addams".

Hobson, David & Anne Hadly, 9 Feb 1809; Thomas Vestal, bm.

Hobson, David & Matilda Lakey, 17 Jan 1829; Jonathan North, bm.

Hobson, David Jr. & Elizabeth Logan, 10 July 1829; Peter Clingman, bm.

Hobson, George & Zilpha J. Williams, 22 Nov 1836; Jesse F. Lakey, bm.

Hobson, John & Suzana Flemmon, 26 Dec 1836; David Hobson Jr., bm.

Hobson, Sammuel & Jude Murphy, 7 Oct 1797.

Hobson, Silas & Marth Pendry, 13 June 1808; David Hobson, bm.

Hobson, Stephen H. & Mary Clingman, 17 Jan 1832; Gabl. Poindexter, bm.

Hobson, Thomas & Rebecah Williams, 20 Jan 1817; Jessee Williams, bm.

Hobson, Thomas & Keziah Reece, 16 Dec 1834; Danl. McGee, bm.

Hobson, William & Bidey Hadly, 10 Nov 1808; Benjamin Hutchens, bm.

Hobson, William & Dorathy B. Wilson, 17 Dec 1828; John Martin Junr., bm.

Hodge, Abner & Polly Waggoner, 12 Sept 1817; John Campbell, bm.

Hodge, Isom & Frances Potter, 20 March 1826; Daniel Hodge, bm.

Hodge, Joseph & C---- McMickle, 17 Dec 1813; Peter McMickle, bm.

Hodge, William & Dorcus Cuningam, 31 March 1825; Elijah Auberry, bm.

Hodges, Aaron & Rebecca Laffoon, 21 July 1831; Wilson Laffoon, bm.

Hodges, Albert A. & Leder Flippin, m 17 Nov 1867 by Thos. J. Lawson, M. G.

Hodges, Andy & Lany Riggs, 26 Dec 1832; Pleasant Hodges, bm.

SURRY COUNTY MARRIAGES, 1779-1868

Hodges, Asa & Clary Dudley, 9 Oct 1830; Joel Kerby, bm.

Hodges, Columbus & Barthilda Scott, 2 Jan 1867; Jesse G. Isaacks, bm; m 3 Jan 1867 by Thos. J. Lawson, M. G.

Hodges, Daniel & Mary V. Nations, 1 Feb 1855; Jacob Nations, bm; m 2 Feb 1858 by Jno. J. McMickle, J. P.

Hodges, Daniel & Sarah Hickman, 7 Dec 1825; Isham Hodges, bm.

Hodges, Drury & Mehaley Gillespie, 13 Jan 1817; James Robertson, bm.

Hodges, Drury & Nancy Gentry, 24 Jan 1863; Ice Snow, bm; m 26 Jan 1863 by R. F. McGuffin, J. P.

Hodges, Evand & Frances Hagins, 16 April 1848; Preston Hodges, bm.

Hodges, Gidion S. & Mary M. Norman, 21 Feb 1854; Mily Burrus, bm; m 29 Feb 1854 by D. R. Cockerham, J. P.

Hodges, Hubard & Martha Hodges, 7 June 1863; A. C. Dunnagan, bm; m 7 June 1863 by Geo. A. Jervis, J. P.

Hodges, Hubbard & Mary Smith, 13 Jan 1829; Jiles Hodges, bm.

Hodges, James & Sally Robertson, 24 Dec 1829; Samuel Kirby, bm.

Hodges, James R. & Amey Ward, 24 Nov 1853; James Nations, bm; m 24 Nov 1853 by Jo. Phillips, J. P.

Hodges, James W. & Sarah Riggs, 22 Sept 1867; m 22 Sept 1867 by H. Laffoon, J. P.

Hodges, Jesse & Peggy Bartley, 18 July 1817; Joseph Hodges, bm.

Hodges, Joel W. & Sally Snow, 10 May 1865; George M. Jarvis, bm; m 14 May 1863 by Geo. A. Jarvis, J. P.

Hodges, Joseph & Mary Noblitt, 11 Sept 1803; James Jervis, bm.

Hodges, Major & Elizabeth Sexton, 12 June 1829; Matthew Hodges, bm.

Hodges, Moses & Mary Potter, 10 April 1821; Drury Hodges, bm.

Hodges, Pleasant & Matilda Cunningham, 4 July 1829; Robert Gentry, bm.

Hodges, Pleasant & Mary Moody, 1 Aug 1864; S. A. Freeman, bm; m 7 Aug 1864 by D. A. Eldridge, J. P.

Hodges, Thomas R. & Rebeca Galespie, 23 Nov 1844; Drury Hodges, bm.

Hodges, Tyre & Elizabeth Burcham, 6 Jan 1853; Thomas D. Davis, bm; m 6 Jan 1853 by Jo. Phillips, J. P.

Hodges, Welcome H. & Sarah Bowers, 28 Sept 1839; Alpheus Harris, bm.

Hodges, William & Rachel Hodges, 16 April 1828; Drury Hodges, bm.

SURRY COUNTY MARRIAGES, 1779-1868

Hodges, William & Emely Lewis, 30 Sept 1846; Elija Bartley, bm.

Hodges, William & Julian Bean, 10 Nov 1855; L. J. Norman, bm; m 10 Nov 1855 by L. J. Norman.

Hodges, William Jr. & Elizabeth Gentry, 11 March 1849; William Cave, Andy Hodges, bm.

Hodgins, Robert & Minerva Hill, 6 May 1867; John S. Green, bm; m 7 May 1867 by Joel Denny, J. P.

Hofines, Adam & Peggy Forkum, 17 Oct 1816; Jacob Hicks, bm.

Hofines, Jacob & Elizabeth Hixt, 15 Feb 1808; William Shepperd, bm.

Holaday, Thomas & Elizabeth Freeman, 11 March 1823; Hadly Reece, bm.

Holand, B. F. & Amanda J. King, 29 March 1866; Charles W. Hurst, bm.

Holbrook, Caleb & Mary Winfrey, 3 Jan 1826; John Winfree, bm.

Holcomb--see also Halcomb.

Holcomb, Branch & Sally Arnold, 16 Feb 1816; William Faircloth, bm.

Holcomb, Dr. D. F. & Ann A. York, 28 Aug 1865; J. F. Brindle, m 8 Sept 1865 by J. F. Smoot, M. G.

Holcomb, Drury & Rhoda Lewis, 29 March 1822; Phillip Holcomb, bm.

Holcomb, George & Nancy Chappel, 15 May 1834; Stephen Pledger, bm.

Holcomb, George & Ann Lang, 10 Sept 1835; James Sheek, bm.

Holcomb, Graham & Permiley McMickel, 28 Aug 1832; John Paysinger(?), bm.

Holcomb, Graham A. & _____ Stockbuyer, 18 Sept 1835; Jas. Armstrong, bm.

Holcomb, John L. & Elizabeth Long, 4 Dec 1849; Philip L. Holcomb, bm.

Holcomb, Leroy & Cloe Elliott, 20 Oct 1802; Thomas Holcomb, bm.

Holcomb, Micajah & Polly Chappell, 11 Feb 1845; James Chappell, bm.

Holcomb, Thomas & Dothe Elliott, 17 July 1797.

Holcomb, Thomas & Susan Sparks, 9 Oct 1833; Leroy Holcomb, bm.

Holcomb, Thomas & Elizabeth Long, 18 Feb 1846; Nathan Long, bm.

Holcombe, Jas. & Frances Glascock, 31 Oct 1803; Phillip Holcomb, bm.

Holcombe, Lewis & Clarinda Johnson, 11 May 1808; William Robinson, bm.

SURRY COUNTY MARRIAGES, 1779-1868

Holcombe, Philip & Margit Joiner, 16 Oct 1800.

Holcombe, Wm & Mary Robinson, 13 Feb 1795.

Holder, Baler & Deborah York, 5 Nov 1813; Abraham Badgett, bm.

Holder, Baler & Deborah York, 12 Nov 1813; John Horn, bm.

Holder, Deasting & Mary Wilson, 17 Sept 1823; Baler Holder, bm.

Holder, Elisha B. & Leatha J. Edmonds, 4 June 1853; Newel J. Harris, bm; m 5 June 1853 by Wilson Laffoon, J. P.

Holder, Henderson & Polly Creed, 13 Nov 1830; James Vhon, bm.

Holder, John & Elizabeth Smallwood, 28 Nov 1820; Michael Idoel, bm.

Holder, John & Susan Hughes, 8 Feb 1832; S. G. Pettitt, bm.

Holder, John & Nancy Howard, 4 May 1837; James P. Fitzgerald, bm.

Holder, William & Elizabeth Isbell, 16 July 1832; Jas. Howard, bm.

Holder, William & Jincy Snow, 22 Dec 1832; John Snow, bm.

Holderfield, John & Mahaley Coale, 3 Aug 1819; William Watson, bm.

Holderfield, Watson & Peggy Venables, 21 Dec 1814; Ralph Holderfield, bm.

Holding, John & _____, 7 Aug 1845; Avery Norman, bm.

Holding, John & Fanny Beard, 31 March 1846; H. G. Hampton, bm.

Holebrook, Robert & Frances Cook, 20 July 1803; Jobe Winfree, bm.

Holeman, Absalom & Hannah Hudspeth, 27 Jan 1794; Thompson Glen, bm.

Holeman, Jon. & Nancy Aln---t, 10 Sept 1806; Dan. Wright, bm.

Holifield, Valentine & Alsey Heckerpeck, 24 Oct 1803; Solomon Harris, bm.

Holifield, Valentine Junr. & Sally Whoton, 8 Dec 1806; Jonathan Dyer, bm.

Holliman, John & Elizabeth Kidner, 15 Sept 1798; William Hollimon Jr., bm; "Stokes County."

Holliman, Mark & Nancy Glen, 23 Feb 1790; Wm. Hollemon, bm.

Hollimon, Wm. Jr. & Sarah Howard, 13 July 1795.

Hollingsworth, Leander & Cristeny Shelton, 22 Feb 1865; Edward McBride, bm; m 23 Feb 1865 by J. Gray, J. P.

Hollinsworth, E. F. & Sarah R. Banner, 9 Dec 1858; H. V. Allred, bm.

SURRY COUNTY MARRIAGES, 1779-1868

Hollinsworth, Joseph & Mary L. Banner, 31 Aug 1847; Winston Fulton, bm.

Hollinsworth, William R. & Susan H. Shaw, 4 April 1867.

Holloway, William & Polley Martin, 25 Aug 1812; Thomas Fuller, bm.

Holstine, Jacob J. & Lucy A. Anderson, 28 July 1849; Allen Denny, bm.

Holt, James & Metilda Thorp, 4 Aug 1823; Carter Hudspeth, bm.

Holyfield, C. C. & Cary A. Snow, 7 July 1866.

Holyfield, Harden & _____, 27 Dec 1832; Benj. F. Bray, bm.

Holyfield, Isaac & Nancy Perry, 25 Dec 1856; m 27 Dec 1856 by W. D. Rutledge, J. P.

Holyfield, Jefferson & Mary Ann Tuggle, 28 May 1859; Tho. J. Doss, bm.

Holyfield, Martin & Jane Odier, 5 Aug 1847; John Holyfield, bm.

Holyfield, Wm. & Rosey Evans, 2 June 1832; Burgess Wood, bm.

Hood, John & Rozeannah Critchlow, 5 May 1795; John Giles, bm.

Hooker, Samuel & Sally Harris, 15 July 1816; Isaac Pike, bm.

Hoots, Hen. & Ann Groace, 13 June 1803; Simon Groace, bm.

Hoots, Jacob & Polly Carver, 11 Jan 1791; George Zeglar, bm.

Hoots, Jacob & Mary Renniger, 16 Oct 1819; John Renniger, bm.

Hoots, John & Frances Taylor, 2 March 1795; Josh Miller, bm.

Hoots, Philip & Mary Morgan, 10 March 1792; John Miller, bm.

Hopkins, John & Rebekah Colvard, 19 April 1809; John Purdom, Thomas Purdom, bm.

Hopper, Edward & Sally Gibbons, 30 March 1819; Hugh Davis, bm.

Hoppers, George & Mary Dillard, 28 Jan 1814; Hugh Davis, bm.

Hoppor, John & Anne Brown, 22 Dec 1806; John Miller, bm.

Hopson, Nicholas & Patsey Stanley, 7 April 1825; Isaac Jester, bm.

Horn, George & Patsey Johnson, 24 March 1822; Joseph Athon, John Johnson, bm.

Horn, Stephen & Nancy Hewett, 14 Nov 1797; Abraham Stoe, bm.

Horter, James & Elender Smith, 16 March 1855; John Mays, bm; m 18 March 1855 by Jno. J. McMickle, J. P.

Horton, Amos & Elizabeth Ludd(?), 25 Jan 1848; William Massy, bm.

SURRY COUNTY MARRIAGES, 1779-1868

Horton, Henry & Rachel A. Edmond, 27 April 1864; Henry H. Jenkins, bm; m 27 April 1864 by A. Simmons, J. P.

Horton, Henry & Sally A. Johnson, 27 April 1855; Vinson Horton, bm; m 27 Aprl 1855 by A. Simmons, J. P.

Horton, Jesse & Pricilla Mahaffe, 15 June 1844; Jas. Horton, bm.

Horton, Vinson & Susannah Johnson, 27 April 1855; Henry Horton, bm; m 27 April 1855 by A. Simmons, J. P.

Horton, William R. & Anniss Hardy, 11 March 1855; Greenville Webb, bm; m 11 March 1855 by A. Simmons, J. P.

Houfhines, Jno. & Mary Tull, 26 March 1800.

Hough, A. S. & Sarah A. Burch, 25 April 1844; Jas. E. Hough, bm. (C. H.).

Houts, Antony & Suzanna Grissom, 1 Aug 1799; Jacob Houts, bm.

Houzars, Heny & _____, 25 Aug 1788; John Harvey Jr., John Harvey, bm.

Howard, Benjamin & Polly Kimbrough, 23 March 1816; MDuke Kimbrough, bm.

Howard, Benjamin & Betsey Walker, 19 Feb 1804; Jesse Lester, bm.

Howard, Hennery Spoon & Sarah Devenport, 13 Dec 1802; Thomas Devenport, bm.

Howard, Jonathan & Elizabeth Walker, 31 Jan 1815; Hensen Atha, bm.

Howard, Joseph & Nancy Early, 15 July 1818; Micajah Reaves, bm.

Howard, Joseph Jr. & Cary Denny, 10 Sept 1836; John Moore, bm.

Howard, Lorensa D. & Elizabeth Hodges, 18 June 1832; Charles Howard, Waitman Sumers, bm.

Howard, Phillip & Elizabeth Fair, 5 Sept 1791; John Truitt, bm.

Howard, Stanwix & Istaney Burress, 20 April 1786; John Fleming, bm.

Howard, Wm. & Sarah Bryan, 10 Sept 1794; Phillip Howard, bm.

Howe, Norval D. & Mary E. Burkheart, 23 Oct 1865; Frederick Burkheart, bm; m 23 Oct 1865 by G. A. Lowe, J. P.

Howel, George & Frances Doudge, 19 June 1831; R. W. Grant, bm.

Howell, David & Mary Thompson, 26 July 1786; Samuel Crocket, bm.

Howell, John & Mary Busey, 22 Aug 1792; Stephen Howell, bm.

Howell, Joseph & Jane Creson, 10 Jan 1802; Abraham Creson, bm.

Howell, Thomas B. & Sarah Ann Hicks, 8 Dec 1834; William Day, bm.

SURRY COUNTY MARRIAGES, 1779-1868

Howerton, Robert & Letefood Higgs, 22 Feb 1855; Robert Briant, bm; m 22 Feb 1855 by A. Simmons, J. P.

Howlet, William & Nancy Kelly, 27 May 1823; Isaac James & Marmaduke Kimbrough, bm.

Huchens, Samuel & Letty Algood, 8 Oct 1830; Henry R. Algood, bm.

Huchins, John & Sally Hunter, 2 April 1851; Samuel Adams, bm.

Huddle, David & Margaret P. Earhart, 7 April 1857; James W. Lockett, bm.

Hudlon, David & Polly Mock, 13 Sept 1815; Stephen Elrod, bm.

Hudson, George & Fanny Blake, 19 Nov 1817; Daniel Stultz, bm.

Hudson, Jas. J. & Miss B. F. Parrish, 8 June 1856; P. C. Javney, bm; M. A. York, wit.

Hudson, John W. & Rachel Mooney, 3 Jan 1856.

Hudson, Meredith & Nancy Creed, 28 Nov 1825; Herod Loftus, bm.

Hudson, Obediah & Sarah Cave, 25 Dec 1813; Ransom Dudly, bm.

Hudson, William & Polley Phillips, 25 July 1807; John Chapman, bm.

Hudspeth, Carter & Fanny Youse, 4 March 1813; Thomas Wright, bm.

Hudspeth, Charles & Elizabeth Glen, 18 Feb 1788; Thompson Glen, bm.

Hudspeth, John & Sarah Weatherman, 21 Feb 1829; John Holcomb, bm.

Hudspeth, Jordon & Polly Collins, 11 Aug 1835; Tho. Tucker, bm.

Hudspeth, Meshack & Mary Teasley, 14 Feb 1830; Jas. Hudspeth, bm.

Hudspeth, Morgan & Mary Rutledge, 16 Jan 1808; William Sweat Junr., bm.

Hudspeth, Thos & Sarah Glen, 4 Jan 1790; Charles Hudspeth, bm.

Hudspeth, Turner & Sally Shores, 3 Sept 1836; A. P. Colvard, bm.

Huff, G. W. & Penelope A. Huff, 2 Feb 1865; m 2 Feb 1865 by A. Simmons, J. P.

Huff, John & Nancy Snow, 3 Dec 1848; Zachariah Williams, bm.

Huff, Joshua & Rachael Martin, 3 March 1807; Jesse Reece, bm.

Huffhines, Phillip & Rachael Early, 1 Dec 1802; William Shepperd, bm.

Hughes, James & Martha Roberts, 12 Oct 1834; Joseph M. Richardson, bm.

Hughes, William & Juda Reece, 15 Nov 1828; Matthew M. Hughes, bm.

SURRY COUNTY MARRIAGES, 1779-1868

Hughlett, Robert & Elizabeth McCraw, 2 June 1819; Nathaniel Bryson, bm.

Hughlett, William & Mary Tate, 28 June 1784; Roger Giddins, bm.

Hull, Gregory & Sally Ann Greenwood, 14 Jan 1835; James Taylor, bm.

Hull, Robert & Nancy Reed, 13 Nov 1838; James Spratlen, bm:

Hull, William & Leatha R. Cobler, 27 Oct 1860; James M. Hill, bm.

Humphreys, Alexander & Lutitia Gillaspie, 4 Dec 1862; A. C. Dunnagan, bm; m 4 Dec 1862 by A. Dunnagan, J. P.

Humphries, David & Martha Word, 2 April 1791; Thos. A. Word, bm.

Hundley, James A. & Jane White, 28 Feb 1854; W. L. Tipton, bm; m 18 Feb 1854 by A. Simmons, J. P.

Hunt, B. F. & Martha Whitaker, 17 Nov 1855; J. J. Hunt, bm. (C. H.).

Hunt, Daniel & Judith Chaffin, 24 Jan 1792; John Lynch, bm.

Hunt, Enoch B. & Mildred E. Franklin, 29 Sept 1834; Nathan D. Hunt, bm.

Hunt, Harvy W. & Hannah C. Mustard, 2 Nov 1853; William M. Bird, bm; m 2 Nov 1853 by A. Simmons, J. P.

Hunt, J. J. & Malsey Moore, 22 Nov 1855; B. F. Hunt, bm; m 22 Nov 1855 by Joel Denny, J. P.

Hunt, Levi & Rachel Deen, 11 Dec 1784; Saml Bryan, bm.

Hunt, Richardson & Caroline Cousins, 22 Sept 1852; Clement Hicks, bm; m 22 Sept 1852 by Wm. R. Lovell, J. P.

Hunt, Timothy & Isabella Duer, 19 Oct 1806; G. Hunt, bm.

Hunter, Benjamin & Anne Longine, 18 Jan 1791; John Hunter, bm.

Hunter, David & Lydia Shores, 10 Jan 1824; Joseph Phillips, bm.

Hunter, John & Jesse Glen, 6 Oct 1818; Josiah Owen, bm.

Hunter, John & Elender Mainline, 3 April 1832; John Colvard, bm.

Hunter, John & Rody Speer, 15 Dec 1799; John Speer, bm.

Hunter, John & Sarah A. Semore, 4 Jan 1860; Elijah Reed(?), bm; m 5 Jan 1860 by C. L. Banner, J. P.

Hunter, Lewis & Milly Pruet, 7 April 1865; William Clark, bm.

Hunter, Mager & Elizabeth Lynch, 1 Jan 1832; Benjamin Calvard, bm.

Hunt, Thomas & Elisabeth Robinson, 15 Sept 1790; John Hunter, bm; Matt Brooks, wit.

Hunter, Thomas & Polly Glen, 5 Nov 1822; H. G. Anderson, bm.

Hurst, James A. & Leah Fulks, 22 May 1851; James C. Fulks, bm.

Hurst, Willia, & Mildred Whitlock, 22 April 1805; George Hurst, bm.

Hurst, William F. & Mary E. Stephens, 30 April 1857; Allen Denny, bm.

Hurt, Joel & Anny Hawkins Kerby, 13 May 1793; Francis Kerby, bm.

Hurt, Joel & Dinah Carter, 16 Oct 1830; Isaac Carter, bm.

Hurt, Ned & Molley Hunt, 17 Aug 1865; Willis Hickerson, bm; m 17 Aug 1865 by Joel Hurt, J. P.

Hurt, Robert & Elizabeth Phillips, 11 Sept 1803; Peter Kerby, bm.

Hurt, Thomas & Nancy Ann Haback, 18 Aug 1852; Wm. T. Moore, bm; (C. H.).

Hurt, William & Frances Cockerham, 8 March 1807; Joel Hurt, bm.

Hutchens, Alexander Balas & _____ Pruett, 28 Oct 1814; John Hutchins, bm.

Hutchens, Benjamin & Hannah Vestal, 8 Sept 1805; Meriday Hutchens, bm.

Hutchens, Benjamin & Rebekah Thompson, 23 Feb 1809; Jonathan York, bm.

Hutchens, Benjamin J. & Margaret Vestal, 7 Sept 1847; Daniel McKie, bm.

Hutchens, Daniel & Lydday Johnson, 5 April 1836; Thompson Hutchins, bm.

Hutchens, Elcanah & Franky Pilcher, 5 April 1822; Morgan Hudspith, bm.

Hutchens, Elkanah & Sarah Reid, 23 April 1821; Frederick Tanner Junr., bm.

Hutchens, Fredk. & Elizabeth Hunter, 13 Oct 1844; Daniel Taylor, bm.

Hutchens, George D. & Jessefy Sneed, 28 March 1848; John Norman Sr., bm.

Hutchens, Green Bury & Charity Bowen, 28 April 1846; Joshua Hutchens, bm.

Hutchins, Isaac & Sarrah Clingman, 22 Sept 1837; James Martin, bm.

Hutchins, Joel & Polly Callaway, 31 Dec 1833; C. W. Williams, bm.

Hutchins, John & Jane Braswell, 26 March 1792; Manning Sumers, bm.

Hutchins, John & Elizebeth Vestal, 1 July 1802; Renny Harding, bm.

SURRY COUNTY MARRIAGES, 1779-1868

Hutchens, John R. & Margaret Matilda Williams 11 Dec 1849; Asa B. Hutchins, bm.

Hutchens, Johnson & Susanna Adams, 15 March 1818; John Hutchens, bm.

Hutchens, Joseph & Susanna Mickle, 1 June 1819; Gideon Johnson, bm.

Hutchens, Josiah & Mary Williams, 20 Oct 1799.

Hutchens, Josiah & Sally Rutledge, 23 Aug 1844; A. Dunagan, bm.

Hutchens, Meriday & Suzanner Fitchgarrel, 23 Dec 1795; Hutchins Stanley, bm.

Hutchens, Nicholas & Lydia Carter, 20 Dec 1809; Thomas Williams Junr., bm.

Hutchens, Patric & Polly Bates, 21 Sept 1838; Strangman Hutchins, bm.

Hutchens, Patrick & Nancey Wealch, 17 March 1837; Samuel Spilman, bm.

Hutchens, Sanders & Miss Eliza F. Simpson, 12 April 1857; J. R. Waugh, bm; m 16 April 1857 by A. Dunagan, J. P.

Hutchens, Sanford F. & Mary Ann Hickman, 19 April 1856; F. M. Walker, bm.

Hutchens, Thomas & Suzanner Hutchins, 30 July 1806; Isaac Williams, bm.

Hutchens, Thomas & Nancy Steelman, 23 March 1821; Jonth. Haines, bm.

Hutchens, Thomas & Rachel Lundy, 6 Aug 1826; Allen Willard, bm.

Hutchens, Thomas J., son of Vestal and Elisabeth Hutchins, & Martha Scott, m 22 Dec 1867 by C. L. Banner, J. P.

Hutchens, William & Milly Purdry, 14 Feb 1832; Allen Willard, bm.

Hutchens, William & Nancy Bullen, 19 June 1863; S. W. Snow, bm; m 21 June 1803 by S. W. Snow, J. P.

Hutchens, William D. & Mary Hobson, 3 April 1850; Asa B. Hutchens, bm.

Hutchings, Strangeman & Mary Holcomb, (no date); Grimes Holcomb, bm.

Hutchins, Calvin & Catherine Yarborro, 21 April 1845; James Hutchins, bm.

Hutchins, James & Nancy Hunter, 8 Jan 1846; Mody A. Hall, bm.

Hutchins, James & Martha A. Roberts, 21 Oct 1864; W. H. Davis, bm.

Hutchins, Jesse & Lyddia Clarke, 25 June 1813; Robert Clarke, bm.

Hutchens, John B. & Elizabeth McCollum, 21 Jan 1814; Talbot Russell, bm.

Hutchins, John W. & Mattilda Caudle, 26 July 1823; Edward Reece, bm.

Hutchins, Joseph & Hannah Stanley, 5 Jan 1811; Aaron Trulove, bm.

Hutchins, Patrick & Polly Faircloth, 10 Dec 1837; Will Woods, bm.

Hutchins, Straingmon & Charrity Williams, 17 July 1799; Saml Ayres, bm.

Hutchins, Strangeman & Polly Rhodes, 7 Aug 1831; Daniel Adams, bm.

Hutchins, Toms. & Rachel Wels, 18 Dec 1795; John Wells, bm.

Hutchins, Vestal & Elizabeth Jester, 1 Feb 1838; Joseph Hutchins, bm.

Hutchins, William & Elizebeth King, 11 July 1799; Thomas Stanfield, bm.

Hutchins, William & Elizabeth Whitehead, 1 Dec 1808; Wm. Brown, Jun., bm.

Hutson, Drury J. & Mary E. McGee, 8 Jan 1865; m 8 Jan 1865 by P. Worth, J. P.

Hutson, Richard & Edney Collins, 7 Jan 1831; Thomas York, bm.

Hutson, Wiley E. & Cintha D. Caudle, 16 Aug 1852; Benjamin McRoberts, bm.

Hyatt, Martin & Maryan Paterson, 17 Sept 1855; Elisha Bowman, bm.

Hylton, Gorden & Lydia Steagall, 31 Jan 1828; Joshua Wilson, bm.

Hynes, Harison & Ann Tuggle, 31 March 1867; Charles Madden, bm; m 31 March 1867 by Marlin Sparger, J. P.

Idoel, Jacob & Nancy Badgett, 5 Oct 1827; Micajah Reeves, bm.

Idoel, Michael & Avey Gallimore, 26 Nov 1822; Jesse Johnson, bm.

Iles, William & Jane Bingham, 11 Dec 1813; Stephen N. Bingham, bm.

Ingram, W. G. C. & Martha F. Wood, 7 July 1867; W. T. Lawson, bm; m 7 July 1867 by Murlin Sparger, J. P.

Inman, Benjamin R. & Rebecca Shelton, 20 March 1852; David Hall, bm.

Inman, Edmund & Sally Lawson, 24 March 1829; Daniel Low, bm.

Inman, J. W. C. & Miss Frances J. Chilton, 29 Dec 1856; S. A. Chilton, bm.

SURRY COUNTY MARRIAGES, 1779-1868

Inman, Thomas & Elmina Gwyn, 26 Oct 1853; Henry Samuel, bm; m 27 Oct 1853 by Wm. Haymore, J. P.

Inman, William & Elizabeth Linvell, 22 Sept 1832; Morris Inman, bm.

Inman, William C., son of Thomas and Frances Inman, and Sarah E. Inman, daughter of Henry and Anna Inman, 21 March 1868; m 22 March 1868 by Wm. Moran.

Inmon, Ira & Mary Shelton, 12 March 185-; Newel Simmons, bm.

Inmon, James M. & Mary Hall, 22 June 1867; m 30 June 1867 by M. A. Hall, J. P.

Inmon, John H. & Sallie A. Cobles, 20 April 1867; m 28 April 1867 by M. A. Hall, J. P.

Inscore, James & Margaret Arnold, 28 July 1827; Richard Wright, bm.

Inscore, Joshua & Amelia Arnold, 18 Dec 1827; Thos. F. Hicks, bm.

Inscore, Lewis & Dicy Calton, 18 Aug 1838; James Inscore, bm.

Inscore, William & Mary Oakly, 2 Sept 1834; Joshua Inscore, bm.

Ireland, Amos & Eliza A. Gross, 7 Jan 1851; Nehemiah Ireland, bm.

Ireland, Nehemiah & Mary Minnish, 21 Dec 1850; Amos Ireland, bm.

Isaacks, Elisha & Miss Elizabeth Callaway, 12 March 1858; John Mays, bm; m 14 March 1858 by Jn. J. McMickle, J. P.

Isaacks, Godfrey & Ferebee Willey, 29 Sept 1856; m 30 Sept 1856 by Lacy Snow, J. P.

Isaacks, F. A. & Basheba Parson, 4 Oct 1866; Aaron Parson, bm; m 4 Oct 1866 by A. H. Kapp, J. P.

Isbell, Hickman & Anny Thorp, 23 Aug 1825; Charles Dudley, bm.

Jacks, Evan & Rachel Cane, 12 Feb 1824; James Hudspeth, bm.

Jacks, Job & Sucky Vanhoy, 6 Feb 1809; J. Whalen, bm.

Jacks, Larkin & Polly Weatherman, 20 Nov 1811; Cornelous Weatherman, bm.

Jacks, Larkin & Nancy Petty, 11 Nov 1822; Zachary Petty, bm.

Jacks, Martin & Susan Shores, 11 April 1836; Drury Holcomb, bm.

Jacks, Richard & Sally Day, 28 Oct 1804; Christian Weatherman, bm.

Jacks, Sollomon & Patsy Gintry, 20 April 1808; George Hedspeth, bm.

Jackson, Aderson & Matilda Griffith, 5 Sept 1833; C. B. Tucker, bm.

SURRY COUNTY MARRIAGES, 1779-1868

Jackson, Caleb & Polly Simmons, 17 April 1848; Jesse B. Carson, bm.

Jackson, Eli & Mary Gallimer, 10 July 1835; Jessa A. Waugh, bm. (C. H.).

Jackson, Elijah & Anne Pickett, 13 Oct 1816; Larkin Strain, bm.

Jackson, George & Franky Chamberlin, 22 April 1827; Isaac Cook, bm.

Jackson, Iredell & Elizabeth Whitlock, 30 May 1831; Neil McLennon, bm.

Jackson, James W. & Adaline M. Belton, 11 May 1854; Ewel Belton, bm; m 11 May 1854 by A. Simmons, J. P.

Jackson, Job & I ¹dia Puckett, 11 April 1818; Eli Cook, bm.

Jackson, Joel & Rebecca Jessup, 23 Jan 1838; John Vawter, bm.

Jackson, John & _____ Spague, 29 Dec 1825; James McDonald, bm.

Jackson, John & Marthy Ogelsby, 26 April 1830; Micajah Oglesby, bm.

Jackson, John & Jane Tucker, 21 Nov 1849; Allen Denny, bm.

Jackson, John H. & Eliza Hollinsworth, 30 Oct 1849; Mordecai Fleming, bm.

Jackson, Martin & Edith Cook, 29 Aug 1826; Newel Jackson, bm. (C. H.).

Jackson, Merida & Mary Morefield, 14 Jan 1834; Wm Chapel, bm.

Jackson, Nathan & Patsy Potter, 23 Nov 1826; William Witch, bm.

Jackson, Newel & Sally Martin, 19 Aug 1832; Wm Jackson, bm.

Jackson, Ruel & Susan Whitlock, 31 Jan 1826; Newel Jackson, bm.

Jackson, Wm. & Celia Gordin, 13 Dec 1834; Martin Gorden, bm.

Jackson, William & Lucy Pike, 9 Dec 1837; Edmund Taylor, bm.

Jackson, William & Hester A. King, 16 Nov 1855; John A. Smith, bm; m 16 Nov 1855 by A. Simmons, J. P.

Jackson, William & Sarah Shelton, 24 Jan 1867; m 25 Jan 1867 by A. Brim, J. P.

Jackson, Wm. R. & Charlotte Bledsoe, 16 Nov 1852; Jacob A. Lewis, bm; m 18 Nov 1852 by H. C. Bray, J. P.

Jacobs, Stanford & Ann M. Sims, 16 Nov 1823; Tolbert Russell, bm.

James, Henry & Mary Harris, 16 March 1867; William Shouse, bm.

James, Jacob & Susan A. Saunders, 19 Nov 1846; Henry Sparger, bm.

Jameson, Charles L. & Emaline Arnold, 8 April 1856; John Arnold, bm.

SURRY COUNTY MARRIAGES, 1779-1868

Jarman, William & Sarah King, 8 May 1856; John F. Kesler, bm; m 8 May 1856 by A. Simmoms, J. P.

Jarell, Albert H. & Jane Tickle, 11 March 1858; Ellis F. Jarrell, bm; m 11 March 1858 by A. Simmons, J. P.

Jarrall, Jno. M. & Juliet Kelly, 8 Dec 1849; Richard E. Reeves, bm.

Jarvis, Abner & Patsey Pall(?), 9 Oct 1812; Levi Jarvis, bm.

Jarvis, Benet & Sarah Masters, 5 March 1803; Abner Rose, bm.

Jarvis, James & Polly Jones, 3 Dec 1822; John Jarvis, bm.

Jarvis, James E. & Mahala Prewit, 11 Aug 1838; Israel Jarvis, bm.

Jarvis, Levi & Rachel Johnson, 5 Sept 1803; Jesse Johnson, bm.

Jarvis, Riel & Caroline Manly, m 19 Feb 1866 by L. J. Stanly, J. P.

Jarvis, William & Elizabeth Jones, 27 Jan 1806; Thomas Ferebee, bm.

Jean, Edmund & Sally Griffith, 11 Oct 1816; William Jean, bm.

Jean, William & Betty Goode, 30 April 1787; Edmond Jean, bm.

Jeffery, James & Betsey Johnson, 23 Nov 1816; Joseph Jackson, bm.

Jenings, William S. & Mary F. McCracken, 4 Aug 1862; James W. Hull, bm; m 4 Aug 1862 by A. Simmons, J. P.

Jenkings, Hiram & Nancy Marsh, 17 May 1826; Isaac Winfrey, bm.

Jenkins, David & Peggy Adams, 30 July 1833; Henry G. Foster, bm.

Jenkins, David F. & Martha E. Etcheson, 1 Sept 1866; Henry Bass, bm.

Jenkins, Elhanan & Anne Miller, 8 April 1810; James Hudspeth, bm.

Jenkins, Francis & Susannah Morrison, 31 March 1819; Barnebus Vinzant, bm.

Jenkins, Hiram, son of Wm & Lucinda Jenkins, & Sarah L. Lancaster, daughter of George Lancaster, m 24 Dec 1867 by Thos. J. Williams, J. P.

Jenkins, Hiram, son of Hiram and Nancy Jenkins, and Delila Stanley, daughter of L. J. and Elizabeth Stanley, m 30 March 1868 by Thos. J. Williams, J. P.

Jenkins, Jesse & Elizabeth Langley, 2 Dec 1831; Thomas Dinkins, bm.

Jenkins, John & Sarah Underwood, 23 June 1828; Benjamin Rose, bm.

Jenkins, R. M. & Sallie E. Lovell, 15 Sept 1865; m 18 Sept 1865 by Miles Foy.

107

Jenkins, William A. & Charity M. Jones, 6 Oct 1866; Daniel J. Cockerham, bm.

Jinkins, David & Anna Bitticks, 21 Oct 1819; Strangeman Hutchens, bm.

Jennings, Thomas & Matilda Manuel, 16 Sept 1846; Edward Jones, bm.

Jentry, Jonathan & Elizabeth Branch, 23 Jan 1851; James Nation, bm.

Jerrell, Rufus A., son of Fountain and Fanny Jerrell, and Susan Sandifer, daughter of Perm and Martha Sandifer, m 6 Oct 1868 by Martin Armsfield, J. P.

Jervis, A. B. C. & Mary S. Scott, 2 May 1857; Miley Burrus, bm.

Jervis, Daniel & Lidia Jones, 8 Oct 1824; John Jervis, bm.

Jervis, George M. & Martha J. Hodges, 9 May 1865; Nicholas Freeman, bm; m 1 June 1865 by Thomas J. Lawson, minister.

Jervis, Jesse G. & Miss Sally Ann Foulks, 4 Oct 1853; Thomas J. Lawson, bm; m 6 Oct 1853 by Jno. J. McMickle.

Jervis, John & Elizabeth Roberts, 28 Nov 1827; Daniel Jervis, bm.

Jervis, Samuel & Sophia D. Hodges, 15 Sept 1845; Gideon Hodges, A. Dunnagan, bm.

Jarvis, William & Martha Badget, 29 Feb 1836; Edward M. Dobson, bm.

Jesop, George W. & Jane Fitzgerald, 19 Nov 1831; Burrel Shelton, bm.

Jessop, Abner & Mary Jackson, 16 Aug 1809; William Pearce, bm.

Jessop, Elam & Anna Hobson, 27 Oct 1845; Hugh Brown, bm.

Jessop, Elijah & Nancy Smith, 18 April 1816; Jona. Unthank, bm.

Jessop, Joseph & Rachael Jackson, 2 Nov 1816; Eli Jackson, bm.

Jessop, Joseph A. & Bethany E. Jessup, 25 Dec 1856; J. J. France, bm; m 25 Dec 1856 by J. Gray, J. P.

Jessop, Thomas & Polly Toys(?), 27 May 1813; John McKiney, bm.

Jessop, William & Elizabeth Cook, 22 Dec 1845; Henderson Cook, bm.

Jessup, Calep & Keziah Bingman, 27 May 1833; Burrell Shelton, bm.

Jessup, Hiram & Sally Jessop, 14 Feb 1837; James Summons, bm.

Jessup, Lee & Mary A. Summons, 18 Jan 1866; Lewis C. Taylor, bm.

Jessup, William S. & Elizabeth Jessup, 23 Jan 1864; Alexander McKinney, bm; m 24 Jan 1864 by J. Gray, J. P.

SURRY COUNTY MARRIAGES, 1779-1868

Jester, Isaac & Rachael Pearce, 3 Jan 1823; Nathan Couch, bm.

Jester, James & Mary Hickman, 4 Feb 1817; John Hickman, bm.

Jester, John & Rachael Adams, 1 Jan 1822; James Adams, bm.

Jester, Nathan & Mary Brown, 4 Oct 1836; James Jester, bm.

Jester, Solomon & Candesia F. Moore, 6 Jan 1861; m 6 Jan 1861 by W. W. Wolff, J. P.

Jester, Williams & Polly Davis, 7 Sept 1832; John Jester, bm.

Jester, Williams & Lucy Sabrina Hinshaw, 27 July 1849; Mark York Junr., bm.

Jinkins, Joel & Katharine Smith, 29 March 1855; C. C. Smith, bm; m by ___ Marshall, J. P., 29 March 1855.

Jinkins, Miner & Nancy Stoutz, 20 Jan 1851; Jo. Dobson, bm.

Jinnings, Jesse & Nancy Nales, 3 Jan 1823; James Fitzgerald, bm.

Johnson, A. M. & Sallie Hopper, 9 Oct 1863; Wm. A. Jenkins, bm; m 15 Oct 1863 by J. H. Lewellin, minister.

Johnson, Alexander & Mary Flinn, 25 Oct 1823; George Flinn, bm.

Johnson, Alfred & Mary Johnson, 26 Dec 1836; John G. Johnson, bm.

Johnson, Ambrus & Lucy Franklin, 28 June 1818; Wm. Bourne Jr., bm.

Johnson, Ambrose M. & Lucinda Snow, 19 Feb 1859; Tyson S. Wilmoth, bm.

Johnson, Ashley & Betsy Brown, 19 Oct 1807; Jonathan Johnson, bm.

Johnson, Baley & Elizabeth Foster, 12 July 1812; Lewis Nolin, bm.

Johnson, Benjamin H. & Rebeca Jones, 9 Jan 1834; Jno Baggerly, bm.

Johnson, Benjamin H. & Mary C. Missie, 6 May 1848; Christian Rinehart Jr., bm.

Johnson, Cader & Franky Haulcomb, 25 July 1807; Wm. Uptegrove, bm.

Johnson, Calvin & Elizabeth Smith, 4 Nov 1828; Hardy Pate, bm.

Johnson, Charles & Gilley Siske, 20 Jan 1829; George Sparks Jr., bm.

Johnson, Charles Jr. & Susanah Nansey(?), 1 April 1812; Elisha Chappel, bm.

Johnson, David & Deborah A. Shinall, 31 Aug 1845; William Love, bm.

SURRY COUNTY MARRIAGES, 1779-1868

Johnson, Edmon & Sarah Kidd, 13 Nov 1855; m 17 Nov 1855 by Drewry McGee, J. P.

Johnson, Edward & Serah Kidd, 13 Nov 1855; James Simpson, bm.

Johnson, Eli & Susanna Hall, 1 Dec 1819; Aaron Matthews, bm.

Johnson, Elisha & Susanna Crouse, 8 Dec 1822; Jonas Johnson, bm.

Johnson, Enoch & Nancy Bray, 19 Nov 1833; Joel Bray, bm.

Johnson, Gideon & Letha Ladd, 12 April 1823; Jesse Johnson, Anderson Johnson, bm.

Johnson, Gideon & Ann Terry, 25 Aug 1823; Benjamin Hutchens, bm.

Johnson, Henderson W. & Melinda Hall, 19 Sept 1865; m 19 Sept 1865 by G. A. Lowe, J. P.

Johnson, Henry & Adaline Barker, 22 May 1849; Isaac Tally, bm.

Johnson, Henson W. & Armitta Jones, 5 Nov 1833; Wm. Zachary, bm.

Johnson, Hutchins & Lucinda Douthit, 12 Jan 1837; Daniel Arnold, bm.

Johnson, Jabez & Lucinda Taylor, 1 March 1853; Newel Johnson, bm.

Johnson, Jacob & Jane Foster, 19 Feb 1852; William Edwards, bm.

Johnson, James & Famey Moore, 18 Nov 1816; Baley Johnson, bm.

Johnson, James & Anna Sneed, 4 April 1826; Zacariah Petted, bm.

Johnson, James & Jemima Reece, 23 April 1836; Anthony Woodhouse, bm.

Johnson, James & Ann Eliza Johnson, 29 Oct 1844; Wm. F. Unthank, bm.

Johnson, James & Sarah Gentry, 27 Dec 1851; William L. Hodges, bm; m 27 Dec 1851 by Drury Hodges, J. P.

Johnson, James & Mary Simpson, 12 June 1860; m by Jos. W. Flippin, J. P.

Johnson, James T. & Fanny Dickerson, 5 June 1835; John Johnson, bm.

Johnson, Jeffery & Delilah Johnson, 7 Dec 1798; Sammuel Johnson, bm.

Johnson, Jeffery & _____ (no date); John W. Longine, bm.

Johnson, Jesse & Lyda Johnson, 6 Dec 1823; Gidion Johnson, bm. (C. H.).

Johnson, Jesse & Marinda Chappel, 1 Sept 1829; Hutchens Johnson, bm.

Johnson, Jesse & Julia Ann Ashburn, 7 Jan 1863; J. E. Reeves, bm.

Johnson, Jesse A. & Elizabeth Gray, 2 Dec 1859; William Mays, bm.

Johnson, John & Polly P. Setleff, 20 Jan 1822; Aaron Matthews, bm.

Johnson, John & Cholea Atken, 5 March 1822; Marmaduke Kimbrough, bm.

Johnson, John & Matilda Linvill, 21 Nov 1829; Samuel Linvill, bm.

Johnson, John & Patience Johnson, 5 Oct 1831; Westly George, bm.

Johnson, John & Marinda Jones, 28 Sept 1833; Edward Jones, bm.

Johnson, John & Isbell Bryan, 2 Aug 1844; Morgan Bryan, bm.

Johnson, John & Nancy Richison, 16 Nov 1852; m 16 Nov 1852 by John Ramey, J. P.

Johnson, John & Rachel Kidd, 27 Jan 1859; James Johnson, bm.

Johnson, John C., son of James H. & Fanny Johnson, and Martha C. Thorp, daughter of Thomas and Eliza J. Thorp, m 24 Dec 1868 by Rev. James Minish.

Johnson, John G. & Linah Messir, 5 Jan 1837; Huchins Johnson, bm.

Johnson, Jonas & Mariann Crouse, 5 April 1823; Hosea Sisk, bm.

Johnson, Jonathan & Sarah Low, 8 July 1802; George Adams, bm.

Johnson, Joseph & Amitintha Jones, 18 Nov 1787; Elisha Cast, bm.

Johnson, Joseph & Elizabeth Brewer, 27 Dec 1807; Amos Chappel, bm.

Johnson, Joseph & Sally Edwards, 23 Aug 1849; John Allen, bm.

Johnson, Joseph & Lucyann Taylor, 20 Feb 1867; Irwin Sutfin, bm; m 21 Feb 1867 by J. A. Bingman, J. P.

Johnson, Joseph F. & Mary Ann Lindley, 10 June 1846; James M. Lindley, bm.

Johnson, Keziah & Mary Jones, 7 June 1834; Newel Johnson, bm.

Johnson, Levi & Sarah Brewer, 11 Nov 1823; Jesse Sisk, bm. (C. H.).

Johnson, Levi & Sally Brassfield, 9 July 1825; Richd. Beeson, bm.

Johnson, Lewis & Milley Johnson, 10 Feb 1812; John Hines, bm.

Johnson, Lewis & Milly Wall, 15 March 1825; Edmund Wooten, bm.

Johnson, Matthew & Martha Danaly, 10 Feb 1846; John Johnson, bm.

Johnson, Minze & Betsey Whitaker, 18 June 1811; Isaac Whitaker, bm.

SURRY COUNTY MARRIAGES, 1779-1868

Johnson, Nicholas & Dianna Hinshaw, 22 July 1829; G. Holcomb, bm.

Johnson, Nicholas & Elizabeth Bovender, 27 Dec 1846; Abraham Thornton, bm.

Johnson, Ransom & Susan Smith, 15 July 1862; Meredith Hodges, bm; m 17 July 1862 by Jno. J. McMickle, J. P.

Johnson, Reuben & Mary Harvil, 23 May 1812; Elisha Chappel, bm.

Johnson, Richard & Harriett Johnson, 29 April 1847; Pleasant C. Hodges, bm.

Johnson, Robert & Theany Knight, 7 Feb 1785; Johnson Whitticor, bm.

Johnson, Rufus & Frances Norman, 4 April 1867; L. J. Gray, bm; m 4 April 1867 by A. Brim, J. P.

Johnson, S. J. M. & Jane Sozars, 18 Nov 1865; Jesse Kidd, bm; m 19 Nov 1865 by R. F. McGuffin, J. P.

Johnson, Samuel & Hannah Brown, 16 March 1803; William Johnson, bm.

Johnson, Samuel & Anne Ramsy, 14 June 1803; Jesse Johnson, bm.

Johnson, Samuel & Polly Johnson, 30 Sept 1830; Joel Daniel, bm.

Johnson, Samuel & Eliza Rottenbury, 26 Feb 1862; Ira Porter, bm.

Johnson, Strangeman & _____, 30 Jan 1830; Ashley Johnson, bm.

Johnson, Thomas & Jane Brooks, 21 June 1785; Isaac Wilkins, bm.

Johnson, Thomas & Sibell Greenwood, 31 Oct 1813; Lewis Voling, bm.

Johnson, Thomas & Rachel Johnson, 30 March 1818; John Howard, bm.

Johnson, Thomas & Nancy Messick, 30 Jan 1832; John F. Dowthit, bm.

Johnson, Wm. & _____, 10 Aug 1792; Jeffery Johnson, bm.

Johnson, William & Tabitha Tailer, 2 Jan 1796.

Johnson, William & Letty Brewer, _____ 1814; Lewis Ried, bm.

Johnson, William & Lucy Roberson, 6 Sept 1808; William Roberson, bm.

Johnson, Wm. A. & Mary K. Axsom, 24 Oct 1867; R. P. Rawley, bm; m 3 Nov 1867 by J. R. Rose, Baptist minister.

Johnson, William F. & Lucinda E. Lindsey, 6 May 1849; Jesse Tutteroe, bm.

Johnston, Joseph & Margeret Graham, 15 May 1783; Robt. Graham, bm.

SURRY COUNTY MARRIAGES, 1779-1868

Johnston, Richard & Rhody Arnold, 28 Sept 1791; Thomas Wilson, bm.

Johnston, William & Sarah Adams, 20 March 1793; Moses Adams, bm.

Joice, James A. & Sally Slaydon, 9 Sept 1854; Joseph Slaydon, bm; m 14 Sept 1854 by Wilson Laffoon, J. P.

Joiner, Elias & Obedience Algood, 4 Nov 1826; Mills N. Joiner, bm.

Joiner, Jiels & Mary Johnson, 2 Aprl 1806; Willis Joiner, bm.

Joiner, Johnathan & Lear Loagin, 13 April 1802; Hugh Logan, bm.

Joiner, Joshaway & Ann Coe, 14 Jan 1805; Jiles Joiner, bm.

Joiner, Mills Nelson & Jane Brown, 26 June 1823; Thomas Kelly, bm.

Joiner, Willis & Sarah Carter, 13 Dec 1797; J. Carter, bm.

Joiner, Willis & Nancy Jater(?), 8 Aug 1826; Thomas Moreland, bm.

Jones, A. R. & Nancy E. Joyce, 14 March 1864; Robt Hill, bm; m 16 March 1864 by James Needham, minister.

Jones, Ambrose W. & Mary Brinkley, 7 Nov 1837; Robt. R. Brinkly, bm.

Jones, Anderson & Polly Young, 30 Sept 1828; William Lyon, bm.

Jones, Archibald & Elizabeth McMillion, 3 May 1838; J. C. Davis, bm.

Jones, Augustine & Cloe Banner, freed people, 28 Dec 1866; m 28 Dec 1866 by M. A. Hall, J. P.

Jones, Augustine S. & Francis C. Herring, 6 Dec 1847; Russel R. Jones, bm.

Jones, Burrell & Elizabeth Brown, 4 March 1817; Isaac Jones, bm.

Jones, Churchwell & Barbary Caviness, 19 Feb 1852; Lewis Stoneman, bm.

Jones, Grances & Eliza Jane McGrady, 5 Sept 1865; m 5 Sept 1865 by J. H. Lewellin.

Jones, George W. & Mary Noonkestl, 24 March 1852; m by B. F. Scott, J. P., 25 March 1852.

Jones, Hugh & Elizabeth Johnson, 4 May 1822; Waller Weaver, bm.

Jones, Jack & Susan Adams, freedmen, m 16 Sept 1866 by L. J. Stanly, J. P.

Jones, Isaac & Rhoda Stephens, 20 Aug 1827; Morton C. East, bm.

Jones, J. H. & Virginia Adams, 14 Dec 1863; S. A. Freeman, bm; m 19 Dec 1863 by Nathan York.

Jones, J. W. & Mary B. Snow, 23 Feb 1867; W. G. Hull, bm; m 24 Feb 1867 by John Jones.

SURRY COUNTY MARRIAGES, 1779-1868

Jones, Jacob & Matilda Chappell, 22 May 1827; Mattw. M. Hughes, bm.

Jones, James & Catharine Speer, 13 May 1797; John Rutledge, William Speer, bm.

Jones, James & Margaret Terry, 7 March 1850; Thomas Sanders, bm. (C. H.).

Jones, James Junr. & Alsey Bills, 8 Dec 1814; Samuel Calliway Jnr., bm.

Jones, James C. & Nancy Haynes, 8 Oct 1859; Stephen Haynes, bm.

Jones, James F. & Amelia Simpson, 4 Nov 1853; George W. Shadrick, bm.

Jones, John & Jane McCarthy, 7 Nov 1833; Wm. D. Somers, bm.

Jones, John A. & Jane Hawks, 13 March 1849; James F. Jones, bm.

Jones, John A. & Elizabeth Stockern, 15 Sept 1853; George A. Shadrick, bm; m 15 Sept 1853 by A. Simmons, J. P.

Jones, John B. & Sarah Noonkerster, m 11 March 1852 by Martin Pyne, J. P. (C. H.).

Jones, John G. & Maleatha Davis, 23 Nov 1845; Logan Roberts, bm.

Jones, John H. & Luvisy Mustard, 18 Sept 1853; N. J. Harris, bm; m 18 Sept 1853 by A. Simmons, J. P.

Jones, Jonathan & Hanah Jarvis, 2 Oct 1830; Woodson Roberts, bm.

Jones, Joshua & Edney Bingham, 31 Aug 1815; Robert Clarke of Rowan County, bm.

Jones, L. B. & Eliza Blackwood, 11 Nov 1862; Henry Dunigan, bm; m 17 Nov 1862 by Thomas Howell.

Jones, Lemuel & _____, 14 Oct 1791; James Jones, bm.

Jones, Lemuel B. & Charity Burch, 11 Dec 1819; Samuel Calloway Jr., bm.

Jones, Mark & Fanny Vaun, 4 Sept 1831; Wm. Elliott, bm.

Jones, Minetree & Nancy Golden, 10 March 1816; William Golden Junr., bm.

Jones, Richard & Betsey Petty, 26 Jan 1807; Reuben _____, bm.

Jones, Robert F. & Nancy E. Gwyn, 2 Feb 1866; W. E. Hill, bm.

Jones, Roland & Rosanna Johnson, 5 April 1823; Enos Windsor, bm.

Jones, Russel R & Mahaly Key, 8 Feb 1849; Augustin Key, bm.

Jones, Samuel & Margarett Poore, 1 Oct 1861.

Jones, Silas & Elizabeth Smith, 23 June 1826; Saml H. Jones, bm.

SURRY COUNTY MARRIAGES, 1779-1868

Jones, Silas & Rozena Smith, 11 Dec 1856; John K. Lunday, bm; m 11 Dec 1856 by Geo. A. Jervis, Esqr., J. P.

Jones, Smith & Nancy Johnson, 19 Nov 1808; Jesse Jones, bm.

Jones, Stephen B. & Temperance W. Marshall, 23 Dec 1852; m 10 Jan 1853 by John Jervis, J. P.

Jones, Toms. & Elizabeth Horn, 14 Dec 1799; Thos Horn, bm.

Jones, Thomas & Nancy Brown, 15 Dec 1811; John Brown, bm.

Jones, Thomas & Sarah Mattecks, 21 Sept 1816; James Steelman, bm.

Jones, Thomas D. & Martha E. Axsom, 3 Aug 1866; William A. Jenkins, bm; m 5 Aug 1866 by John K. Rose, minister of the Baptist denomination.

Jones, Vance & Elizabeth Ellis, 24 Dec 1808; Jesse Jones, bm.

Jones, Wily & Elizabeth Butterey, 19 March 1808; Jn. Thomson, bm.

Jones, William & Nancy Matterson, 25 March 1826; Joseph Beeman, bm.

Jones, William & Lucinda Dosson, 22 Feb 1846; James A. Fowlks, bm.

Jones, Wm. W. & Miss Sarah L. Doss, 8 March 1854; J. H. Jones, bm; m 9 March 1859(?), by Job Hamlin, J. P.

Jones, William Spencer & Anna Kimbrough, 16 Oct 1815; Lewis Williams, bm.

Jourden, George & Abigail Nicholson, 21 Dec 1847; R. H. Blackwood, bm.

Joyner, Charles A. & Sarah Ann North, 2 Feb 1848; Alvers Pilcher, bm.

Joyner, David & Catharine Coe, 27 April 1799; Hampson Glen, bm.

Joyner, Giles & Salley Phillips, 7 Dec 1837; John W. Cornelius, bm.

Joyner, John & Elizabeth Dixson, 19 Jan 1832; Wm. Harding, bm.

Joyner, Jonathan & Nancy Matthews, 3 Aug 1818; Mills Joyner, bm.

Joyner, Joseph & Nancy Whitlock, 20 Sept 1804; Joshua Joyner, bm.

Joyner, Zachariah & Rebeckah Spence, 28 April 1833; Giles Joyner, bm.

Jurney, Peter & Nancy A. Reeves, 14 Jan 1861; m 16 Jan 1861 by Jesse Roberts.

Kapp, A. H. & Mary F. Thompson, 13 April 1858; C. H. Kapp, bm.

Kearby, Jesse & Jean Martin, 24 Aug 1802; Samuel Martin, bm.

SURRY COUNTY MARRIAGES, 1779-1868

Kee, William & Sarah Davis, 30 Oct 1815; Joel Underwood, bm.

Keen, Sampson & Mary Braizer, 21 May 1803; William Brazier, bm.

Keesee, William F. & Jane Coatney, 1 March 1854; Joseph W. Warner, bm; m 1 March 1854 by A. Simmons, J. P.

Keeter, Samuel & Nancy Hollomon, 16 June 1849; Jesse Keeter, bm.

Keeton, William L. & Jane Joyner, 29 March 1833; John H. Chinn, bm.

Kell, Thomas & Lydia Lakey, 22 Sept 1816; Thos. Holcomb, bm.

Keller, Samuel & Nancy Whitlock, 15 March 1821; James Wm. Crouse, bm.

Kelley, John & Caroline Brubaker, 16 April 1846; George C. Davis, bm.

Kelly, Andw. & Mary Hutchens, 12 March 1819; Thomas Vestal, bm.

Kelly, Jno. Junr. & Mildred Sater, 10 Aug 1813; Wm. D. Kelly, bm.

Kelly, Leonard D. & Rebekah Creson, 11 May 1822; Joseph Steelmon, bm.

Kelly, Richard & Parthenia Marshall, 26 Dec 1829; Th. Lambert, bm.

Kelly, Wm. C. & MaryJane Miller, 14 Dec 1847; Joseph F. Buthrell, bm.

Kenley, Thomas J. & Mary Jennings, 29 Nov 1854; Levi Milgrim, bm.

Kennedy, A. W. & Miss Kezziah Cockerham, 27 Jan 1855; L. J. Norman, bm.

Kennedy, Columbus & Elizabeth Golden, 29 _____ 1860; S. Venable, bm

Kennedy, Plesant B. & Mary Thompson, 29 Jan 1854; Wilmington Kennedy, bm; m 3 Feb 1854 by G. Bryan, J. P.

Kennicks, David & Sarah Rector, 1 May 1804; Peter Rector Jur., bm.

Kerby, Edmund S. & Elizabeth C. Uptegrove, 7 Jan 1832; P. S. Martin, bm.

Kerby, James & Nancy Dickens, 27 July 1865; B. J. Dickens, bm; m 29 July 1865 by B. J. Dickens, J. P.

Kerby, Joel & Frances Robert, 24 March 1836; John Bryan, bm.

Kerby, John & Suzanner Lain, 25 Feb 1805; John Poindexter, bm.

Kerby, John & Eliza Hagan, 28 Aug 1855; J. Love, bm.

Kerby, John & Eliza Keath, 27 Jan 1856; J. Calver Tuburt, bm.

Kerby, Samuel & Edy Low, 6 Feb 1830; Giles Hodges, bm.

SURRY COUNTY MARRIAGES, 1779-1868

Kerby, Samuel & Cely Dickins, 4 Dec 1864; B. J. Dickins, bm; m 4 Dec 1864 by J. Low, J. P.

Kerby, Joseph & _____, 11 Aug 1791; Richd. Kerby, bm.

Kerby, Samuel & Elizabeth Garner, 28 July 1807; Leonard Davis, bm.

Kerr, Absalom & Sarah Martin, 3 Sept 1796; Thos. W. Poindexter, Samuel Martin, bm.

Kerr, Archibald M. & Sarah Ann Fitzgerald, 25 April 1831; H. C. Bray, bm.

Kerr, John & Sarah Scott, 23 Dec 1803; George Martin, bm.

Kerr, Reuben & Eliza. Setliff, 16 Dec 1797; Absalom Kerr, bm.

Kerr, Wesly & Sophiah Hall, 18 Feb 1834; Jonathan Fry, bm.

Kersey, Drury & Elizabeth Roberts, 7 March 1826; Pleasant Venables, bm.

Kersey, John & Lucinda Ashworth, 6 Aug 1851; Andrew J. Breeding, bm.

Kester, James & Martha Omerer, 9 Sept 1847; Martin D. Word, bm.

Key, A. S. & Ellin Whitaker, 30 Dec 1862; John W. Key, bm; m 31 Dec 1862 at the house of Litle Whiteackers by John Jones.

Key, A. S. & Mary F. Denny, 17 Nov 1864; John Jones, bm; m 17 Nov 1864 at the house of Edmond Denny, by John Jones.

Key, Archelis & Sarah Denney, 7 Dec 1809; Charles Latham, bm.

Key, Augustin & Clarissa R. Herring, 22 Sept 1852; Russel R. Jones, bm. (C. H.).

Key, Hesikier & Huldy E. Moore, 27 Aug 1866; Jesse Kidd, bm; m 26 Aug 1866 at the house of Hulday Moores, by John Jones.

Key, Iredell & Emsey Whitaker, 25 Jan 1832; F. K. Armstrong, bm.

Key, James R. & Nancy P. Edmond, 14 March 1857; Henry T. Sheppard, bm.

Key, John A. & Nelly Pain, 29 Dec 1820; Rue Key, bm.

Key, John A. & Emily Chandler, 1 July 1858; Thos. D. Davis, bm.

Key, John K. & Belinda Fulk, 26 Oct 1859; William J. Key, bm.

Key, Joseph & Mary Ann Marsh, 21 Nov 1849; Jonathan Bledsoe, bm.

Key, L. J. & Ellen E. Denny, 24 Jan 1867; m by John Jones at the house of Edmond Denny, 29 Jan 1867.

Key, Lewis & Elizabeth Turner, 8 Dec 1845; Nathan Alberty, bm.

Key, Lewis & Miss Elizabeth Hutson, 4 Dec 1854; Jesse Bullin, bm.

Key, Lewis A. & Elizabeth Jones, 27 Oct 1835; James McKinney, bm.

SURRY COUNTY MARRIAGES, 1779-1868

Key, Linsey M. & Nancy Stone, 24 June 1832; Milbourn Key, bm.

Key, Martin & Sarah Bullin, 6 Sept 1860; m 8 Sept 1860 by A. Whitaker, J. P.

Key, Milbourn & Elizabeth Monkins, 5 March 1833; Isaac A. Suttle, bm.

Key, Rece & Sally Bullen, 19 June 1836; William Bullen, bm.

Key, Russel R., son of William S. & Lydia D. Key, and R. B. Denny, daughter of Joel and Nancy Denny, m 3 March 1868 by John Jones.

Key, Samuel & Patsey Forester, 31 Aug 1837; Lindsey Key, bm.

Key, Samuel C. & Miss Nancy White, 31 Aug 1855; Edmond Bullen, bm; m 2 Sept 1855 by W. D. Rutledge, J. P.

Key, William & Lomey Forrester, 23 Dec 1809; Charles Latham, bm.

Key, Wm & Dicy Whitaker, 30 Dec 1831; Watson Holyfield, bm.

Key, William & Polly Wood, 23 June 1835; Wm. Butler, bm.

Key, William & Lydia D. Jones, 19 March 1839; Lewis A. Key, bm.

Key, William & Etha Linville, 20 June 1867; Valentine Hollyfield, bm; m 25 June 1867 by H. Laffoon, J. P.

Key, William J. & Sarah J. Kay, 26 Nov 1867; m 28 Nov 1867 by John Jones at the house of William Keys.

Keys, Achillis & Amelia Merrion, 6 Dec 1809; Daniel Merrian, (bond signed Achilles Dotherage).

Keys, Joseph & Lucy Smith, 23 Oct 1826; Jesse Rece, bm.

Keys, Silus & Patsy Kidd, 12 Feb 1823; Larkin Kanady, bm. (C. H.).

Kid, Jesse James & Anner Greenwood, 3 Jan 1816; Jesse Johnson, bm.

Kidd, James & Polly Wilkes, 11 March 1847; Watson Holyfield, bm.

Kidd, Jesse, son of Alen & Nancy Kidd, & Nancy Johnson, daughter of Enoch and Nancy Johnson, m 23 April 1868 at my house, by John Jones.

Kidd, John M. & Rebeca E. Suiter, 2 Aug 1851; no bm.

Kidd, William A. & Polly Suitir, 1 May 1852; T. F. Prather, bm.

Kieth, Wm. & Sarah F. Harris, 25 Aug 1860.

Killion, Isaac & Edith Phillips, 12 Oct 1823; Littleton Noles, bm.

Killion, William & Jemima Roseberry, 31 Aug 1825; Benjamin Moore Jr., bm.

Kimbrough, George & Catharine Young 12 Feb 1786; John Allen,bm.

SURRY COUNTY MARRIAGES, 1779-1868

Kimbrough, John & Amy Joyner, 27 June 1837; George Carver, bm.

Kimbrough, Marmaduke & Patsey Young, 14 Oct 1801; Ormon Kimbrough, bm.

Kimbrough, Ormon & Elizabeth Davie, 13 Oct 1795.

Kineda, Aaron & Tempy Marshal, 16 Jan 1831; William Norman, bm.

King, Anderson D. & Rebeca Warf, 27 July 1863; William Golden, bm; m 27 July 1863 by Wm. Golden, J. P.

King, Austin & Sintha Vaughn, 14 Aug 1847; Martin Carrier, bm.

King, Benager & Elizabeth Roynolds, 28 Feb 1851; John Snody, bm; m by Wright Johnson, minister.

King, Caleb & Nancy E. Shelton, _____ 186-.

King, Charles S., son of Russel and Pheby King, and Ida V. Dehart, daughter of Isaac and Mary Dehart, m 30 Oct 1868 by Thomas Schaub, J. P.

King, Chester B. & Henrietta Sufferbarger, 24 May 1864; William King, bm.

King, Doctor & Margret Edwards, 6 June 1852; Edward Gwynn, bm.

King, Henry & Matilda Hicks, 21 Dec 1859; William Mays, bm.

King, Jeremiah & Polley Freeman, 16 Nov 1804; John Summers, bm.

King, Jesse & Mary Bowden, 4 Jan 1801; William King, Richard King, bm.

King, John & Margaret Gymon, 19 Jan 1830; A. Steele, bm.

King, John & Nancy Love, 26 Nov 1858; Gilbert A. Love, bm.

King, Nathaniel & Catharine Gentry, 12 Sept 1850; William Chamberlain, bm.

King, Richard & Darkus Rafield, _____ 1804.

King, Shirel & Lucinda Ally, 17 Sept 1850; Mathew Hodge, bm. (C. H.).

King, William & Margret Aten, 16 Oct 1811; Alexander King, bm.

King, William & Lettitia Kesler, 6 Oct 1856; William Jarman, bm; m 6 Oct 1856 by A. Simmons, J. P.

King, William Riley & Jane Jessup, freed people, 2 May 1867; Alfred Jessup, bm.

Kinly, Joshua & Mary Ann Jemmery, 18 Aug 1851; Iredell Mabre, bm.

Kirkbride, Wm. P. & Martha Wells, 5 Sept 1848; Wm. H. Carter, bm.

Kirkman, John & Patsey Buron, 12 Feb 1860; Marshall Harrison, bm.

Kirkman, Noah & Nicy Whitaker, 1 May 1844; A.L. Whitaker, bm.

SURRY COUNTY MARRIAGES, 1779-1868

Kirkmand, Andrew V., son of William and Elisa J. Kirkmond, & Lucinda Adkins, daughter of Thomas and Elisa Adkins, m 12 March 1868 by M. A. Hall, J. P.

Kittle, John S. & Rachel Phillips, 8 Feb 1850; Richard Logan, bm.

Kittle, Joseph & Frany Leibengood, 26 May 1858; D. C. Wolff, bm.

Kittle, William & Polly Hall, 16 June 1821; Absolam Matthews, bm.

Knott, Abraham & Peggy Parker, 30 Sept 1818; Thomas Rains, bm.

Krouse, Henry & Edney Stablefield, 4 Dec 1790; Claiborn Gentry, bm.

Kyle, James & Jemimah Holyfield, 26 June 1808; Edwin Chaffin, bm.

Lackey, Benjamin W. & Belinda Cook, 28 Sept 1844; Gideon J. McMickle, bm.

Ladd, Constant & Mary McNally, 25 Aug 1788; Richd. Goode, bm.

Ladd, Thomas & Elizabeth B----, 7 Jan 185-; Alfred Long, Jesse M. Cary, bm.

Ladd, Wm. & Betsey Bowers, 3 Jan 1822; Amos Ladd, bm.

Lael, Jacob Jr. & Matilda Ann Layel, 26 Feb 1854; T. H. Maxwell, bm.

Laffoon, Hardin & Sally Lewis, 21 June 1850; James M. Gordan, bm. (C. H.).

Laggoon, Henderson & Nancy Brassfield, 2 Feb 1836; Stephen Laffoon, bm.

Laffoon, James W. & Basheba Bowles, 28 Sept 1848; James Bowles, bm.

Laffoon, Mark & Nancy Bray, 25 Nov 1847; James W. Laffoon, bm.

Laffoon, Matthew & Sarah Riggs, 12 Feb 1816; James Fitzgerald, bm.

Laffoon, Stephen & Nancy Mays, 12 May 1836; Andrew McCraw, bm.

Laffoon, Stephen D. & Harretta Horten, 25 March 1854; Reubin Bray, bm; m 26 March 1854 by John J. McMickle, J. P.

Laffoon, William & Mary Venable, 4 Jan 1825; Pleasant Venables, bm.

Laffoon, Wilson & Rebeca Venable, 9 Sept 1831.

Laffoon, Wilson & Margrett Haynes, 11 Dec 1837; Anderson Dunnagan, bm.

Laftice, Ambrose J. & Arteminsey Adkins, 14 April 1849; James D. Laftice, bm.

Lain, Alexander & Elizabeth Gray, 28 Dec 1817; Daniel H. McGee, bm.

SURRY COUNTY MARRIAGES, 1779-1868

Lain, George W. & Manda Fillips, 8 March 1862; m by William Golden, bm.

Lain, James & Julina Pelmon, 14 July 1823; Daniel McGee, bm.

Lain, Jesse & Nancy Stone, 10 Aug 1815; John Chandler, bm.

Lain, Taylor & Lucy Kearby, 17 Dec 1798; David Poindexter, bm.

Lakey, Abraham & Nancy Philips, 5 June 1823; Isaiah Stewart, bm.

Lakey, James & Mary Head, 13 Aug 1804; Francis Lakey, bm.

Lakey, Maner & Elizabeth Speer, 22 Oct 1800; Jno. Douling, bm.

Lakey, Mark & Charlott Williamson, 30 March 1817; Wm. Hobson, bm.

Lakey, Solomon & Susannah Normon, 28 July 1847; Jesse F. Lakey, bm.

Lamb, Hiram & Elizabeth Fulk, 14 Sept 1820; Abraham Badgett, bm.

Lambert, Elisha & Sally Johnson, 31 May 1831; Daniel Low(?), bm.

Lambert, John C. & Mary Hanes, 1 Oct 1850; James S. Hanes, bm.

Lambert, William & Polly Lambert, 29 March 1828; John Crouse, bm.

Lambert, William & Katharin Lewis, 29 April 1831; Henry Marshall, bm.

Lambert, Woodford & Anne Love, 9 Dec 1823; Jonathan Taylor, bm.

Lambert, Loftin H. & Elizabeth B. Perkins, 21 Nov 1853; David Bowers, bm; m 21 Feb 1852 by A. Simmons, J. P.

Landreth, Benjamin & Nancy Ayers, 21 Dec 1837; James Deen, bm.

Landreth, David M. & Permelia Denton, 23 Oct 1851; Jeremiah Denton, bm.

Landreth, Thomas & Rosy Walk, 29 March 1859; George Musgrove, bm.

Lane, Archabald & Elizabeth Hall, 6 Feb 1816; Absalom Kerr, bm.

Lane, David & Liddy Roberson, 18 Aug 1831; Nathaniel Roberson, bm.

Lane, William & Abigal Prichard, 13 Aug 1816; Saml Clark, bm.

Langly, Alexander & Jane Harvil, 18 May 1834; James Dickson, bm.

Lanier, Washington & Elisabeth Hicks, 18 Nov 1784; Miles Hicks, bm.

Lanchaster, Wm. & Rhody Smith, 26 Aug 1784.

Lapish, John A. & Mary Fletcher, 26 Feb 1848; George D. Williams, bm.

SURRY COUNTY MARRIAGES, 1779-1868

Lash, Harmon & Jemima Coe, 19 Dec 1808.

Lash, James & Mary Scott, 7 March 1814; Henry Sater, bm.

Lash, Nathaniel & Hennadel Woodfork, 19 Dec 1825; Richard Purycoff(?), bm.

Lash, Wm. A. & Nancy Hardin, 24 May 1829; John Conrad, bm.

Lashmet, Elias & Mary Padgett, 23 Feb 1790; Alexander Linn, bm.

Laster, George W., son of James and Mary Laster, and Elizia Norman, daugher of William and Nancy Norman, m 22 Oct 1868 by Rev. J. K. Rose, Baptist minister.

Laurence, Claybourn & Mary Hudspeth, 24 Dec 1784; George Hudspeth, bm.

Lavender, John & Jane Baker, 16 June 1825; Wm. Green, bm.

Lawrence, Richd. & Sally Barbour, 23 Sept 1817; David Buckhannon, bm.

Lawson, Alexander & Susanah Forkner, 16 March 1819; Martin Lawson, bm.

Lawson, Allen & Malitha Fensdale, 14 July 1848; Isham Riddle, bm.

Lawson, Anderson & Mary E. Sisk, 3 Sept 1856; John W. Vennable, bm; m 3 Sept 1856 by A. Simmons, J. P.

Lawson, Edmond & Mary Bennett, 13 May 1849; James Goyen, bm.

Lawson, James & Agnes Dannelly, _____ 186-.

Lawson, Thomas Jackson & Lydia Jarvis, 31 Dec 1850; Zael Williams, bm.

Lawson, William & Catharine Griffin, 11 March 1849; Pleasant Griffin, bm.

Leach, Rodney & Rachel Tate, 28 Nov 1818; Squire Glen, bm.

Lee, Benjamin & Susana Brown, 1 June 1805; William Rich, bm.

Lee, Joseph & Betsy Johnston, 24 Dec 1821; Conell James, Farfax Athon, bm.

Leeke, Wilson & Vicy Carter, 2 May 1824; Milton Carter, bm.

Lawson, Woody & Mary Lawson, 26 Dec 1850; Starlin Taylor, bm. (C. H.).

Lendin, Azariah & Elizabeth Holder, 5 Jan 1824; Jesse Holder, bm.

Lenear, Lewis & Marende Snider, 11 April 1867; Solomon W. Young, bm.

Lenoir, Rufus T. & Sally L. Gwyn, 16 Feb 1857; m 18 Feb 1857 by James Purvis.

Lester, Jesse & Mary Walker, 20 May 1787; David Owen, bm.

SURRY COUNTY MARRIAGES, 1779-1868

Lewellin, Thomas & Jane Roberts, 8 May 1851; John Robertson, bm.

Lewis, Albert & Malinda Head, 24 Jan 1850; Bennet Head, bm. (C. H.).

Lewis, Alex. D. & Sarah Ann Pardue, 28 Sept 1849; Benjamin Tucker, bm.

Lewis, Asa & Betsy Shinn, 21 Sept 1822; Thomas B. Wright, bm.

Lewis, Chapman & Jemima Perdue, 31 Aug 1829; R. Gilliam, bm.

Lewis, Charles & Eady Stone, 17 Dec 1830; Daniel Tully, bm.

Lewis, Fredrich & Milley Ross, 12 Feb 1799; John Ross, bm.

Lewis, Harden & Sarah Ann Parker, 4 April 1859; T. V. Hamlin, bm.

Lewis, James & Nancy Jackson, 17 Feb 1824; Thomas H. Poindexter, bm.

Lewis, James Martin & Mary Boswell, 29 March 1790; Joseph Herndon Jun., William Meridith, bm.

Lewis, Jesse & Frances A. Nations, 8 Sept 1855; T. V. Hamlin, bm; m 11 Sept 1853 by James Haynes, J. P.

Lewis, Joel & Miriam Eastham, 24 March 1786; Silvanus Pipes, bm.

Lewis, Kendrack & Mary Gallian, 25 Jan 1827; Julius Dickins, bm.

Lewis, Lemuel & Vilenty Poe, 8 Sept 1823; Thos Norman, bm.

Lewis, Warner & Susanna Bengum, 10 April 1809; Charles Lewis, bm.

Lewis, William & Mary Lockhart, 13 Sept 1820; Zachary Petty, bm.

Lewis, William & Caty Poined, 18 May 1823; Drury Holcomb, bm.

Lewis, William T. & Mary Ann Marien, 17 Dec 1849; Reuben Dunagan, bm.

Lewis, William T., son of Eleaner & Mehala Lewis, & Elizabeth E. Harbor, daughter of Martha Harbor, 16 Nov 1868.

Lewis, Willie & Polly Dumsigan, 21 Oct 1825; Elijah Gillaspie, bm.

Liddle, William Jr. & Elisa P. Porter, 18 Feb 1864; John Dent, bm; m 18 Feb 1864 by A. Simmons, J. P.

Lindly, James M. & Sarah M. Felts, 11 Oct 1848; E. T. Burgiss, bm.

Lindly, Thomas & Rossanna Harp, 6 Aug 1824; Alvin J. Duvall, bm.

Lindsay, Johnson & Fanny Willard, 12 Sept 1835; Thos. D. Gibbs, bm.

Lindsey, Anderson & Sally Moody, 14 Oct 1806; Abner Searcy, bm.

SURRY COUNTY MARRIAGES, 1779-1868

Lindsey, John Y. & Lucy Thorpe, 10 Dec 1836; Josiah Cowles, bm.

Lindsey, Francis W. & Mary Hurst, 14 July 1854; Jno. Q. A. King, bm; m 14 July 1854 by A. Simmons, J. P.

Lindsey, Leonard & Winney Patterson, 9 Sept 1818; Joseph Bray, bm.

Lindsey, Pinkney & Fanny Jacks, 11 Feb 1849; Shadrac Myers, bm.

Lindsey, Thomas & Sally Finch, 24 June 1826; James Kelly, bm.

Lindsey, William M. & Sarah Ann Edwards, 4 Sept 1845; Lewis Cash, bm.

Lineback, Daniel & _____, (no date); Phillip Howard, bm.

Lineback Emanuel & Rosanah Brown, 14 Nov 1857; L. W. Brinkly, bm.

Lineback, John & Abby Hall, 23 Dec 1799; Joseph Hall, bm.

Lineberry, A. W. & Cely Galespie, 9 Feb 1846; A. Dunnagan, bm.

Lineberry, Peter & Elizabeth Lain, 4 Dec 1855; Jacob Coller, bm.

Link, John W. & Sarah Casper, 7 Sept 1858; Ed. Bullin, bm. (C. H.).

Linn, Alexander & Precilla Spiers, 17 April 1787; Michael Turrage, bm.

Linvil, Franklin & Nancy E. Haymore, 22 Aug 1853; Pleasant Haymore, bm; m 25 Aug 1853 by A. Dunnagan, J. P.

Linville, Berry & Jane Slaydon, 21 Nov 1855; Wilcher Slaydon, bm; m 22 Nov 1855 by D. M. McGee, J. P.

Linville, Henry & Cleo White, 2 July 1864; James Major, bm; m 5 July 1864 by A. Dunnagan, J. P.

Linville, Hiram & Charity East, 24 Jan 1827; Hughes East, bm.

Linville, John & Levica Dooling, 17 Aug 1837; William Bowles, bm. (C. T.).

Linville, Moses & Henrietta White, 10 Oct 1832; John Seagrove, bm.

Linville, Ruel & Adaline Hemmons, 3 May 1862; James D. Creasy, bm; m 4 May 1862 by J. Gray, J. P.

Lion, John & Sarah Duglis, 4 Jan 1803; John Mikles, bm.

Lions, John & Polly Mathews, 28 Aug 1832; William Stewart, bm.

Lions, Meredith & Pereline Tolen(?), 18 Dec 1845; James Lions, bm.

Lions, William & Matilda Harris, 15 Aug 1850; Martin Payne, bm.

Little, Abraham & Peggy Starr, 11 Dec 1788; Lewis Little, bm.

Little, Lewis & Elizabeth Call, 27 Feb 1790; Jno Miller, bm.

SURRY COUNTY MARRIAGES, 1779-1868

Little, Peter & Nancy Richtor, 1 Nov 1793; Lewis Little, bm.

Litterel, Richard & Ann McClure, 20 Nov 1786; Reason Harbin, bm.

Liverton, Daniel & Jean Williams, 6 Oct 1797.

Logain, John W. & Mary Ann Hutson, 31 May 1867; m 1 June 1867 by Miles Foy, minister.

Logan, Anderson Littleberry & Ethalindy Rogers, 20 Dec 1821; James Melton, bm.

Logan, George & Rhody Hudspeth, 21 April 1808; Drury Holcomb, bm.

Logan, George Junr. & Polly Upthegrove, 6 Dec 1819; William Rash, bm.

Logan, Isaac & Elizabeth Philips, 18 Dec 1845; Richard S. Phillips, bm.

Logan, James & Mary Lynch, 6 Sept 1788; John Logan, bm.

Logan, John & Miriam Rash, 18 Jan 1791; Hugh Logan, bm.

Logan, John & Justian Creed, 7 Sept 1813; Edward Sweatt, bm.

Logan, John & Liddia Burender, 5 Sept 1818; Squire Glen, bm.

Logan, John & Delany Douglass, 29 Aug 1820; John Phillips, bm.

Logan, John & Rebekah Flynn, 7 Aug 1822; Thomas Flynn, bm.

Logan, Major & Polly Melton, 24 Jan 1821; Squire S. Glen, bm.

Logan, Partrick & Elizabeth Bevendor, 26 Dec 1811; Isham Melton, bm.

Loggains, Major & Elizabeth Clayton, 22 Aug 1789; Britain Clayton, bm.

Loggins, Thomas & Lucy Ann Wall, 4 Nov 1864; T. E. Mickey, bm.

London, Amos & Sarah Billis, 10 Feb 1793; Jams. Jackson, Lewis Wheliss, bm.

London, John & Amelia Cheek, 23 April 1800; Benj. H. Martin, bm.

Long, Daniel & Sarah Binkley, 30 May 1816; Jno. Money, bm.

Long, Frederick & Catherine Binkney, 15 Dec 1818; Henry Shore, bm.

Long, Fredrick Jr. & Rachael Starr, 16 June 1802; Fredrick Long, bm.

Long, George & Ann Davis, 31 Dec 1784; Robt Lanier, bm.

Long, George & Nancy Belletton, 8 Nov 1810; Jackson Davis, bm.

Long, George & Marry Culton, 6 March 1837; Isaac Vestal, bm.

Long, George D. & Elizabeth Vestal, 7 Feb 1850; Joseph B. Helton, bm.

Long, Henry & Jemimah Kinion, 8 June 1806; Frederick Long, bm.

Long, Henry & Nelly Holcomb, 20 April 1822; John Money, bm.

Long, Henry & Zilpha Ronard, 21 Nov 1837; John Long Jr., bm.

Long, Isaac & Rosanna Steelmon, 17 March 1846; John A. Long, bm.

Long, Isaac Jr. & Sarah Jane Prior, 28 Jan 1846; Thos Holcomb, bm.

Long, James F. & Sally E. Marion, 15 July 1863; L. N. Marion, bm.

Long, John & Betsey Griffin, 12 Nov 1804.

Long, John & Elizabeth Turner, 16 Jan 1816; Thomas Hally, bm.

Long, John & Nancy Davis, 1 June 1827; Solomon Vestal, bm.

Long, John A. & Bethana Vestal, 17 March 1846; Isaac Long, bm.

Long, Jonathan & Ruthey Hill, 1 June 1816; Thomas Halley, bm.

Long, Joshua & Sarah Morten, 26 Dec 1837; Jesse May, bm.

Long, Nathan & Nancy A. Ireland, 18 Feb 1846; Thos Holcomb, bm.

Long, Tobias & Fanny Frick, (no date); Archibald Carmichael, bm.

Long, Wm. & Polly Welch, 30 Sept 1811.

Long, William & _____, 20 Nov 1819; Adam Wagoner, bm.

Long, William & Polly Rennard, 10 April 1828; Joseph Bevins, bm.

Longbottom, Elijah & Rachel Money, 22 Oct 1847; James Day, bm.

Longbottom, Manen & Malissa Chandler, 22 Aug 1860; John Cane, bm; m 23 Aug 1860 by L. B. Bledsoe, J. P.

Longine, James & Ruth Holcomb, 19 Nov 1808; William Cannon, James Faircloth, bm. (C. H.).

Longine, John & Nancey Phillips, 23 Dec 1788; John Thos. Longine, bm.

Longine, John Thos & Sarah Bohannan, 16 Nov 1790; Francis Poindexter, bm. (C. H.).

Longine, Thomas & Mary Ransom, 1 Sept 1788; John Thos Longing, bm.

Love, Anderson & Louisa Love, 20 Aug 1856; m 27 Aug 1856 by W. E. Davis, J. P.

Love, David & Nancy Rarder, 18 Nov 1818; John Love, bm.

Love, Elexander, son of Malpark & Marget Love, & Elizabeth Neal, m 29 Oct 1868 by Isaac Armfield, J. P.

Love, Elijah & Elisa J. Vormon, 4 Dec 1856; James R. Snody, bm.

SURRY COUNTY MARRIAGES, 1779-1868

Love, Isaiah & Peggy Chinault, 2 Feb 1818; Richd. Chinall, bm.

Love, James Madison & Leanah Love, 11 March 1851; Thomas Love, bm; m 11 March 1851 by Jo. Phillips, J. P.

Love, John & Patsy James, 6 Feb 1787; James Love, bm.

Love, John & Polly Rarden, 15 Aug 1818; David Love, bm.

Love, Mason & Margaret Bingman, 17 March 1835; John Hicks Junr, bm.

Love, Thomas Jr. & Mary Evans, 5 April 1820; Ruel Jackson, bm.

Love, William & Jane Pruett, 17 May 1828; Archabald Taylor, bm.

Love, Wm & Matilda Payn, 1 July 1859; Kenny Low, bm.

Love, William & Mahaly Love, m 17 Oct 1855 by J. Gray, J. P.

Loveless, Andrew & Rebekah Holeman, 6 Oct 1795; George Wilkins, bm.

Lovell, Edward Jr. & Nancy Scott (no date); Benjamin Pettitt, bm.

Lovell, Edward F. & Polly Scott, 1 Oct 1864; T. E. Mickey, bm; m 2 Oct 1864 by Miles Foy.

Lovell, Hiram & Sarah Campbell, 12 Jan 1830; Andrew Cain, bm.

Lovell, John & Felema High, 16 July 1855.

Lovell, Joshua & Ann Odeal, 14 Sept 1825; Lender Armstrong, bm.

Lovell, William & Sarah Upthagrove, 17 March 1814; William Epperson, bm.

Lovill, Armstead & Nancy Coe, 13 Jan 1816; Francis Pettit, bm.

Lovill, E. F. & Josephine T. Marion, 12 Sept 1866; F. Booker, bm; m 12 Feb 1866.

Lovill, Edwd & Lucy Badgett, 29 Dec 1794.

Lovill, James & Sarah Poindexter, 3 June 1807; Samuel Martin, bm.

Lovill, James H. & Elizabeth Franklin, 11 Dec 1852.

Lovill, William & Jane Tate, 3 Feb 1834; Frederick Crouse, bm.

Lovill, Wm. R. & Eliza S. Reves, 29 Aug 1837.

Loving, William & Mahala Going, 19 April 1856; Edmond Bullen, bm; m 20 April 1856 by D. G. Bodenhamer.

Low, Anuel & Martha Davis, 6 Feb 1866; Stephen Low, bm; m 6 Feb 1866 by B. J. Dickins, J. P.

Low, Elias & Lydiann Payne, 30 Sept 1854; Jackson Low, bm; m 1 Oct 1854 by John Ramey, J. P.

Low, Elisha & Elijah Ramey (sic), 8 Jan 1833; Elijah Ramey, bm.

SURRY COUNTY MARRIAGES, 1779-1868

Low, Isaac & Matilda Muneus, 23 March 1836; John Ramy, bm.

Low, Jacob & Effy Galyen, 2 May 1849; Byram Gallyer, bm.

Low, James & Elizabeth Brown, 2 Jan 1817; Absalom Matthews, bm.

Low, James & Patsy Minhis, 26 March 1818; David Defrees, bm.

Low, Kenny & Julianny Stewart, 18 May 1853; Isaac Low, bm; m 19 May 1853 by Martin Payne, J.P.

Low, Kirby, & Rebeccah Galyer, 20 March 1854; Elias Low, bm.

Low, Kenny & Delia Ann Flippin, 5 July 1859; Wiley Dilkin, bm.

Low, Samuel & Salley Hayes, 9 Dec 1810; William Potter, bm.

Low, Samuel & Jane Williams, 14 March 1851; Wiley Dickens, bm.

Low, William & Lucy Nichols, 15 Feb 1820; Peter Muncens, bm.

Lowder, Samuel & Betsy Ratliff, 14 Dec 1808.

Lowe, John H. & Jestin Kiddle, 2 Aug 1859.

Lowe, Samuel & Caroline Nation, 1 Jan 1868.

Lowe, Stephen & Polly Knuckels, 1 March 1826; Revel Bentley, bm.

Lowe, Tarleton B. & Mary Davidson, 15 Jan 1851; Andrew Burge, bm.

Lowell, Thos & Lucy Lyon, (no date); Jas Fitzgerald, bm.

Lowery, Hilbard & Matilda Tucker, 13 Feb 1864; John Snow, bm; m 31 Feb 1864 by Geo. A. Jervis, J. P.

Lowrey, Edward & Mariah Clouse, 31 Oct 1850; Wm. W. Hicks, bm. (C. H.).

Lowrey, John W. & Catharine Williamson, 15 Oct 1851; Westly M. Smith, bm; m 15 Oct 1851 by Lemmon Shell, J. P.

Lowry, John & Hannah Vance, 9 Feb 1787; Samuel Vance, bm.

Loyd, Benjamin & Elizabeth Childress, 11 Oct 1786; Thomas Gordon, bm.

Luark, John & Ann Holt, 11 Aug 1797; Michael Warden, bm.

Luffman, Caleb W. & Sarah A. Horace, 29 Dec 1864; Amferd Horace, bm; m 29 Dec 1864 by D. A. Eldridge.

Luffman, Mark H. & Bosthenia C. Johnson, 25 Oct 1837; George A. Jervis, bm.

Luffman, Milton & Lucy Perdue, 28 May 1836; Wm. Farrington, bm.

Luffman, Silas & Sally Hodges, 16 Jan 1849; Samuel Jones, bm.

Lugert, Enos & Caroline Davis, 2 Jan 1831; John Davis, bm.

Lundy, Elijah & Rhoda Wills, 14 July 1806; Thomas Whitlock, bm.

SURRY COUNTY MARRIAGES, 1779-1868

Lundy, Elisha, of the State of Virginia, & Elizabeth A. Axsom, 21 April 1853; John Setliff, bm; m 21 April 1853 by H. M. Waugh, J. P.

Lundy, Ezekiel & Elizabeth Yeats, 26 Aug 1810; Benjamin Howard, Robert Freeman, Mark Shelton, bm.

Lundy, James & Sarah Lundy, 20 Aug 1853; Kerby Low, bm; m by Wm. Hodges, J. P.

Lupes, James & Patsy Calton, 17 March 1816; Joel Carter, bm.

Lyle, James & Ruthy West, 30 Nov 1831; Mathew West, bm.

Lynch, John & Patience Glen, 4 Jan 1788; Jo. Williams, bm.

Lynch, John & Honor Logan, 9 Feb 1791; James Logan, bm.

Lynch, John & Polly Flynn, 14 Jan 1817; Isham Milton, bm.

Lynch, Larkin & Elizabeth Hunter, 25 July 1833; Wm. Spilmon, bm.

Lyon, Robert & Polley Parnell, 25 Nov 1807; William Lyon, bm.

Lyon, Stephen H. & Judy Wilkerson, 29 May 1830; Joseph Richerson, bm.

Lyon, William & Sarah Freeman, 2 July 1804; Robert Freeman, bm.

Lyons, Absalum & Sarah Frankling, 7 Feb 1817; Brison Cook, bm.

Lyons, John & Melvina Lundy(?), 25 Dec 1835; Anderson Melton, bm.

McAtee, Thomas & Sarah Starr, 12 March 1802; Adam Starr, Thomas Watkins, bm.

Macay, William S. & Miss Mildred A. Hunt, 27 Nov 1853; J. H. A. Speer, bm; m 30 Nov 1853 by Wm. O. Reid, minister.

McBride, David & Eleanor Ridgeway, 14 Sept 1802; William Purdom, bm.

McBride, George T. & Eliza Nance, 1 June 1833; Saml Edwards, bm.

McBride, Gray & Emily Henderson, m 4 Jan 1857 by Wm. H. Pardue.

McBride, J. J. & Nancy Young, m 26 Sept 1867 by W. M. Hicks, J. P.

McBride, Samuel & Mary Cook, 6 Dec 1801; Isaac Cook, bm.

McBride, Wakeman & _____, (no date); William Purdom, bm.

McBride, William & Jane Hill, 25 Aug 1810; Wakeman McBride, bm.

McBride, William P. & Mary King, 1 Nov 1864; Anderson Linch, bm; m 3 Nov 1864 by J. Gray, J. P.

McBride, Wm. & Jez. Ann Frost, 18 May 1830; John McBride, bm.

McCallister, John & Sally Caudle, 7 Aug 1814; Martin Couper, bm.

McCallem, David & Sarah Walker, 9 Sept 1848; William McCollum, bm.

McCann, James & Mary Richardson, 13 Jan 1866; Wm. Richardson, bm; m 15 Jan 1866 by Rev. R. Sparks.

McClamack, James & Elizabeth Cornell, 22 Sept 1807; John Cornell, bm.

McCollem, Wm. & Polly King, 3 Aug 1823; Eli Jessop, bm.

McCollum, Thomas & Nancy Stanley, 5 Sept 1787; John McBride, bm.

McCollum, William & Dianer Galespie, 9 Oct 1847; Thomas Davis, bm.

McCraw, Andrew & Elizabeth Brassfield, 9 Sept 1837; Wilson Laffoon, bm. (filed under Macraw).

McCraw, Francis & Elizabeth Payne, 16 June 1838; Richard Snow Senr., bm.

McCraw, Francis & Sallie Newman, 23 Nov 1862; Jacob W. McCraw, bm; m 23 Nov 1862 by G. A. McCraw, J. P.

McCraw, G. A. & M. V. Lamkin, 24 March 1862; J. W. Rawley, bm.

McCraw, George & Willey Maclain, 26 May 1838; Richard Snow Senr, bm.

McCraw, Jacob A. & Sally Davis, 27 Feb 1822; C. W. Perkins, bm.

McCraw, Jacob W. & Nancy Spencer, 1 May 1851; Francis M. McCraw, bm.

McCraw, James W. & Sarah Golden, 7 April 1846; William Golding, bm.

McCraw, Jefferson & Mahaly Snow, 14 April 1850; Christopher Carter, bm. (C. H.).

McCraw, Mordacai H. & Nancy Golding, 21 May 1855; Levi Jones, bm.

McCraw, Waller & Leanah Edwards, 31 March 1845; Francis McCraw, bm.

McCraw, Waller & Matilda Roberson, 20 Jan 1848; James Greenwood, bm.

McCraw, William R. & Rosey Branscom, 15 May 1848; J. W. McCraw, bm.

McCraw, William W. & Mary Cove, 8 Feb 1833; James L. Bray, bm.

McDade, John & Rebekah Surat, 10 July 1815; John Turner, bm.

McDaniel, Allen & Elizer Carey, 7 April 1846; Vollet Yale, bm.

Mc Daniel, Colley & _____ (no date, during admn. of Gov. Ashe); Samuel Howard, bm.

McDaniel, H. P. & Eveline Baldwin, 31 Dec 1866; Watson Marshall, bm; m 2 Jan 1867 by M. A. Hall, J. P.

SURRY COUNTY MARRIAGES, 1779-1868

McDaniel, Ruben & _____ (no date); James Mears, bm.

McDonal, John & Paulina McCraw, 6 Dec 1833; B. F. Bray, bm.

McGahey, Daniel & Nancy Forkner, 24 June 1815; Samuel Forkner, bm.

McGahee, Alexander & Sally Roseberry, 6 April 1831; Henry C. Bray, bm.

McGee, A. W., son of John McGee, and Sarah Davis, daughter of Jessee Davis, _____ 186-.

McGee, Alson & Louisa McKinney, 31 Dec 1856; S. H. Jones, bm; m 1 Jan 1857 by James Needham, J. P.

McGee, Danel & Susan Dunbar, 9 Dec 1857; Smily Whittington, bm; m 10 Dec 1857 by Wilson Laffoon, J. P.

McGee, Drury & Sarah Venables, 16 Jan 1828; Ralph Holderfield, bm.

McGee, Drury & Permelia Taylor, 1 Sept 1856; Iredell Venable, bm.

McGee, James L., son of Harmon & Leanna O. McGee, and Nancy Stanly, daughter of Garrett & Mima Stanly, m 14 Jan 1868 by R. S. Pilson, J. P.

McGlaulin, Thomas & Lucy Wallander, 14 Sept 1823; Andrew Fulk, bm.

McGraw, James & Lidda A. Love, 5 Jan 1867; m 6 Jan 1867 by A. Brim, J. P.

McGuire, Olvy & Mary Ann Mofield, 3 Nov 1834; Jno Robinson, bm.

McGuire, Robert & Prudence Swaim, 28 May 1811; John McGuire, bm.

McIntire, William & Keziah Parsons, 27 June 1867; m 28 June 1867 at the house of Keziah Parsons, she is the daughter of Vinson Ball; m by J. E. Turner, J. P.

McKaughan, B. D. & E. M. Stanly, 14 Sept 1860; J. F. Anthony, bm; m 25 Sept 1860 by L. J. Norman, J. P.

McKay, Neill & Joesphene Cranor, 14 Nov 1852; m 14 Nov 1852 by M. T. Folger, J. P.

Mackey, John & Mary Reynolds, 31 Jan 1819; Peter Dowel, bm.

McKie, John Jr. & Caroline Davis, 13 Nov 1849; N. B. Dozier, bm.

Mackie, Robert & _____, 8 Dec 1817; John Mackey, bm.

Mackie, William & Luddy Vestal, 23 Aug 1850; Christian Royal, bm.

Mackie, William & Theresa M. Goughy, 26 March 1834; Theopilus Hauser, bm.

McKiney, Aaron & Lidea Norman, 23 March 1845; Henry Norman, bm.

SURRY COUNTY MARRIAGES, 1779-1868

McKiney, Achiles & Nancy J. Key, 19 Aug 1865; L. G. Waugh, bm; m 25 Aug 1865 by John Jones, at the house of Lewis Key.

McKinny, David & Rachel Garrott, 27 Dec 1830; Garrott Copeland, bm.

McKinney, Jesse & Phebe Gillespie, 16 April 1859; Joseph Gordon, bm.

McKinny, Fountain B. & Martha Moore, 5 June 1834; Wm. P. Tucker, bm.

McKinny, Granville & Emezet J. Ferris, 13 Feb 1856; Pleasant Haymore, bm; m 14 Feb 1856 by W. E. Davis, J. P.

McKinny, John & Sarah Roard, 18 May 1814; Thomas Jessop, bm.

McKiny, E. H. & S. S. Scott, m 29 Aug 1865; B. F. Scott, bm.

McKiny, James & Lucinda Kees, 24 Jan 1833; Edward M. Dobson, bm.

McKnight, William & Tilly Holeman, 27 May 1793; Jeremiah Allen, bm.

McLean, Thomas G. & Elizabeth N. Glass, 21 Oct 1851; Samuel L. Gilmer, bm.

McLemore, John & Ruth Steelman, 7 April 1810; James Hudspeth, bm.

McLemore, Wright & Sarah Ransome, 16 May 1795; George Hudspeth, bm.

McMachan, Morgan & Roseannah Railsback, 27 Feb 1799; Jonathan Bryan, bm.

McMickle, C. C. & Roseltha P. Kapp, 5 Dec 1856; Jno. J. McMickle, bm; m 9 Dec 1856 by G. Bryan, J. P.

McMickle, Gideon J. & Sarah Cockerham, 16 Dec 1834; St. Clair McMickle, bm.

McMickle, Gideon J. & Susan Green Wood, 10 April 1837; Bryson Darnall, bm.

McMickle, John & Vianna Martin, 8 April 1820; James Spencer, bm. (C. H.).

McMickle, Peter & Jennet Clee, 27 May 1814; Joseph Hodges, bm.

McMickle, Saintclair & Polly Woodruff, 26 Oct 1809; Peter McMickle, bm.

McMickle, William G. & Catharine Russell, 11 Sept 1826; Eli Rees, bm.

McMillian, F. B. & Susan T. Dodge, 16 Oct 1850; R. M. Allison, bm.

McMillon, Greenville & Sarah Combs, 5 April 1853; James McMillon, bm.

McMillen, John & Martha Gwyn, 20 Aug 1864; James D. Dean, bm; m 20 Aug 1864 by G. A. McCraw, J. P.

SURRY COUNTY MARRIAGES, 1779-1868

McMillian, Dudley & Polley Allen, 9 May 1821; William Allen, bm.

McMillon, James L. & Sarah McMillon, 6 Sept 1854; Calvin P. Smith, bm; m 6 Sept 1854 by A. Simmons, J. P.

McMillon, Pierce & Aby Allen, 27 May 1847; Aaron Gwyn, bm.

McMilon, John & Elizabeth _____, m 26 Jan 1860 by C. L. Banner, J. P.

McMilon, Joseph, son of Harmon & P. H. McMilan, and Nancy Harris, daughter of Eli Harris, m 3 Sept 1868 by Thomas Schaub, J. P.

McMilon, William and Elizabeth Boyd, 11 May 1862; see Hiatt, William.

McMullin, James & Margaret Pettegene, 19 May 1793; Isham Young, bm.

McPeeak, Henry & Emeline Sutfin, 17 Oct 1858; Wm. R. McPeeack, bm.

MacPherson, Wm. & Sarah Owins, 15 June 1797; Ephraim Williams, bm.

McPerson, Wm. & Nancy Wily, 24 Aug 1824(?); Stephen McPherson, bm.

McRoberts, Benjamin, son of John and Bency McRoberts, and Amy F. Williams, daughter of Mary Childris, m 8 Nov 1868 by John H. Lowe, J. P.

Mabbitt, John & Nelly Martin, 14 March 1814; Virtue Sweatt, bm.

Mabe, Arnold & Sarah F. Carner, 29 Aug 1863; J. Smart, bm; m 28 Aug 1863 by Wilson Laffoon.

Maber, Iredell & Malinda Dunkin, 1 July 1851; Wm. M. Hicks, bm.

Maberry, Samuel & America Boyd, 19 Nov 1859; Saml. L. Gilmer, bm.

Mabury, William & _____, 8 July 1848; Andrew Goard, bm.

Mabry, Alfred & Emley Dalton, 28 Sept 1862. (C. H.).

Macey, Reuben & Lucy Petty, 20 Oct 1802; Stephen Mankin, bm.

Madon, Charles & Sarah Venable, 24 Dec 1858; Jacob Stuart, bm.

Mahaffy, Jesse & Charity Woolff, 9 July 1851; Watson Holyfield, bm.

Mainard, Horace & Tennesse Harvill, 28 Nov 1844; Alexander Hall, bm.

Maneus, Peter & Nancy Senter, 13 Feb 1818; Wm. Cunningham, bm.

Mankins, Jackson D. & Mary Adaline Copeland, 12 Feb 1852; Jas. L. Copeland, bm.

Mankins, James & Catharine Marsten, 3 Jan 1824; Asa Reaves, bm. (C. H.).

SURRY COUNTY MARRIAGES, 1779-1868

Mankins, James & Elizabeth Walker, 29 Aug 1826; Pleasant Venable, bm.

Mankins, John & Patsy Kerby, 16 Feb 1798; Jesse Mankin, bm.

Mankins, Simeon & Elizabeth S. Caloway, 21 Aug 1859; J. K. Smith, bm.

Mann, Roland H. & Lucinda Ballard, 19 Aug 1849; Phillip Holcomb, bm.

Marion, Adam & Sally Reeves, 19 May 1824; Jeremiah Marion, bm.

Marion, Adam, son of Isaac and Anny Marion, & Esther Baker, daughter of James and Elizabeth Reed, m 26 Jan 1868 by C. H. P. Whitaker, J. P.

Marion, Azriah & Sarah Franklin, 9 Sept 1861.

Marion, Henry W. & Miss Permelia Whitaker, m 19 Jan 1860 by R. E. Reeves, J. P.

Marion, Irvin & Nancy Hill, 6 Nov 1838; A. Whitaker, bm.

Marion, Isaac & Anna Whitaker, 12 May 1831; Watson Holyfield, bm.

Marion, Jesse & Rachel Bass, 25 May 1844; William Ring, bm.

Marion, Jesse & Letty Childress, 31 April 1854; Amos Reid, bm; m 15 April 1854 by John Hamlin, J. P.

Marion, John M. & Candece Denny, 19 Feb 1838; John Draughon, bm.

Marion, Joseph, son of Jeremiah Marion, and Nancy Copeland, daughter of Freeman Copeland, m 11 Feb 1851 by H. C. Bray, J. P.

Marion, Mat, son of Isaac and Anna Marion, and Sarah J. Collins, daughter of Anthony & Nancy Collins, m 20 Dec 1868 by Thos. J. Williams, J. P.

Marion, Moses & Elizabeth Forrester, 7 April 1821; George Blair, bm.

Marion, Moses & Polly Coe, 26 May 1828; Ezekiel Watson, bm.

Marion, Robert & Polly Alberty, 1 June 1823; Peter Graves, bm.

Marion, William Jr. & Pasia Gillaspy, 7 April 1846; Jeremiah Marion, bm.

Marion, William & Miss Thirsey Copeland, 21 Nov 1853; Melvin W. Copeland, bm; m 25 Dec 1853 by H. C. Bray, J. P.

Markland, Jonathan & Nelly Padgett, 14 April 1787; Robert Markland, bm.

Markland, Joseph & Polly Bowles, 23 Jan 1790; Robert Markland, bm.

Marler, John & Mary W. Poindexter, 18 Dec 1834; John J. Poindexter, bm.

Marlor, Thomas & Sarah Germon, 23 Aug 1789; John McCollum, bm.

Marmon, David & Rhoda McWiller(?), 29 Jan 1808; Joseph Marmon, bm.

Marmon, Joseph & Sally Hatley, 27 Sept 1811; Thos Marman, bm.

Marmon, Thomas & Jemimah Esteel, 27 Oct 1804; John Beaty, bm.

Marsh--see also Mash

Marsh, Asbury, son of Nancy Marsh, and Mary Williamson, daughter of Park and Lettie Williamson, m 22 Jan 1868 by Joseph Aresom, J. P.

Marsh, Daniel & Catharine Childress, 28 Oct 1845; Jonathan Childress, bm.

Marsh, Ezekiel & Liddy Whitaker, 18 July 1798; Jeremiah Wilmon, Phillip Howard, bm.

Marsh, Henry A., son of William M. and Susan P. Marsh, and Manerva Scott, daughter of Jos. H. & Permelia Scott, m 15 Dec 1868 by John H. Lowe, J. P.

Marsh, Israel & Salley Mash, 2 Nov 1795; Samuel Marsh, bm.

Marsh, James & Meriah White, 28 July 1832; H. C. Bray, bm.

Mash, Jerry & Elizabeth Norman, 6 Aug 1856; John S. Douglass, bm.

Marsh, John & Nancy East, 13 Nov 1817; Minor Marsh, bm.

Marsh, Minor & Hetley Brown, 23 Jan 1832; Jesse Brown, bm.

Marsh, Miner & Polly Brown, 2 April 1836; Abraham Bowles, bm.

Marsh, Miner & Nelly Norton, 1 July 1808; Thos Marsh, bm.

Marsh, Pleasant & Keziah Dunnagan, 29 March 1838; William Marsh, bm.

Marsh, Samuel & Peggy Wright, 24 March 1792; Thomas Wright, bm.

Marsh, Thomas & Rachael Summers, 1 Sept 1794; John Marsh, Jr., bm.

Marsh, Thomas & Martha Phipps, 6 Oct 1820; Leonard Ray, bm.

Marsh, Thos & Prudence Smith, 6 Nov 1831; Henry H. Marsh, bm.

Marsh, William & Edith Paul, 15 Oct 1817; Thos Marsh, bm.

Marsh, Wm. & Lucretia Brown, 27 July 1833; Pleasant Venable, bm.

Marsh, William & Susannah Dunagan, 30 Oct 1844; Jefferson Hickman, bm.

Marsh, William & Sarah A. Phillips, 28 Dec 1866; J. M. Jenkins, bm.

Marsh, William H. & Sallie Melton, 14 Aug 1865; Thos. Moore,bm; m 14 Aug 1865 by R. F. McGuffin, J. P.

SURRY COUNTY MARRIAGES, 1779-1868

Marsh, Willis & Miss Elizabeth M. Smith, 28 Dec 1853; Isaiah Whitaker, bm; m 9 Jan 1854 by Jas. Jones, J. P.

Marshal, William C., son of Richard and Susannah Marshal, and Elina T. Johnson, daughter of Lewis & Dealia Johnson, m 22 Dec 1868 by A. Simmons, J. P.

Marshall, Aaron & Temperance Williams, 12 Aug 1800; Richd. Wilbourn, bm.

Marshall, Archibald & Matilda Carlton, 27 March 1847; Jesse F. Atwood, bm.

Marshall, Edward & Mary Abbott, 10 Jan 1845; Wm. Marsh, bm.

Marshall, Gabriel & Mary Douthit, 23 Jan 1844; Bryson Darnall, bm.

Marshall, Garland C. & Sophrony N. Hutchins, 29 Oct 1867; S. D. Critz, bm; m 31 Oct 1867 by A. Simmons, J. P.

Marshall, H. B. & Celia Willis, 13 Dec 1855; by 13 Dec 1855 by R. Marshal, J. P.

Marshall, John & Irementa Boyd, 24 April 1862; E. W. McMillion, bm; m 24 April 1862 by Wm. R. Bray, J. P.

Marshall, John, son of Joseph and Ann Marshall, and Martha D. McCracan, daughter of Thomas & Wilmoth McCracan, m 24 Sept 1868 by Thomas Schaub, J. P.

Marshall, John M. & Chistena Sparger, 4 Dec 1844; Jno. H. Jackson, bm.

Marshall, Moses & Mary Roberts, 11 Feb 1830; J. Callaway, bm.

Marshall, Robert & Martha Pucket, 26 May 1831; Joshua Lester, bm.

Marshal, Wm. & Nancy West, 28 April 1827; E. L. Marshall, bm.

Marshall, William & Charlotte Willis, 28 Dec 1837; Greenville Willis, bm.

Marshall, Simon & Sarah Reece, 27 Oct 1812; Jesse Reece, bm.

Marshall, Thomas & Elizabeth Loudon, 13 Aug 1817; William Marlin, bm.

Martin, Barret Lewis & Mary Martin, 24 Nov 1806; Benj. H. Martin, bm.

Martin, Burrel & Luvania Mathis, 14 Aug 1804; James Mathews, bm.

Martin, Daniel H. & Malinda Reece, 7 Dec 1844; John McKie, bm.

Martin, Gilbert & Elizabeth Baker, 11 May 1850; John Martin, bm.

Martin, Henry & Sally Linkins, 22 Aug 1832; James P. Childress, bm.

Martin, Henry H. & Martha McMickle, 27 Dec 1830; E. M. Spencer, bm.

Martin, Hiram & Catharine Mackie, 15 Feb 1831; Alvis Reece, bm.

SURRY COUNTY MARRIAGES, 1779-1868

Martin, James & Mary A. Dobson, 14 Feb 1839; Jessa A. Waugh, bm.

Martin, Jas. C. & Sarah Thompson, 27 March 1849; J. R. McLean, bm.

Martin, James F. & Martha W. Kerr, 5 May 1831; Pleasant Henderson, bm.

Martin, James S. & Matilda Hawkins, 21 Aug 1867; Richard Martin, bm.

Martin, Job & Caroline Meteldea Pledge, 4 Jan 1796; W. Pledger Poindexter, Saml Martin, bm.

Martin, Jobe & Marita Martin, 21 Feb 1791; Valn. Martin, bm.

Martin, John & Francis Lynch, 19 Oct 1785; Goldman Kimbrough, bm.

Martin, John Jr. & Leroy Hanes, 26 March 1835; John Myres, bm.

Martin, Matthew & Ann Moore, 10 March 1787; Parish Sims, bm.

Martin, Meredith & Rosey Hanes, 6 Nov 1827; Zachariah Sawyers, bm.

Martin, Reps & Nancy Poindexter, 20 Sept 1848; T. P. Hampton, bm.

Martin, Richard & M. R. Roby, 26 Oct 1858; J. E. Reeves, bm; m 27 Oct 1858 by Dexter A. Snow, Evangelist for the Church of Christ, Snowville, Va.

Martin, Robert & Amelia Wright, 12 Jan 1786; John Wright Jr., bm; consent from John Wright, father of Amelia, 10 Jan 1786.

Martin, Samuel & Elizabeth Scott, 18 Aug 1811; John Coe Jr., bm.

Martin, Samuel A., son of Henry and Elizabeth Martin, and S. V. Marion, daughter of R. E. and Pegy Marion, m 15 Sept 1870 by M. Baldwin, minister.

Martin, Simon & Ruth Mackey, 28 Sept 1818; Peter Dowell, bm.

Martin, Thos. S. & Ann C. Poindexter, 6 Nov 1844; Jno. P. Clingman, bm.

Martin, William & Mary Head, 14 Feb 1846; William Martin, bm.

Martin, William & Mariam Hauser, 1 April 1851; John H. Martin, bm.

Martin, Wm. & Mary Elkins, 16 Aug 1856; m 16 Aug 1856 by B. F. Scott, J. P.

Martin, Williams & Mary Lewis, 15 Dec 1847; Ephraim Hough, bm.

Martindale, John & Elizabeth Carmichael, 2 Dec 1822; Starling Carmichael, bm.

Mash, Clabourn & Elisabeth Carter, 26 Oct 1803; Jeremiah Mash, bm.

SURRY COUNTY MARRIAGES, 1779-1868

Mason, John & Sarah Toads, 2 July 1795; Michael Finniege, bm.

Massy, Peeples & Amy Perkins, 18 May 1815; Sterling Lanier, bm.

Master, James & Elizabeth Poe, 17 July 1792; George Hudspeth, bm.

Master, Nicholas & Elizabeth McDaniel, 22 Sept 1786; James Masters, bm.

Masters, John & Menerva Johnson, 15 Nov 1835; Isaac D. Wright, bm.

Masters, William & Margeret Cockerham, 30 Nov 1807; James Callaway, bm.

Masters, William or Johnson, Joseph, & Elizabeth Brewer, 27 Dec 1807; Amos Chappel, bm.

Mathews, Absalom & Ametty Poindexter, 28 Sept 1830; Thomas F. Prather, bm.

Mathews, Alexander & Cathrain Long, 31 Aug 1850; Littlebery Mathews, bm.

Mathews, Benjamin & Darkes Speer, 27 Feb 1828; John G. Pettitt, bm.

Mathews, Bradly & Martha Day, 2 Dec 1816; David Day, bm.

Mathews, H. H. & Mary Ann Sutfin, m 23 Sept 1865 by J. S. Green, J. P.

Matthews, Harrison & Elizabeth Boomdn(?), 19 Aug 1833; Abraham G. Philips, bm.

Mathews, Hezekiah Jr. & Rebeca Mathews, 26 Sept 1846; Hezekiah Mathews Senr., bm.

Mathews, William & Frances Brinkly, 8 Dec 1847; John Hill, bm.

Mathis, Hezekiah & Mary Lion, 2 May 1804; John Lion, bm.

Mathis, James & Prisilla Flyn, 27 July 1828; Benet Creed, bm.

Mathis, Enoch Solomon & Nancy Hopkins, 14 Jan 1810; Philip Howard, Marmaduke Kimbrough, bm.

Mathis, Rubin & Drusiller Martin, 16 Jan 1794; John Bovender, bm.

Mathis, William & Elizebeth Lyons, 10 May 1833; William Stewart, bm.

Mathis, William & Martha Lewis, 5 Sept 1849; Littleberry Mathis, bm.

Matthews, Aaron & Meddey Johnson, 9 Feb 1817; Absalom Mathews, bm.

Matthews, Benjamin & Elizabeth Melton, 28 Aug 1833; Daniel Speers, bm.

Matthews, Chesley & Maryan Glazebrooks, 24 June 1816; James Chappel, bm.

SURRY COUNTY MARRIAGES, 1779-1868

Matthews, Jacob & Phebe Willard, 14 Jan 1823; Landon Trulove, bm.

Matthews, James & Elizabeth Martin, 11 Sept 1818; Hezekiah Matthews, bm.

Matthews, James & Rebekah Tull, 17 May 1824; Landon Truelove, bm.

Matthews, William & Catherine Tull, 20 July 1825; Charles Trulove, bm.

Maudlin, Charles & Mary Holt, 16 Feb 1818; Joseph Johnson, bm.

Maxwell, J. H. & Laura F. York, 13 March 1860.

Maxwell, R. H. & E. C. Cumings, 2 June 1864; Wm. Whitecer, bm; m 2 June 1864 by D. A. Eldridge, J. P.

May, Martin & Rebecca Cranfill, 1 Sept 1831; Jo. Reavis, bm.

May, Jesse & Elisabeth Jinkins, 27 May 1835; Henry Jinkins, bm.

May, Samuel & Lydia Hoots, 21 Oct 1837; Mark May, bm.

May, William & Mary Daner, 5 Dec 1829; Martin May, bm.

Mayberry, George W. & Elizabeth Monday, 19 Nov 1859; Saml. L. Gilmer, bm.

Mayes, Goodin & Phebe Johnson, 20 Nov 1784; John Johnson, bm.

Mayes, John & Susan Callahan, 3 Jan 1860; m 5 Jan 1860 by Jno. J. McMickle, J. P.

Maynard, Henry & Jane Holcomb, 20 July 1846; Jesse Jinkins, bm.

Maynard, Thaddeus & Polly Steelmon, 23 Sept 1819; Jonathan Haines, bm.

Mays, Fleming & Polly Pilmon, 6 July 1828; D. Walker, bm.

Mays, George & Carline Hodges, 2 Feb 1864; A. Dunnagan, bm.

Mays, Joel & Mary Norman, 2 Feb 1856; John Mays, bm; m 14 Feb 1856 by Jno. J. McMickle, J. P.

Mays, Shelton & Patsy Laffoon, 25 Sept 1834; Jonathan Barass, bm.

Medley, Jas. H. & Sarah Ann Riggsby, 7 Feb 1857; Jas. Oneal, bm.

Meers, Thoms. & Elezebeth Isbell, 22 April 1798; James Mathews, bm.

Meglehorne, George & Elizabeth Carpenter, 8 Feb 1853; John Ramey, bm; m 17 Feb 1853 by John Ramey, J. P.

Mehaffy, Thomas & Betsey Moyers, 19 Nov 1806; John Reid, bm.

Mehaley, Garrett & Lorana Day, 11 July 1807; James Callaway, bm.

Melton, Amon & Nancy Mosir, 16 July 1836; Joel Dyer, bm.

Melton, Anderson & Elizabeth Bledsow, 25 Dec 1835; John Lyons, bm.

Melton, Elijah & Mary Suthard, 29 March 1814; Isaac Bledsoe, bm.

Melton, Robert & Susanna Cook, 3 March 1811; Chas. Carter, bm.

Melton, William & Litchey Melton, 26 June 1812; Daniel Bills Jr., bm.

Melton, William & Syntha Speer, 21 Jan 1837; William Randolph, bm.

Meridith, James K. & Rhoda A. Farmer, 25 Feb 1867.

Meredith, William & Rebeccah Noblet, 17 Aug 1792; Airs Hudspeth, bm.

Merion, Joseph & Nancy Copeland, 8 Feb 1851; James L. Copeland, bm.

Merrion, Daniel & _____, 21 Feb 1810; Presley Lawless, bm.

Merrion, Jeremiah & Mary Howard, 30 June 1822; George Wooten, bm.

Messer, Leonard & Melinda Windsor, 2 May 1808; James Whitlock, bm.

Messick, Elisha & Mary Jones, 24 Oct 1837; Wiley Messick, bm.

Messick, Henry P. & Nancy Martin, 29 Jan 1836; Elisha Messick, bm.

Messick, Ira B. & Nancy Emeline Wells, 27 Feb 1847; Elisha Messick, bm.

Messick, Leonard J. & Mary Ann Brown, 24 Aug 1848; Elisha Messic, bm.

Messick, Lewis R. & Mary Talbert, 31 Jan 1848; L. J. Messick, bm.

Messic, Wilie & Rebecca Brown, 1 March 1845; James B. Johnson, bm.

Messick, Wm. J. & Polley E. Naylor, 27 April 1835; Thomas B. Naylor, bm.

Miars, Jacob & Nancy Haynes, 23 Jan 1827; George Miars, bm.

Micheals, William & Elizabeth Taylor, 8 March 1831; Thomas Ooten, bm.

Michel, William & Elizabeth Speer, 14 Oct 1833; Osrel M. Spilman, bm.

Mickey, J. L. & Barbara Hunt, 9 Oct 1857; J. C. Barr, bm; m 11 Oct 1857 by Adam Scott, J. P.

Mickle, Elijah & Elizabeth Cash, 4 Dec 1824; John Collins, bm.

Mickle, Thomas & Jemima Kelly, 9 Oct 1834; Vestal Hutchens, bm.

Mickle, William & Betsy Greenwood, 13 Oct 1813; Lewis Noland, bm.

Mickle, William & Elizabeth Casy, 17 July 1856.

Midkiff, David & Mary Thorp, 24 May 1853; Thomas Lowry, bm; m 29 May 1853 by Isaac Armfield, J. P.

Midkiff, Ephraim & Lucy Forkner, 2 Nov 1847; John Midkiff, bm.

Midkiff, John & Sally Griffith, 10 Jan 1846; Elisha Banner, bm.

Midkiff, Joseph & Levina Boyd, 6 Aug 1854; Jackson Baker, bm.

Midkiff, Joseph & Nancy Griffith, 22 Dec 1844; John Midkiff, bm. (C. H.).

Midkiff, Samuel M. & Rebeca Jane Porters, 6 Feb 1864; Charles Poore, bm.

Midkiff, William H., son of John and Sarah Midkiff, and Isabellar N. Smith, daughter of Larken and Mary Smith, 28 July 1868.

Mihaffy, Richard & Elizabeth Hector, 23 Dec 1811; Thos. Mihaffy, bm.

Mikels, Isaac & Temperance Hutchans, 25 July 1846; Hugh Brown, bm.

Mikels, Joel & Martha Normon, 21 Oct 1820; William Rhodes, bm.

Mikels, Jesse & Nancy Davis, 3 Oct 1833; Joel Hutchins, bm.

Mikels, Thomas & Martha Diar, 18 Dec 1791; Thos. Stanfield, bm.

Mikels, William & Winny Norman, 18 Sept 1823; Amos S. Hutchens, bm.

Mikles, John & _____, 179-; Thomas Hudspeth, bm.

Mikles, John & Winney Martin, 22 Aug 1825; William Norman, bm.

Mikles, Thomas & _____, 21 May 1794; John Mikles, bm.

Mikles, William & _____, 10 Aug 1844; George Mikels, bm; Joshua Patterson, wit.

Milgrum, Levi & Emily W. Campbell, 25 June 1855; Emmett T. Campbell, bm.

Millar, Adom & Elender Scantlin, 9 Aug 1800; William Garner, bm.

Miller, Carter & Elizabeth C. Jefferson, 5 Nov 1845; Thomas Patterson, bm.

Miller, Dan. & Sally Dillard, 11 April 1808.

Miller, Frederick & Judith Ridings, 28 March 1809; John Miller, bm.

Miller, Henry & Mary Grabel, 30 May 1826; Eli Cook, bm.

Miller, Henry G. & Nancy Boling, 30 July 1809; Richd. E. Hazelwood, bm.

Miller, Jacob & Jane Walker, 1 Feb 1792; Zepheniah Dowden, bm.

Miller, Jacob & Sarah Phillips, 28 Oct 1806; George Griffith, bm.

Miller, John & Ellender Garner, 19 Aug 1797; William Garner, bm.

Miller, John & Polly Hudspeth, 14 Sept 1807; Jos. Hudspeth, bm.

Miller, John & Jane Carmichael, 1 April 1824; Charles Shelton, bm.

Miller, John Martin & Elizabeth Humphris, 11 June 1788; Zepheniah Dowden, bm.

Miller, John W. & Margaret Holcomb, 11 Feb 1833; Greenberry Hardin, bm.

Miller, Matthias & Elizabeth Richards, 18 Feb 1795.

Miller, Peris M. & Caroline Anderson, 15 Jan 1837; David Arnold, bm.

Miller, Peter & Christeny Danner, 31 Dec 1813; Jacob Shores, bm.

Miller, Nicholas & Nancy Smith, 23 Aug 1825; Vachel Craft, bm.

Miller, Thos & Elizabeth Paul, 12 July 1845; James Angel, bm.

Miller, Wm. H. & Catharine Mortin, 14 Dec 1845; A. Q. Reece, bm.

Mills, Daniel & Mahala Harrison, 30 Dec 1832; Wm. G. Haynes, bm.

Mills, James P. & Sarah E. Johnson, 22 Dec 1866; Samuel Y. Simpson, bm.

Mills, Peter & Mary Stanley, 12 Feb 1822; William Rhodes, bm.

Minefee, Benjamin S. & Elizabeth McCraw, 15 Oct 1834; Thomas B. Wright, bm.

Mines, Robert & Hanah Hiet, 3 July 1814; Moses Adams, bm.

Minish, A. W. & N. C. McDaniel, 22 Sept 1866; E. B. Walsh, bm; m 7 Oct 1866 by M. V. Sherrill.

Minish, Isaac W. & Lucretia C. Lines, 25 Jan 1851; Thomas D. Minnish, bm.

Minish, James & Elizabeth Salomon, 7 Dec 1827; George Messick, bm.

Minish, James Jr. & Polly Henderson, 11 Dec 1831; John Whitlock, bm.

Minish, Joshua & Martha Messick, 19 May 1838; James Minish, bm.

Minish, Thomas & Polly Padget, 27 Jan 1805; Isaac Minish, bm.

Minish, Thomas & Judith Padgett, 12 Jan 1821; James Minish, bm.

SURRY COUNTY MARRIAGES, 1779-1868

Minish, William A. & Maryan Jarvis, 1 May 1856.

Minter, George, son of Flem and Lucy Minter, and Ann Hiotte, m 15 Nov 1868 by D. C. Stinson.

Mires, Barnett & Anna Reece, 7 Jan 1845; C. W. Williams, bm.

Mires, Charles & Martha Vass, 28 Dec 1837; John Thompson, bm.

Miridith, Daniel & Hannah Cooke, 12 Jan 1787; Benjamin Burch, bm.

Mirs, Peter & Mary Thompson, 1 Aug 1856.

Mise, Shepherd and Elizabeth Maze, 12 Sept 1838; A. J. Gordon, bm.

Missel, Thomas & Sarah Godfrey, 20 March 1848; William J. Messel, bm.

Mitchel, William & Jane Burge, 2 Jan 1855; J. H. Dobson, bm; m 2 Jan 1855 by Drury Hodges.

Mitchell, James & Franky Mitchell, 22 Dec 1824; Arter Lurle(?), bm.

Mitchell, James V. & Mary Barham, 28 Dec 1854; Henry T. Stump, bm.

Mitchell, Moses & Elizabeth Windsor, 16 April 1833; James A. Windsor, bm.

Mitchell, Robert & Sally Mickle, 6 Sept 1821; Wm. Mickle, bm.

Mitchell, William & Franky Cave, 4 Jan 1864; A. H. Freeman, bm; m 4 Feb 1864 by A. Dunnagan, J. P.

Mock, Andrew & Mildred McBride, 24 Nov 1816; John K. Gammond, bm.

Mock, Daniel & Elizabeth Joiner, 1 Oct 1814; Joseph Sater, bm.

Mock, David & Elizabeth Owen, 25 Dec 1821; Samuel Bolejack, bm.

Mock, George & Margrett Haixt, 20 Dec 1814; Jacob Haixt, bm.

Mock, Heinrich (Henry) & Catherine Black, 25 Oct 1787; Peter Mock Jr., bm.

Mock, Henry & Nancy Gibbs, 8 Dec 1819; John Miller, bm.

Mock, Lewis & Mary Denny, 20 Nov 1819; Isaac Brown, bm.

Mock, Peter & Polly Binkley, 12 Oct 1813; Adam Black, bm.

Mock, William & Anna Static(?), 6 Dec 1825; Solomon Elrod, bm.

Mofield, Gabriel & Sally Robinson, 12 Sept 1833; Nathan Price, bm.

Moles, Flemon & Emley Dolton, 23 Aug 184-; Ruben McPeak, bm.

Molin, Denas & Lydia Kays, 10 July 1790; Joseph Keys, Jr., bm.

Monday, Hail & Catharine Donner, 1 Oct 1829; Adam Donner, bm.

SURRY COUNTY MARRIAGES, 1779-1868

Money, Daniel & Tennessee Johnson, 14 June 1845; E. L. Hamby, bm.

Money, David & Martha Ross, 28 May 1848; Eph. L. Hamby, bm.

Money, Goldman & Elizabeth Anthoy, 10 Dec 1831; Howel Money, bm.

Money, Hardy & Letha Marshall, 24 Dec 1835; Tho. H. Money, bm.

Money, Henry & Tallitha Brineger, 19 March 1829; Jacob Wagner, bm.

Money, Henry J. & Susannah Pendrega, 3 Oct 1844; William Collins, bm.

Money, Howel & Elizabeth Shores, 22 Feb 1823; Isaac Money, bm.

Money, Howel & Nancy Morison, 27 Feb 1862; Philip Shore, bm; m 27 Feb 1862 by W. H. Pardue.

Money, Isaac & Elizabeth Parsons, 17 March 1837; Charles Dudley, bm.

Money, James & Ann Pendri, 24 Sept 1805; Adam Brinnagar, bm.

Money, James & Elizabeth Ivins, 3 Dec 1850; James Ashly, bm.

Money, John & Lydia Austelle, 7 Sept 1817; William Money, bm.

Money, Johnson & Nancy Tucker, 1 June 1822; John Money, bm.

Money, Moses & Caroline Norman, 14 Sept 1844; Harison Sisk, bm.

Money, Thomas & Betsey Roswell, 27 Dec 1821; William Money, bm.

Money, Thomas H. & Prudence Money, 13 July 1834; Ephraim Hamby, bm.

Money, William & Catherine Miller, 23 Dec 1818; John Shores, bm.

Money, Zebulon & Susanah Spurling, 10 Sept 1838; Thos. F. Anthony, bm.

Moniro, Henry & Emily Cloud, 12 Oct 1856; Columbus Fleming, bm; m 12 Oct 1856 by A. Simmons, J. P.

Monjoy, James L. & Mary A. E. Showalter, 4 Dec 1853; Russell Rupe, bm; m 4 Dec 1853 by A. Simmons, J. P.

Monkers, Calvin & Eliza Fortner, 16 April 1855; James Bartley, bm; m by John Ramey, J. P., 19 April 1855.

Monson, Samuel & Clarey Hudspeth, 18 Jan 1785; John Colvard, bm.

Montgomery, Caswell P. & Cristina A. Bowmon, 28 Dec 1847; Alford P. Bowmon, bm.

Montgomery, Crafton & Francis Finley, colored, 30 Aug 1860.

Montgomery, Floyd & Emeline Mankins, 2 Jan 1866; Madison Montgomery, bm.

Montgomery, Milton & Mary Deatherge, 27 Feb 1844; W. A. Miller, bm.

Montgomery, Samuel & Luemma Wilson, 7 Feb 1853; Andrew J. Simkins, bm.

Moody, J. R. & Elitha Calkeham, 25 Oct 1856; J. W. Cokerham, bm.

Moody, John R. & Sarah Snow, 7 April 1833; James Jones, bm.

Moody, Pleasant B. & Elizabeth Moody, 3 March 1835; F. B. Jones, bm.

Moody, R. & Laticy Cockerham, 3 Aug 1865; J. R. Moody, bm; m 3 Aug 1865 by C. H. Kapp, J. P.

Moody, Thomas B. & M. Z. Wright, 13 Jan 1860.

Moody, W. R. & M. A. Cunningham, 14 Sept 1864; Pleasant Hodges, bm; m 17 Sept 1864 by Geo. A. Jervis, J. P.

Mooney, Martin & Amelia Jones, 26 Jan 1833; George Burris, bm.

Mooney, William & Celia Donathan, 13 Sept 1865; Elijah Donathan, bm.

Mooneyham, Joel & Lucey Seales, 8 April 1814; Thomas Marsh, bm.

Moor, John & Nancy Desorn, 12 Jan 1832; John M. Gorden, bm.

Moore, Alford & Tabbitha Peak, 8 June 1852.

Moore, Andrew & Cattern Lemmon, 23 Dec 1786; Joseph Reed, bm.

Moore, B. F. & Mary E. Sanders, 18 Dec 1856; m 18 Dec 1856 by A. Dunnagan, J. P.

Moore, Benja. & Elizabeth Moles(?), 1 March 1820; J. Fitzgerald, bm.

Moore, Charles & Nancy White, 20 Dec 1818; James Johnson, bm.

Moore, Edward & Elizabeth, 15 Aug 1823; George Crisman, bm.

Moore, Edward & Sarah Cunningham, 2 Jan 1858; Joseph Nations, bm.

Moore, Eligia & Elisabeth Franklin, 28 July 1855; Isaac Whitaker, bm; m 29 July 1855 by Joel Denny, J. P.

Moore, Elijah & Alsey Denney, 16 Aug 1805; Thos. Johnson, bm.

Moore, F. L., son of William and Nancy Moore and Rachel E. Banner, daughter of Elisha and Elisa Banner, m 22 June 1868 by Marquis L. Wood, minister.

Moore, Gabriel & Mary Franklin, 10 Sept 1829; Jno. F. Poindexter, bm.

Moore, Galahew & Rheda Larrener, 25 Aug 1816; George Smith, bm.

Moore, Gordon D. & Nancy Rogers, 6 Nov 1859; Stephen Moore, bm; m 6 Nov 1859 by E. Banner, J. P.

Moore, Henry & Mary Ann Griffin, 6 Sept 1845; John Ashburn, bm.

SURRY COUNTY MARRIAGES, 1779-1868

Moore, Henry W. & Rolly Moore, 24 Dec 1852; Cohull W. Martin, bm; m 25 Dec 1852 by Martin Payne, J. P.

Moore, Jacob, son of Diner Moore, and Sarah Clark, persons of color, 28 Dec 1867.

Moore, James & Patsey Portice, 28 Dec 1831; John Whitaker, bm.

Moore, James & Barbary Walker, 25 March 1847; Drury H. Copeland, bm.

Moore, James & Mary Lawson, 29 Jan 1867; Jno. M. Cloud, bm.

Moore, James C. & Martha Scott, 21 April 1853; Wm. A. Moore, bm; m 21 April 1853 by E. Banner, J. P.

Moores, James L. & Mary G. Shores, 15 July 1867; Henry H. Moore, bm; m 17 July 1867 by A. Whitaker, J. P.

Moore, Jesse & Rosa Griffy, 5 Oct 1833; Robert McGuin, bm.

Moore, Jesse F. & R. Ann Banner, 11 Aug 1861; m 13 Aug 1861 by Jesse Roberts.

Moore, Joel & Mary Tucker, 6 Dec 1798; Tommus Clanton, bm.

Moore, John & Catharine Boatright, 12 Dec 1788; Alexander Bowles, bm.

Moore, John & Mary Beaman, 21 March 1793; Edward Clanton, bm.

Moore, John & Nancy Whitaker, 28 March 1808; Isaac Copeland, bm.

Moore, John, son of Malinda Moore, and Hannah Davidson, daughter of Lewis and Phebe Davidson, m 23 July 1868 by Marquis L. Wood, minister.

Moore, John Jr. & Sally Howard, 30 July 1836; Anderson Whitaker, bm.

Moore, John V. & Nancy J. Burnett, 3 June 1858; J. R. Waugh, bm.

Moore, John W. & Mary B. Freeman, 15 Sept 1864; Pleasant Hodges, bm; m 15 Sept 1864 by F. J. Lawson.

Moore, Lewis & Menerva Jane Davis, 31 Aug 1863; William Whitaker, bm.

Moore, Samuel & Elizabeth Gaines, 1 Dec 1788; Ambrose Gaines, bm.

Moore, Samuel D. & Matilda Franklin, 29 Oct 1827; Seth Hickerson, bm.

Moore, Thomas & Mary Phillips, 9 Aug 1821; Benjamin Moore, bm.

Moore, Thomas & Nancy Underwood, 12 Jan 1828; Andrew Webster, bm.

Moore, Thomas H. & Elizabeth Key, 8 Nov 1865; H. G. Anthony, bm; m 9 Nov 1865 by R. F. McGuffin, J. P.

Moore, Thomas J. & Elizabeth Shores, 15 Dec 1836; W. H. George, bm.

SURRY COUNTY MARRIAGES, 1779-1868

Moore, William & Rebecca Keziah, 4 Oct 1798; Jonathan Dagley, bm.

Moore, William & Celia Dudley, 14 Feb 1846; Logan D. Roberts, bm.

Moore, Wm. F. & Elizabeth McGlacham, 11 June 1867; Joseph Branick, bm; m 11 June 1867 by B. J. Dickins, J. P.

Moorefield, Frederick & Polly Fulk, 20 April 1858.

Moorefield, John & Pauline Fulk, 16 Feb 1856; Arch. Farrar, bm; m 16 Feb 1856 by W. E. Davis, J. P.

Moran, James & Chrischanica Vissmon, 27 Dec 1859; Henry Shelton, bm.

Morefield, Gabriel & Sally Vestel, 16 Oct 1810; Wm. Cannon, bm.

Morefield, William & Nancy Ashley, 17 Aug 1805; John Morefield, bm.

Moreland, Joseph & Sarah Thornton, 17 May 1797; Wm. Thornton, bm.

Morgan, Theophilus & Elizabeth Burkins, 11 Jan 1828; Archabald Felts, bm.

Morgan, Thomas & Mary Hollinsworth, 5 Jan 1859; James Shelton, bm.

Morris, Daniel & Mary Downey, 17 Sept 1804; David Morris, bm.

Morris, Jesse & Martha Boling, 13 Jan 1848; James H. Unthank, bm.

Morris, John & Saraah Derrett, 1 April 1836; John Wright, bm.

Morris, John & Rody Branscom, 16 March 1854; John D. Stuart, bm; m 16 March 1854 by A. Simmons, J. P.

Morris, Simon T. & Jane Bowman, 15 April 1851; Andrew J. Brim, bm.

Morris, Shadrach & Nancy Allin, 24 Feb 1824; Jesse Johnson, bm.

Morris, Thomas & Susanah Appleton, 4 Jan 1786; John Colvard, bm.

Morris, William & Catharine Bass, 31 Aug 1817; Joel Brown, bm.

Morris, William & Lucindy Trulove, 21 Oct 1830; Laurence Morris, bm.

Morrison, Alfred, son of Andrew and Matilda Morrison, and Mary E. Ruberry(?), daughter of Thomas and Rachel Perlite, m 4 May 1868 by Rev. James Minish.

Morrison, James & Sally Sparks, 13 Nov 1836; Henry Waldridge, bm.

Morrison, Jesse & Nancy West, 19 April 1837; James Morrison, bm.

Morrison, Lewin, son of Jesse and Nancy Morrison and Susan T. York, daughter of Ham and Mary York, m 10 Dec 1868 by Rev. R. W. Pegram.

Morrow, James & Susanah Watson, 31 Dec 1785; Claborn Watson, bm.

Morse, Joseph B. & Polly Nichols, 16 Sept 1828; Jas. Clanton, bm.

Morten, Henry P. & Elizabeth Houser, 25 Aug 1834; A. M. Kerr, bm. (filed under Martin).

Morton, James & Elisabeth Sumers, 6 Oct 1802; Daniel Marsh, bm.

Morton, Patrick & Rachel Hammons, 10 Dec 1810; Benjamin Bledsoe, John Stanley, bm.

Morton, Thos. & Rachel Williams, 18 March 1832; Thomas Ransom (?), bm.

Moseley, West & Rebeckah Shore, 17 Nov 1797; Edmund Paul, bm.

Mosely, Theophilus & Sally Galaspy, 3 Jan 1834; Thos. Roberts, bm.

Moser, Joseph E. & Rebeckah A. Carlile, m 31 March 1861 by W. W. Wolff, J. P.

Moser, Michael & Patsy Bolejack, 6 Feb 1833; John B. Edmondson, bm.

Mosley, Henry & Martha Gates, 17 June 1846; Anderson Dunnagan, bm.

Mosley, James H. & Thusay M. Hurt, 21 Nov 1863; E. D. Nicholson, bm; m 26 Nov 1863 by D. A. Eldridge, J. P.

Mosley, James H. & Rebecca W. Dunbar, 11 Jan 1864; Tyre Creed, bm; m 12 Jan 1865 by Wilson Laffoon, J. P.

Mosley, West & Malinda Forkner, 27 Nov 1831; (C.H.).

Moss, Henry & Melchia Petticoart, 14 April 1786; David Anders, bm.

Mosser, Christian & Elizabeth Fister, 24 May 1788; Edward Bartlet, bm.

Motley, B. H. & Pauline J. Womack, 11 July 1859; Allen M. Womack, bm.

Moxley, Daniel & Mary Shores, 3 March 1844; Samuel Brooks, bm.

Muemilon, Leftedge & Nancy A. Merida, 3 Jan 1853; Joshua Ayers, bm.

Muller, Stephen & Polly Rigsby, 4 July 1807; Jacob Siger, bm.

Mullins, James S. & Sarah J. Reace, 3 March 1858; Ervin Moore, bm; m 3 March 1858 by A. Simmons, J. P.

Mullis, Ambrose & Mary Wooten, 27 Jan 1830; Stephen Mullis, bm.

Mullis, George & Polly Green, 12 March 1822; Thomas Minish, bm.

Muncus, Elisha & Cinthia Hendrick, 21 June 1814; Hardin Franklin, bm.

Mundy, James J. & Emboset Thompson, m 20 Dec 1865 by Murlen Sparger, J. P.

Munkus, Henry & Jane Ramey, 23 Nov 1813; Gentry Hodge, bm.

Munkus, Sandferd & Nancy Bartley, 3 Dec 1833; David Lane, bm.

Munrow, John G. & Anne Johnston, 15 Aug 1811; Charles Johnson, bm.

Munsey, James W. & Emmarly Kirk, 25 Oct 1849; Nehemiah Findley, bm.

Murphey, Joseph Jr. & Prudence Chamberlain, 12 Dec 1789; Richard Murphy, bm.

Murphey, Joseph & Catharine Thompson, 11 Nov 1802; Joseph Murphey Jr., bm.

Murphey, Stephen & Hannah Cliff, 14 Dec 1796; Johnson Whitaker, bm.

Murphy, Franklin & Jane Murphy, 19 March 1865; Torler Lane, bm.

Murphy, Greenbury & Mary Law, 5 April 1859; Barnet Low, bm.

Murphy, Joseph & Agness Devenport, 19 Jan 1798; Samuel Hobson, bm.

Murphy, Joseph & Betsy Wordline, 21 Dec 1825; Moris Stinson, bm.

Murphy, M. F. & M. C. Tolbart, 13 July 1866; m 13 July 1866 by D. A. Eldridge.

Murphy, Richard & Jean Yourk, 2 Sept 1800; Daniel Pilsher, bm.

Murphy, Zachary & Nancy Wilks, 15 Dec 1850; John North, bm. (C. H.).

Myars, George & Mary Ashley, 24 Aug 1819; John Hutchins, bm.

Myers, James H. & Pamelia Carter, 10 July 1847; Charles A. Joyner, bm.

Myers, John & Rebekah Brown, 4 Nov 1802; Andrew Davis, bm.

Myers, Peter & Ruth Finney, 24 Dec 1792; Daniel Sebastine, bm.

Myers, William A. & Sarah Wohlford, 29 June 1846; Wm. H. Moore, bm.

Myers, Zedekiah & Polly Mullice, 30 April 1836; Lewis Cash, bm.

Myres, John & Marilda Wells, 10 Dec 1833; John Wells, bm.

Nall, Robert & Mary Franklin, 12 Feb 1796; Mesheck Franklin, bm.

Nance, John & Sarrah Anthony, 14 July 1838; Zebidee Money, bm.

Nance, Littleton & Priscilla Moor, 13 July 1833; Jesse Moor, bm.

Nance, Richard & Mildred Merrion, 9 Dec 1822; Sampson Fleming, bm.

Nantz, William & Deborah Atkins, 23 June 1811; Robert Atkins, bm.

Nations, James & Eliza Hodges, 1 Jan 1835; Daniel Riggs, bm.

Nations, Jesse & Creasy Johnson, 14 March 1846; Wm. M. Riggs, bm.

Nations, Thomas & Rebekah Riggs, 5 June 1814; Peter Graves, bm.

Naylor, Joseph & Mary Hawkins, 13 Aug 1844; John W. Naylor, bm.

Naylor, Thomas B. & Sarah Vestal, 17 Oct 1831; John Dejarnett, bm.

Neall, Wm. M. & Lizzie F. Durham, _____ 1867.

Needham, Christian & Lucinda B. Perkins, 1 Nov 1845; Jefferson Hickmon, bm.

Needham, Elijah, son of James and Martha Needham, and Sallie Johnson, daughter of Hiram and Lidia Johnson, m 22 Dec 1867 by Wm. Y. Tucker, J. P.

Needham, James H. & Julia Ann Boyles, 30 Sept 1858; John H. Boyes, bm; m 30 Sept 1858 by J. H. Caudle.

Needham, Jessee M. & Ary Ancilvania Glasby, 19 Dec 1852; S. D. Davis, bm. (C. H.).

Needham, John W. & Deborah Ann Patterson, 26 Feb 1846; John O. Gossett, bm.

Needham, S. A. & Letha J. Simmons, 5 Dec 1852; William H. Taylor, bm; m 5 Dec 1852 by William Hill, J. P.

Neeley, James & Salley Kerby, 4 Nov 1804; Francis Kearby, bm.

Neese, Hezekiah & Dory Leath, 26 July 1829; William Grubb, bm.

Nelson, William & _____, 21 Oct 1820; Conaway Stone, bm.

Nelson, William R. & Suphroney B. Shaver, 16 June 1863; W. H. Davis, bm; m 16 June 1863 by A. Simmons, J. P.

Nester, Jacob & Nancy Philips, 7 April 1856; Tobias Philips, bm.

Nester, Joshua & Perlina Goard, 23 Nov 1854; John Nester, bm; m 23 Nov 1854 by A. Simmons, J. P.

Nester, Zion & Elizabeth Ayers, 26 Aug 1851; John Nester, bm.

Netherland, Benjamin & Thodocia Bramblet, 16 Feb 1788; Wm. Shepperd, George Pettit, Jno. Bruce, James Gibbons, bm.

Newby, John H. & Mariah Landrum, 8 Sept 1864; Wm. R. Bray, bm; m 8 Sept 1864 by Wm. R. Bray, J. P.

Nichols, Benjamin & Elizabeth Miers, 13 July 1791; Jacob Edlemon, bm.

Nichols, Bird & Huldah Childres, m 14 Sept 1860 by S. W. Roberts, J. P.

Nichols, Edmon & Jestine Parker, 8 Sept 1839; Esquire Barker, bm.

Nichols, George & Lucinda Dewyean(?), 14 Aug 1832; Jeremiah Morrow, bm.

Nickols, Jefferson & Nancy Franklin, 3 April 1852; Tyre Simpson, bm; m 12 April 1852 at the residence of T. V. Hamlin, by T. V. Hamlin, J. P.

Nichols, John & Nancy Simpson, 29 Jan 1846; Edmond Nicholds, bm.

Nichols, Morgan & Sarah Smith, 29 Oct 1848; Bennet Smith, bm.

Nichols, Richard & Nancy Patterson, 2 Oct 1823; Jesse Fleming, bm.

Nichols, William & Julia A. E. Poindexter, 17 Nov 1847; Thomas D. Cartright, bm.

Nicholson, Cornelius & Sarahann Sitliff, 26 Jan 1856; Israel P. Axsom, bm; m 30 Jan 1856 by Martin Axsom, J. P.

Nicholson, Micajah & Betsy Woodroof, 2 Nov 1818; Ephraim Nicholson, bm.

Nicholson, Ephraim & Prudence Woodruff, 24 Feb 1816; Philip Philips, bm.

Nicholson, Jacob & Nancy Jacks, 21 Jan 1838; Wm. Chamberlin, bm.

Nichols, Wm. J. & Mary Ann West, 4 April 1851; m 6 April 1851 by J. A. Davis.

Nicholson, John M. & Clarissa B. Parks, 7 Jan 1850; E. C. Jones, bm.

Nicks, Calvin S. & Eliza Houzzy, 24 July 1850; James Harvell, bm.

Nicks, Joseph & Delila Holden, 29 Dec 1828; Reuben Johnson, bm.

Nixon, F. M. & Martha Thompson, 3 Jan 1866; Wm. P. Nixon, bm; m 4 Jan 1866 by A. H. Kapp, J. P.

Nixon, Joseph & Elizabeth Windsor, 14 Oct 1833; John Walker, bm.

Nixon, Nathan & Mary Nixon, 8 Feb 1831; Larkin Kenada, bm.

Nixon, Thomas Jr. & Matilda Wilmoth, 26 Nov 1847; Jas. Jones, bm.

Nixon, Thos L. & Elizabeth Nixon, 31 Jan 1845; Thos Nixon Jr., bm.

Nixon, Thos. P. & Nancy Smith, 6 Sept 1860; John Thompson, bm; m 9 Sept 1860 by Jno. J. McMickle, J. P.

Nixon, Wm. P. & Francis Nixon, 24 Oct 1866; Wm. R. Nixon, bm; m 25 Oct 1866 by A. H. Kapp, J. P.

SURRY COUNTY MARRIAGES, 1779-1868

Noble, Coleman & Sarah Chappel, 24 Dec 1803; Ralph Shaw, bm.

Noble, John & Rhoda Jones, 26 March 1808; W. M. Shaw, bm.

Noble, Joshua & Hester Chappel, 7 Oct 1805; W. M. Shaw, bm.

Noblitt, Joseph & Cristena Williason, 31 Dec 1802; G. Holcomb, Wm. Noblett, bm.

Noland, Charles & Polly Whitlock, 9 Nov 1814; Thomas Dobbins, bm.

Noland, Daniel & Mary Wilson, 22 Dec 178-; James Noland, bm.

Noonkester, Daniel & Sally Hall, 10 Nov 1847; George W. Reece, bm.

Noonkester, Michael & Mary Hawks, 15 July 1830; Solomon Hawks, bm.

Norman, Clements & Ann Wolf, 12 July 1828; Lewis Wolf, bm.

Norman, Columbus & Sally Ann McJames, 7 Nov 1849; James F. Jones, bm.

Norman, David C. & _____, 12 Jan 1833; Zachariah A. Joyner, bm.

Norman, Greenbury & Jain Gallion, 5 Dec 1820; Thomas Gallion, bm.

Norman, Hardy & Metildy Branner, 14 Jan 1839; Henry Norman, bm.

Norman, Henry & Sarah Joyner, 2 May 1824; Nathaniel Norman, bm.

Norman, Isaac & Abagal Riggs, 8 Dec 1829; Eleaner Lewis, bm.

Norman, Isaac & Nancey Burk, 28 Jan 1838; Ambrose Fletcher, bm.

Norman, Isaac & Nancy Johnson, 8 Feb 1847; Elisha Banner, bm.

Norman, James & Mary Snow, 6 Oct 1828; Charles S. Early, bm.

Norman, James & Patience Donner, 8 March 1830; Jacob Donner, bm.

Norman, James H. & Hettie Hicks, _____ 1867.

Norman, Jesse & Elizabeth Isaacks, 9 Sept 1850; Deep Snow, bm. (C. H.).

Norman, John & Elizabeth Alva, 8 May 1828; John Myers, bm.

Norman, John & Celia Crumel, 25 Nov 1829; John Cassaday, bm.

Norman, John & Nancy Allen, 3 Aug 1833; Hugh Martin, bm.

Norman, L. J. & Peggy Mash, 16 Jan 1864; Ephraim Galyear, bm; m 17 Jan 1864 by Wm. J. Combs, minister.

Norman, Martin V. B., son of Thurman and Mary Ann Norman, and Nancy Caroline Brooks, daughter of Harden and Cassa Brooks, m 5 Dec 1868 by Rev. J. F. Roberts.

Norman, Matthew & Sally Franklin, 14 May 1844; Wilson Norman bm.

SURRY COUNTY MARRIAGES, 1779-1868

Norman, Meredith T. & Nancy Thompson, 22 Jan 1853; William M. Norman, bm; m 22 Jan 1853.

Norman, Nathaniel & _____, 13 Feb 1833; John Norman, bm.

Norman, Peter & Elizabeth Odel, 14 May 1831; Joseph Boyd, bm.

Norman, Preston & Emma Robertson, m 21 June 1866 by James H. Lewellin, M. G.

Norman, Solomon & Letitia Williams, 16 Nov 1865; L. J. Gray, bm; m 16 Nov 1865 by G. A. Lance, J. P.

Norman, Thomas & Janes Wiles, 14 June 1809; James Wiles, bm.

Norman, Thomas & Lucy Monday, 15 Jan 1811; Jesse Williams, bm.

Norman, Thomas, son of Henry Norman, and Charlotte Blackborne, m 9 Sept 1868 by Rev. Wm. Harris.

Norman, William & Agga Isaacs, 9 Oct 1827; Samuel Isaacs, bm.

Norman, William & Miss Judy Hodges, 24 Jan 1855; Jesse Davis, bm.

Norman, Wm. C. & Rebecca M. Colvard, 30 Dec 1845; Francis Wood, bm.

Norman, Wm. M. & Letitia Holyfield, 9 March 1860; m 15 March 1860 by D. M. Cooper, J. P.

Norman, William R. & Faithy Poor, 4 Feb 1860; Samuel D. Poore, bm; m 4 Feb 1860 by C. L. Banner, J. P.

Norman, Wilson H. & Sophia Willey, 20 Jan 1862; Godfrey Isaacks, bm; m 21 Jan 1862 by Lacy Snow, J. P.

Normon, John & Nancy Apperson, 30 Jan 1850; H. W. Bynum, bm. (C. H.).

Normon, Stanley & Hannah Bass, 3 Oct 1820; John Bovender, bm.

Normon, Thomas & Mary Baker, 14 Sept 1819; John Marshall, bm.

Norris, James W. & Mary Gilbert, 14 April 1837; John C. Davis, bm.

North, Jonathan & Anna Hobson, 14 Oct 1822; John Vestal, bm.

North, Thomas & Rachel Vestal, 19 Dec 1823; William Douglass, bm.

Norton, James & Tempy Childress, 22 April 1856; Larken Norton, bm; m 24 April 1856 by John E. Stanly, J. P.

Norton, Jesse & Gilley Bledsoe, 2 Aug 1823; James Bray, bm.

Norton, Larken & Eliza Steel, 5 March 1850; D. F. Steel, bm. (C. H.).

Norton, Nicholas & Ruth White, 19 Feb 1852; Larkin North, bm. (C. H.).

Nunn, Andrew J. & Scena Hurst, 18 Feb 1855; Sylvester Breeding, bm; m 18 Feb 1855 by A. Simmons, J. P.

SURRY COUNTY MARRIAGES, 1779-1868

Nunn, Martin & Sarah Cox, 3 Jan 1865; Lewis Taylor, bm. (C.H.).

Nunn, W. H. & Ruth Adams, _____ 1867, m by Alexander Moran.

Odel, James & Patty Collier, 24 Aug 1823; John Perkins, bm.

Odel, James & Sally Caviness, 9 Nov 1859; Geo. W. McCraw, bm.

Odell, Jefferson & Liney Jane Hampton, 6 Dec 1851; m 10 Feb 1852 by Joel Denny, J. P.

Odell, Solomon & Sarah Childress, 17 June 1829; Stephen H. Lyon, bm.

Odle, Squire J. & Sarah Hazelwood, 9 Feb 1860; m 9 Feb 1860 by C. L. Banner.

Odle, George & Elizabeth Maze, 3 July 1849; John Kimbrell, bm.

Oglesby, Shadrach & Nancy Roberts, 24 Oct 1831; Jas. Tucker, bm.

Oglesby, Thomas & Polly Easley, 18 Feb 1819; Hardin P. Franklin, bm.

Olinger, Christian P. & Susannah E. Price, 2 Sept 1853; Robert J. Harris, bm; m 3 Sept 1853 by A. Simmons, J. P.

Oliver, Elijah & Polley Hicks, 15 Aug 1800; William Jeffery, bm.

Oliver, Ezekiel & Sarah Brown, 18 Nov 1799; Joshaway Brown, bm.

Oliver, Jesse & Elizabeth Swinney, 19 Aug 1812; Allen Willard, bm.

Oliver, Joseph & Winaford Marsh, 29 March 1823; Littleton Noles, bm.

Oliver, William & Nancy East, 2 Nov 1826; John Moody, bm.

Olliver, Wm. & Agness East, 25 Nov 1801; John Dindino, bm.

Omarey, Moses & Sarah Dolehide, 15 Jan 1847; Henry Johnson, bm.

Onale, Hennery & Anna Wadkins, 12 Feb 1805; Wm. Forrester, bm.

Oneal, Elias & Caroline Doss, 18 Dec 1855; Little Adkins, bm; m 18 Dec 1855 by J. Copeland, J. P.

Oneal, Elias & Miss Cynthia June Watson, 17 Feb 1855; Jos. Oneal, bm.

Oneal, James & Jerusha A. C. Wall, 11 Sept 1860; m at house of Crofford Walls, by John Jones, 13 Sept 1860.

Oneal, Lemuel & Lucinda Rigsby, 12 Jan 1844; Benjamin Carpenter, bm.

Oquin, Edmond & Catherine Wiles, 22 Sept 1829; G. Sprinkel, bm.

Orrell, William & Cynthia Brookshire, 24 Nov 1830; Thos. Phelps, bm.

Orton, Joseph & Lizy Dennis, 5 Nov 1816; Stephen Wood, Jr., bm.

Osbon, Elias & Margaret Blackborn, 4 Jan 1844; Wm. E. Swaim, bm.

Osborn, William & Rhoda Jacks, 25 Oct 1845; Shadrack Myers, bm.

Owen, Flemming A. & Cornelia Kelly, 21 Aug 1867; Joseph M. Owen, bm.

Owen, Franklin D. & Julia Venable, 27 Sept 1853; m 30 Sept 1853 by H. Steele.

Owen, James B. & Sharlotte Moore, 30 Nov 1856; John H. Owen, bm; m 30 Nov 1856 by A. Simmons,J. P.

Owen, John R. & Patsey Tipton, 30 Nov 1856; James B. Owen, bm; m 30 Nov 1856 by A. Simmons, J. P.

Owen, Peyton & Eliza Marion, 25 June 1844; Leonard Scott, bm.

Owen, Josiah & Polly Phillips, 20 March 1820; John Phillips, bm.

Owen, William E. & Nancy F. Sturdivant, m 15 Sept 1852 by Wm. Hill, J. P.

Owens, Abel & Eliza Cane, 24 July 1856; m by J. Gray, J. P.

Owens, Juriah & Malinda McMillion, 15 March 1837; Vernon Surratt, bm.

Owens, Wm. & Nancy Nelson, 6 July 1823; James McKinney, bm.

Owins, Albert & Fatima Barker, 24 May 1862; Thomas T. Barker, bm.

Pace, Alfred & Milly Bray, 21 Sept 1817; Moses Bray, bm.

Pace, Edmund & Sarah Walker, 25 Dec 1782; David Bray, bm.

Pace, John & Elizabeth Pigg, 11 March 1809; John White, bm.

Pace, Peter & Lissa Revell, 24 Nov 1866; m 26 Nov 1866 by Miles Foy.

Pack, Jonathan & Susan Ann Bowman, 12 May 1859; Samuel Hooker, bm; m 12 May 1859 by Elisha Banner, J. P.

Packs, John & Hannah Southard, 26 April 1806; John Darnell, bm.

Padget, John & Polly Sawer, 9 Jan 1810; Thomas Minish, bm.

Padgett, Jacob C. & Lydia Wright, 16 March 1824; Amos A. Cowles, bm.

Paff, John D. & Lurainey Jackson, 23 Oct 1817; Isam Owens, bm.

Pain, John & Sally Cockerram, 15 Dec 1832; Joseph Cockerrum, bm.

Pain, William & Abigail Jordan, 19 April 1827; Moses Marshall, bm.

Painter, Isaac & Evalina J. Bell, 24 Nov 1828; Lee Nuckolls, bm.

Painter, Sidney C. & Mary G. Bitting, 4 Dec 1867; m by Lee C. Brown, Pres. Min.

Palmer, James & Nancy Flyn, 22 March 1845; William E. Cook, bm.

Pardew, L. R., son of Wm. and Louzena Pardue, and Prudence Lyons, daughter of _____ Crouse, m 15 Nov 1868 by Rev. W.J. Combs.

Pardue, J. M. G. & Mary A. York, 10 Aug 1863.

Pardue, Joel & Janetty Sparks, 30 Oct 1845; William Holcomb, bm.

Pardue, Lilston A. & Harriet N. Welch, 10 Dec 1844; Jeremiah Pardue, bm.

Pare, Iham & Katharine Merchant, 17 March 1864; Warren Bolt, bm; m by Wm. R. Bray, J. P.

Parker, Edmund & Nancy Hickmon, 4 March 1819; John Roberts, bm.

Parker, George & Elizabeth Richards, 17 Feb 1803; Will Armstrong, bm.

Parker, Jas. & Polly Everton, 18 May 1805; Johnsey Gaith, bm.

Parker, John & Polly Pennion, 12 Feb 1821; Hickmon Isbell, bm.

Parker, John & Mary E. Collins, 20 Aug 1856; Calvin Mabe, bm; m 20 Aug 1856 by A. Simmons, J. P.

Parker, Joseph & Polly Hickmon, 15 Dec 1830; Ed Parker, bm.

Parker, Lemuel & Sarah Richards (no date); Will Armstrong, bm.

Parker, R. T. G. & Mary H. Coe, 30 Jan 1845; A. J. Coe, bm.

Parker, Squire & Betsy Morgan, 15 Oct 1810; John Mills, bm.

Parker, Wiett & Elizabeth Kezzel, 12 Feb 1849; Allgias Dunnagan, bm.

Parker, Wm. & Airy _____, 9 Sept 1796; Solomon Parker, bm.

Parker, Wm. R. & Patsy Hodge, 25 Nov. 1826; Ed Parker, bm.

Parker, William W. & Sarah Ann Tayler, 12 March 1859; James S. Hill, bm.

Parks, John & Elizabeth Arnold, 24 March 1814; Daniel Arnold, bm.

Parks, Francis & Mary Brown, 22 July 1816; John Setliff, bm.

Parnel, Burrell & Nancy Martin, 11 May 1819; Jesse _____, bm.

Parrish, W. W. & Sally Paune, 24 Dec 1863; Wm. Spencer, bm; m 24 Dec 1863 by Wm. Golden, J.P.

Parson, J. C. & Kezasiah Ball, 8 Sept 1853; Jas. Nichols, bm; m 8 Sept 1853 by Robert Wilbourn, Baptist minister.

Parson, Richard & Elizabeth Spence, 1 Feb 1817; John Thornton, bm.

Parsons, Aaron, son of Allen & Adeny Parsons, and Francis Isaacks, daughter of Ashby and Catharine Isaacks, m 23 Jan 1868 by Rev. William J. Combs.

Parsons, Dudley & Keziah Hickman, 23 Feb 1835; Wm. H. Moore, bm.

Parsons, Marion, son of Allen and E. D. Parsons, and Rebeca E. Isaacks, daughter of Samuel and Nancy Isaacks, m 16 Dec 1868 by Rev. William J. Combs.

Parsons, William & Cora V. Cleburn, m 26 Dec 1860 by C. L. Banner, J. P.

Partin, William & Elizabeth Partin, 17 Dec 1845; Thomas Hamlin, bm.

Pary, Elisha & Vaney Kerby, 23 Dec 1862; Isaac Landy, bm; m 23 Dec 1862 by J. Low, J. P.

Pass, E. H. & Elizabeth Hopper, 25 Feb 1865; Jas. J. Pedjo, bm; m 26 Feb 1865 by J. H. Lewellin.

Patrick, Elisha & Elizabeth Reavis, 13 July 1811; Jesse Whitticor, bm.

Patterson, Benjamin & Mary Jackson, 12 Feb 1817; Jesse Patterson, bm.

Patterson, Benjamin & Catherine Creson, 24 Aug 1822; James Patterson, bm.

Patterson, Chambers C. & Synthia Haynes, 20 Sept 1819; Jonth. Haines, bm.

Patterson, David & Mica Holder, __ Sept 1825; Baler Holder, bm.

Patterson, Gilbert & Mary McBride, 25 April 1807; Joshaway Carter, bm.

Patterson, Green & Missouri A. Walton, 6 Oct 1867; m 24 Nov 1867 by A. Whitaker, J. P.

Patterson, Harrison & Sarah E. Whitaker, 2 Jan 1867; C. N. Stutts, bm; m 6 Jan 1867 by A. Whitaker, J. P.

Patterson, Henry D. W. & Lucinda E. Harrison, 28 Dec 1853; m by W. E. Davis, J. P., 27 Dec 1853.

Patterson, James & Betsy Spere, 3 Dec 1813; James Johnson, bm.

Patterson, James & Nancy Holcomb, 10 Oct 1826; Thos. Williams, bm.

Patterson, James & Elizabeth Wiles, 16 Jan 1846; Robert C. Whitiker, bm.

Patterson, Jesse & Nancy Brown, 19 Jan 1811; Joseph Brown, bm.

Patterson, Jesse & Mary Creson, 28 July 1818; Benjamin Patterson, bm.

Patterson, Jesse & Nancy Bowen(?), 30 May 1824; Jesse Creed, bm.

Patterson, Jesse & Nancy Dough(?), 26 May 1838; Thomas Vestal Jr., bm.

Patterson, Joel & Sarah Hardin, 5 Aug 1801; Renny Harding, bm.

Patterson, Joel & Sally Patterson, 8 Sept 1833; Thomas Hutchins, bm.

SURRY COUNTY MARRIAGES, 1779-1868

Patterson, John & Edy Johnston, 14 Nov 1797; Shadrack Holcomb, bm.

Patterson, John S. & Sarah Blume, 8 Nov 1833; Henry G. Hampton, bm.

Patterson, Joshua & Polly Williams, 20 Dec 1819; John Stockton, bm.

Patterson, Julius A. & Harriet N. Tuttle, 21 Oct 1857; m 21 Oct 1857 by Jesse Roberts, M. G.

Patterson, M. L. & Minerva J. Jessop, 30 Dec 1863; John C. Davis, bm.

Patterson, W. E. & Margret F. Sparger, m 25 April 1868 by R. T. N. Stephenson.

Patterson, Wiley & Drucinda Davis, 28 Dec 1825; Newell Jackson, bm.

Patterson, William & Keziah Patterson, (no date), Wm. Patterson Sen., bm.

Patterson, William & Rebecca Davis, 6 April 1844; Winston Fleming, bm.

Patterson, William C. & Cynthia Nayler, 13 Jan 1822; Jno. S. Clingman, bm.

Patterson, William C. & Caroline Mainard, 17 Feb 1833; John G. Pettit, bm.

Paul, Nathan & Jane Ranard, 15 Nov 1845; James W. Angel, bm.

Paul, Thomas & Seba Walker, 23 Jan 1821; Robert Kid, bm.

Paul, William & Lucy Kid, 29 Dec 1818; Robert Kidd, bm.

Payne, Barnet & Sary Cave, 19 May 1857; Thos. Dicken, bm; m 19 May 1857 by J. Low, J. P.

Payne, Bartlet, son of Richard and Ann Snow, and Mary Wood, daughter of Michael and Amey Wood, m 7 Jan 1868.

Payne, Edward & Elizabeth Snow, 12 Dec 1848; Levi Payne Jr., bm.

Payne, Gideon & Lucy Ann Spencer, 4 June 1851; James M. Stewart, bm.

Payne, Henry & Jane Coal, 3 Feb 1858; Barnet Payne, bm; m 8 Jan 1858 by Wm. Hodge, J. P.

Payne, Henry & Mary A. Brim, 27 Feb 1867; no bm.

Payne, Jackson & Eliza Hanks, 14 Oct 1839; Barnet Payne, bm.

Payne, Jackson & Margaret Hawks, 28 Aug 1848; Shadrack Stewart, bm.

Payne, Jesse S. & Elizabeth A. Hood, 2 Dec 1850; Wm. H. Norman, bm. (C. H.).

Payne, Levi & Julian Hanks, 23 Jan 1845; Stephen Payne, bm.

SURRY COUNTY MARRIAGES, 1779-1868

Payne, Levi & Martha Golden, 15 Feb 1847; William Golden, bm.

Payne, Stephen & Sibana Hansk, 23 Jan 1845; Levi Payne, bm.

Payne, Stephen, son of Barnett & Luvinca Payne, and Lourena F. Williams, daughter of Enoch & Rachell Williams, m 31 Dec 1868 by William H. Beamer, J. P.

Payne, Thomas & Sarah Lyons, 23 Jan 1823; Jacob McCraw, bm.

Payne, William & Sarah Stonemon, 18 Aug 1851; Mitchel Snow, bm; m 18 Aug 1851 by Martin Payne, J. P.

Peace, Alford M. & Martha M. Pettitt, 29 March 1825; Samuel D. Kelly, bm.

Peak, Nathan & Catharine Logan, 2 Jan 1786; Christopher Kechely, bm.

Peal, John W. & Nancy Boman, 19 June 1855; m 21 June 1855 by R. Marshall, J. P.

Pell, Timothy & Sarah Dunigan, 11 June 1823; William Marsh, bm.

Pearce, David & Sarah A. Walls, 3 Oct 1850; James Shadrach, bm. (C. H.).

Pearce, John & Elizebeth Roop, 6 Dec 1803; Jonth. Haines, bm.

Pearce, Newton & Sally Parker, 3 Aug 1829; Peter Haines, bm.

Pearce, William & Hannah Jessop, 8 Feb 1819; Joseph Jessop, bm.

Pearce, William & Anne Bales, 26 Aug 1821; Richard Cox, bm.

Pearman, James & Mary Porter, 23 Nov 1850; James Spencer, bm. (C. H.).

Pearman, Samuel & Doutha Sowers, 18 Dec 1826; Stephen Sanders, bm.

Pearman, Thomas & Sarah Porter, 18 June 1854; Stephen Malary, bm; m 18 June 1854 by A. Simmons, J. P.

Peden, Moses & Martha Smith, 13 Sept 1788; Jesse Bennet, bm.

Peel, Alexander & D. H. Marsh, 10 March 1867; Martin Peel, bm.

Peel, Daniel T. & Elizabeth J. Chilton, 21 March 1867; E--- A. Peel, bm.

Peel, Eli Martin, son of Jesse and Elizabeth Peel, and Margaret Bullen, son of William and Sally Bullen, m 8 Oct 1868 by Richard _____, J. P.

Peel, George E. & Serena Marsh, 25 July 1832; S. V. Chilton, bm.

Peel, H. A. & Margaret Jane Edwards, 29 Aug 1866; m 2 Sept 1866 by Jos. H. Lewellin, M. G.

Peel, James H. & Mary Gillaspy, 17 Feb 1834; George E. Peel, bm.

Peel, Jesse & Elizabeth Freeman, 10 Jan 1828; Stephen Chilton, bm.

SURRY COUNTY MARRIAGES, 1779-1868

Peel, Thomas & Polly Holyfield, 23 Oct 1858; Wesley Fowler, bm.

Peel, William & Miss Nancy Brinkly, 4 May 1854; Newel Wall, bm.

Peele, Jesse L. & Martha E. Taylor, 24 Dec 1860; m 25 Dec 1860 by Wm. R. Bray, J. P.

Pegram, R. W. & Miss Pheba Ann Bryan, 5 Dec 1855; James Holyfield, bm.

Peirce, Jesse & Sally Lakey, 13 March 1820; Frank Lakey, bm.

Peirce, John & Rhody Murphey, 13 Oct 1833; David Baker, bm.

Pell, Jonathan & Mary Jane Cook, 25 April 1860; m 25 April 1860 by J. Gray, J. P.

Pell, William H. & Sarah L. Cook, 30 July 1864.

Pellig, William & Mary Cogshall, 3 Oct 1812; William Kell, bm.

Pendry, John & Elizebeth Arnal, 25 March 1802; Wm. Cannon, bm.

Pendry, Jonathan & Polly Wiles, 16 Feb 1818; Thomas Wiles, bm.

Pendry, Thomas & Liney Vanhoy, 13 Oct 1828; Jonathan Pendry, bm.

Pennington, Isaac & Mary Freemon, 2 Sept 1818; John Kennida, bm.

Penright, Silas & Nelly Whitacre, 15 March 1835; Jesse E. Sheek, bm.

Perdew, John & Rodey Austin, 7 Jan 1829; Major Austin, bm.

Perdue, Thomas & Elizabeth Day, 10 Feb 1848; Jno Perdue, bm.

Perdue, Will & Elizabeth Henderson, 6 Nov 1837; Joshua Minish, bm.

Perkins, C. W. & Susannah Lemmons, 20 Sept 1825; Jesse Copeland, bm.

Perkins, James & Midia Canada, 16 Nov 1833; Tho. Porteet, bm.

Perkins, John & Deborah Davis, 21 Jan 1813; Thos Perkins, bm.

Perkins, Leonadus & Jane Spargur, 23 Sept 1857; m 23 Sept 1857 by Jesse Roberts, M. G.

Persons, Allen & Edney Brown, 3 Dec 1829; Adam Wagner, bm.

Petite, Thomas & Rachel Painer, 8 May 1828; John Whitehead, bm.

Petree, Adam & Lucy Pryor, 29 Feb 1812; Abner Pryor, bm.

Pettet, Thomas & Keziah Robinson, 26 Jan 1809; Wm. Bells,bm.

Pettiford, Isaac & Mary Ann Lester, 9 Feb 1846; Ithamer Lester, bm.

Pettijohn, Jacob & Delilah Aldridge, 26 Feb 1791; Thos. Mason, bm.

SURRY COUNTY MARRIAGES, 1779-1868

Pettijohn, Peter & Nancy Vandevor, 19 Jan 1789; George Vandevur, bm.

Pettit, George & Martha Poindexter, 23 Nov 1785; Francis Poindexter, bm.

Pettit, George & Mary Longine, 21 Sept 1811; Benjamin Pettitt, bm.

Pettit, Benjamin & Charlotte Martin, 18 March 1813; Thomas Sprinkle, bm.

Pettitt, Francis P. & Patty McCammon, 7 Dec 1821; Tyre Glen, bm.

Pettitt, Robert & Ann Shetliff, 1 Aug 1800; John Apperson, bm.

Pettit, Thos. & Sally Hogdon (Slogdon?), 21 April 1811; Jno. Arnold, bm.

Pettitt, Thomas & Lucy Chandler, 5 Nov 1814; Isaac Killion, bm.

Pettit, William & Jane Ridings, 7 Oct 1816; Thomas Epperson, bm.

Pettitt, William & Sarah Binkley, 26 April 1847; Solomon Philips, bm.

Petty, Elijah & Letty Lewis, 18 Jan 1832; Philip Holcomb, bm.

Petty, Elisha & Polly Harp, 7 May 1833; John Collins, bm.

Petty, Watson & Lydia Macey, 8 Sept 1828; Zeno Worth, bm.

Pettyjohn, William & Sarah Hendrix, 23 Dec 1828; Wm. West, bm.

Pfaff, Jacob & Sarah Inman, 28 April 1828; William S. Ferington, bm.

Pfaff, Thomas & Nancy Inman, 1 Oct 1828; J. L. Pfaff, bm.

Philips, Abner & Nancy Cockerham, 8 Jan 1866; H. Cockerham, bm.

Philips, Ezekiel & Betsey Brown, 20 Dec 1808; Wm. Hudson, bm.

Philips, James & Nancy Cox, 2 Jan 1857; Preston Philips, bm; m 2 Jan 1857 by A. Simmons, J. P.

Philips, John & Rachel Hopson, 20 Aug 1831; Thomas Flin, bm.

Philips, Merrel & Eliza. Stubelfield, Stokes County, 16 Jan 1797; John Purdom of Stokes Co., bm.

Philips, Ozwell & Elizabeth Bolling, 23 Nov 1816; James Flynn, bm.

Philips, Philip & Sussannah Spencer, 2 Feb 1809; Abner Phillips, bm.

Philips, Solomon & _____, 11 May 1785; Andrew Phillips, bm.

Phillips, Abraham & Sarah Rideans, 18 Feb 1799; John Phillips, bm.

Phillips, Abram & Rachel Spillmon, 1 Oct 1848; Solomon R. Doss, bm.

SURRY COUNTY MARRIAGES, 1779-1868

Phillips, Andrew & Quintala Waddle, 20 Oct 1830; Robert Mackie, bm.

Phillips, Edmon & Mary Chinn, 1 Dec 1806; John Williams, bm.

Phillips, James & Peggy Vanderpool, 22 Dec 1837; James Spratlen, bm.

Phillips, John & Agness Jentry, 28 Jan 1799; Matthew Phillips, bm.

Phillips, John & Alcy Merrion, 17 Feb 1819; Thomas Moore, bm.

Phillips, John & Colly Tate, 7 Dec 1824; Jonathan W. Shores, bm.

Phillips, Joseph & Mary Davis, 18 Oct 1832; Tyre Glen, bm.

Phillips, Joseph & Nancy Shinalt, 17 Oct 1851; E. Crane, bm.

Phillips, Joseph & Agnes Rhoads, 12 May 1821; Benjamin Mathess, bm.

Phillips, Lewis & Elizabeth Dowling, 15 May 1811; Lewis Noland, bm.

Phillips, Lewis & Eliza Jane Dezern, 22 Dec 1854; Thomas Norman, bm; m 24 Dec 1854 by J. Whitaker, J. P.

Phillips, R. S. & Nancy Normon, 11 Feb 1849; G. D. Hamby, bm.

Phillips, Richard & Ann Loagin, 2 Oct 1804; Jonathan Joyner, bm.

Phillips, Solomon L. & Frances Lynch, 25 March 1847; Joel R. Stow, bm.

Phillips, Thos & Ellender Miles, 18 Oct 1809; George Phipps, bm.

Phillips, Thomas J. & Keziah Williams, 15 Nov 1848; A. Q. Reece, bm.

Phillips, Wade & Polley Carter, 15 Dec 1798; Benjamin Carter, bm.

Phillips, Wesley & Elisebeth Cox, 10 April 1853; Lewis C. Quesonberry, bm; m 10 April 1853 by A. Simmons, J. P.

Phillips, William & Sarah Glen, 2 Nov 1824; William Phillips Senior, bm.

Phillips, William & Mary Scott, 14 Dec 1850; Thomas Hauser, bm. (C. H.).

Phillips, William & Sally Adams, 30 Oct 1866; Mose Adams, freedman, bm.

Phillips, William L. & Jenny Dooling, 20 Dec 1819; William Rash, bm.

Phipps, George & Keziah Anthony, 2 July 1807; R. Holcomb, bm.

Phlieger, David & Mary Colfer, 3 Oct 1859; Wm. W. Breeding, bm.

Pierce, Chaffin & Ann Bohmnon, 15 Feb 1848; N. B. Dozier, bm.

SURRY COUNTY MARRIAGES, 1779-1868

Pierce, John & Ruth Steelmon, 5 April 1812; Charles Steelmon,bm.

Pigg, William & Sarah Mosier, 3 Aug 1812; John Deal, bm.

Pigg, Wm. W. & Caroline Winfry, 22 Oct 1837; Wm. D. Somers, bm.

Pike, Elias & Poley Slator, 28 June 1825; Benjamin Pike, bm.

Pike, Hugh & Marthy Love, 21 Dec 1855; m by J. Gray, J. P.

Pike, Thomas & Nancy Love, 6 June 1835; Andrew H. Burch, bm.

Pike, William & Martha Jones, 6 May 1848; William R. Hollinsworth, bm.

Pilcher, Daniel & Icey Hutchins, 20 Nov 1819; John Eddleman, bm.

Pilcher, James & Lydia Carrender, 23 Jan 1816; Archibald Whitehead, bm.

Pilcher, James Jr. & Nancy Hill, 10 Sept 1785; John Thos Longine, bm.

Pilcher, John & Edith Carnder, 13 March 1817; James Pilcher, son of Daniel, bm.

Pilcher, Joseph & Catharine Aceborn(?), 19 Sept 1829; G. A. Holcomb, bm.

Pilcher, Sefus & Ruthy Carter, 22 Oct 1848; Charles A. Joyner, bm.

Pilson, R. J. & Lydia J. Bowles, 20 Nov 1858; G. W. Boyce, bm.

Pilson, William L. & Milly Poindexter, 25 Feb 1867; B. W. Badgett, bm; m 27 Feb 1867 by N. Alberty.

Pinion, Thomas & Patsey Gowen, 27 Oct 1822; Martin Lawson, bm.

Pinion, William & _____, 13 Nov 1832; Wilson Holyfield, bm.

Pinix, William G. & Polly Dickerson, 3 Dec 1827; William F. Atwood, bm.

Pinkley, Peter (signed Peter Brinkley, German), & Christina Kreiger, 26 July 1788; Adam Geiger, bm.

Pinnell, Wm. A. & Elizabeth Crocket, 30 Aug 1846; Wm. M. Nance, bm.

Pinnix, George & Adaline C. Shore, 6 Feb 1850; Overton Pinnix, bm.

Pinnix, Robert Burton & Anna Long, 8 April 1816; Jno. Money, bm.

Pique, Joseph & Nacy Farrel, m 16 March 1867 by W. Golding, J. P., James H. Pressley, bm.

Pledger, Stephen & Mary Holcomb, 21 Sept 1830; Phillip W. Green, bm.

Plowman, John & Phebe Burris, 6 Nov 1831; Christopher Weatherman, bm.

SURRY COUNTY MARRIAGES, 1779-1868

Poe, Alvis & Nancy Lewis, 3 Jan 1827; Edward Marshall, bm.

Poe, Edmund & Sarah Parker, 30 Nov 1794; James Masters, bm.

Poindexter, Alexander & Sally Doulass, 10 Nov 1832; Francis P. Vest, bm.

Poindexter, Arche & Rebecker Flinn, 12 Sept 1800; J. G. Poindexter, bm.

Poindexter, Dandridge, & Martha H. Freeman, 21 Jan 1826; Wm. Hamlin, bm.

Poindexter, David T. & Lucretia Bledsoe, 29 Oct 1856; W. A. Bray, bm; m 30 Oct 1856 by L. Hankins, J. P.

Poindexter, Francis & Polly Boman, 7 March 1812; Jesse Brown, bm.

Poindexter, Francis Anderson & Rosannah Ferrier, 22 July 1820; Isaac Jarret, bm.

Poindexter, Isaac C. & M. A. M. Houser, 15 Nov 1866; H. M. Scott, bm; m 19 Nov 1866 by N. S. Chaffin.

Poindexter, John & Mary Carr, 18 Sept 1799; Wm. Forrester, bm.

Poindexter, John & Jane Martin, 6 Aug 1805; Jesse Martin, bm.

Poindexter, Leroy & Sallie White, 1 June 1867; W. L. Pilson, bm.

Poindexter, Richard R. & Shaba White, 15 Oct 1866; W. R. Poindexter, bm; m 13 Oct 1866 by N. A. Alberty.

Poindexter, Robert A. & Mariann Flinn, 27 Sept 1806; Benjamin Pettit, bm.

Poindexter, Robert A. & Charlotte Pettitt, 12 May 1819; Thomas Apperson, bm.

Poindexter, Thomas & Sally Nance, 25 May 1823; Landon Trulove, bm.

Poindexter, Thomas J. & Lucy W. Morton, 21 July 1847; Abraham M. Stow, bm.

Poindexter, Thomas W. P. & Elizabeth Lowell, 23 Nov 1797; Samuel Martin, bm.

Poindexter, Wm. A. & Mary Taylor, 23 July 1835; Thos. H. Poindexter, bm.

Poindexter, William H. & Miss Nancy White, 2 April 1857; W. D. Rutledge, bm; m 2 April 1857 by W. D. Rutledge, J. P.

Poindexter, William J. & Margaret Brown, 25 May 1861; m 30 May 1861 by L. J. Stanley, J. P.

Poindexter, W. J. & Sallie March, 18 Aug 1866; A. L. Gates, bm.

Pool, R. C. & Elizabeth J. Hunt, 2 Oct 1866; S. J. McMickle, bm; m 4 Oct 1866 by J. N. Barker, parson.

Poor, Addom & Elizabeth Sanders, 14 Oct 1823; William Dove, bm.

Poor, Allen & Jane Jones, 27 June 1852; John Poor, bm.

Poor, Thomas & Nancy Dudly, 26 Aug 1827; John Guinn, bm.

Poor, William & Cloe Gwynn, 8 Aug 1826; Peyton Wilson, bm.

Poore, Allen & Peaga Gwynn, _____ 18--; Thomas Forkner, bm.

Poore, Charles, son of Thomas and Nancy Poore, and Ladoskey McGee, daughter of John and Nancy McGee, m 1 March 1868 by C. L. Banner, J. P.

Poore, George & Rebecca Venable, 15 Sept 1833; John Gwyn, bm.

Poore, George & Luan For, 28 June 1845; John Poore, bm.

Poore, Samuel D. & Mary J. Durham, 25 Dec 1864; William Poore, bm.

Pope, C. C. & Polly J. Fults, 25 Jan 1865; Creed Fults, bm; m 25 Jan 1866 by W. Golden, J. P.

Porter, Alexander & Matilda J. Jones, 30 Dec 1853; James M. Pool, bm; m 30 Jan 1853 by A. Simmons, J. P.

Porter, Dudley & Hester Coe, 14 March 1789; Benj. Arnold, bm.

Porter, Stephen & Victory Davidson, 21 Dec 1866; James R. Fulford, bm.

Porter, Ira & Mary Ann Elizabeth Nichols, 10 Jan 1846; Absalom Devenport, bm.

Porter, Jordan & Josaphene Britten, 2 Dec 1850; David Shuts, bm. (C. H.).

Portes, Allen & Anny Reed, 30 Aug 1822; Isaac Reed, bm.

Portes, Allen & Sarah Jones, 25 Dec 1850; Levy Gwyn, bm. (C. H.).

Portes, John & Francis McKinny, 21 Dec 186<u>5</u>; m 25 Dec 186<u>6</u> by Joh- Jones, Baptist minister.

Portes, Silas & Rachel Ried, 28 June 1853; Mason W. Keller, bm; m 28 June 1853 by A. Simmons, J. P.

Portes, Uriah & Sarah Reed, 12 Aug 1827; Daniel Haymore, bm.

Poston, Charles & Anna Starr, 13 Feb 1797; Adam Starr, bm.

Poston, George & Sarah Bretton, 16 Feb 1851; Richard Hines, bm.

Poteet, Squire & Cloah Petit, 12 Dec 1802; George Petit, bm.

Potter, Gideon & Tabitha Hodge, 3 Dec 1822; Jona. Unthank, bm. (filed under Patter).

Pottes, Hendly & Rachel Boys, 11 Oct 1827; Obed N. Boys, bm.

Powel, John & Nanceay Reaves, 12 April 1798; John Reaves, bm.

Prather, Thomas F. & Charity Briggs, 15 Oct 1834; Jesse A. Waugh, bm.

SURRY COUNTY MARRIAGES, 1779-1868

Prather, Thomas W. & Mary R. Banner, 5 Dec 1859; John W. Rawley, bm.

Pratt, Elisha & Mary Dickenson, 11 Nov 1817; John Sims, bm.

Prewet, Anderson & Lucy Clanton, 4 Feb 1833; John G. Pettit, bm.

Price, John & Ann Carlton, 30 Sept 1831; Thomas Arnold, bm.

Price, Samuel & Elizabeth Merimon, 13 Dec 1786; John Colvard, bm.

Price, William & Rachel Head, 17 Oct 1804; Wm. Forrester, Thomas Rollins, bm.

Price, William D., son of Duke and Rachael Price, and Rebecca Ann Cain, daughter of Andrew and Elizabeth Cain, m 28 May 1868 by C. D. Hill, J. P.

Prichett, William & Sally Shelton, 29 April 1865; Watson Marshall, bm; m 30 April 1865 by James Needham, M. G.

Priddy, Lewis & Elizabeth Tyler, 19 May 1807; Jacob Black, bm.

Pride, Oliver & Mary Davis, 27 Aug 1787; Leonard Richards, bm.

Primm, Enoch & Polly Logan, 7 March 1818; George Logan, son of Hugh, bm.

Prim, James & Hathy Cook, 2 Sept 1829; Enoch Prim, bm.

Primm, Joshua & Nancy Killion, 10 Sept 1817; Caleb Primm, bm.

Primm, Joshua & Nancy Killion, 5 Aug 1818; Thomas Pettit, bm.

Primm, Alexander P. & Judeth Ann Peek, 26 Nov 1849; Isaac A. Gardner, bm.

Primm, Caleb & Polly Arney, 15 July 1814; James Primm, bm.

Primm, David & Katharine Edwards, 21 Feb 1855; Thomas J. Kinley, bm; m 21 Feb 1855 by A. Simmons, J. P.

Primm, John & Malinda J. Husk, 18 Aug 1849; Wm. R. Bray, bm.

Primm, Joshua & Betsey Speer, 21 Dec 1807; Joseph Kelley, bm.

Phofet, Arraton & Gemmima Bingham, 21 May 1816; Stephen Bingham, bm.

Pruett, James M. & Lew F. McHane, 31 May 1866; m 21 May 1866 by Murlin Sparger, J. P.

Pruette, Jesse & Tobitha Legins, 26 July 1828; Joseph Steelmon, bm.

Pruit, Thomas & Charlotte Wishan, 15 June 1821; David Baity, bm.

Pruitt, Hardin & Paulina Tayler, 27 Feb 1863; m 1 March 1863 by D. McGee, J. P.

Pruitt, Jacob & Sarah Cockerham, 19 Sept 1864; Jno. M. Cloud, bm; m 21 Sept 1864 by James Minish, J. P.

Pruitt, William & Elizabeth Hollinsworth, 6 April 1858; m 8 April 1858 by Drewry McGee, J. P.

Pucket, Doctor F. & Elizabeth White, 17 July 1854; John Willis, bm; m 17 July 1854 by A. Simmons, J. P.

Pucket, Elijah & Sally Pucket, 14 Aug 1852; Read Pucket, bm; m 26 Aug 1852 by Martin Payne, J. P.

Pucket, Hugh & Elisabeth Golding, 15 March 1861.

Pucket, James & Martha Snow, 23 June 1855; William Golden, bm.

Pucket, Levi J. & Sarah E. Holsey, 26 Aug 1854; George M. Isley, bm; m 26 Aug 1854 by A. Simmons, J. P.

Pucket, Lewis & Catherine Webb, 6 Aug 1846; Chroet Webb, bm.

Pucket, Riley & Matilda Snow, 17 Oct 1853; Gabl. McCraw, bm; m 27 Oct 1853 by B. F. Scott, J. P.

Pucket, Samuel & Elizabeth Guilpin, 21 March 1837; John Pack, bm.

Puckett, David & Elizabeth Warden, 4 Feb 1833; Anderson Taylor, bm.

Puckett, Ephrem & Jennett McBride, 10 Aug 1865; John Puckett, bm.

Puckett, Isham & Ruth Cain, 24 March 1816; Solomon Cain, bm.

Puckett, Jacob & Sarah Marshal, 11 March 1825; William Phillips, bm.

Puckett, John & Sarah J. Stovall, 24 April 1862; Samuel D. Critz, bm; m 24 April 1862 by A. Simmons, J. P.

Puckett, Moses & Elisabeth Puckett, 13 June 1818; Benjamin Taylor, bm.

Puckett, Ruel & Cary Puckett, 25 Aug 1848; Pleasant Puckett, bm.

Puckett, Zachariah & Edith Jackson, 26 July 1817; Wm. Unthank, bm.

Purdom, Elijah & Caty Shepperd Rough, 28 July 1802; George Tull, bm.

Purdom, Henry & Aggy Andrews, 30 Aug 1808; Joseph Sater, bm.

Purdom, Mark & Polly Bittaton, 30 Dec 1814; Anvell Mock, bm.

Purdom, Thomas & Elizabeth Aldridge, 15 Jan 1809; Thomas Colvard, bm.

Purdom, William & Mary McBride, 21 Nov 1795; John Purdom, bm.

Purdue, I. M. G. & Mary A. York, 10 Aug 1863; E. H. York, bm. (C. H.).

Purkins, James & Lucy Conley, 5 Aug 1850; James Haynes, bm.

Quesinberry, Franklin S. & Louemma Tipton, 13 Aug 1858; Joseph Quesinberry, bm.

SURRY COUNTY MARRIAGES, 1779-1868

Quesinberry, Lewis C. & Sarah Cox, 16 Nov 1851; Preston Phillips, bm.

Quesinberry, Wm. & E. J. Shepperd, 13 Jan 1844; Franklin Huett, bm.

Quin, William & Mahala Linvill, 25 May 1836; John Linvill, bm.

Quinn, John & Agnes Muckmillion, 5 Nov 1820; Pierce Quinn, bm.

Rachels, James & Jane Hutson, 21 Feb 1849; Ralph Holyfield, Jr., bm.

Raiden, Jeremiah & Nancy Warden, 2 Jan 1817; Alexander Watson, bm.

Railsback, Daniel & Charity Little, 27 July 1795; Isaac Ellis, bm.

Railsback, Daniel & Elizabeth Dossee, 29 Feb 1796; Aaron Stinson, bm.

Raines, Jonathan & Lettitia Paton, 1 June 1847; Michael Nookester, bm.

Ralls, Hector & Sally Stone, 4 Dec 1818; Edward Lovill, bm.

Ramey, Benjamin & Nancy Pelley, 10 March 1785; Joseph Ramey, bm.

Ramey, Daniel J. & M. M. Thompson, 3 July 1858; m by G. Bryan, 8 July 1858.

Ramey, Elijah & Priscilla Jervis, 28 March 1832; Train Branick, bm.

Ramey, John & Susannah Elrode, 22 Nov 1785; Joseph Ramey, bm.

Ramey, Joseph Jr. & Mary Stewart, 17 Jan 1807; Robt. Ship, bm.

Ramsey, James & Mary Ann Warner, 30 Nov 1845; David E. Graham, bm.

Randolph, William & Dolly Poindexter, 22 Nov 1816; William Pettet, bm.

Ransom, Benjamin & Elizebeth Degearn, 22 Sept 1806; Wm. Fomested, bm.

Rarden, James & Elender Chandler, 22 Sept 1813; Lazarus Ritter, bm.

Rash, John & Elizabeth Logan, 7 Nov 1788; John Logan, bm.

Ratliff, Elias & Elisabeth Farmer, 22 Dec 1810; Levi Rees, bm.

Ratliff, Harden M. & _____, 15 Oct 1839; Hezekiah Smith, bm.

Ratliff, John H. & Amey Chinall, 3 March 1854; Randol Chinall, bm; m 3 March 1854 by A. Simmons, J. P.

Ratliff, Phineas & Christiana Rogers, 5 Aug 1828; Ezekiel Rogers, bm.

SURRY COUNTY MARRIAGES, 1779-1868

Raussau, David & Nancy Shores, 30 Sept 1801; Abraham Washington Shores, bm.

Rawley, Darious & Purlina McCraw, 19 Dec 1838; Thos. B. Wright, bm.

Rawley, J. C. & Elizabeth Mitchell, 12 March 1861; m 13 March 1861 by Jesse Roberts.

Rawley, William & Mary Davis, 7 Nov 1837; Darius Rawley, bm.

Rawlin, Peter & Elizabeth Russell, 9 May 1845; Thomas Brown, bm.

Ray, Jackson & Lydia Ray, 26 Feb 1845; Richard Ray, bm.

Ray, Spottswood D. & Sarah Kelly, 19 Aug 1858; John Owen, bm.

Ray, William T. & Caroline Walker, 17 Feb 1846; Henry I. Money, bm.

Reade, Isaac & Charlotty Desern, m 31 Dec 1856 by John Jervis, J. P.

Reavis, Abel & Polly Garner, 30 Oct 1808; Henry A. Garner, bm.

Reavis, Anderson & Elizabeth Foot, 30 Jan 1850; Henry Jinkins, bm.

Reavis, Asa & Polly Reavis, 2 Feb 1839; Joseph Reavis, bm.

Reavis, Edward & Mary Haddocks, 13 Oct 1795; Jesse Reavis, bm.

Reavis, Edward & Sarah Reavis, 16 Feb 1793; Pinson Wiles, bm.

Reavis, James & Mary Gibbons, 7 Dec 1845; Joseph Reavis, bm.

Reavis, Jesse & Mary Gibbons, 6 Oct 1806; Joshua Brown, bm.

Reavis, Jesse & Mary Garman, 5 April 1830; Joel Reavis, bm.

Reavis, Joseph & Nancy C. Powel, 6 May 1848; James S. Hanes, bm.

Reavis, Joseph & Sally Vestal, 2 Dec 1828; Wm. Dickinson, bm.

Reavis, Samuel & Nancy Wilkins, 28 Dec 1817; Archibald Garner, William Harris, bm.

Reavis, William & Jane Steelmon, 2 Feb 1813; George Steelmon, bm.

Rector, Jesse of Grayson, Va., & Margret Winford, 29 Jan 1802; Peter Rector, of Rowan Co., bm.

Rector, William & Julina Collins, 27 July 1865; H. M. Waugh, bm; m 31 July 1865 by B. J. Dickens, J. P.

Redding, Allen & Sarrah Sparks, 11 Nov 1833; William Reading, bm.

Redpoth, Benjamin & Nancy Lumas, 18 Dec 1837; Lorrenzor Wright, bm.

Reece, Abraham & Ruth Hadly, 28 Dec 1802; Joel Reece, bm.

Reece, Abraham & Mary Owen, 20 Dec 1826; Jesse Reece, bm.

SURRY COUNTY MARRIAGES, 1779-1868

Reece, Abraham Jr. & Jane York, 10 Dec 1822; Daniel Rees, bm.

Reece, Abraham M. & Jane Hurt, 18 Sept 1833; Anthony Woodhouse, bm.

Reece, Alvis & Mary Hobson, 15 Nov 1831; Thomas Vestal, bm.

Reece, Alvis & Gragery MacKie, 8 May 1844; Daniel H. Martin, bm.

Reece, Edward & Judy Hutchins, 22 Aug 1823; John Vestal, bm.

Reece, Edward & Ann D. Reece, 12 Aug 1850; Aquila Speer, bm.

Reece, Eli & Sarah Crommel, 13 Nov 1817; Daniel Reese, bm.

Reese, Franklin & Matilda Hurt, 28 Sept 1835; John S. Philips, bm.

Reece, Hiram & Elizabeth Hurt, 2 Aug 1844; John J. Woodruff, bm.

Reece, Jesse & Peggy Hadly, 15 April 1807; Abraham Reece, bm.

Reece, Joel & Sarah Martin, 14 Jan 1804; Levi Rees, bm.

Reece, John & Elizabeth Critchfield, 15 Sept 1820; Daniel Reece, bm.

Reece, Martin & Mary Cockerham, 12 Jan 1855; John Hamlin, bm; m 17 Jan 1855 by John Jervis, J. P.

Reece, Miles & Rebecca Mackie, 12 Sept 1835; Wilson Reece, bm.

Reece, Noah & Nancy Gibes, 4 Jan 1844; John C. Gibes, bm.

Reece, Samuel & Malinda Calloway, 16 Dec 1844; James York, son of Nimrod, bm.

Reece, Thomas & Pheroby Thornton, 5 Jan 1814; Simon Marshall, bm.

Reece, Thomas H. & Lear Greenwood, 6 Jan 1818; Daniel Reece, bm.

Reece, Wily & Elmida Hinshaw, 26 April 1838; Jos. Johnson, bm.

Reed, Amos & Sibby Kidd, 8 Dec 1853; m 9 Dec 1853 by E. Reeves, J. P.

Reed, Helry & Mary Ladd, 2 April 1823; Joseph Horton, bm.

Reed, Irvin, son of Jacob and Tabitha Reed, and Martha E. Atkerson, daughter of Johnson and E. H. Atkerson, m 9 Feb 1868 by Jas. H. Lewellin, minister.

Reed, Isaack & Elizabeth McGlaughlin, 9 April 1819; Jacob L. Fulk, bm.

Reed, Jacob & Tabitha Linvill, 9 April 1824; James Reed, bm.

Reed, James & Betsey Holderfield, 2 Nov 1825; James York, bm.

Reed, Jesse & Eliza McKinny, 21 June 1859; John H. Brinkley, bm.

SURRY COUNTY MARRIAGES, 1779-1868

Reed, John & Sally Mehaffy, 21 Dec 1806; Thomas Mehaffy, bm.

Reed, John & Mary Freeman, 16 Jan 1841.

Reed, John & Louisa Portee, 20 June 1845; James Moore, bm.

Reed, John & Delphia R. Ashburn, 15 March 1867; Denson A. Ashburn, bm; m 18 March 1867 by A. Whitaker, J. P.

Reed, Preston & Thersey Marion, 12 June 1855; D. M. Cooper, bm; m 12 June 1855 by D. M. Cooper, J. P.

Rees, Eli & Mattilda Greenwood, 10 Oct 1825; Abrm. Reece, bm.

Rees, Daniel Jr. & Sarah York, 17 Oct 1819; Nimrod York, bm.

Reese, Thomas & Pheroby Thornton, 5 Jan 1814; Simon Marshall, bm.

Reese, Zachariah & Mary Davis, 20 July 1821; Jonathan York, bm.

Reet, William & Susannah Nance, 16 Nov 1836; Michael W. McGuire, bm.

Reeves, J. S. & Dortha N. Nott, 14 Jan 1855; M. C. Reeves, bm.

Reeves, John & Sarah Smith, 29 Nov 1825; Jacob Ideol, bm.

Reeves, J. D. & Elener Howard, 8 June 1811; Jeremiah Early, bm.

Reeves, Micajah & Elizabeth Early, 2 Feb 1817; Richard E. Reeves, bm.

Reeves, Zachariah & Sally Ann Whitaker, 2 Feb 1848; Richard E. Reeves, bm.

Reid, J. F. & Nancy Whiteker, 27 June 1860; m 28 June 1860 by P. Worth, J. P.

Reid, John & Mary Edds, 3 Feb 1858; Harrison Eddes, bm.

Reede, Amos & Sibby Kidd, 8 Dec 1853; Jesse Coe, bm.

Repass, Joel & Ellin Kidd, 2 Sept 1857; William S. Kidd, bm.

Resdon, Fieldin L. & Lucy Brown, 29 Oct 1803; Elijah Snap, bm.

Renagar, William & Sally Wooten, 15 Oct 1835; John Wooten, bm.

Rennals, Henry & Mary Jones, 4 Oct 1812; Jonathan Harral, bm.

Rennigar, Peter & Catharine Garmer, 17 April 1815; Henry Rennigar, George Renniger, bm.

Rennegar, Peter & Sarah James, 25 Dec 1831; David Grover, bm.

Revis, John & Catherine Macy, 11 May 1827; Samuel Whitlock, bm.

Reynolds, C. M. & M. J. Mourning, 10 May 1867; m 10 May 1867 by J. A. Bingham, J. P.

Reynolds, David B. & Ellen R. Jones, 4 Dec 1833; John Jones, bm.

Reynolds, Dudley & Mary King, 23 Feb 1859; Stephen King, bm.

SURRY COUNTY MARRIAGES, 1779-1868

Reynolds, Fleming R., son of David Reynolds, and Eliza Reed, daughter of James and Lucinda McKinney, m at the house of D. B. Reynolds, 11 Oct 1868 by John Jones.

Reynolds, George & Mary Hadly, 12 April 1812; Thomas Reynolds, bm.

Reynolds, Hadly & Margaret Martin, 14 Jan 1838; Nathan Bond, bm.

Reynolds, John T. & Ezenth Fowler, 14 March 1865; m by P. Worth, J. P.

Reynolds, Johnson & Debby Love, 9 Dec 1817; Isaiah Love, bm.

Reynolds, Jonas & Mary Hanes, 18 March 1827; George Reynolds, bm.

Reynolds, Jonas F. & Nancy Shelton, 4 April 1867; m 4 April 1867 by A. Brim, J. P.

Reynolds, Jonas & Elizabeth Wilson, 1 Oct 1833; Thomas Hobson, bm.

Reynolds, Masberry, son of Charles and Nancy Reynolds, and Alviny Burnett, daughter of Henry & Mary A. Burnett, m 14 Nov 1868 by Thomas Schaub, J. P.

Reynolds, Nathaniel & Rachel Gowin, 22 Dec 1820; Henry Sparger, bm.

Reynolds, Peter & Catharin Love, 29 Nov 1825; Thomas Love, Jr., bm.

Reynolds, Verlin & Jane Smith, 14 March 1865; Wm. R. Hollinsworth, bm.

Reynolds, William & Hannah Love, 8 Nov 1808; William Love, bm.

Reynolds, William & Patience Hadley, 22 Nov 1819; Jesse Reece, bm.

Reynolds, William & Sarah Love, 28 Dec 1831; Thomas Lambert, bm.

Reynolds, William L. & Mary Simmons, 30 Dec 1861; m 2 Jan 1862 by J. Copeland, J. P.

Rhoads, David & Rachel Delany, 29 Oct 1826; William Spillman Jr., bm.

Rhoads, Richard W. & Rhodey Williams, 14 July 1832; Thomas B. Naylor, bm.

Rhodes, George A. & Sarah A. Ayers, 4 June 1860; Richard Landrum, bm.

Rich, David R. & Sarah Steelman, 9 Nov 1846; Jas. M. Johnson, bm.

Richards, Felix & Mehetable Jarvis, 6 Oct 1802; Lennard Snow, bm.

Richards, John & Pricilla Colvard, 23 Dec 1791; Richard Speer, bm.

Richards, Morris & Sally Dezarn, 17 April 1834; Wm. D. Somers, bm.

Richardson, Culland & Elizabeth Meumillion, 5 Feb 1838; Samuel Muemillion, bm.

Richardson, James & Elizabeth Ayers, 17 Sept 1854; John Bays, bm; m 17 Sept 1854 by A. Simmons, J. P.

Richardson, Jesse & Rutha Jones, 27 Jan 1794; Lemuel Jones, bm.

Richardson, Lemuel & Martha Ayers, 19 Nov 1837; James D. Deen, bm.

Richardson, Wm. T. & Nancy York, 26 Dec 1862; James M. Ward, bm; m 20 Dec 1862 by Thomas Howell.

Richerson, Daniel & Jane Sparks, 3 Aug 1862; Isaac Londy, bm.

Richerson, James & Mary Vernum, 6 Feb 1844; James Vernum, bm.

Richerson, Joseph & Mary A. Owens, 23 Oct 1865; m 26 Oct 1865 by Saml. Forkner, J. P.

Richerson, Joseph & Charlottee Galyer, 5 Nov 1846; Larcan Canady, bm.

Riddle, Asa & Perlina Steal, 27 Dec 1854; Daniel Haymore, bm; m by Wm. Haymore, J. P., 28 Dec 1854.

Riddle, Franklin, son of Ayre and Betsy Riddle, & Elizabeth Armstrong, daughter of Hugh and Nancy Armstrong, m 27 Dec 1868 by John H. Lowe.

Riddle, John & Mary Keen, 1 April 1789; William Douthit, bm.

Ridenhour, Joseph & Pheba Ann Thompson, 3 Dec 1859; Wm. F. Scott, bm; m 3 Dec 1859 by E. Banner, J. P.

Ridge, William & Sarah Horn, 17 Feb 1797; Moses Moore, bm.

Ridgeway, Saml & Eliza. Gaton, 22 April 1799; Osburn Ridgeway, bm.

Ridings, Isaac & Susannah Chin, 7 June 1818; Squire Glen, bm.

Ridings, Jesse & Mary Poindexter, 16 Dec 1804; William Phillips, bm.

Ried, David & Jenny Moore, 22 June 1853; J. W. Creed, bm; m 22 June 1853 by D. M. Cooper, J. P.

Riggan, R. H. & Lucy Hodges, 27 Jan 1860; m 2 Feb 1860 by Jos. Venable, J. P.

Riggins, Francis & Polly Carpender, 5 Oct 1853; Jesse Davis, bm; m 6 Oct 1853 by John Ramey, J. P.

Riggins, Joseph M. & Mary Hodges, m 7 April 1852 by Wilson Laffoon, J. P. (C. H.).

Riggs, Daniel & Mary Jane Haymore, 5 Sept 1856; Jas. L. Gillaspie, bm; m 7 Sept 1856 by Wilson Laffoon, J. P.

SURRY COUNTY MARRIAGES, 1779-1868

Riggs, James, son of Jesse and Lydia Riggs, and Midiam Marion, daughter of William and Patience Marion, m 10 Dec 1868 by M. G. Harbour, J. P.

Riggs, Jesse & Lydia Hodges, 28 Oct 1830; Andrew Hodges, bm.

Riggs, John & Patsey Peterson, 11 July 1825; John York, bm.

Riggs, John & Sinthy Lawson, 21 Jan 1826; Newel Jackson, bm.

Riggs, Wiley & Julia Ann Haymore, 26 Jan 1859; Joseph S. Gordon, bm.

Rights, John & Lucy Wiles, 1 Jan 1813; Lewis Wiles, bm.

Rigsby, Henry & Nancy Southard, 31 Dec 1833; Welcome Hodges, bm.

Rilay, Michael & Sarah Black, 5 March 1796; Fredrick Black, bm.

Riley, James & Martha Cast, 25 Feb 1789; Robert Fraizer, bm.

Riley, John & Sarah Ellsberry, 12 Aug 1797; Benjamin Elsberry, bm.

Riley, William & Jane Jessup, colored, 2 May 1867; m by Wm Moran.

Rinehardt, Christian & Leah Martin, 13 Oct 1835; James A. Windsor, bm.

Rinhart, Frederick & Rachel Holcomb, 16 April 1836; Isaac Shores, bm.

Ring, Adam, son of Martin and Rachel Ring, and Mary Matildia Shore, daughter of Benjamin and Rebecka Shore, m 27 Dec 1868 by R. T. N. Stephenson.

Ring, Augustine & Martha Ashburn, 6 Jan 1866; Adam Ring, bm.

Ring, Enoch & Sarah Daken, 14 Dec 1854; Harvey Denney, bm; m 15 Dec 1854 by Joel Denny, J. P.

Ring, Martin & Nancy Whitaker, 14 Jan 1863; R. E. Marion, bm.

Ring, Thomas & Nancy Nance, 27 March 1824; Sampson Fleming, bm.

Ring, William & Elizabeth Draughon, 4 March 1839; Milton Bray, bm.

Ring, William & Rebecca Evans, 21 Oct 1845; William Ashburn, bm.

Ring, William, son of Martin and Celia Ring, and Jane Blanset, m 22 Oct 1868 by John Jones.

Ritchey, Moses & Susannah Hill, 15 Nov 1823; Charles Welch, bm.

Ritner, Fredrick & Elizabeth Shimmel, 22 Dec 1800; John Miller, bm.

Roark, John & Elizabeth Gibbs, 25 Oct 1806; Henry Linvill, bm.

Roberds, Edmon & Nutty Roberson, 28 July 1805; Peter Elcer(?), bm.

SURRY COUNTY MARRIAGES, 1779-1868

Roberson, James & Sarah Ann Sadler, 12 Aug 1844; Thomas Roberson, bm.

Roberson, James & Elizabeth Hodge, 13 Nov 1810; Anthony Foster, bm.

Roberson, John & Lucinda McGuire, 14 Dec 1828; Martin Costephens, bm.

Roberson, Nathaniel & Lucy Lane, 18 Aug 1831; David Lane, bm.

Roberson, Peter & Elizabeth Hall, 19 May 1810; Chesley Roberson, Lewis Hall, bm.

Roberson, Pleasant & Miss Elizabeth Hodges, 18 March 1858; Moore Snow, bm; m 21 March 1858 by Geo. A. Jervis, J. P.

Roberson, Thomas & Elizabeth Hatcher, 8 Sept 1858; N. York, bm; m 8 Sept 1858 by Nathan York.

Roberson, William & Talitha Walker, 5 June 1830; Philip W. Green, bm.

Roberts, Ambrose & Miss Phebe A. Phillips, 17 Dec 1853; S. W. Roberts, bm.

Roberts, Daniel C. & Elizabeth Witcher, 28 Feb 1837; Nathan D. Hunt, bm.

Roberts, George & Elizabeth Reaves, 6 April 1831; John Reavis, bm.

Roberts, John & Nansey Cockerham, 9 March 1806; Richd. Welborn, bm.

Roberts, John & Nancy Caroline Spence, 5 March 1855; John R. Mosely, bm.

Roberts, John & Nancy Lyon, 24 Jan 1813; James McCraw, bm.

Roberts, Jonathan & Polly Davis, 28 March 1808; Leonard Davis, bm.

Roberts, Jonathan & Sary Taylor, 12 May 1839; Thos. B. Wright, bm.

Roberts, Logan D. & Susan M. Fleming, 16 Dec 1854; Thomas Roberts, bm.

Roberts, Richard & Nancy Bryson, 31 July 1810; Jas. McCraw, bm.

Roberts, Rufus & Lucy A. Cox, 16 Feb 1853; Thomas Smith, bm.

Roberts, Thomas B. & Nancy Winfrys, 28 March 1838; John Jervis, G. W. Roberts, bm.

Robins, John & Elizabeth Ball, 4 July 1844; Iredell Prevett, bm.

Robinson, Philip & Catharine Phillips, 25 Oct 1826; William Hunter, bm.

Roby, Absalom & Rosana Hampton, 20 April 1836; Henry G. Hampton, bm.

SURRY COUNTY MARRIAGES, 1779-1868

Roby, Wm. A. & Elizabeth Welch, 30 July 1831; Nathan T. Grant, bm.

Rogers, Allen & Ruth Kittle, 29 Oct 1817; Levi Rogers, bm.

Romyea, John & Nancy Speer, 21 Oct 1799; Calvin Wheaton, bm.

Rone, Haywood & Nancy Bird, 24 April 1859; Vichtler Lane, bm.

Ronnard, James & Fanny Brittain, 16 Jan 1835; William Song(?), bm.

Roop, Chester B. & Matilda Shealter, 12 March 1867; M. L. Haley, bm; m by Wm. R. Bray, J. P.

Roop, Jacob & Margery Olliver, 3 March 1801; John Dinkins, bm.

Roop, John & Febe Pilcher, 18 Dec 1804; John Dinkins, bm.

Roop, William H. & Sarah M. Hawley, 24 Sept 1862; J. F. Meredith, bm; m 24 Sept 1862 by A. Simmons, J. P.

Roope, Martin & Mary Pilcher, 26 June 1812; John Oliver, bm.

Rose, Abner & Sally Summers, (no date, ca. 1805); Kezia Rose, bm.

Rose, Benjamin & Rebekah Sutlif, 31 May 1813; Alexander Apperson, bm.

Rose, Major & Jane Olvy, 16 April 1846; William Hambric, bm.

Rose, Rezia & Rhoda Critchfield, 19 Sept 1805; Wm. _____, bm.

Rose, Sterling & Rebeca Howell, 19 Nov 1836; Benjamin Rose, bm.

Roseberry, William & Margret James, 6 July 1824; Ralph Holderfield, bm.

Ross, William & Nelly Davis, 28 June 1822; Thomas Nations, bm.

Rose, Wm. J. & Nancy Morris, 30 Dec 1844; John Rose, bm. (C.H.).

Robhauss, Conrad & Anna Stoner, 10 July 1794; Heinrich Ahel, bm.

Rothenberry, Seth & Arinah Adkins, 26 March 1833; Jason Jackson, bm.

Rotin, Timothy & Nancy Pullen, 25 March 1833; Daniel Carlan, bm.

Rottenberry, John & Willey Richardson, 14 March 1856; m 15 March by Isaac Armsfield, J. P.

Rottenberry, John & Ratchal Celly, 21 March 1828; Stinlin Taylor, bm.

Roughton, Amer & Sarah West, 18 Jan ____; Lewis Mock, bm.

Roughton, Elisha & Nany Brown, 21 Aug 1817; Richard Jacks, bm.

Roughton, James & Elendor Messicks, 14 Sept 1807; Henry Brown, bm.

SURRY COUNTY MARRIAGES, 1779-1868

Rowzee, Paschal & Matilda Williams, 28 Feb 1826; D. L. Williams, bm.

Roy, Leondard & Anne Fips, 26 Dec 1818; Littleberry Fips, bm.

Royal, Henry & Sally Weathermon, 19 July 1822; James Hudspeth, bm.

Royal, Lodiwick & Jane Faircloth, 29 Nov 1826; William Williard, bm.

Royal, Thomas & Martha Normon, 14 May 1818; Thomas Vestal (FC), bm.

Rudder, John & Sarah Welch, 10 Oct 1827; Asa Vestal, bm.

Runnegar, Jacob & Tenea Iram(?), 19 Nov 1817; John Waggoner, bm.

Rupard, Caloop & Lillis L. Cary, 3 Jan 1856; m 3 Jan 1856 by Wm. H. Purdue.

Rupe--see also Roop

Russ, William & Ann Rogers, 7 Feb 1834; Geo. A. Jervis, bm.

Russell, Abner & Sarah Allgood, 17 Dec 1831; James West, bm.

Russell, John & Nancy Sparks, 11 Sept 1824; Joel H. Burch, bm.

Rutledge, Enos & Sarah Bowen, 2 June 1821; Nathan Rutledge, Morgan Hudspeth, bm.

Rutledge, Jacob & Nancy Morgenson, 22 April 1799; Thomas Donniley, bm.

Rutledge, Joel & Mary Steelman, 16 June 1803; James Rannard, bm.

Rutledge, John & Valentine Murphey, 23 May 1797; Thos. Donniley, bm.

Rutledge, Joseph & Phebe Gough, 23 Dec 1816; Gilliam Wiles, Charles Steelman Jr., bm.

Rutledge, Nathan & Isabella Rhoades, 13 Sept 1823; Enos Rutledge, bm.

Rutledge, Wm. W. & Catharine Creson, 10 Dec 1828; Joseph Steelman, bm.

Ryals, Uriah & Rachael Denny, 16 June 1848; Jorden Denny, bm; W. W. Wolff, wit.

Ryon, Patrick & Polly Durham, 12 Sept 1805; Robert Ahle, bm.

Sailes, M. L. & Phebe Wright, 26 April 1864; m 27 April 1864 by James Minish.

Sale, M. D. & Phebe Bright, 26 April 1864; A. L. Hendrix, bm.

Sales, William & Betsey Johnston, 17 March 1812; Samuel Binge, bm.

Sales, William & Caroline Dickerson, 23 April 1844; Jas. E. Hough, bm.

SURRY COUNTY MARRIAGES, 1779-1868

Sater, Joseph & Polly Purdom, 8 March 1804; Giles Hudspeth, Benjamin Purdom, bm. (filed under Saer).

Salmon, James & Fanny Blade, 29 Oct 1808; James Fraizer, bm.

Salmons, David & Eliza Shore, 10 April 1850; Jacob Whitlock, bm.

Salmons, Elisha & Lucy Ellet, 17 Jan 1847; Campbell W. Salmons, bm.

Salmons, Josiah F. P. & Grace Vanhoy, 1 Jan 1846; William Pinnix, bm.

Sammons, David & Nancy Pettijohn 7 Aug 1823; John N. Messicks, bm.

Sampson, William H. & Sinthy M. Warden, 27 Dec 1854; Johnston Warden, bm; m 27 Jan 1854 by A. Simmons, J. P.

Sams, Green L. & Emely McKinny, 6 Aug 1865; William A. Sams, bm; m 8 Aug 1865 by James S. Green, J. P.

Samuel, Edmund & Susanah Hill, 15 March 1788; Augustin Samuel, bm.

Samuel, Henry & Thirza Forkner, 15 Jan 1829; C. H. Hill, bm.

Sanders, Hardy & Elizabeth Jones, 2 March 1789; James Sanders, bm.

Sanders, Isaac & Winny Cole, 9 Sept 1814; Reece Davis, bm.

Sanders, James & Elizabeth Riley, 28 July 1786; Edward Riley, bm.

Sanders, Jesse & Martha A. Marshall, 2 Jan 1854; Thomas Evans, bm; m by Jesse Roberts.

Sanders, John Jr. & Hannah A. Walton, 2 June 1825; John A. Jenkins, bm.

Sanders, Stephen & Franky Bratton, 21 May 1818; Wm. McCraw, bm.

Sanders, William N., son of James and Edy Sanders, and Louiza Colar, daughter of Solomon and Mary Collers, m 23 Dec 1868 by John H. Caudle.

Sapp, Caleb & Polley Loagin, 28 July 1795; Hugh Logan, bm.

Saser, Enock & Frances Harless, 28 Dec 1830; James Harless, bm.

Sattenfield, John & Mary Haga, 7 _____ 1786; John Rosingbum, bm.

Satterfield, John D. & Lucinda Allred, 12 March 1864; William H. Davis, bm; m 15 March 1864 by John B. Stenson, minister of the M. E. Church.

Satterfield, John D. & Jennie Adkerson, 6 Dec 1866; W. E. Patterson, bm; m 9 Dec 1866 by Jas. H. Lewellin, Min.

Saunders, James K. & Mary Ann Weatherpond, 20 Nov 1859; Jno. L. Worth, bm.

SURRY COUNTY MARRIAGES, 1779-1868

Savage, Kendal & Sarah Jarvis, 5 March 1803; Abner Ross, bm.

Savage, William H. & India Lambert, 26 Nov 1857; H. C. Culler, bm; m 26 Nov 1857 by Adam Scott, J. P.

Sawers, John & Sarah Tansy, 5 Feb 1813; Calop Jessop, bm.

Sawers, Menter & Shental(?) Puckett, 4 July 1827; Thornton Bremmer, bm.

Sawyers, James & Elizabeth Pucket, 31 July 1857; John Pucket, bm.

Sawyers, John & Hannah Simmons, 7 Nov 1845; Henderson Cook, bm.

Sawyers, Meriman & July Ann Sawyers, 12 Aug 1847; George W. Reece, bm.

Sawyers, Thomas Clayton & Ann Adams, 27 Feb 1866; Wm. Waugh, bm.

Scales, Anderson, son of Lina Scales, and Ann Hopper, daughter of Liza Hopper, colored, 18 Jan 1868; m 26 Jan 1868 by Wm. Y. Tucker, J. P.

Schaub, Levi & Mary M. McCraw, 16 Aug 1858; Jas. Davis, bm.

Scott, Benjamin & Elizabeth Normon, 12 April 1831; F. P. Vest, bm.

Scott, Daniel Jr. & Catharine Coe, 23 May 1818; Francis Pettitt, bm.

Scott, Daniel W. & Elizabeth Flin, 9 March 1821; William Kettle, bm.

Scott, Edward & Mary Martin, 18 Feb 1799; Samuel Martin, bm.

Scott, Francis & Mary Hawl, 4 Aug 1805; Thomas Scott, bm.

Scott, Greenville & Lucy S. Roberson, 29 May 1854; Richard Barnard, bm; m 29 May 1854 by R. Marshall, J. P.

Scott, Henry & Elizabeth Philips, 3 March 1863; Peyton Owen, bm.

Scott, Henry W. & Hulda Mankins, 25 March 1861; m 2 April 1861 by L. J. Norman, J. P.

Scott, Jesse & Sarah Kerr, 25 Jan 1818; Robert Scott, bm.

Scott, Jesse & Louisa Miller, 29 Nov 1847; Alfred Snow, bm.

Scott, John & Reachel Horton, 10 May 1804; Daniel Scott, bm.

Scott, John & Sally Trulove, 10 Nov 1854; William Phillips, bm; m 11 Nov 1854 by Wm. R. Lovill, J. P.

Scott, Robert & Polly Martin, 28 March 1818; William Garner, bm.

Scott, Samuel & Harriet Scott, 25 June 1835; John Brickell, bm.

Scott, Samuel & Mary Spainhower, 23 March 1845; Daniel C. Wolff, bm.

SURRY COUNTY MARRIAGES, 1779-1868

Scott, Shade F. & Louiza Payne, 3 Nov 1851; James M. Stuart, bm; m 3 Nov 1851 by Martin Payne, J. P.

Scott, Thomas P. & Sally T. Franklin, 16 Aug 1810; Edward Lovill Jr., bm.

Scott, William F. & Mary A. Belton, 19 May 1857; John W. Rawley, bm; m 19 May 1857 by E. Banner, J. P.

Scott, William P. & Amy Hunt, 21 Oct 1854; Adam H. Scott, bm; m 26 Oct 1854 by Wm. R. Lovill, J. P.

Seals, Burrel & Locky McGraw, 28 March 1817; William Mash, bm.

Seany, Samuel & Catron Wishon, 2 Jan 1805; Fridrich Dannad, bm.

Sears, Michael & Sarah C. Lynch, 23 March 1848; George D. Williams, bm.

Seasar, James & Eliza Ann Stuart, 27 Aug 1846; colored; Elisha Banner, bm.

Seaser, Peter, son of Masrin & Judith Seaser, and Silvany Simmons, daughter of Frank and Mary Simmons, 8 Jan 1868; m by J. A. Bingman, J. P.

Seasor, William F. & Mass Hill, 20 May 1847; H. Samuel, bm.

Seazer, Jacob & Sally Hill, 8 Nov 1856; m 13 Nov 1856 by Drewry McGee, J. P.

Senter, John & Hallin Stanley, 17 May 1826; Peter Muncan, bm.

Senter, Solomon & Nancy Spencer, 6 July 1854; Oliver Stanliff, bm; m 6 July 1854 by W. M. Freeman, J. P.

Senter, Stephen & Polly Jonson, 24 Dec 1814; William Lyon, bm.

Sermones, Martin & Mary Ann Stevenson, 10 May 1847; Isaac Ogle, bm.

Settles, Isaac & Julian Holder, 20 June 1834; Wm. D. Somers, bm.

Seward, Samuel & Alce Gentry, 22 Oct 1789; Jonathan Thompson, bm.

Shadrick, George W. & Adaline Jones, 7 Nov 1853; Thomas J. Bradner, bm; m 7 Nov 1853 by A. Simmons, J. P.

Shan, Ralph & Polly Carter, 29 April 1804; Coleman Noble, bm.

Sharitz, Reuben A. & Mariah T. Repass, 23 Aug 1856; Eli Rider, bm; m 23 Aug 1856 by A. Simmons, J. P.

Sharp, Lewis Mercian, son of William and Meley Sharp, and Beckey Oston, daughter of James and Rebecker Oston, 15 Nov 1868; m by Thomas Schaub, J. P.

Sharpe, Thomas M. & Sarah J. Clement, 27 Dec 1837; Jesse A. Waugh, bm.

Shauss, Frederick & Elizabeth Helsenbeck, 21 Sept 1787; Frederick Helsebeck, bm.

Shaver, Andrew & Lydia Dudley, 18 Jan 1845; Isaiah Tally, bm.

Shaver, Joel & Any Oneals, 5 Nov 1834; John J. Angell, bm.

Shaw, Isaac & Nancy Whitaker, 5 March 1827; Ralph Shaw, bm.

Shaw, Nicholas & Rosanna Petty, 7 Nov 1822; William Burgiss, bm.

Sheehan, Jeremiah & Mary E. Morgan, 3 May 1852; Robert J. Harris, bm. (C. H.).

Sheek, Albert & Elizabeth C. Gilliam, 25 Dec 1855; E. Williams, bm.

Sheek, Daniel & Gene Williams, 29 Jan 1838; Thomas Brann, bm.

Sheek, Jesse E. & Sally Long, 8 Sept 1835; James Sheek, bm.

Sheek, Wiley & Maryetta C. Gillam, 21 Aug 1854; L. M. Gillam, bm; m 28 Aug 1854 by W. W. Albea.

Sheeks, David & Elizabeth Howard, 18 Jan 1790; Martin Bridgefaverall, bm.

Sheler, Thomas G. & Levina Wade, 23 March 1863; William L. Bird, bm; m 23 March 1863 by A. Simmons, J. P.

Sheles, Winston & Arritter Wood, 4 Feb 1847; Thompson Hutchens, bm.

Shelley, Richard & Elizabeth Thornton, 10 April 1797; Wm. Thornton, bm.

Shelton, Burrel & Lucinda Vaugn, 23 Jan 1868; m 23 Jan 1868 by C. D. Hill, J. P.

Shelton, Edward F. & Eveline Kirkman, 11 Sept 1857; m 12 Sept 1857 by Isaac Armfield, J. P.

Shelton, Elies & Luisa Phileps, 14 Feb 1833; Hugh Glen, bm.

Shelton, George & Magdaline Shaub, 30 Sept 1813; William Logan, bm.

Shelton, Henry & Mary Gray, 16 Dec 1850; James W. Jackson, bm.

Shelton, James & Jane Shelton, 26 Dec 1859; J. M. Owen, bm.

Shelton, James W. & Melinda E. Griffith, 26 Sept 1865; William A. Deatherage, bm; m 26 Sept 1865 by G. A. Lowe, J. P.

Shelton, Jeremiah Gra. & Nancy Flecher, 16 July 1800; Jeremiah Shelton, bm.

Shelton, John & Sally Bray, 21 Aug 1823; Charles Shelton, bm.

Shelton, Joseph & Usley Stone, 14 May 1818; Ambers J. Gregory, bm.

Shelton, Philip, son of William and Nancy Shelton & Martha Ann Snody, daughter of William & Julia Snody, 28 May 1868; m 7 June 1868 by M. A. Hall, J. P.

SURRY COUNTY MARRIAGES, 1779-1868

Shelton, Robert L. & Sarah B. Scott, 24 Jan 1855; Adam M. Reece, bm; m 24 Jan 1855 by A. Simmons, J. P.

Shelton, Stephen & Mildred Head, 4 Nov 1816; Jesse Stewart, bm.

Shelton, William & Nancy Deathrage, 28 Feb 1829; Daniel Love, bm.

Shelton, William & Mahala F. Nunly, 2 Dec 1859; Jas. J. Rogers, bm.

Shelton, William B. & Delfina Kirkman, 3 April 1855; John Shelton, bm; m 3 April 1855 by Wm. Haymore, J. P.

Shenall, Benjamin & Nany Rachels, 11 May 1839; Richard Shenall, bm.

Shinault, Benjamin & Micky P. Hutson, 3 Dec 1862; James Lemuel McGee, bm; m 3 Dec 1862 by S. W. Snow, J. P.

Sheppard, Nathan & Elizabeth Chapman, 22 March 1790; Phillip Howard, bm.

Shepherd, Wm. & Elizabeth Sawyers, 6 Sept 1828; Wm. Easley, bm.

Shermer, Peter & Mary Vhore, 25 June 1801; John Binkley, bm.

Shiffer, Ezekiel & Margaret Curry, 15 Oct 1791; Edward Edwards, bm.

Shin, Levi & Hannah de Bord, 30 Aug 1797; George Hoppes, bm.

Shin, Levi & Nelly Walker, 4 Nov 1834; Asa Lewis, bm.

Shinalt, Richard Jr. & Sarah Bidsall, 7 Aug 1818; Reuben Shinall, bm.

Shinault, Henry A. & Sally Ann Shinault, 30 April 1865; Wm. Doss, bm; m 1 May 1865 by John Jones at my house.

Shinall, Reuben & Nancy W. Childress, 19 Oct 1858; Winston Fulton, bm.

Shinnault, James & Mahala Gallyer, 23 Oct 1864; Anderson Gallyer, bm; m 23 Oct 1864 by B. J. Dickens, J. P.

Shipp, John & Elizabeth Oglesby, 20 Jan 1816; Wm. Davis, bm.

Shore, Daniel & Elizabeth Dudley, 18 Jan 1848; Alstin Poplin, bm.

Shore, Henry & Elizabeth Love, 12 Dec 1788; Jacob Shore, bm.

Shore, Henry & Rachael Parsons, 1 Oct 1818; Fredrick Long, son of George, bm.

Shore, Jacob & Catharine Hooser, 23 July 1787; Jacob Hauser (German signature), bm.

Shore, Jacob & Cinthy Harp, 10 Dec 1833; Jourden Hudspeth, bm.

Shore, James & Susan Mathews, 31 Jan 1847; Henry Marshall, bm.

Shore, John & Margit Groce, 12 Nov 1804; Jonathan Sprinkle, bm.

SURRY COUNTY MARRIAGES, 1779-1868

Shore, John B. & Unus Rees, 11 Jan 1846; William Hunter, bm.

Shore, Martin & Lucinda Chappell, 30 March 1850; George Pennix, bm.

Shore, W. T. & Mary Ashbourne, 14 Jan 1856; C. P. Fulk, bm.

Shore, William & Betsey Plowman, 23 April 1821; Fredrick Tanner Jr., bm.

Shore, William & Mary Jeffery, 7 Oct 1835; Charles Johnson, bm.

Shore, William & Elizabeth Elmore, 2 Nov 1848; Abednigo Stokes, bm.

Shores, Benjamin & Amanda M. Houston, 6 March 1867; A. A. Crissman, bm; m 10 March 1867 by John Jones.

Shores, David & Patsy Sisk, 12 March 1820; John Shores, bm.

Shores, David & Rachel Clanton, 10 April 1827; Joseph Steelmon, bm.

Shores, David & Sarah Canady, 10 Dec 1844; Martin Shores, bm.

Shores, Henry & Rebeckah Logan, 7 Dec 1813; George Shelton, bm.

Shores, John & Mary McGuire, 9 July 1814; John McGuire, bm.

Shores, John B. & Janett Johnson, 1 Oct 1830; John C. Hampton, bm.

Shores, John C. & Sarah Rose, 17 Aug 1844; Sterling Rose, bm.

Shores, Jonathan William & Fanny Philips, 23 Oct 1819; George Shelton, bm.

Shores, Lewis F. & Elizabeth W. Grigg, 1 Sept 1851; Henry Steele, bm.

Shores, Martin & Nansey Cunningham, 14 Nov 1835; Thomas J. Moore, bm.

Shores, Reuben & Lucinda Woodruff, 12 April 1833; Henry G. Hampton, bm.

Short, Newton P. & Ann E. Hines, 8 Nov 1867; Albert N. McGee, bm.

Shouse, Henry & Elizabeth Null, 17 Jan 1788; Daniel Shous, bm.

Shouse, Philip & Elitha Haymore, 31 Aug 1846; William Moore, bm.

Shouse, William A. & Mary Moore, 26 Dec 1866; m 2 Jan 1867 by M. A. Hall, J. P.

Showalter, Henry B. & Elizabeth Turpin, 25 Nov 1850; Robt S. Gilmer, bm. (C. H.).

Shropishire, Jeremiah & Dicy F. Lewis, 22 Feb 1858; Ellis F. Jarrell, bm.

Shugart, Eli & Jean Hardin, 5 May 1801; Thomas Harding, bm.

SURRY COUNTY MARRIAGES, 1779-1868

Shugart, Russell & Silva Williams, 5 Feb 1821; Jesse Atwood, bm.

Shugart, Thomas & Lyda Mackie, 28 Dec 1845; Edward J. Reece, bm.

Shugart, William & Ruth Bond, 20 Feb 1814; William Mackie, bm.

Shular, Andrew & Katarine Matilda Fulks, 3 Aug 1849; Thomas S. Fulks, bm.

Sigler, David & Margarett Beck, 4 Feb 1797; Sentleger Beck, bm.

Sigler, John & Agnus Wials, 8 July 1791; Lawrence Sigler, bm.

Sillivan, Benjamin & Elizabeth Marshall, 5 Nov 1815; Richard Sillivan, bm.

Simcock, Thomas & Narcissa Underwood, 19 Nov 1834; George Crissman, bm.

Simkins, Andrew J. & Amanda J. Wilson, 7 Feb 1853; Samuel Montgomery, bm.

Simmons, Alpha & Francis Bays, 31 Oct 1837; James Badgett, bm.

Simmons, Amer & Nancy Armstrong, 12 Sept 1846; Joseph Hollinsworth, bm.

Simmons, David J. & Elizabeth Adams, 21 March 1862; E. B. Simmons, bm; m 25 March 1862 by John Jones.

Simmons, Floyd, son of Vilet Floyd, and Mary Tucker, daughter of William and Sarah Tucker, 15 April 1868; m 15 April 1868 by J. A. Bingman, J. P.

Simmons, Franklin & Martha M. Ball, 21 Jan 1863; m 22 Jan 1863 by Nathan Nixon, Esqr.

Simmons, Gabriel J. & Mary E. Taylor, 30 July 1864; W. M. Cook, J. P.

Simmons, James, son of Mahaly & Eliza Banner, 4 Jan 1868; m by C. L. Banner, J. P.

Simmons, Joel & Tempie E. Harris, 19 April 1866; m 29 April 1866 by H. N. Wolfe, J. P.

Simmons, John & Betsey Hammons, 21 Jan 1811; William Unthank, bm.

Simmons, John A. & Mesia Harrison, 18 Jan 1848; Columbus Thompson, bm.

Simmons, Nathan & Michkey A. Taylor, 29 Aug 1863; William H. Taylor, bm.

Simmons, Peter & Nancy Armstrong, 11 Feb 1819; Eli Cook, bm.

Simmons, Preston & Sarah Q. Seal, 18 Oct 1866; m 22 Oct 1866 by M. A. Hall, J. P.

Simmons, Samuel & Margaret Cocklrece, 1 Sept 1847; John A. Simmons, bm.

Simmons, Thomas & Jemima Linville, 31 March 1862; Alfred Cook, bm; m 1 April 1862 by J. Gray, J. P.

SURRY COUNTY MARRIAGES, 1779-1868

Simmons, William & Polly Haymore, 28 Aug 1832; Allen Canter, bm.

Simmons, William & Maislanna Greenwood, 21 May 1839; Moses Tilly, bm.

Simms, Robert & Elisabeth Gentry, 9 June 1822; James Hicks, bm; (filed under Limms).

Simons, Charles, son of John & Elizabeth Simons, and Rebecca Hodges, daughter of Andrew and Delala Hodges, 24 March 1868; m 29 March 1868 by Thos. J. Lawson, M. G.

Simons, Iredell & Sealy Venable, 8 March 184-; Samuel Forkner, bm.

Simkins, Floyd & Sarah Sumpter, 10 June 1855; Amon Moore, bm; m 10 June 1855 by A. Simmons, J. P.

Simpson, C. F. & Lucinda Ann Sawyers, 22 Dec 1864; Alfred Adkins, bm; m 22 Dec 1864 by John Jones.

Simpson, Henry & Celia Simpson, 16 Nov 1855; Andrew J. Bobbitt, bm.

Simpson, Isum & Elizabeth Reed, 23 Dec 1849; John Nichols, bm.

Simpson, James & Elizabeth Copeland, 18 Jan 1845; John Sawyer, bm.

Simpson, John & Matilda Harris, 20 Nov 1845; John Nichols, bm.

Simpson, Joseph & Nancy Mills, 30 Dec 1865; Ice Snow, bm; m 31 Dec 1865 by R. F. McGuffin, J. P.

Simpson, Richard & Lockey Greenwood, 13 Dec 1849; Wm. Lewis, bm.

Simpson, Samuel Y., son of James & Elizabeth Simpson, & Cornelia Francis Key, daughter of Lewis A. & Elizabeth Key, m 1 Jan 1868 by John Jones.

Simpson, Tyre & Martha Nickals, 3 Feb 1853; William S. Key, bm; m 3 Feb 1853 by A. Dunnagan, J. P.

Sims, John & Franky Creed, 23 Oct 1814; Ransom Dudley, bm.

Sims, Randolph & Mary Bates, 26 July 1814; George Baits, bm.

Sims, William & Nancy Padgett, 14 March 1849; Henry Tucker, bm.

Sink, Stephen W. & Mandy M. Stone, 17 Oct 1846; Thomas D. Ashworth, bm.

Sisk, Allen & Betsey Edwards, 14 Nov 1809; Jesse Sisk, bm.

Sisk, Daniel & Rebekah Macalgen, 26 Oct 1803; Hew Macalgen, bm.

Sisk, Daniel & Betsey Johnson, 25 March 1816; Allen Sisk, bm.

Sisk, James & Nansey Manner, 23 Sept 1812; Thomas Hinshaw, Richard Allin, bm.

Sisk, James & Nancey Row, 1 Feb 1850; Aleson Jackson, bm.

Sisk, Jesse & Ferryby Harvill, 11 Aug 1797; Thomas Allen, bm.

185

Sisk, John & Polly Southard, 8 Jan 1819; Thomas Jacks, bm.

Sisk, Terrel & Elizabeth Collens, 14 Feb 1816; Etheldred Edwards, bm.

Sizemoore, Levi & Elizabeth Delph, 7 Aug 1848; Algias Dunnagan, bm.

Sizemore, Isham & Precilla Hamlin, 31 Jan 1820; Daniel Reece, bm.

Skidmore, Abraham & Katharine Burns, 8 March 1786; Henry Skidmore, bm.

Skows, William & Jean Fender, 30 June 1839; Hezekiah Smith, bm.

Slade, William & Nancey Franklin, 1 March 1821; James Stephens, bm.

Slater, William F. & Sarah J. Harsh, 12 Jan 1855; William H. Garnes, bm; m 12 Jan 1855 by A. Simmons, J. P.

Slaton, Wilcher & Elizabeth Linvill, 18 July 1854; Henry M. Freeman, bm; m 18 July 1854 by D. M. Cooper, J. P.

Slusher, George A. & Mary Mundy, 20 Dec 1865; m 20 Dec 1865 by Marlin Sparger, J. P.

Slusher, LaFayette & Louisa Ballinger, 7 Aug 1863; S. J. Slusher, bm; m 7 Aug 1863 by Wm. R. Bray, J. P.

Slusher, Solomon Jr. & Luiza Compton, 11 Sept 1852; William Mabry, bm; m 11 Sept 1852 by A. Simmons, J. P.

Slusher, William & Elly D. Long, 24 April 1837; John Pack, bm.

Samllwood, Jonathan & India Howard (no date); Stephen Ring, bm.

Smith, --- ph & Elizabeth West, 21 June 1791; John Harvey, security.

Smith, Albert & Lemina J. Adams, 29 Sept 1865; James A. Chilton, bm; m 1 Oct 1865 by G. A. Lowe, J. P.

Smith, Alexander & Nancy Sparks, 22 July 1796; Joseph Smith, bm.

Smith, Bartholomew & Polly Hodges, 29 Aug 1831; William Hodges, bm.

Smith, Bennet & Rebeckah Cotton, 3 Oct 1829; Michael Swain, bm.

Smith, Charles Jr. & Nancy Golden, 10 July 1826; William D. Smith, bm.

Smith, Conrod & Ruthey Marshell, 15 Oct 1826; James Smith, bm.

Smith, Drewry & Elizabeth Low, 18 March 1846; Gideon Barker, bm.

Smith, Durant & Elizabeth Keys, 11 Oct 1825; Hadly Rees, bm.

Smith, Easley & Patsey Low, 28 Dec 1836; B. Smith, J. K. Munchus, bm.

Smith, Fremon & Lucy Jane Dezern, 12 May 1849; Jn. H. Dobson, bm.

SURRY COUNTY MARRIAGES, 1779-1868

Smith, Garret & Hannah Whitaker, 5 Feb 1833; Thomas Stanly, bm.

Smith, George P., son of George & Sarah Smith, & Rebecca F. Sawyers, daughter of James and Elizabeth Sawyers, 21 Jan 1868, m by A. Simmons, J. P.

Smith, Henry & Elmina Whitaker, 24 Dec 1832; J. G. Pettit, bm.

Smith, Henry, son of Freeman and Sally Smith, & Frances Simpson, daughter of Isham & Elizabeth Simpson, 20 March 1868, m by Jessee Lewis, J. P.

Smith, Henry G. & Nancy E. Barker, 28 Dec 1865; m 31 Dec 1865 by Saml. Forkner, J. P.

Smith, J. W., son of Ewell & Massy Smith, & Jane Beamer, daughter of Reuben and Sarah Beamer, m 18 Oct 1868 by Martin H. Armfield, J. P.

Smith, Jackson, son of Samuel & Elizabeth Smith, and Louiza B. Freeman, daughter of Elisha & Mary Freeman, 8 Dec 1868; m by D. F. Poindexter, J. P.

Smith, Jacob & _____, 17 Aug 1798; Spenser Stevens, bm.

Smith, Jacob & Lydia Morefield, 22 March 1815; William Swaim, bm.

Smith, James M. & Dianer D. Hodges, 26 July 1860; m by Jno. J. McMickle, J. P.

Smith, James S. & Arnette Kimble, 9 July 1846; Greenville Willis, bm.

Smith, Jesse & Judith Lankester, 12 Aug 1786; John Lankester, bm.

Smith, John & Martha Colvard, 31 March 1793; Isham Young, bm.

Smith, John & Eliza. Speer, 9 Aug 1797; Elias Turner, bm.

Smith, John & Elizabeth Awberry, 7 Dec 1819; Catlet Smith, bm.

Smith, John & Siddy Dunnigan, 22 March 1836; Samuel Wall, bm.

Smith, John H. & Rachel Hunter, 4 Nov 1836; James C. Moore, bm; m 4 Nov 1856 by E. Banner, J. P.

Smith, John W. & Eliza Blakley, __ Oct 1866; R. E. Reeves, bm.

Smith, Jonathan & Elizabeth Marsh, 2 May 1856; Isaiah Whitaker, bm; m 11 May 1856 by John E. Stanly, J. P.

Smith, Joseph & Elizabeth West, 21 June 1791; John Harvey, bm.

Smith, Joseph & Leatha Boyd, 7 Oct 1852; William Boyd, bm; m 7 Oct 1852 by A. Simmons, J. P.

Smith, Laban & Milly Morris, 26 April 1828; John Davis, bm.

Smith, Levi & Celia Marsh, 18 Dec 1856; m 23 Dec 1856 by G. Bryan, J. P.

Smith, Lewis & Martha Booman, 1 Oct 1839; William Epperson, bm.

SURRY COUNTY MARRIAGES, 1779-1868

Smith, M. & Nancy Burcham, 26 Dec 1864; m 26 Dec 1864 by J. Love, J. P.

Smith, Moses & Sealy Low, 22 May 1851; Wiley Dickins, bm; m 22 May 1851 by W. M. Freeman, J. P.

Smith, Pleasant & Cynthia Ashley, 10 April 1833; Alexander Ballard, bm.

Smith, Robert & Anna Calvert, 18 Nov 1817; John Shore, bm.

Smith, Samuel & Ann Richardson, 11 June 1855; Bartholomew Smith, bm.

Smith, Thomas & Sarah Griffin, 21 Oct 1804; Robt. Hawkins, bm.

Smith, Tho. & Susan Tiler, 20 Aug 1837; Jacob Nickolson, bm.

Smith, Thomas & Sarah Jane Prather, 30 Aug 1853; James C. Norman, bm; m by Jesse Roberts.

Smith, William & _____, (no date); Wm. Mickle, bm.

Smith, William & Nancy Speer, 8 Oct 1800; Thomas Lanier, bm.

Smith, William & Elender Griffith, 18 Feb 1818; Evan Davis, bm.

Smith, William & Sarah Aran, 5 Oct 1820; Jesse McKinney, bm.

Smith, William & Nancy Auberry, 18 Feb 1834; William Galyar, bm.

Smith, William & Elizabeth E. Joyner, 2 Nov 1847; M. A. Vestal, bm.

Smith, William & Elvina Warden, 17 Jan 1867; Riley Warden, bm.

Smith, William H. & Parthenia McMillan, 30 Nov 1858; William Hendricks, bm.

Smith, William R. & Lucinda Vipperman, 29 June 1855; m 5 July 1855 by Wright Johnson, M. G.

Smith, Williamson & Leathy Moore, 25 Jan 1824; Galihew Moore, bm.

Smith, Wright & Lidia Brunt, 22 Dec 1818; David Smith, bm.

Smith, Wyett T. & Susanah Bean, 15 April 1848; Elisha Edwards, bm.

Smith, Zachariah & Rebekah Moore, 23 Nov 1813; Jacob Smith, bm.

Smith, Zion & Sarah E. Williamson, 28 Sept 1865; m 28 Sept 1865 by Joel Hurt, J. P.

Smithermon, Andrew & Lucinda Carr, 31 May 1819; William Garner, bm.

Smithers, Columbus & Sarah Landreth, 27 Sept 1856; Isaac Collins, bm; m 27 Sept 1856 by A. Simmons, J. P.

Smythers, Stephen & Jane Arnold, 19 Oct 1851; William Smythers, bm.

Sneed, Alexander & Tempy Safly, 15 Jan 1811; Gideon Flynn, bm.

SURRY COUNTY MARRIAGES, 1779-1868

Snoddy, J. H. & Frances Collins, 2 Aug 1865; m 2 Aug 1865 by G. A. Lowe, J. P.

Snoddy, John & Hannah Love, 5 Jan 1831; Archi Taylor bm.

Snody, Joel & Jemima Johnson, 28 Jan 1847; Isaac Norman, bm.

Snody, Samuel & Susanah Love, 16 Nov 1854; m 16 Nov 1854 by A. Dunnagan, J. P.

Snody, William A. & Anney Lambert, 26 March 1856; Wm. M. Hall, bm; m 27 March 1856 by Wm. Haymore, J. P.

Snow, A. L. & R. E. Jones, 23 Dec 1865; m 26 Dec 1865 by Jas. H. Lewellin, min.

Snow, Alfred & Mary Jenkins, 15 Oct 1844; Wm. Stepp, bm. (C.H.).

Snow, Benjamin & Tamer Freeman, married 10 Oct 1846; acknowledged before Lacy Snow, J. P., 9 Aug 1866. (C. H.).

Snow, Byrd & Mary B. Herring, 3 March 1859; Lewis Martin, bm.

Snow, Deep & Cerepta Wiley, 23 Dec 1850; Meridith T. Norman, bm. (C. H.).

Snow, Fielding & Jane E. Bodenhamer, 23 Aug 1854; Henry M. Freeman, bm; m 23 Aug 1854 by D. M. Cooper, J. P.

Snow, Fountain & Sarah Helen, 1 Dec 1823; Lot Wilmoth, bm.

Snow, Frost & Mary Golding, 10 Dec 1866; L. J. Norman, bm.

Snow, Henry, son of Thomas Snow, & Lizzie m. Axsom, daughter of Jos. & Mary Axsom, 31 aug 1868; m 8 Sept 1868 by F. H. Jones, M. G.

Snow, James & Alley Cove, 20 Dec 1820; Frost Snow, bm.

Snow, James & Polly Walker, 10 May 1834; James Mankins, bm.

Snow, James & Elizabeth Holensworth, 18 Aug 1844; Ice Snow, bm.

Snow, James M. & America Davis, 23 Sept 1865; m 27 Sept 1865 by T. J. Lawson, M. G.

Snow, James S. & Matildah Snow, 23 Feb 1846; William H. Tucker, bm.

Snow, James S. & Mary Cockerham, 11 Aug 1859; Stephen Venable, bm.

Snow, John & Franky Easley, 10 Dec 1812; Woodson Easley, bm.

Snow, John & Elizabeth Golding, 3 Dec 1832; P. Venable, bm.

Snow, John & Sarah Beamer, 6 May 1835; Joseph Forkner, bm.

Snow, John & Margaret Snow, 20 Dec 1860; T. V. Hamlin, bm; m 20 Dec 1860 by D. M. Cooper, J. P.

Snow, John & Sarah Lowe, 12 Feb 1867; Thomas M. Snow, bm; m 26 Feb 1867 by James A. Calley, J. P.

Snow, Johnson & Mary M'Colum, 20 Feb 1844; Calvin Johnson, bm.

SURRY COUNTY MARRIAGES, 1779-1868

Snow, Lafayette & Nancy Pope, 4 Oct 1854; William McMillon, bm; m 4 Oct 1854 by A. Simmons, J. P.

Snow, Larkin C. & Mary Ann Gregory, 28 April 1863; Jas. S. Pedigo, bm; m 28 April 1863 by A. Dunnagan, J. P.

Snow, M. W. & Eliza Ann Cordell, 24 Dec 1860; Jesse Thompson, bm.

Snow, Michael & Matilda Spencer, 22 Dec 1852; m 26 Dec 1852 by Martin Payne, J. P.

Snow, Revel & Cloah Willmorth, 7 April 1818; Richard Wright, bm.

Snow, Richard & An Payn, 19 Aug 1858; m 19 Aug by B. F. Scott, J. P.

Snow, Ruel & Frances Golding, 28 Dec 1835; William C. Snow, bm.

Snow, Saml. & Sarah Fletcher, 17 March 1805; Frostin Snow, bm.

Snow, Samuel & Emily Gwyn, 26 Dec 1866; Samuel D. Critz, bm; m 27 Dec 1866 by J. T. Johnson, J. P.

Snow, Simpson W. & Matilda Coe, 7 Nov 1849; John H. Dobson, bm.

Snow, Terrel B. & Caroline Moseley, 8 June 1844; Lewis W. Bray, bm.

Snow, Thomas & Betsey Wilmoth, 21 Jan 1812; James Tucker, bm.

Snow, Thomas J. & R. W. Jones, 23 Feb 1866; Richard Wilmoth, bm.

Snow, Thomas T. & Elizabeth Gates, 27 Jan 1846; Tyson S. Wilmoth, bm.

Snow, William & Salley Tucker, 12 April 1808; James Tucker, bm.

Snow, William & Rebekah Masters, 6 Jan 1818; Thomas Snow, bm.

Snow, William & Sarah Christian, 24 Oct 1827; Miller Easley, bm.

Snow, William & Rebecca Mays, 29 Aug 1856; Godfrey Isaacs, bm.

Snow, William C. & Martha Bowles, 17 Aug 1836; Hanan Bray, bm.

Snow, William M. & Nancy Gates, 23 Jan 1845; James S. Snow, bm.

Snow, Zeachel & Sarah Thompson, 28 Nov 1866; m 29 Nov 1866 by Wm. Y. Tucker, J. P.

Solomon, John & Lucy Pritchett, 7 Nov 1818; Laveter J. Solomon, bm.

Somers, Watemon & Charity Franklin, 9 Jan 1834; Wm. G. Haynes, bm.

Somonas, Willson & Mary E. Beamer, 12 July 1857; m 12 July 1857 by B. F. Scott, J. P.

Songer, Francis M. & Susannah Loucks, 9 Sept 1852; W. F. Lucado, bm; m 9 Sept 1852 by A. Simmons, J. P.

Sopsher, Jeremiah & Dicy B. Lewis, 22 Feb 1858.

SURRY COUNTY MARRIAGES, 1779-1868

South, James H. & Jane Varnum, 16 Feb 1854; Samuel South, bm; m 18 Feb 1854 by John Ramey, J. P.

South, Jesse C. & Elizabeth Hodges, 15 Sept 1846; Samuel Smith, bm.

South, John Riley & Catherine Davis, 11 June 1865; Creed South, bm; m 11 June 1865 by Jack Lowe.

Southard, John M. & Phebe Baugass, 18 April 1836; John H. Dobson, bm.

Southard, Levi W. & Kiziah Reece, 25 Sept 1838; Martin P. Southard, bm.

Southard, Martin & Elizabeth Southard, 5 March 1807; Henry Southard, bm.

Southard, Martin & Ruth E. Ball, m 22 Feb 1852 by Robert Wilbourn, M. G.

Southard, Micajah & Polly Wallace, 8 Jan 1811; Henry Davis, bm.

Southard, Umberson & Mary Catharine Ball, 1 Sept 1858; Martin Southard, bm.

Southerd, Levi & Sarah L. Isaacks, 2 Sept 1851; William Southerd, bm; m 11 Nov 1851 by David R. Cockerham, J. P.

Southerland, Dillard & Melley Ann Parker, 20 Feb 1862; T. F. Prather, bm; m 20 Feb 1862 by A. Dunnagan, J. P.

Sowder, Adam & Liona Harless, 3 Feb 1851; Michael Poff, bm.

Soyars, Joseph & Nancy Jane McGuffin, 2 July 1860; J. E. Reeves, bm.

Spain, Berry & Betsey Matthews, 21 May 1808; William Tull, bm.

Spain, William & Perthenea Ann Potts, 4 May 1835; Absolom Mathews, bm.

Spainhour, Isaac & Nancy Scott, 22 Dec 1853; E. F. Lovill, bm.

Spainhower, Emanuel & Basheba Jane Brown, 30 Oct 1845; Benjamin Cullar, bm.

Spainhower, Jeremiah & Lucinda Venable, _____ 1833; William P. Tucker, bm.

Spainhower, John V., son of John W. & Lidia M. Spainhower, & Charlotte L. Crouse, daughter of Henry & Henrietta Crouse, 10 Feb 1868; m 14 Feb 1868 by Joel Denny, J. P.

Sparger, Henry & Mary A. Cook, 2 Dec 1846; J. A. Bingman, bm.

Sparger, James & Mary Francis Page, 22 March 1846; Joseph Hollinsworth, bm.

Sparger, John & Nancy Jane Cook, 10 Jan 1854; B. W. Mathas, bm; m 10 Jan 1854 by Wm. Haymore, J. P.

Sparger, Mullin & Betheany Cook, 6 Dec 1838; Tho. B. Wright, bm.

SURRY COUNTY MARRIAGES, 1779-1868

Sparger, Wm. A. & Mary E. Fulton, 23 Dec 1867; James C. Gilmer, bm.

Sparger, William S. & Sarah M. Witcher, 18 Dec 1854; Daniel Haymore, bm; m 19 Dec 1854 by R. Marshall, J. P.

Spargur, Henry W. & Susanna Roberts, 25 Oct 1816; William McCraw, bm.

Spargur, John & _____, ____ 1818; Eli Cook, bm.

Spargur, William & Nancy Bryson, 6 July 1817; John Bryson, bm.

Sparkes, James & Letha Ann Bryan, 29 Oct 1846; Francis Wood, bm.

Sparkes, Joseph & Martha Edwards, 28 Jan 1815; Richard Gentrey, bm.

Sparkes, William & Elizabeth Gentry, 4 Jan 1813; Wiley Craft, bm.

Sparks, Athanasious & Sally Brinigan, 12 April 1857; Moses Austill, bm.

Sparks, Benjamin & Eliza. Hicks, 18 Jan 1797; John Allen, bm.

Sparks, George & Fany Lindsey, 1 Dec 1829; Charles Johnson Jr., bm.

Sparks, Jonathan & Rachel Swain, 26 Nov 1817; William Sparks, bm.

Sparks, Mathew & Sarah Elmore, 20 Feb 1808; Wm. West, bm.

Sparks, Thomas & Cathorine Swaime, 28 Feb 1837; William Z. Sparkes, bm.

Sparks, William & Lethey Speer, 1 Aug 1816; Thomas Arnold, bm.

Sparks, William & Mary Benge, 5 Sept 1844; George Sparks, bm.

Speer, Andrew & Elizabeth Murphy, 29 July 1788; Richd. Speer, bm.

Speer, Drury & Betsey Flyn, 2 Aug 1808; John Stewart, bm.

Speer, Elisha & Peggy Potts, 14 March 1851; Lewis Phillips, bm.

Speer, Jacob & Tempe Pruit, 26 Dec 1803; Abraham Pruit, bm.

Speer, James J. & Elizabeth Hadley, 25 Sept 1820; Isaac Callaway, bm.

Speer, John & Elizabeth Steelmon, 12 Oct 1784; Matthias Steelmon, bm.

Speer, John & Mary Sprinkel, 26 Oct 1801; Jonathan Sprinkle, bm.

Speer, John & Elizabeth Aldridge, 9 Oct 1820; John Bridgman, bm.

Speer, Leavan & Mary Martin, 27 April 1802; William Chanler, bm.

SURRY COUNTY MARRIAGES, 1779-1868

Speer, Levi & Sarah Dixon, 18 Nov 1815; Isaac Brewbaker, bm.

Speer, Levi & Elizabeth Pettitt, 8 March 1819; Absalom Mathews, bm.

Speer, Richard & Ruth Richards, 19 Dec 1785; Leonard Richards, bm.

Speer, Robert, son of Thomas Speer, & Polly Fair, 3 May 1818; Peter Cook Jr., bm.

Speer, Robert Jr. & Caroline M. Gwyn, 20 May 1857; Mitchel B. Tate, bm; m 20 May 1857 by Jesse Roberts, M. G.

Speer, Samuel & Ruth Eddlemon, 16 Sept 1812; Hugh Logan, bm.

Speer, Samuel & Nancy Speer, 6 Dec 1848.

Speer, Thomas & Beaney Burke, 22 March 1832; Benjamin Mathis, bm.

Speers, George & Charlot Ingram, 9 July 1795; John Speer, bm.

Spelmon, John & Reacael Eddlemon, 1 July 1809; Thornton Dowling, Samuel Speer, bm.

Spence, Lewis & Frances Brim, 11 June 1833; Robert Lowe, bm.

Spence, Uriah & Sarah Monday, 26 Feb 1857; m 26 Feb 1857 by Jesse Roberts, M. G.

Spence, Wiley & Elizabeth McKie, 12 Dec 1837; George Reynolds, bm.

Spence, William & Hannah Morris, 24 Dec 1792; David Spence, bm.

Spencer, Hiram & Nancy Dobbins, 28 Dec 1833; Daniel Dobbins, bm.

Spencer, James & Sarah Martin, 19 Nov 1807; Benj. H. Martin, bm.

Spencer, James & Mary Ann Stewart, 20 March 1845; Richard Hawks, bm.

Spencer, John & Sally Andrew, 14 Dec 1821; James Spencer, bm.

Spencer, John & Martha Gray, 22 Aug 1827; James Spencer, bm.

Spencer, Sion & Keziah York, 21 Dec 1826; James Callaway, bm. (C. H.).

Spencer, Uel & Suffiah Stockner, 18 June 1846; Richard Hawks, bm.

Spencer, William & Susanah Deen, 12 Dec 1833; Dickerson Taleaferro, bm.

Spencer, William Jr. & Nancy Thomason, 13 May 1817; William Spencer Sr., bm.

Spencer, William D. & Mahala Ann Hall, 22 Aug 1849; Abner Davis, bm.

SURRY COUNTY MARRIAGES, 1779-1868

Spencer, William H. & Eunice Reece, 24 Oct 1826; Winston Somers, bm.

Spencer, William H. & Sarah Davis, 5 Aug 1847; William R. Davis, bm.

Spicer, J. B. & Letty Bryant, 10 Feb 1862; C. H. Kapp, bm; m 13 Feb 1862 by G. A. McCraw, J. P.

Spiers, William & Ruth Philips, 9 Dec 1793; Alexander Lynn, bm.

Spiers, William & Sarah Petree, 24 Aug 1797; Adam Boyer, John Spiris, bm.

Spilman, Samuel & Aley Hutchins, 13 Jan 1824; Elkanah Hutchins, Michael Warden, bm.

Spilmon, Lovill M. & Sarah Dinkins, 19 Dec 1820; James Pilcher, bm.

Spray, William & Sucky Godfrey, 20 Oct 1807; Thos. Pardue, bm.

Sprinkel, Henderson & Elizabeth Whiticeker, 25 Nov 1845; William Whiticker, bm.

Sprinkel, Jonathan & Fanny Clanton, 28 Nov 1810; Samuel Sprinkel, bm.

Sprinkel, Joseph & Polly Carter, 14 March 1830; Hiram Phillips, bm.

Sprinkel, Moses & Mary Clanton, 19 Dec 1798; James McCallom, bm.

Sprinkel, Samuel & Ruth Norman, 18 Dec 1807; John Binkley, bm.

Sprinkle, A. J., son of James and Nancy Sprinkle, & Rebecca Mosley, daughter of Henry and Martha Mosley, m 26 Dec 1868 by D. F. Poindexter, J. P.

Sprinkle, George & Elizabeth Scott, 30 Sept 1828; Henry Scott, bm.

Sprinkle, Michael & Peggy Pendry, 9 July 1836; Ellis Sprinkle, bm.

Sprinkle, Peter & Ann Matucks, 10 Feb 1805; Benj. P. Garner, bm.

Sprinkle, Tho. A. & Martha Jane Moore, 7 April 1860; Thomas Moore, Jr., bm; m 12 April 1860 by D. M. Cooper, J. P.

Sprinkle, William & Elizabeth Hoppers, 24 Aug 1827; James Hudspeth, bm.

Sprouse, Robert & Elisebeth Dozier, 13 Dec 1845; John J. Woodroof, bm.

Stafford, William H. & Sarah A. Burtin, 11 May 1847; Settle T. Allred, bm.

Stale, Robert & Milly Johnson, 10 March 1832; J. Armstrong, bm.

Stallings, Henry & Keziah Bond, 2 Nov 1849; William Bond, bm.

Stamper, Asa & Betsey Fender, 5 July 1821; Joshua Jones, bm.

SURRY COUNTY MARRIAGES, 1779-1868

Stamper, Dilyerd & Margarett Ross, 20 Sept 1823; Henry Waddle, bm. (C. H.).

Standfield, James & Nancy Turner, 20 Feb 1806; Thomas Standfield, bm.

Standfield, Mason & Elizabeth Kidd, 27 Apr 1806; James Stanfield, bm.

Standley, Garrotte & Jemima Smith, 23 Jan 1827; William Standley, bm.

Standley, John & Sally Butcher, 30 Oct 1825; Jesse Stanley, bm.

Stanfield, Samuel & Catharine Gross, 14 April 1796; Thomas Stanfield, Henry Shore, bm.

Stanfield, Thomas & Elizabeth Michaels, 28 Aug 1791; John McCollum, bm.

Stanfield, William A. & Nancy Purkins, 11 Feb 1867; R. E. Wright, bm; m 11 Feb 1867 by J. H. Nation, J. P.

Stanley, Elijah & Rachel Hutchens, 20 Dec 1822; Peter Mills, bm.

Stanley, John Hutchins & Ann Hoppis, 13 July 1795; Jesse Stanley, bm.

Stanley, Jona. & Seney Holder, 5 March 1833; William Moore, bm.

Stanley, Thomas & Lucinda Pare, 5 Feb 1814; John Thomason, bm.

Stanley, William & Margarett Hutchens, 26 Oct 1810; Joseph Hutchens, bm.

Stanly, Alfred & Lucy Wilmoth, 19 Nov 1836; Jesse Stanly, bm.

Stanly, Henry & Suentha Butcher, 19 Feb 1851; William Bowles, bm.

Stanly, Henry & Cathorine R. Rutledge, 6 Sept 1856; Thomas Steele, bm; m 7 Sept 1856 by H. M. Waugh, J. P.

Stanly, Hiram & Sally Stanly, 19 June 1836; John C. Stanly, bm.

Stanly, Hiram & Adaline Coe, 10 Oct 1856; T. V. Hamlin, bm; m 16 Oct 1856 by M. Y. Folgar, J. P.

Stanly, Jesse & Sally Wilmoth, 11 Feb 1837; John E. Stanly, bm.

Stanly, Jesse Smith & Francis White, 13 Jan 1851; Jno. E. Stanley, bm.

Stanly, Lemuel J. & Elizabeth Hardy, 26 March 1846; Chatwell V. Butcher, bm.

Stanly, Nathan A. & Nancy Jenkins, 22 Dec 1851; Lemuel J. Stanly, bm; m 23 Dec 1851 by A. H. Dobson, J. P.

Stanly, William & Nancy Kyle, 17 Feb 1824; John Bowles, bm.

Stanliff, John & Suzanah Hawks, 15 March 1845; Andrew Hawks, bm.

Star, Jasper & Alse Watkins, 18 Oct 1796; Thomas Watkins, bm.

Starbuck, John & Beely Garrett, 3 March 1811; William Unthank, bm.

Starling, J. W. A. & Sarah Axsom, 28 Nov 1866; J. M. Starling, bm.

Starling, John W. & Marry Odur, 16 Oct 1827; William G. Haynes, bm.

Starr, Adam & Keziah Watkins, 11 March 1802; Thomas McAtee, Thomas Watkins, bm.

Stealman, James & Mary Howell, 10 Sept 1792; Stephen Howel, bm.

Steel, Doctor Franklin & Prudence Nicholson, 12 Jan 1848; John J. Angel, bm.

Steel, John & Elizabeth Pettitt, 12 Aug 1823; Elijah Thompson, bm.

Steel, Thomas & Mary Stone, 14 Nov 1806; Josiah Vanderpool, bm.

Steel, Thomas & Sally Southard, 29 July 1837; James Wright, bm.

Steelman, Charles & Nancy Hoppos, 28 July 1807; Joel Rutledge, bm.

Steelman, Charles & Sally McNight, 26 Feb 1829; James West, bm.

Steelman, Charles & Jane Danner, 1 Jan 1845; Saml. Hammons, bm.

Steelman, George & Anna Dixon, 19 July 1824; Silas Vestal, bm.

Steelman, Joseph & Mary Creson, 30 Nov 1816; Charles Creson, bm.

Steelman, Joseph & Ruth Steelman, 16 Aug 1838; Jesse MacKie, bm.

Steelman, Samuel & Ann B. Williamson, 4 March 1832; Samuel Connor, bm.

Steelmon, Charles & Mary Herrold, 25 Jan 1797; William Cain, bm.

Steelmon, George & Rebecker Foot, 19 March 1805; John Rutledge, bm.

Steelmon, James & Mary Reavis, 2 July 1817; Assa Reavis, bm.

Steelmon, James & Choley Ashby, 20 Aug 1819; George Steelmon, John Steelmon, bm.

Steelmon, James & Caty Rennegar, 9 Oct 1828; Charles Steelmon, Edward Milstead, bm.

Steelmon, John & Hannah Gough, 30 March 1812; Abraham Cunningham, bm.

Stephens, Bird & Polly Parker, 21 Nov 1829; Thos. Kelly, bm.

Stephens, James & Elizabeth Skidmore, 3 Nov 1785; Henry Speer, bm.

Stephens, James & Betsy Pike, 17 Aug 1825; John Dickson, bm.

SURRY COUNTY MARRIAGES, 1779-1868

Stephens, John & Hannah Kays, 25 July 1831; Samuel Barnee, bm.

Stephenson, R. T. N. & Mary F. Burns, __ Oct 1866; R. E. Reeves, bm.

Stevens, William & Margaret Speer, 10 July 1790; Shadrack Speer, bm.

Steveness, John & Rutha Franklin, 11 Dec 1821; John McDade, Marmaduke Kimbrough, bm.

Stewart, Isaiah & Elizabeth Petit, 19 Nov 1810; John Cor Jr., bm.

Stewart, Jacob & Nancy Soyers, colored, 23 Feb 1856; m 23 Feb 1856 by Elisha Banner, J. P.

Stewart, John & Hollon Head, 9 April 1804; Frances Lakey, bm.

Stewart, William & Sally Hill, 23 Feb 1827; Thomas Beverus, bm.

Stewart, William & Katharine Logan, 9 June 1849; John Logan, bm.

Stewart, William A. & Nancy S. Williams, 28 Jan 1834; Zachariah Pettet, bm.

Stinson, Aaron & Mary Shelton, 21 Aug 1797; Joshua Stinson, bm.

Stinson, Aaron & Jemmima Coe, 11 Feb 1826; William C. Bird, bm.

Stinson, Mosses & Lizebeth Masters, 26 July 1797; James Mathews, bm.

Stockton, William P. & Sarah Eaton, 7 April 1818; Marmaduke Kimbrough, bm.

Stoe, John & Rachel Upthegrove, 28 March 1808; Jessee Horn, bm.

Stoefer, Daniel E. & R. C. Fultz, 11 Feb 1864; m 11 Feb 1864 by B. F. Scott, J. P.

Stoker, John & Amelia Anthony, 25 Marcy 1826; Moses Austill, bm. (C. H.).

Stokes, Abednego & Mary Felts, 16 April 1836; Josiah Cowles, bm.

Stokes, Charles & Mary Henshaw, 18 Dec 1830; Edmond Parker, bm.

Stokes, Jarman & Luesy Parker, 9 Dec 1830; Charles Stokes, bm.

Stokes, Richard & Elizabeth Jackson, 9 Dec 1829; J. Breenen, bm.

Stokes, Wm. & Indiana Holcomb, 19 Oct 1833; Wm. R. Sparks, bm.

Strother, John B. & M. M. T. Tiffney, 16 Aug 1848; W. E. Kerkbride, bm.

Stuart, Isaac B. & Eliza A. Harold, 12 Jan 1860; m 12 Jan 1860 by B. F. Scott, J. P.

Steward, Shaderick & Polly Payne, 1 Jan 1833; Thomas Payne, bm.

Stuart, Wilks & Betsy Hill, black woman, 28 June 1815; Michael Hill, bm.

Stuart, William & Lucy Volentine, colored, m 21 Feb 1861 by C. L. Banner, J. P.

Stubblefield, Stephen & Elizabeth Phillips, 3 Sept 1789; William Holliman, bm.

Studivant, James & Fempy Haynes, 17 Dec 1844; Isaac Laseter, bm. (C. H.).

Stuerd, William & Areter Bovender, 7 July 1850; John J. Martin, bm. (C. H.).

Stultz, Daniel & Nancy Hutson, 9 May 1808; Peter Binkly, bm.

Stultz, George & Hannah Forkum, 7 Sept 1815; Peter Forkum Jr., bm.

Stultz, Henry & Sarah Nichols, _____ 179-; Chasper Stuls, bm.

Stultz, Jacob & Polly Hudson, 22 Dec 1812; William Griffith, bm.

Stultz, Nathaniel & Miss Eliza York, 26 March 1857; Philip McCarter, bm.

Stutes, Amon & Agnes Pendleton, 15 Aug 1846; Richard Hines, bm.

Sugert, Enos & Caroline Davis, 2 Jan 1831; John Davis, bm. (filed under Lugert).

Sult, Francis & Elizabeth Wirick (Mirick?), 29 Nov 1832; William Grubb, bm.

Sumers, Watiman & Winney Durham, 8 March 1811; Nathan Pigg, bm.

Summers, Johnson & Sarah London, 29 June 1788; Mannering Summers, bm.

Summers, Mannering & Sarah McCollum, 22 Nov 1788; Thomas McCollom, bm.

Summers, Thomas & Jane McCollum, 24 April 1791; Mannering Summers, bm.

Sumner, Absalom & Prisila Jackson, 9 Aug 1811; Jacob Carson, bm.

Sumner, Isaac & Jane Hanks, 21 March 1847; Lewis Stoneman, bm.

Surrat, Joseph M. & Elizabeth Slater, 27 Aug 1828; Hampton Hudson, bm.

Surrat, Wiley & Hannah Coltrane, 23 Nov 1829; James Spencer, bm.

Surratt, John T. & Nancy Combs, 27 Feb 1830; Wm. Carter Jr., bm.

Surratt, Vinson & Tempy McMillan, 29 March 1838; Joseph McMillan, bm.

Surrence(?), Franklin & Polly Davis, 8 Sept 1836; Mosses Wooten, bm. (C. H.).

Sutfin, Burge & Rebecca Keeth, 7 June 1846; John C. Keeth, bm.

Sutfin, John & Sarah Smith, 18 Sept 1859; Elijah Sutphin, bm; m 18 Sept 1859 by E. Banner, J. P.

Sutphin, Asa & Vinette Goard, 25 May 1863; William Suthpin, bm; m 25 May 1863 by A. Simmons, J. P.

Sutphin, Henderick & Elizabeth Thompson, 1 Nov 1846; Thomas Sutfin, bm.

Sutphin, John H. & Lenina Mabery, 19 Nov 1859; Samuel L. Gilmer, bm.

Sutphin, Wiley & Jane Nester, 1 May 1844; James Nester, bm.

Sutphin, William & Virginia S. Quisinbury, 3 Sept 1855; Elijah Sutphin, bm; m 3 Sept 1855 by A. Simmons, J. P.

Sutphin, William O. & Martha J. Atkins, 26 June 1864; Samuel Atkins, bm; m 7 July 1864 by M. A. Hall, J. P.

Swaim, Abraham & Mary Vestell, 26 April 1818; Shaerrel Chappell, bm.

Swaim, John & Mary Adams, 8 Dec 1822; Sherill Chappal, bm.

Swaim, Jonathan & Sarah Ann Collins, 5 Feb 1850; Simon Adams, bm. (C. H.).

Swaim, Michael & Elizabeth McGuire, 26 April 1828; John Swaim, bm.

Swaim, Michael & Mary Carlton, 1 July 1850; William Carlton, bm.

Swaim, Solomon D. & Sarah Waggoner, 14 Aug 1828; James Armstrong, bm.

Swan, Robert & Elizabeth Brindle (no date); Daniel Adams, bm.

Sweat, Edward & Rhoda Carter, 20 Dec 1795; Elias Turner, bm.

Sweat, George & Elizabeth Moreland, 23 May 1806; William Sweat, bm.

Swift, J. W. & Sally Norman, 19 Aug 1867; m 21 Aug 1867 by A. H. Kapp, J. P.

Swinney, Harden & Winney Vancyk, 20 April 1837; John Rinchet, bm.

Swinney, William & Milley Griffin, 1 Feb 1875; Stephen Green bm.

Swinny, Edmond & Sarah Willard, 27 June 1807; John D. Bruce, bm.

Tague, Henry & Patsy Buey, 26 July 1807; Jesse Sterdant, bm.

Talbert, James & Mary Mathews, 18 Feb 1851; John Huchens, bm.

SURRY COUNTY MARRIAGES, 1779-1868

Talbert, Levi & Sintha Calvard, 21 Jan 1829; Ambrose T. Chappell, bm.

Talburt, James & Elizabeth Howard, 21 Nov 1817; Elisha Chappell, bm.

Taliaferro, Charles & Jane Whittrek, 27 Feb 1822; Jona. Unthank, bm. (C. H.).

Talliaferro, Benjamin & Adra Snow, 4 June 1791; David Humphreys, bm.

Talliaferro, Benjamin & Lucy Harris, 28 Nov 1825; Jesse Copeland, bm.

Tally, Daniel & Celia Lewis, 10 July 1830; John Seagrove, bm.

Tanner, Jacob & Sarah Smith, 30 May 1821; Morgan Hudspeth, bm.

Tansey, Eli & Edith Hiatt, 1 Sept 1814; Thomas Beales, bm.

Tate, Alexander & Milla Ryans, 8 Dec 1826; Pleasant Venable, bm.

Tate, Francis & Salley Davies, 4 April 1837; Thomas Davis, bm.

Tate, James & Susannah Pennion, 8 Oct 1823; Joshua Parker, bm.

Tate, James & Rebecca Wilmouth, 3 July 1845; John R. Burrus, bm.

Tate, James & Sarah E. Baker, 18 June 1867; J. W. Cummins, bm; m 20 June 1867 by A. Whitaker, J. P.

Tate, James & Eliza Wilson, 10 March 1869; Edmond Nichols, bm.

Tate, John & Tilda Glenn, 1 March 1825; David Owen, bm.

Tate, Mitchell B. & Amelia Gwynn, 8 Sept 1852; John H. Stuart, bm.

Tate, Uriah & Lucinda J. Jones, 6 Oct 1853; James W. Fulk, bm; m 6 Oct 1853 by A. Simmons, J. P.

Tayer, Jacob Jr. & Matilda Ann Tayer, 26 Feb 1854; m 26 Feb 1854 by D. R. Cockerham, J. P.

Tayler, Edmond M. & Nancy Danily, 13 Feb 1859; Charles Poor, bm.

Tayler, Lewis & Priscilla F. Cook, 3 Dec 1862; m 7 Dec 1862 by C. Thompson, J. P.

Taylor, Anderson & Susan Pitman, 13 Dec 1834; James Taylor, bm.

Taylor, Archibald & Lucinda Owen, 4 April 1831; Thomas Lambert, bm.

Taylor, Benjamin Jr. & Nancy Canter, 24 March 1827; William Matthews, bm.

Taylor, Daniel & Rebeca Taylor, 17 Oct 1849; Jacob James, bm.

Taylor, Edmon & Tempy Haymour, 31 March 1819; Jacob Riner, bm.

Taylor, Evan & Jarmele Scott, 27 Feb 1867; n 31 March 1867 by Elisha Banner, J. P.

SURRY COUNTY MARRIAGES, 1779-1868

Taylor, Henry G. & E. F. Taylor, 17 June 1867; m 23 June 1867 by M. A. Hall, J. P.

Taylor, Hugh & Lucinda Deathridge, 23 Dec 1830; Robert A. Canter, bm.

Taylor, James & Susanna Speer, 30 Dec 1821; Joshua Bridgeman, bm.

Taylor, James & Lucinda Denton, 26 Dec 1822; Welcom Garrett, bm.

Taylor, James & Nancy Hyett, 13 Nov 1830; B. D. Gardner, bm.

Taylor, James J. & Nannie Thompson, 30 June 1866; m 1 July 1866 by William Rawley.

Taylor, James Smith & Susanna Fleming, 30 Dec 1818; Jesse Flemons, bm.

Taylor, John J. & P. S. Spainhour, 24 Sept 1867; Richard M. Taylor, bm; m 24 Oct 1867 by Miles Foy.

Taylor, Jonathan & _____, 4 Feb 1826; Archi Taylor, bm.

Taylor, Lewis C. & Nancy J. Jessup, 3 June 1867; m 9 June 1867 by M. A. Hall, J. P.

Taylor, Luke & Mary Ann Taylor, 8 Aug 1799; David Poindexter, bm.

Taylor, Mark & Susanna Matthews, 10 Nov 1813; Littleberry Spain, bm.

Taylor, Mark & Fanny Trulove, 14 Dec 1850; Wm. Martin, bm. (C. H.).

Taylor, Matthew Jr. & Frances Martin, 14 July 1816; Mark Taylor, bm.

Taylor, Starling & Elizabeth Taylor, 21 Aug 1819; John Taylor, bm.

Taylor, Thomas & Sarah Taylor, 26 April 1830; Stirlin Taylor, bm.

Taylor, Thomas & Polly Donelly, 9 Nov 1835; J. Anderson Taylor, bm.

Taylor, Turner R. & Jane Sparger, 24 Feb 1848; Henderson Cook, bm.

Taylor, William B. & Christena Deatherage, 10 March 1835; Joseph M Richardson, bm.

Taylor, William H. & Martha J. Taylor, 26 Jan 1854; m 26 Jan 1854 by Elisha Banner, J. P.

Taylor, William H. & Hannah Shelton, 11 Sept 1854; John Shelton, bm; m 11 Sept 1854 by William Haymore, J. P.

Taylor, William J. & Susan Surface, 19 June 1855; Thomas G. Hardwick, bm; m 19 June 1855 by A. Simmons, J. P.

Tearney, Gilbert & Mary Dean, 9 May 1829; James Spencer, bm.

SURRY COUNTY MARRIAGES, 1779-1868

Templeton, Thomas & Mary Wigfield, 23 June 1792; Isam Welch, bm.

Terrell, Julius & Ruth Flemming, 25 May 1849; Ruel Jackson, bm.

Terry, William & Rawsey E. Chapell, 1 April 1862; Albert A. Eaton, bm; m 3 April 1862 by Wm. R. Bray, J. P.

Tharp, John & Keron Forkner, 25 Jan 1827; John Gwyn, bm.

Tharp, Joseph & Frances Chamberlin, 11 Sept 1836; John Beaty, bm.

Thomas, Henry & Susan E. Krouse, 20 Dec 1832; B. D. Gardner, bm.

Thomas, Henry & Elizabeth Combs, 3 June 1852; William A. Edwards, bm.

Thomas, John & Nancy Johnson, 14 April 1823; Jesse Johnson, bm.

Thomas, John & Phebe Combs, 19 Feb 1852; Thomas Combs, bm.

Thomas, Levi & Jane Gwyn, 27 Nov 1856; John Thomas, bm; m 27 Nov 1856 by A. Simmons, J. P.

Thomas, Robert & Mary Ayres, 27 Dec 1849; William Edwards, bm.

Thomason, David & Lettice Welmoth, 25 Feb 1808; William Hamlin, bm.

Thomason, George W. & Nancy Spencer, 11 April 1812; Joseph Spencer, bm.

Thompson, Aaron & Sarah Ann Thompson, 12 Jan 1864; William P. Nixon, bm; m 14 Jan 1864 by Wm. J. Combs, M. G.

Thompson, Andrew G. & Sarah M. Hicks, 14 Aug 1849; Allgias Dunnagen, bm.

Thompson, Calvin & Jane Marshall, 2 April 1832; Joseph Cockerham, bm.

Thompson, Charles T. & Mary A. Alltiser, 6 Jan 1853; Edmonson Alltiser, bm.

Thompson, Columbus & Mary A. Cockrum, 20 July 1853; John P. Marsh, bm.

Thompson, Elihu J. & Frances Edwards, 6 Jan 1854; Cicero Williams, bm; m by John C. Thompson.

Thompson, Elijah & Rebecah Hodges, 2 Nov 1851; Calvin Gentry, bm; m 13 Nov 1851 by John Ramey, J. P.

Thompson, Ezekiel, son of Ben Roberts and Hannah Tucker, & Emily Kennidy, daughter of Ben Thompson and Nannie Snow, 18 Jan 1868, m 30 Jan 1868 by Wm. Y. Tucker, J. P.

Thompson, Frederick & Nancy Cocker, 24 Dec 1784; William Allen, bm.

Thompson, Greenville & Margaret A. Aust, 19 Sept 1853; Thomas J. Jennings, bm; m 19 Sept by A. Simmons, J. P.

SURRY COUNTY MARRIAGES, 1779-1868

Thompson, Hardin & Nancy Vass, 10 July 1834; Greensville Willis, bm.

Thompson, Harvey G. & Sophia E. Cline, 1 May 1854; William McLean, bm; m 1 May 1854 by A. Simmons, J. P.

Thompson, James & Hannah Nixon, 12 Feb ____; Elijah Thompson, bm.

Thompson, James P. & Joyesy Harbor, 2 Dec 1851; Jeremiah Tolbert, bm.

Thompson, Jesse & Thurzy Nations, 5 Nov 1854; Calvin Gentry, bm; m by E. Ramy.

Thompson, Jesse K. & Elizabeth Tucker, 11 Nov 1829; E. Thompson, bm.

Thompson, John & Frances Roges, 29 July 1847; Michael Noonkester, bm.

Thompson, John & Ann Bryan, 21 Sept 1865; F. M. Nixon, bm; m 24 Sept 1865 by John J. McMickle, J. P.

Thompson, John C. & Sarah Thompson, 25 Jan 1849; Pleasant R. Cockerham, bm.

Thompson, John D. & Sealy Murglorhorn, 22 Aug 1864; John Cobble, bm; m 25 Aug 1864 by John C. Thompson, J. P.

Thompson, Joseph & Martha Bryan, 8 Jan 1851; Henry C. Booker, bm.

Thompson, Nelson & Rachel C. Massey, 30 Dec 1858; Greenville Willis, bm.

Thompson, Nicholas & Jane Cockerham, m 6 Feb 1860; certified by John C. Thompson, J. P., 27 Aug 1866.

Thompson, Stephen & Polly Marsh, 12 Feb 1828; William Marsh, bm.

Thompson, Stephen & Peggy Snow, 31 Oct 1856; M. W. Snow, bm.

Thompson, W. H. & Mary Pardue, 6 March 1862; J. M. Pardue, bm; m 6 March 1862 by Jas. Minish, M. G.

Thompson, William J. & Micky Galyean, 2 Dec 1854; Calvin Gentry, bm; m by E. Ramy, M. G.

Thomson, Jonathan & Rebekah Dagley, 13 Feb 1792; Zepheniah Dowden, bm.

Thonbury, William & Elizabeth Cox, 14 Oct 1850; Wm. M. Hicks, bm. (C. H.).

Thore, John H., son of N. and Francis Thore, & Callie F. Burres, daughter of John & Axes Burres, 4 Feb 1868 by R. T. N. Stephenson.

Thornberry, William & Elizabeth Slaughter, 3 Sept 1846; Jerry Slaughter, bm.

Thornton, Eli & Rebekah Hinshaw, 29 June 1823; James Thornton, bm.

SURRY COUNTY MARRIAGES, 1779-1868

Thornton, James & Sarah Johnson, 20 Dec 1820; Simon Marshill, bm.

Thornton, John & Jane Slater, 3 Sept 1808; James A. Thornton, bm.

Thornton, Thomas & Betsey Athan, 19 Feb 1818; Thomas Colvard, bm.

Thurmond, Thomas J. & Sarah Franklin, 11 Feb 1834; Enoch B. Hunt, bm.

Tickle, Lindsay & Martha N. Dunbar, 11 March 1867; James Mosley, bm; m 12 March 1867 by J. T. Johnson, J. P.

Tickle, James & Minerva Jane Herold, 19 Nov 1863; Smiley Whittington, bm; m 19 Nov 1863 by Wilson Laffoon, J. P.

Tilley, John, son of John and Lucinda Tilley, & Matilder Combs, daughter of Stephen & Malinder Combs, 17 Dec 1867; m 19 Dec 1867 by Rev. William J. Combs.

Tilley, Peter L. & Mary A. Patterson, 22 May 1856; Joel F. Tilley, bm.

Tilly, Thomas J. Jr., & Delila Chandler, 4 July 1854; John Griffith, bm; m 4 July 1854 by R. Marshall, J. P.

Tippett, Hillory H. & Mary Ann Unthank, 11 April 1838; Jno. W. Lewis, bm.

Tipton, William F. & M. A. F. Clark, 22 July 1867; W. J. Wuesenberry, bm; m 22 July 1867 by Murlin Sparger, J. P.

Todd, Thomas & Polly Zachary, 3 June 1811; David Zachary, bm.

Toffar, John Sensin & Sarah Willy, 25 Sept 1827; Christopher Willy, bm.

Tomson, Tobias & Mary Loagan, 20 Jan 1801; Hugh Logan, bm.

Tomson, William & Ann Nelson, 30 Dec 1800; John Skidmore, bm.

Tow, A. H. & Mary F. Bowers, 3 June 1865; William A. Johnson, bm; m 3 June 1865 by W. Golden, J. P.

Tranue, Robert & Hannah Griffuth, 29 Aug 1820; Mantur D. Word, bm.

Treece, George & Hanner Sentichfield, 6 March 1810; Henry Frick, bm.

Trese, Jacob & Frances Alberty, 21 Feb 1817; Moses Alberty, bm.

Triplet, Tolbert & Martha Morgan, 18 March 1851; Rufus Hampton, bm.

Triplet, William & Polly Chappel, 22 April 1809; Richard Jacks, bm.

Triplet, William & Mary Day, 30 April 1834; Bradley Mathews, bm.

Triplett, James & Louisa Mathews, 11 April 1838; James Chappell, bm.

SURRY COUNTY MARRIAGES, 1779-1868

Triplett, Joel & Susanna Sillevant, 1 Oct 1822; Bradley Matthews, bm.

Triplett, Thomas & Peggy Williams, 25 Feb 1818; Richard Jacks, bm.

Trivitt, Andrew & Almeda Barnes, 21 Dec 1849; Newton Barron, bm.

Troy, Henry & Nancy Carrow, 21 Dec 1829; Shadrach Oglesby, bm.

Truelove, Austen & Rebecca Poyndexter, 25 May 1836; Thomas Colvard, bm.

Truelove, Charles & Sarah Flynn, 23 April 1819; Jesse Fleming, bm.

Truitt, Eli & Nancy Colvard, 9 March 1799; John Colvard, bm.

Truitt, Jesse & Pricilla Speer, 10 Sept 1787; John Truitt, bm.

Truitt, Lazarus & Sarah Cranfield, 4 Nov 1823; David Baity, Jr., bm.

Truitt, Saxagotha & Holland Joiner, 28 Jan 1799; Eli Truitt, bm.

Trulove, Charles & Lusannee Flyn, 13 July 1824; Jacob Matthews, bm.

Trulove, Samuel & Elizabeth Morris, 23 July 1831; William Morris, bm.

Trulove, William & Sarah Matthews, 22 June 1814; John Bovender, bm.

Tucker, Aaron A. & Sophia A. Norman, 9 Oct 1865; J. K. Rose, bm; m 11 Oct 1865 by J. W. Rose, M. G.

Tucker, Ben, son of Charles & Matilder Tucker, & Cresy Thompson, daughter of Ezekiel & Cilvina Thompson, m 30 Jan 1868 by Wm. J. Tucker, J. P.

Tucker, Benjamin J. & Marsy C. West, 11 March 1845; Isaac Shore, bm.

Tucker, Branch & Lucey Blakey, 12 June 1803; Edward Moore, bm.

Tucker, Churchwell B. & Rozannah McKiney, 11 July 1823; Edward Moore, bm.

Tucker, David & Caty Day, 18 March 1806; Benjamin M. Tucker, bm.

Tucker, David J. & Jane Hughes Tilly, 27 Aug 1845; Charles Tilly, bm.

Tucker, James & Anna Cave, 8 Jan 1810; John Seagroves, bm.

Tucker, James B. & S. A. Cockerham, 17 Dec 1873; consent from her father, M. F. Cockerham.

Tucker, John, son of Thomas & Lucy Tucker, & Martha E. Kidd, daughter of Jesse & Martha Kidd, 25 July 1868; m by A. Simmons, J. P.

SURRY COUNTY MARRIAGES, 1779-1868

Tucker, Thomas B. & Matilda Moore, m 30 Jan 1853 by Jo. Phillips, J. P.

Tucker, William Y. & Sarrah Thompson, 31 July 1854; Byrd Snow, Jr., bm.

Tuggle, Claboun & Hannah Sayers, colored, 26 Nov 1866; m by Elisha Banner.

Tuggle, Wyat, son of Isaac and Fanny Gunter, and Caroline Banner, daughter of Hainer Banner & Alf Davis, 30 Dec 1868, m 30 Dec 1868 by Joe. A. Bingman, J. P.

Tulbert, William & Mary Howard, 4 Jan 1816; Elisha Chappel, bm.

Tull, Artha & Ruth Jones Matthews, 13 Oct 1817; Squire Glen, bm.

Tull, Henry & Mary Freeman, 14 Aug 1826; James Matthews, bm.

Tull, Lave & Raney Matthews, 10 March 1823; Landon Trulove, bm.

Tull, William & Sarah Mathis, 27 Jan 1807; Abel Grace, bm.

Tull, William & Thursy Joyner, 3 March 1833; Daniel Binkley, bm.

Tumon, Henry & Ann Simmons, 18 Nov 1829; Newel Jackson, bm.

Turman, Joseph & Sarenah Hilmsman, 1 Aug 1846; Nathaniel Runnels, bm.

Turman, William & Mary Turman, 27 Sept 1831; William McPeak, bm.

Turner, Elias & Sarah Davie, 27 Nov 1797; Ormon Kimbro, bm.

Turner, Elias & Elizabeth Chapmon, 1 Aug 1818; George Kimbrough, bm.

Turner, James M. & Careen Hill, 2 Sept 1863; A. J. Whalen, bm; m 2 Sept 1863 by A. Simmons, J. P.

Turner, John & Sally Kimbrough, 3 Feb 1819; George Kimbrough, bm.

Turner, Matthew & Betsey McClover, 20 May 1787; Thomas Jobe, bm.

Tuttle, John & Mariah Jarrell, 11 Dec 1860; m 11 Dec 1860 by B. F. Scott, J. P.

Tuttle, Thomas & Mary Jane Moore, 27 Oct 1860; m 30 Oct 1860 by Wm. R. Bary, J. P.

Uptegrove, Isaac & Rebekah Lovill, 11 May 1819; Francis Pettitt, bm.

Uptegrove, William & Mary Lovill, 3 June 1807; Isaac Uptegrove, bm.

Vanderpool, L. Berry & Nancy Cummins, 11 March 1836; Joshua Cummins, bm.

SURRY COUNTY MARRIAGES, 1779-1868

Van Eaton, William L. & Judith C. Hunt, 24 Dec 1845; Jas. W. _____, bm.

Vanhoy, Abram & Jane Ross, 7 Oct 1847; Henry Marshall, bm.

Vanhoy, James & Judy Burroughs, 9 Dec 1833; Henry J. Money, bm.

Vanhoy, John & Jinsy Sutle, 23 Dec 1844; Obadiah Collens, bm.

Vanhoy, William & Sally Jacks, 30 May 1808; John Whaling, bm.

Vannatter, John & Nansey Macguier, 4 May 1813; John Whitlock, bm.

Varnam, Nehemiah & Susanah Smith, 19 Jan 1854; Isaac Low, bm; m 19 Jan 1854 by W. M. Freeman, J. P.

Vaughan, John & Elizabeth Key, 1 Oct 1847; A. H. Dobson, bm.

Vaughn, Archalaus & Elizabeth Smith, 10 March 1856; William H. Smith, bm.

Vaughn, Gideon Y. & Stacy Stone, 11 Jan 1867; m 16 Jan 1867 by Joel Denny, J. P.

Vaughn, James & Lutrisa Holder, 23 Feb 1828; Jeremiah Hatcher, bm.

Vaughn, John & Susannah Jones, 4 Jan 1835; David Jones, bm.

Vaughn, John Y. & Manervia Flinchum, 28 Dec 1865; m 9 Jan 1866 by James S. Green, J. P.

Vaughn, Johnson & Matilda Hunt, 11 May 1848; James Vaughn, bm.

Vaughn, Minnetree J. & Nancy Jane Moore, 12 Oct 1846; John Burcham, bm.

Vaughn, Parson & Catharine Easter, 16 April 1846; Lewis Easter, bm.

Vaun, Samuel & Nancy Tanner, 22 Nov 1814; Jona. Unthank, bm.

Vawter, John M. & Polly M. Campbell, 11 Aug 1834; George W. Campbell, bm.

Veanble, Daniel & Mary Owens, 18 July 1838; Watson Holyfield, bm.

Venable, James & Susan R. Franklin, 13 Jan 1862; Pleasant Venable, bm; m 16 Jan 1862 by Lemuel J. Stanly, J. P.

Venable, Iredell & Lucinda Taylor, _____ 1850; Charles Thompson, bm. (C. H.).

Venable, Jefferson & Mary Ann Love, daughter of Thomas Love, m 11 July 1868 by Jno. Banner, J. P.

Venable, Joab & Rebecca T. Lewis, 13 Nov 1852; m 18 Nov 1852 by Drury Hodges, J. P.

Venable, Martin & Frances Forkner, _____ 182-; P. Venable, bm.

Venable, Stephen & Kesiash Jones, 5 May 1860; Pleasant Venable, bm.

SURRY COUNTY MARRIAGES, 1779-1868

Venable, Thomas & Prissey Forkner, 22 Dec 1809; Jesse Smith, bm.

Venable, William & Susan Brinkley, 23 March 1864; James Reid, bm.

Venables, Isham & Anny Creed, 9 June 1816; Watson Holderfield, bm.

Venables, William & Sarah Smith, 10 June 1829; Jesse Venables, bm.

Venerable, Joshua & Elizabeth Snow, 2 Aug 1849; Isham Venable, bm.

Vennable, Jesse & Nancy Bowles, 29 Jan 1823; Jesse C. Cockerham, bm.

Vennible, Francis M. & Lusetty L. Lawrence, 5 April 1864; William A. Gregg, bm; m 17 April 1864 by James Needham, M. G.

Venzaunt, Garrel & Polley Shores, 24 July 1802; William Patterson, bm.

Vernon, Ewel & Piercy Leonard, 22 Dec 1864; Wiley Vernon, bm; m 22 Dec 1864 by G. A. McCraw, J. P.

Vernon, Thomas & Nancy Hicks, 18 Nov 1784; Thomas Adams, bm.

Vernon, Wiley & Elizabeth McCraw, 25 Dec 1856; Leroy Spencer, bm; m 25 Dec 1856 by A. Simmons, J. P.

Vernorn, George W., son of Nemiah & Lucinda Vernorn, & Mary M. Hamlin, daughter of Thomas V. & Sarah Hamlin, **m** 2 Jan 1868 by L. J. Norman, J. P.

Vernum, James & Elizabeth Hardy, 21 March 1844; David H. Thompson, bm.

Vest, Francis P. & Elizabeth W. Davis, 24 Feb 1828; John G. Pettitt, bm.

Vest, Wesley N. & Martha G. Gordan, 24 March 1866; m 29 March 1866 by S. H. Holsabeck.

Vestal, Adam & Elizabeth Long, 6 Dec 1834; Jesse Vestal, bm.

Vestal, Alexander & Delanah Gross, 5 April 1844; James Callaway, bm.

Vestal, Bartholomew & Patsey Davis, 23 Feb 1819; William Vestal, bm.

Vestal, Daniel & Nancy Davis, 20 Sept 1828; David Vestal, bm.

Vestal, David & Mary Longine, 11 Aug 1791; John Thos. Longine, bm.

Vestal, Davis & _____, 2 Aug 1838; James Garges, bm.

Vestal, Davis & Elizabeth Mikels, 12 March 1846; Wm. Martin, bm.

Vestal, Isaac & Nancy Dickinson, 2 Dec 1834; James Johnson, bm.

SURRY COUNTY MARRIAGES, 1779-1868

Vestal, James & Ann Casada, 4 Oct 1791; Thomas Vestal, bm.

Vestal, James & Anna Whitehead, 27 Feb 1816; John Vestal, bm.

Vestal, James & Sally Reese, 7 March 1819; John Casstevens, bm.

Vestal, Jesse Jr. & Susanna Sanders, 14 Jan 1829; Christopher Weatherman, bm.

Vestal, John & Mary Vestell, 22 March 1822; Asa Vestal, bm.

Vestal, John & Rachael Hopson, 27 Sept 1822; John Adams, bm.

Vestal, John & Elizabeth Vestal, 9 Nov 1837; John Hobson, bm.

Vestal, Silas & Bershaba Jones, 17 July 1817; Zachariah Jones, bm.

Vestal, Solomon & Nancy Long, 30 March 1824; Jesse Vestal, bm.

Vestal, Thomas & Ann Martin, 4 Oct 1791; Jams. Vestel, bm.

Vestal, Thomas & Mary Hinshaw, 7 Sept 1801; Jacob Hinshaw, bm.

Vestal, Thomas & Gracy Swaim, 15 Nov 1831; Alvis Reece, bm.

Vestal, Thomas Jr. & Biddy Williams, 4 Dec 1821; Jesse Williams, bm.

Vestal, William & Sally Miller, 26 Jan 1814; Neal Bohannon, bm.

Vestel, Jesse & Elizabeth Miller, 2 Jan 1812; Isaac Vestal, bm.

Vestel, John & Saly Royal, 6 June 1835; Joshua Sheek, bm.

Vestell, Jesse & Martha Casady, 27 Dec 1794; James Casady, bm.

Vestle, George & Sarah An Holcomb, 16 Jan 1865; m 16 Jan 1865 by D. A. Eldridge, J. P.

Via, Lewis & Mary F. Gothard, 4 Aug 1846; Jno. W. Hancock, bm.

Viar, George & Joan Jenny, 25 July 1854; Allen Denny, bm.

Viech, John & Elizabeth Pettitt, 16 Dec 1818; Moses Brown, bm.

Viers, John & Elviria Whitaker , 4 May 1847; Elisha Banner, bm.

Vinzant, Barnabas & Elizabeth Buckhannan, 25 Sept 1834; Major Austill Jr., bm.

Wabbleton, Joseph & Agnus Hartley, 2 Aug 1785; George Long, bm.

Waddill, George & Betsy Atwood, 25 Jan 1816; Jesse Atwood, bm.

Waddill, Kinchen & Elizabeth Bates, 21 Jan 1830; James Steelman, bm.

Waddill, Richard & Mary Wiles, 23 Sept 1802; Thomas Wiles, bm.

Waddle, Calvin & July Isabel Havens, 22 Oct 1850; James Shadrach, bm. (C. H.).

Waggoner, Adam & Sarah Whitehead, 26 Feb 1838; Joel Whitehead, bm.

SURRY COUNTY MARRIAGES, 1779-1868

Waggoner, David & Catharine Sperlin, 29 March 1830; Jacob Waggoner, bm.

Waggoner, Daniel & Nancy Hoppers, 27 June 1837; Moses Swaim Jr., bm.

Waggoner, Jacob & Mary Brannager, 11 Dec 1819; Leroy E. Holcomb, bm.

Wales, Jacob & Nancy Denny, 20 Sept 1819; George Denny, bm.

Wales, Samuel & Mary Sigler, 4 June 1791; Jno. Sigler, bm.

Walk, Alexander & Francis Allen, 9 Sept 1860; m 9 Sept 1860 by Elisha Banner, J. P.

Walk, Jesse & Nancy Davis, 28 April 1834; James Davis, bm.

Walk, Martin & Sarah Hendrick, 26 July 1858; James Cox, bm.

Walker, Dabney & Mary Binkly, 16 July 1821; Neal McClennon, bm.

Walker, David & Mary Reece, 21 June 1802; Robert Walker, bm.

Walker, David & Melley Penix, 24 Sept 1809; John Martin, bm.

Walker, John & Mary Jones, 5 Dec 1834; John E. Roberts, bm.

Walker, Rasmus & Sarah Richardson, 3 Sept 1839; John Calven Thompson, bm.

Walker, Richard & Keziah Reece, 7 Jan 1805; Eli Reece, bm.

Walker, Robert & _____, 24 Sept 1807; Jacob Nixon, bm.

Walker, William & Mary Lowrey, 21 April 1778; John Lowrey, bm; consent from Isabella Lowry.

Wall, Alcena & Adaline Fulk, 25 Dec 1860; A. A. Culler, bm; m 25 Dec 1861 by W. W. Wolff, J. P.

Wall, Anderson & Emiline Nusum, 5 July 1854; Isaac Barr, bm; m 5 July 1854 by W. W. Wolff, J. P.

Wall, Crawford & Lucinda Freeman, 25 Feb 1834; Allen Kidd, bm.

Wall, Dred Ira & Frances Ann Adkins, 27 Feb 1836; m 28 Feb 1856 by Jas. M. Flippin, J. P.

Wall, F. B. & Sarah Hauser, 4 Jan 1847; S. C. James, bm.

Wall, Henry J. & Lucinda Williamson, 22 Oct 1853; O. H. P. Wall, bm.

Wall, Irey & Verinda Rottenbury, 6 July 1851; Paskell Adkins, bm; m 6 July 1851 by William Haymore, J. P.

Wall, James A. & Milly Bullin, 31 Oct 1855; m ___ Nov by Erasmus Canter.

Wall, James B. & Mary E. Midkiff, 2 Feb 1867; Russel F. Wall, bm; m 3 Feb 1867 by John Jones, at the house of old Mrs. Midciff.

Wall, John & Unity Callahan, 19 April 1831; Peyton Tally, bm.

SURRY COUNTY MARRIAGES, 1779-1868

Wall, Michael & Nancy Johnson, 14 May 1810; Nathan Holt, bm.

Wall, Miles & Elizabeth Bruner, 10 Feb 1862; Henry J. Wall, bm.

Wall, Minzy & Elizabeth Brady, 5 Nov 1851; Martin Hiett, bm; m 5 Nov 1851 by J. L. Fulk, J. P.

Wall, Newell J. & Lucinda Brinkley, 15 Dec 1852; m 16 Dec 1852 by Wilson Laffoon, J. P. (C. H.).

Wall, Samuel & Mary Dunagan, 4 March 1820; Robert Poor, bm.

Wall, Samuel W. & Irina Copeland, m 15 April 1852 by John Jones.

Wall, Thomas H. & Sarah Shores, 25 Dec 1827; David Owen, bm.

Wall, William & Elizabeth Atkins, 21 June 1825; Alexander Evens, bm.

Wall, William & Vicy Whitaker, 24 Dec 1855; H. M. Whitaker, bm; m 24 Dec 1855 by John Hamlin, J. P.

Wall, William P. & Lemesa Hall, 4 Sept 1855; m 5 Sept 1855 by John Banner, J. P.

Wallace, D. C. & Caroline O. Hudson, 29 June 1858; Joseph Soyars, bm.

Wallace, John & Catharine Blalock, 9 Jan 1787; Thomas Hudspeth, bm.

Wallace, Thomas & Prudence Painion, 6 Aug 1820; John Griffith, bm.

Waller, George & Margaret Slate, 15 Dec 1858; Stephen D. Smythes, bm.

Waller, John & Elizabeth Porter, 12 April 1862; Hubberd Bratton, bm; m 12 April 1862 by A. Simmons, J. P.

Walles, Isham & Polly Jones, 29 Sept 1822; Edmond Taylor, bm.

Wallism James B. & Eviline Collings, 22 July 1844; Henry Grean, bm.

Waran, William & Elizabeth Sugarts, 20 Sept 1818; James Hargrove, bm.

Ward, Anderson & Sarah E. Privett, 23 Dec 1855; Frederick Coatney, bm; m 23 Dec 1855 by A. Simmons, J. P.

Ward, Chesley & Malinda Dicken, 11 March 1854; James Bartley, bm; m 11 March 1854 by John Ramey, J. P.

Ward, John H. & Mary Wall, 11 Jan 1859; N. A. Wolff, bm.

Ward, Levin Jr. & Elizabeth Brock, 13 Feb 1822; Joseph M. Hauser, bm.

Ward, William & Elizabeth E. Hawks, 20 April 1863; Abraham Hawks, bm; m 26 April 1863 by Wm. Golden, J. P.

Warden, Elija & Mary Stinson, 27 July 1825; Robert Warden, bm.

Warden, Elijah & Aggy Chandler, 26 July 1826; Greenville Barker, bm.

Warden, John Wesley, son of Izaah & Perlina Warden, & Almeda Donathan, daughter of Benjamin & Arrena Donathan, 8 Dec 1867; m by P. Worth, J. P.

Warden, Johnston & Sarah Patterson, 3 June 1852; Hugh Jinkins, bm.

Warden, Michael & Doshey Hardwick, 18 Sept 1812; Jonathan Haines, bm.

Warden, Robert & Billsy Pilcher, 20 Jan 1821; Levil Spilmon, bm.

Warden, William, son of Isaiah & Paulina Warden, & Charlotta Jackson, daughter of Lewis & Mary Bledsoe, 9 Nov 1867; m 10 Nov 1867 by P. Worth, J. P. (licesnse states that groom is colord and bride is white).

Warner, Jacob & Ann Robruth, 27 Sept 1853; David H. Poindexter, bm; m 27 Sept 1853 by A. Simmons, J. P.

Warren, James R. & Nancy Stow, 12 May 1845; Calvin J. Cowles, bm.

Warters, Cary, son of Burrel & Barbary Lacy, & Elizabeth Reynolds, 8 March 1868; m by C. L. Banner, J. P.

Watkins, David & Darkus Silvey, 16 Nov 1808; Thomas Watkins, bm.

Watkins, William & Polly Lawless, 2 Sept 1811; Josiah Vanderpool, bm.

Watson, Alexander & Susanna Jessop, 21 March 1817; Thomas Lockhart, bm.

Watson, Amos & Amelia Bays, 17 Jan 1828; Obediah M. Bays, bm.

Watson, Claebourn & Nancy Hester, 27 Aug 1785; Sowell Frazer, Isaac Gray, bm.

Watson, Edmond & Margarett Gwyn, 8 March 1862; William Poore, bm.

Watson, Ellock & Mary Ann Morgan, 18 July 1854; Jesse Morgan, bm.

Watson, John & Jane Lavender, 2 Sept 1820; Samuel Simmons, bm.

Watson, John & Charlotte Lindsay, 10 Sept 1845; Robert Hines, bm.

Watson, Lemuel & Mary B. Johnson, 30 July 1844; Blemmon Haymore, bm.

Watson, Sanford & Sally Ann Edmonds, 29 July 1862; David Watson, bm; m 20 July 1862 by Wm. J. Lewis, J. P.

Waugh, H. M. & Nancy B. White, 22 Dec 1856; Jno. E. Lundy, bm.

Waugh, James R. & Elizabeth M. Martin, 18 April 1860; m 18 April 1860 by Isaac W. Avent.

SURRY COUNTY MARRIAGES, 1779-1868

Waugh, William & Eliza Churcher, 19 Feb 1867; L. J. Norman, bm.

Wauhop, James W. & Matilda McCraw, 1 March 1827; John McGilbary, bm.

Weathermon, Christopher & Patsy Vestal, 9 March 1825; Solomon Vestal, bm.

Weathermon, Cornelius & Caty Runager, 20 Nov 1811; Larkin Jacks, bm.

Weatherman, James & Elizabeth Arnold, 24 Dec 1827; John Hudspeth, bm.

Weatherman, Samuel & Mary Morgan, 24 July 1845; Martin Jacks, bm.

Weatherman, William & Elizabeth Riel, 17 April 1819; James Hudspeth, bm.

Weaver, Abraham & Nacy Campble, 14 Dec 1803; James Evens, bm.

Weaver, John & Nancy Murphy, 4 Sept 1832; Watson Holyfield, bm.

Webb, Andrew & Charlotte Padgett, 7 March 1844; Jacob Horton, bm.

Webb, Caleb & Mary Hedspeth, 11 Dec 1797; Absalom Holiman, bm.

Webb, Charles W. & Mary Martin, 24 Feb 1859; Isaac Webb, bm; m 24 Feb 1859 by M. L. Wood, M. G.

Webster, James & Nancy Lambert, 13 Aug 1814; Samuel McCraw, bm.

Webster, William & Charata Bass, 11 May 1826; John Cassdas, bm.

Weddle, William & Clementine Fortune, 25 July 1835; Wesley Smith, bm; m 23 July 1855 by A. Simmons, J. P.

Weeks, John & Susanah Huff, 13 Aug 1846; Chapman D. Weeks, bm.

Weeks, Robert & Sarah Houchen, 13 July 1846; Raleigh Sutfin, bm.

Welch, Charles McK. & Mary Atkins, 15 Dec 1823; James Turner, bm.

Welch, David & Sarah Rutledge, 8 July 1820; Enos Rutledge, bm.

Welch, Elza & Leanna Franklin, 20 March 1820; Wm. Lewis Franklin, bm. (C. H.).

Welch, James & Fany Revil, 24 Aug 1802; Daniel Jefferson, bm.

Welch, James & Mahala Dixon, 28 March 1829; Thos. C. Davis, bm.

Welch, Samuel C. & Ann Brown, 25 Jan 1845; Alexander Bolin, bm.

Welch, William & Polly Kimbrough, 26 April 1820; George Kimbrough Jr., bm.

Weldon, James & Mary Ploughman, 10 Jan 1822; Fredrick Tanner, Jr., bm.

Welkor, Adam & Nancy Fletcher, 28 Nov 1793; John Fletcher, bm.

SURRY COUNTY MARRIAGES, 1779-1868

Wells, George & Matilda Fair, 14 Aug 1846; Ira Crutchfield, bm.

Wells, James & Phebe Southard, 15 May 1864; M. D. Sale, bm; m 15 May 1864 by D. A. Eldridge, J. P.

Welmon, John & Rutha Twiney, 2 Oct 1787; Leonard Richards, bm.

Welsh, Ephraim & Elizabeth Miller, 1 Feb 1792; David Welsh, bm.

West, James & Nancy Algood, 1 Feb 1827; William Shores, bm.

West, Lewis & Mary Williams, 30 Nov 1795; Benjamin Williams, bm.

West, Will & Elvira Money, 22 June 1844; Henry B. Tucker, bm.

West, William & Margerett Sparks, 4 Jan 1799; Joseph Smith, bm.

West, William Jr. & Elizabeth Austill, 11 Feb 1832; James Armstrong, bm.

Westrope, John & Hannah Bryan, 18 Aug 1784; Daniel Bryan, bm.

Wetherford, William D. & Priscilla B. Samuels, 18 Oct 1838; Richard Marshall, bm.

Wharton, Frank, son of Andy & Sarah Wharton, & Sarah Luvina Stone, daughter of Wm. Banner, 1 Feb 1868; m 2 Feb 1868 by Joel Denny, J. P.

Whealess, Allen & Elizabeth Durham, 15 Sept 1803; Jesse Johnson, bm.

Whitaker, Abraham & Lydia Whitaker, 14 April 1840; Edmund Whitaker, bm.

Whitaker, Anderson & Susan Hughes, 31 July 1832; J. G. Pettitt, bm.

Whitaker, David & Vergarina Whitaker, 1 Jan 1853; Jourden Whitaker, bm; m 3 Jan 1853 by E. F. Lovill, J. P.

Whitaker, Edmond & Disey Safley, 9 Aug 1816; Jonathan Whitaker, bm.

Whitaker, Elisha & Nancy Williamson, 5 Nov 1835; Edward M. Dobson, bm.

Whitaker, Green & Elizabeth Howard, 5 Sept 1837; James L. Somers, bm.

Whitaker, Isaac & Malsey Howard, 3 Sept 183-; Jonathan Whitaker, bm.

Whitaker, Isaac & Margaret M. Lovell, 6 May 1846; Watson Holyfield, bm.

Whitaker, Isaac Jr. & Anny Fulk, 5 Jan 1837; Isaac Whitaker Sr., bm.

Whitaker, Isasah & Sally Smith, 11 May 1852; Wm. White, bm. (C. H.).

Whitaker, Jackson & Hanner Bass, 8 Oct 1846; John M. Edwards, bm.

SURRY COUNTY MARRIAGES, 1779-1868

Whitaker, James M. & Delphia A. Key, 6 Nov 1864; Erasmus Canter, bm; m 7 Nov 1864 by E. Canter, J. P.

Whitaker, Jesse & Mary Campbell, 3 Sept 1816; Elijah Desern, bm.

Whitaker, Jiles & Lucy C. Adkins, 27 April 1865; m 30 April 1865 by James Needham, M. G.

Whitaker, John & Polly Cummins, 27 Oct 1820; Aaron Bass, bm.

Whitaker, John & Julia Leagins, 6 Jan 1849; John R. Burrus, bm.

Whitaker, Johnson & Sarah Stafford, 7 Sept 1784; Thomas Whitaker, bm.

Whitaker, Jonathan & _____, 29 Dec 1835; Melton Cain, bm.

Whitaker, Jordon & Rebekah Evans, 18 Dec 1825; Alexander Evans, bm.

Whitaker, Jourdon & Elizabeth Harrison, 5 Jan 1846; Tho. F. Hampton, bm.

Whitaker, Jourdon & Nancy Evans, 27 Aug 1853; m 1 Sept 1853 by John Hamlin, J. P.

Whitaker, Josiah & Patsey Sneed, 5 Feb 1831; Jordan Whitaker, Edmond Whitaker, bm.

Whitaker, Lorenzo D. & Riney Fitzgerald, 15 Dec 1831; Haden Swinny, bm.

Whitaker, M. R. & Lydia R. Whitaker, 13 Nov 1851; Zaml. H. Belejack, bm.

Whitaker, Silas & Elizabeth Caudle, 16 April 1840; Isaac Whitaker Sr., bm.

Whitaker, Silas & Jalila Shores, 8 Jan 1853; Anderson Whitaker, bm.

Whitaker, Thomas & Rachael E. Biggs, 3 March 1850; James Simpkins, bm. (C. H.).

Whitaker, Wesley, son of Wm. & Nancy Whitaker, & Sarah A. Nicholson, daughter of John & Setliff Nicholson, 3 Jan 1868; m 5 Jan 1868 by R. T. Pilson, J. P.

Whitaker, Westly & Elizabeth Holderfield, 6 Dec 1837; Anderson Whitaker, bm.

Whitaker, William & Nancy Harrison, 11 March ____; William Whitaker, bm.

Whitaker, William & Mary Whitaker, 18 Dec 1825; Alexander Evans, bm.

Whitaker, William & Patsey Oliver, 17 Oct 1837; Green Whitaker, bm.

Whitaker, William & Frances Draughn, 24 Oct 1855; John Hamlin, bm; m ___ Oct, by Erasmus Canter.

Whitaker, William & M. S. Harben, 11 May 1858; M. Y. Folger, bm.

SURRY COUNTY MARRIAGES, 1779-1868

Whitaker, William Hampton & Mahala Whitaker, 19 Jan 1848; L. H. Burrus, bm.

White, Albert & Margaret Moore, 11 Aug 1821; John White, bm.

White, Albert & Polly Wilmouth, 11 April 1846; Thos. B. Roberts, bm.

White, Albert & Margret Stanley, 4 Jan 1867; m 21 Jan 1867 by S. W. Roberts, J. P.

White, Harden & Nancy Axum, 5 Nov 1837; Albert White, bm.

White, Joel, son of Joel White and Sally Nicholds, daughter of Dudley Nicholds, m 23 Sept 1851 by H. C. Bray, J. P.

White, John C., son of Joseph & Mary White, & Emily R. Gray, daughter of Jeremiah & Elizabeth Gray, 28 April 1868; m 29 April 1869 by John H. Lowe, J. P.

White, Joseph W. & Mary Johnson, 12 Jan 1844; George H. Stovall, bm.

White, Riley & Sally Nickals, 18 Sept 1831; Walter Aikin, bm.

White, Robert & Nancy Snow, 11 Oct 1836; Calvin Snow, bm.

White, Robert, son of John White Jr., & Elizabeth White, daughter of Joseph White, m 17 April 1853 by H. C. Bray, J. P.

White, Robert Jr. & Elizabeth White, 15 April 1853; James White, bm.

White, W. J. & Sarah White, 25 Jan 1861; m 26 Jan 1861 by L. J. Norman, J. P.

White, William & Malinda Haines, 9 April 1829; William Dickerson, bm.

White, William & Araminta C. Alberty, 8 Oct 1867; m 8 Oct 1867 by R. C. White, J. P.

Whitehead, Francis & Sarah Ann Deboard, 26 Jan 1792; William Whitehead, bm.

Whitehead, James & Mary Happas, 24 Jan 1819; Michael Fender, bm.

Whitehead, Joel & Pegy Weatherman, 11 July 1834; George Holcomb, Jr., bm.

Whitehead, John & Rosannah Hampton, 12 Jan 1805; Thos. Hampton, bm.

Whitehead, John & Patsey Royal, 28 April 1831; John Brindle, bm.

Whitehead, William & Sarah Bailey, 23 April 1794; Francis Whitehead, bm.

Whiteker, William & Jane Bray, 20 July 1833; Isaac Whitaker, bm.

Whithead, Francis & Nancy Vestal, 6 March 1823; Peter Dowell, bm.

Whitiker, William & Sarah Carter, 8 Feb 1844; Alfred Pendry, bm.

Whitington, James W. & Mary Wilson, 8 Jan 1851; Jesse M. Needham, bm.

Whitlock, Benjamin & Margarett Rawley, colored, 26 Dec 1866; Samuel D. Critz, bm.

Whitlock, Charles & Celia Roberts, 22 April 1822; Dickerson Taliaferro, bm.

Whitlock, Ephraim & Epsy Cook, 4 Sept 1845; Gideon Johnson, bm.

Whitlock, Jacob & Susan Salmons, 10 Nov 1849; Josiah F. P. Salmons, bm.

Whitlock, James & Mary Seasor, colored, 2 Aug 1866; m 9 Aug 1866 by J. T. Johnson, J. P.

Whitlock, John & Hannah Padgett, 10 Jan 1819; Thomas Minish, bm.

Whitlock, John & Libby Paul, 26 July 1835; Josiah Cowles, bm.

Whitlock, Matthew & Katharine Fair, 15 Aug 1845; Ira Crutchfield, bm.

Whitlock, Oliver B. & Susan Lindsey, 10 Nov 1850; Jesse M. Casey, bm.

Whitlock, Samuel & Theney Bowles, 28 July 1829; William Gentry, bm.

Whitlock, Thomas & Mary Ponsonbay, 17 May 1799; Bonnet Wood, bm.

Whitlock, William & Nancy Myres, 4 Jan 1823; Ashley Johnson, bm.

Whitt, A. L. & Cintha M. Hill, 4 Jan 1866; Gideon Y. Vaughn, bm.

Whitt, Wiley & Nancy Ashburn, 23 July 1831; Henry Moore, bm.

Whittington, Smiley & Mary McGee, 18 Oct 1848; Anthony Collins, bm.

Whitworth, Isaac & Nancy Keston, 1 Sept 1850; Wm. Moore, bm. (C. H.).

Wicker, Thomas & Polly Farriss, 17 Feb 1851; Charles Faries, bm.

Wickham, F. A. & Nancy L. Moore, 4 Sept 1864; Jas. F. Hicks, bm; m 4 Sept 1864 by Wm. R. Bray, J. P.

Wilbern, Richard & Susannah Roberts, 9 April 1791; Thos. C. Burch, bm.

Wilborn, Harrison C. A. & Milly Harris, 8 July 1850; John Welborn, bm.

Wilborn, John R. & Nancy Nailer, 30 Oct 1847; Elisha Felts, bm.

Wilbourn, Richard & Sarah Jane McMickle, 30 Aug 1855; m by A. J. Roberts.

Wilbourne, Elliott & Nancy Snow, 17 Aug 1858; m 17 Aug 1858 by A. J. Roberts, J. P.

SURRY COUNTY MARRIAGES, 1779-1868

Wiles, Enoch & Anna Patteson, 13 March 1847; James B. Patteson, bm.

Wiles, James & Anne Bingham, 10 Jan 1810; William Wiles, bm.

Wiles, John & Bridgett Martin, 26 July 1814; Joel Reece, bm.

Wiles, Lewis Jr. & Catharine Gough, 22 Jan 1820; Samuel Gough, bm.

Wiles, Luke & Mary Hobson, 2 Nov 1807; David Hobson, bm.

Wiles, Nathan & Mary Jane Patterson, 18 Nov 1847; James Patterson, bm.

Wiles, Richardson & Sally Atwood, 7 March 1822; John Wiles, bm.

Wiles, Stephen & Rachel Steelman, 30 March 1809; John Rutledges, bm.

Wiles, Thomas & Elizabeth Steelmon, 30 June 1818; Lewis Wiles, bm.

Wiles, Thomas Jr. & Susanna Waddle, 13 Sept 1822; Thomas Wiles, Sr., bm.

Wiley, William Wilbourn & Elizabeth Thornton, 24 Oct 1844; John Thornton Jr., bm.

Wilkins, George & _____, 25 Dec 1794; John Garner, bm.

Wilkins, John & Elizabeth Royal, 12 Oct 1847; Will Wilkins, bm.

Wilkinson, James & Polly Lyon, 4 ____ 1829; Jnon. Zachary, bm.

Wilkinson, William & Christenia Lyon, 1 April 1828; C. B. Oglesby, bm.

Willard, Allen & Nancy Hutchins, 6 Jan 1816; Patrick Hutchins, bm.

Willard, Elkanah & Matilda Bovender, 27 Sept 1850; Samuel Irvin, bm. (C. H.).

Willard, Jonathan & Keziah King, 29 Dec 1809; Augustine Willard, bm.

Willard, William & Nancy Brown, 27 Sept 1848; Samuel Irvin, bm.

Willey, Christley, & Margaret Snow, 8 Jan 1827; Job Southard, bm.

Willey, Westley & Nancy P. Isaacks, 17 Feb 1858; Wilie Willey, bm.

Willey, Wiley & Charity Cockerham, 10 Feb 1849; Deep Snow, bm.

Williams, Azel & Phebe Hodges, 22 Feb 1847; Pleasant Hodges, bm.

Williams, Benjamin & Catharine James, 14 Dec 1788; James James, bm.

Williams, C. W. & Nancy Johnson, 20 Dec 1834; Isaac W. Hutchins, bm.

SURRY COUNTY MARRIAGES, 1779-1868

Williams, Elisha & Rhoda Thomson, 20 Sept 1806; Jno. Thompson, bm.

Williams, Ephraim & Mary Ann Doulling, 23 May 1799; John Williams, bm.

Williams, Ephraim & Harriet J. Michael, 22 Sept 1849; Nicholas Williams, bm.

Williams, George & Mary Milraney, 3 March 1808; Joseph Milraney, bm.

Williams, George H. & Martha E. Baily, 25 Dec 1834; Elias H. Baily, bm; m 25 Dec 1854 by A. Simmons, J. P.

Williams, H. M. & Julina Bedsour, 21 June 1866; m 21 June 1866 by Wm. Golding, J. P.

Williams, Henry E. & Elizabeth White, 30 July 1853; James P. White, bm.

Williams, Henry H. & Judith Parker, 10 Feb 1859; Martin V. Barker, bm.

Williams, Henry H. & Sarah McCraw, 7 Nov 1862; Geo. W. McCraw, bm; m 8 Nov 1862 by Wm. Golden, J. P.

Williams, Henry Janes & _____, 13 Feb 1804; James Williams, bm.

Williams, Hiram & Jane Brown, 9 April 1866; m 12 April 1866 by T. J. Lawson, M. G.

Williams, Ira & Mary McKenny, 11 Oct 1860; Hiram Williams, bm.

Williams, Isaac & Dice Ridings, 24 Aug 1812; Wm. D. Kelly, bm.

Williams, Isaac & Nancy Jester, 15 Nov 1827; James Adams, bm.

Williams, Isaac & Mary Bagnell, 6 Sept 1852; James C. Norman, bm; m 6 Sept 1852 by A. Simmons, J. P.

Williams, J. H., son of Enoch & Rachel Williams, & Eliza A. Stourt, daughter of M. P. and Frances Harold, 16 Jan 1868.

Williams, James & Levina Matax, 6 July 1807; Thomas Clanton, bm.

Williams, James & Ann Gallimore, 7 Jan 1824; Jacob Donathan, bm.

Williams, James & Nancy Ridenhour, 28 Aug 1860; m 2 Sept 1860 by S. W. Roberts, J. P.

Williams, James N. & Elizabeth Pierce, 1 Feb 1845; Chaffin Pierce, bm.

Williams, Jesse & Nancy Douling, 12 March 1807; G. Martin, bm.

Williams, Joel & Elizabeth Gregory, 5 Dec 1834; John Goodrum, bm.

Williams, Joel & Margaret Land, 6 Nov 1862; Hiram Williams, bm; m 6 Oct 1862 by John Jones.

Williams, John & Sally Doulling, 25 March 1801; Toms. Williams, bm.

SURRY COUNTY MARRIAGES, 1779-1868

Williams, John & Rebekah Woottan, 16 March 1805; R. Woottan, bm.

Williams, John & Margit Williams, 2 April 1805; John Williams, bm.

Williams, John & Agness Ridins, 1 Oct 1806; G. Martin, bm.

Williams, John & Nancy Jones, 21 May 1809; Labourn Williams, bm.

Williams, John & Sabrilla Brown, 9 April 1843; Walter K. Franklin, bm.

Williams, John Jr. & Elizabeth Clingman, 3 Sept 1830; Josiah Cowles, bm.

Williams, Jonathan & Temperence Welbourn, 12 Aug 1831; Wm. Williams, bm.

Williams, Joshua L. & Sarah Hutchins, 1 Oct 1836; Isaac Hutchens, bm.

Williams, Kade M. & Sarah Matthews, 31 Aug 1833; Joshua Williams, bm.

Williams, Leroy & Martha Donathan, 26 July 1863; William Butcher, bm; m 26 July 1863 by P. Worth, J. P.

Williams, Lewis & Nancey Yourk, 7 Sept 1833; Jonathan Williams, bm.

Williams, Nathaniel & Jemima Allen, 1 March 1828; Shadrach Morris, bm.

Williams, Nehemiah & Cynthia Bowden, 5 Oct 1807; Fredrick Black, bm.

Williams, Phillip & Anne Vest, 18 Feb 1808; Isaac Vest, bm.

Williams, Reazen & Mary Douthit, 5 March 1785; John Giles, bm.

Williams, Richard & Elizabeth Chessure, 26 Oct 1799; Jas. Canter, bm.

Williams, Robert & Cynthea S. Kennedy, 3 July 1848; Jno. M. Cloud, bm.

Williams, Samuel & Drinda Peake, 9 Aug 1856; m 9 Aug 1856 by B. F. Scott, J. P.

Williams, Thomas & Elizabeth Harding, 4 Nov 1793; Renny Harding, bm.

Williams, Thomas & Mary Lakey, 2 Aug 1845; Thos. A. Patterson, bm.

Williams, Thomas & Curlistia Reece, 19 Feb 1851; Thos. A. Patterson, bm.

Williams, Thomas Jr. & Luceanna Holcomb, 27 Sept 1819; Josiah Hutchens, bm.

Williams, Wiat & Sally Absher, 14 Feb 1847; Robert Hines, bm.

Williams, William & Leda Noble, 16 July 1808; Wm. Shaw, bm.

SURRY COUNTY MARRIAGES, 1779-1868

Williams, William & Elizabeth Fulfred, 24 March 1866; Charles Guyn, bm.

Williams, Zachariah & Polley Phillips, 21 Sept 1836; William Harding, bm.

Williamson, Joseph & Mary Bass, 10 March 1820; Samuel Callaway, bm.

Williamson, Parker & Lettitia Jackson, 11 Dec 1835; John H. Dobson, bm.

Williamson, William & Jeney McGlammory, 28 July 1827; Ralegh Shelton, bm.

Williamson, William & Mary Whitaker, 17 Oct 1838; Jorden Whitaker, bm.

Willson, Isom & Julian Davis, 16 Feb 1862; m 16 Feb 1862 by J. Low, J. P.

Willson, Martin & Matilda Wilson, 15 Oct 1853; William Dicken, bm; m 16 Oct 1853 by John Ramey, J. P.

Wilmoth, Ambrose & Lucinda Whitaker, 30 Aug 1856; Smith Stanly, bm.

Wilmoth, Ezekil & Martha Hodges, 25 Oct 1852; m 27 Oct 1852 by John J. McMickle, J. P.

Wilmoth, Lot & Lucinda Snow, 4 Nov 1820; Thomas Snow, bm.

Wilmoth, Lot & Fanny Potter, 27 Dec 1822; Thomas Snow, bm.

Wilmoth, Stephen & Mary Lasiter, 18 July 1859; Jas. Butcher, bm.

Wilmoth, Tyson S. & Sarah Snow, 30 April 1858; Jno. S. Snow, bm; m 2 May 1858 by J. S. Snow, J. P.

Wilmoth, William & Mary Wolf, 28 April 1827; Frederick Wolff, bm.

Wilmouth, Calvin & Sarah Harris, 29 Nov 1854; Sarah Harris, bm; m 30 Nov 1854 by D. R. Cockerham, J. P.

Wilmouth, Stephen & Elizabeth Snow, 5 March 1816; Thomas Snow, bm.

Wilmouth, Tyson S. & Elizabeth Snow, 12 Nov 1845; Anderson Dunnagan, bm.

Wilmouth, William & Anna Franklin, 21 Aug 1822; William Franklin, bm.

Wilson, Daniel & Mary Creb, 10 Nov 1838; John McRoberts, bm.

Wilson, George & Mary Adams, 10 Jan 1787; William Adams, bm.

Wilson, George C. & Betsey Hill, 14 Oct 1822; Hiram Phelps, bm.

Wilson, Isom & Joelian Davis, 16 Feb 1862; John Collins, bm.

Wilson, Jerrimiah & Kezia Murphy, 9 March 1862; B. J. Dickens, bm; m 9 March 1862 by J. Low, J. P.

SURRY COUNTY MARRIAGES, 1779-1868

Wilson, Jesse & Willy Galyan, 11 March 1831; Wm. Aubery, bm.

Wilson, John H. & Areny Felts, 23 Dec 1851; Jacob Johnson, bm.

Wilson, Joshua & Fanny Wall, 3 Feb 1834; Benjamin Taylor Sr., bm.

Wilson, Lazarus & Catharine Goen, 27 Dec 1829; Willes Wilson, bm.

Wilson, Paton & Elizabeth Hammons, 24 Jan 1828; Samuel Griffity, bm.

Wilson, Robert W. & Thursey Calton, 18 Sept 1853; David Burge, bm; m 18 Sept 1853 by A. Simmons, J. P.

Wilson, William & Patty Charles, 18 Dec 1786; Joel Charles, bm.

Wimbish, John H. & Rebekah L. Williams, 16 Sept 1810; Thomas L. Williams, bm.

Windle, John W. & Mary L. Clark, 7 Oct 1855; John Quesenbury, bm; m 7 Oct 1855 by A. Simmons, J. P.

Windsor, Amos & Mary McDaniel, 20 Dec 1823; Stephen Wells, bm. (C. H.).

Windsor, Daniel & Sally Arnold, 14 Dec 1808; Wm. Wright, bm.

Windsor, Elisah A. & Clarissa Johnson, 13 Dec 1849; Henry W. Casey, bm.

Windsor, Enos & Nancy Jones, 14 Oct 1816; Aquilla Windsor, bm.

Windsor, James A. & Nancy Walker, 14 March 1837; David Arnold, bm.

Windsor, James R. & Susan Minish, 4 Aug 1836; Bennet Windsor, bm.

Windsor, Jesse & Lucinda Denney, 20 Nov 1835; Berry Stroud, bm.

Windsor, Samuel B. & Sarah Morgan, 14 March 1848; Jesse M. Casey, bm.

Winfree, Caleb & Polly Hamlin, 5 Dec 1809; Wm. Hamlin, bm.

Winfree, Job & Elizabeth Canaday, 30 Jan 1807; Jesse Canaday, bm.

Winfry, Thomas & Mary Hadlye, 2 Nov 18--; Joel Burch, bm.

Winston, John & Sabellow Mozby, 21 Feb 1788; Joseph Mozby, Daniel Evans, bm.

Wiseley, Joseph R. & Mary E. Keister, 18 Sept 1854; J. A. Bennett, bm; m 18 Sept 1854 by A. Simmons, J. P.

Wishon, Adam & Nancy Miller, 13 Oct 1810; Leonard Wishon Jr., Henry Hoots, bm.

Wishon, Coon Rood & Sarah Sene, 29 July 1805; John Brinkley, bm.

Wishon, John & Nancy Johnson, 2 March 1829; Isham Baity, bm.

SURRY COUNTY MARRIAGES, 1779-1868

Wishon, Philip & Caty Hoots, 4 Feb 1821; David Baity, Joseph Reniger, bm.

Wishon, Samuel & Barbara Spikard, 4 July 1812; Henry Renniger, Joseph Renniger, bm.

Witcher, Lacy & Elizabeth Lyon, 4 March 1829; William Wilkinson, bm.

Witcher, William & Julina Burch, 18 March 1834; Wm. D. Somers, bm.

Wolff, Henry A. & Rachel Isaacs, 10 Feb 1845; Wm. R. Wilmoth, bm.

Wolff, N. A. & Alethea D. Gordon, 9 Feb 1863; William W. Wolff, bm.

Wood, Alexander & Elizabeth Pucket, 24 Aug 1854; John Bays, bm; m 24 Aug 1854 by A. Simmons, J. P.

Wood, Andrew & Lucinda Holderfield, 4 Nov 1839; Jesse Coe, bm.

Wood, Benj. F. & Elizabeth A. Bingmon, 8 Jan 1867; A. J. Bobbitt, bm; m 9 Jan 1867 by R. F. McGuffen, J. P.

Wood, Bennet & Betsy Whitlock, 30 Nov 1799; Thomas White, bm.

Wood, Burgess & Cary Holyfield, 4 Jan 1825; Thomas Wood, bm.

Wood, Clinton & Luritta Mills, 18 Jan 1860; m 18 Jan 1860 by Jas. S. Snow, J. P.

Wood, Francis & Nancy Sparks, 4 Jan 1838; Kinchin Goss, bm.

Wood, Francis & _____, 20 Oct 1849; Josiah L. Roughton, bm.

Wood, Henry & Mary Smith, 10 Jan 1840; Jesse Coe, bm.

Wood, James & Nancy Mankins, 9 Oct 1835; William Standly, bm.

Wood, James & Nancy Stanly, 12 Oct 1835; Thomas Standly, bm.

Wood, John & Frances Bryant, 13 Aug 1805; Stephen Wood, bm.

Wood, John & Elizabeth Mahaffy, 11 March 1819; Wesley Armstrong, bm.

Wood, John & Massy Bray, 27 July 1835; Wm. Bullin, bm.

Wood, John & Elizabeth Wilmouth, 13 April 1844; William Bullen, bm.

Wood, John R. & Micky Ann Adkins, 8 July 1866; m by Mgr. Harbur, J. Peace.

Wood, John W. & Nancy Lambert, 20 Dec 1854; William R. Epperson, bm; m 21 Dec 1854 by W. Haymore, J. P.

Wood, Joseph & Lurana Mason, 27 March 1837; James Armstrong, bm.

Wood, Obediah & Frances Charles, 7 Sept 1785; Jesse Scott, bm.

Wood, Peter & Pantha Merut Coe, 4 July 1851; James Wood, bm.

SURRY COUNTY MARRIAGES, 1779-1868

Wood, Robert & Lucy Ann Golding, 18 Dec 1851; Nicholas Butcher, bm; m 18 Dec 1851 by J. H. Dobson, J. P.

Wood, Silas & Mary Strange, 17 Feb 1866; John J. Jenkins, bm.

Wood, Solomon & Jane Lane, 10 Feb 1854; Frost Beamer, bm; m 16 Feb 1854 by B. F. Scott, J. P.

Wood, Thomas & Polly Bullen, 14 March 1839; Charles Bullen, bm.

Wood, William H., son of Henry B., and Mary Wood, & Margret Brannock, daughter of Wilson and Lucinda Brannock, 19 Dec 1867 by Thos. J. Lauson, M. G.

Wood, William R. & Peggy Stanly, 7 May 1833; Jesse Coe, bm.

Woodde, Naaman & Ruth Carter, 24 Nov 1804; William Woodde, bm.

Woofruff, Abner & Nansey Burch, 27 Oct 1809; Sinclare McMikle, bm.

Woodruff, Cornelius & Betsy Hurt, 29 Dec 1809; Peter McMicel, bm.

Woofruff, David & Elizth. Davis, 15 April 1818; Micajah Nicholson, bm.

Woodruff, Joel M. & Lydia C. Walker, 21 Dec 1849; Barzillia Spear, bm.

Woodruff, Moses & Elizabeth Collins, 29 June 1806; Obadiah Martin, bm.

Woodruff, Moses & Charity Cockerham, 12 Feb 1822; David Woodruff, bm.

Woodruff, Moses C. & Sarah Ann Copeland, 19 March 1856; John Hamlin, bm.

Woodruff, Richard P. & Nancy Phillips, 19 May 1831; William Woodruff, bm.

Woodruff, Samuel & Keziah Burch, 11 Dec 1819; Samuel Callaway, bm.

Woods, William & Betsey Binkley, 17 Feb 1824; Joshua Harris, bm.

Woodruff, William B. & _____ Johnson, 9 Sept 1845; Reuben W. George, bm.

Woodside, John & Sally Bagby, 21 Feb 1816; Thomas Bagby, bm.

Woolfesberger, Philip & Rachael Sumner, 14 Aug 1807; Achillis Deatherage, Thos. A. Word, bm.

Wooten, George Sr. & Betsey Brassfield, 16 April 1825; Benjamin Baker, bm.

Wooten, Jesse & Rosanna Wooten, 7 July 1828; William Harp, bm.

Wooten, John & Sarah Haynes, 20 Feb 1813; John Masters, bm.

Wooten, Richard & Leah Wooten, 26 Jan 1830; John Vooten, bm.

SURRY COUNTY MARRIAGES, 1779-1868

Wooten, Thomas & Presilla Martin, 8 April 1827; James Matthews, bm.

Wooten, Thomas & Ailsey Fleming, 10 Sept 1829; Jonathan North, bm.

Wooten, William & Matilda Griggory, 1 March 1820; Gabriel Gregory, bm.

Wooton, Isaac & Mahala Bass, 7 Sept 1843; William Doss, bm.

Wooton, Lewis & Martha Pucket, 9 Oct 1819; Horatio Barker, bm.

Wooton, Riley & Dotia Harison, 10 Jan 1823; James York, bm.

Wooton, Thomas & Sarah Fletcher, 3 Sept 1833; Bartholomew Marion, bm.

Wooton, Ward & Ursula Nance, 1 Sept 1832; Littleton Nance, Peter Doudge, bm.

Wootton, John T. & Matilda C. Coalman, 24 Feb 1855; Shepard Curry, bm; m 24 Feb 1855 by A. Simmons, J. P.

Word, James & Nancy Forkner, 11 Oct 1816; Thomas A. Word, bm.

Word, Thomas & _____, _____ 180-; James Hanna, bm.

Word, Thomas Adams & Jestianer Dickenson, 15 Feb 1792; James Bryson, bm.

Wording, John & Rachel Puckett, 18 Nov 1849; Isham Puckett, bm.

Worth, John L. & Evelina R. A. Davis, 11 Nov 1863; Ice Snow, bm; m 12 Nov 1863 by W. Alex Smith.

Wray, Andrew & Hannah Walker, 6 Nov 1786; Robert Walker, bm.

Wright, Aaron & _____, 16 Nov 1792; David Riggs, Thos. York, bm.

Wright, Daniel & Lydia Gorden, 22 Nov 1851; Joseph Gordon, bm; m 22 Nov 1851 by A. R. Cockhem, J. P.

Wright, Isaac D. & Love Douge, 14 Jan 1839; Welborn Wright, bm.

Wright, James & Elizabeth Moody, 19 Jan 1853; Cicero Williams, bm; m 19 Jan 1853 by D. R. Webster, J. P.

Wright, James G. & Susan Baugus, 29 July 1837; Thomas Steel, bm.

Wright, John & Eliza Wheeler, 26 April 1829; Hardin P. Franklin, bm.

Wright, Samuel W. & Mary A. Dakin, 17 Aug 1857; m 17 Aug 1857 by John R. Patterson, J. P.

Wright, Thomas B. & Sally Armstrong, 16 June 1824; James Hicks, bm.

Yeates, William & Elizabeth Miller, 15 March 1787; George Carver, bm.

York, Adam & Polly Woodruff, 31 Dec 1832; Ed. M. Dobson, bm.

York, Cornelius & Loueasy Phillips, 18 Aug 1858; m 18 Aug 1858 by A. J. Roberts, J. P.

York, Enock H. & Keziah Cummings, 5 Feb 1867; John W. York, bm; m 5 Feb 1867 by Joel Hurt, J. P.

York, J. D. & Elizabeth Macglean, 18 Nov 1860.

York, James & Maryann Chrisman, 15 Oct 1832; Bilson B. Burnham, bm.

York, James Jr. & Mary B. Poindexter, 20 Sept 1848; Richard E. Reeves, bm.

York, Joel D. & Lydia Eley Maxwell, 10 Oct 1866; John W. York, bm; m 11 Oct 1866 by Joel Hurt, J. P.

York, John & Piggy Wadden, 6 May 1806; Richard York, bm.

York, John D. & Mary Fleming, 1 Jan 1835; Lewis Gadberry, bm.

York, John W. & Margaret Kemmer, 4 March 1867; Sinclair J. McMickle, bm. m 4 March 1867 by Joel Hurt, J. P.

York, Jonathan & Rebekah Hinshaw, 9 April 1807; Joel York, bm.

York, Lewis & Elizabeth Darnall, 6 Sept 1845; Daniel York, bm.

York, Mark & Clary Durham, 2 Jan 1810; James Johnson, bm.

York, Mark & Mamcy Gadberry, 29 Oct 1833; F. K. Armstrong, bm.

York, Mark A. Jr. & Adeline E. Crumpler, 13 March 1851; Leon H. Cash, bm; m 12 March 1851 by N. H. Blackwood, J. P.

York, Nathan & Elizabeth Johnson, 28 March 1854; T. H. Crumpler, bm; m 29 March 1854 by John Robertson, M. G.

York, Nathan & Sally Ann McGuffin, 30 Aug 1860; F. H. Jones, bm; m 30 Aug 1860 by F. M. Jones.

York, Nimrod & Mary Reese, 20 Sept 1818; Mark York, bm.

York, Thomas & Christina Panther, 15 Dec 1822; Benjamin Moore, bm.

York, William & Tempy Glen, 26 Aug 1829; James York, bm.

Young, Franklin & Genny Eldridge, 24 July 1855; m 24 July 1855 by D. R. Cockerham, J. P.

Young, Isham & Nancy Harvey, 11 March 1802; David Welch, bm.

Young, Noah & Herret Auberry, 31 Jan 1845; Gideon Barker, bm.

Young, William & Margett McCord, 19 Oct 1789; James McCord, bm.

Young, William M. & Rebecca C. Morlin, 2 March 1845; Owen Bartlett, bm.

Zachary, Alfred & Jane Powers, 28 Jan 1859; J. E. Reeves, bm.

Zachary, David & Margaret Todd, 9 May 1811; Joel Gargus, bm.

INDEX

-----, ----- 1, 5, 14,
  15, 16, 17, 19, 21,
  22, 23, 24, 27, 28,
  30, 34, 39, 43, 45,
  49, 51, 56, 59, 62,
  65, 66, 70, 71, 76,
  77, 78, 79, 80, 81,
  82, 83, 84, 88, 94,
  97, 98, 99, 110, 112,
  114, 117, 124, 126,
  129, 130, 131, 133,
  140, 141, 150, 152,
  153, 161, 163, 168,
  187, 188, 192, 201,
  208, 210, 215, 218,
  219, 223, 225
Airy 156
B.J. 48
Elizabeth 133
Harriet 9
Hetty 67
Jas. W. 207
Jesse 156
Lucinda 56
Mahalia 10
Martha 6
Reuben 114
Silvanus 4
William 83
Wm. 176
Aakins, Caroline 57
Abbott, Mary 136
Absher, John B. 42
  Sally 220
Aceborn, Catharine (?)
  163
Adams, Abigail 33
  Abraham 1
  Ann 26, 179
  Caroline 77
  Ceasor Womack (?) 2
  Cinda 2
  Daniel 104, 199
  Edmund 47, 48
  Elisebeth 55
  Elizabeth 23, 33, 184
  Firman 1
  George 1, 25, 51, 65,
    111
  Hannah 91
  Harvy J. 43
  Henry 53
  Henry Wilkerson (?) 2
  J.S. 32
  James 66, 109, 219
  Jas. 1, 33
  Jesse 17
  Joel S. 21
  John 1, 209
  John A. 2
  Lemina J. 186

Adams, (cont.)
  Lidy J. 43
  Lydia 25
  Margaret 26
  Margret 65
  Marinda Agurs 2
  Mary 199, 221
  Mos. 70
  Mose 162
  Moses 26, 113, 142
  Nancy 1
  Peggy 107
  Peter Carter (?) 77
  Rachael 109
  Rhoda 2
  Ruth 154
  Sally 50, 162
  Sally A. 2
  Samuel 1, 100
  Sarah 25, 113
  Sendarilla 1
  Simon 199
  Susan 113
  Susanna 103
  Thomas 208
  Virginia 113
  William 89, 221
Addams, Moses 94
Addleman, Marget 32
Adkerson, Jennie 178
Adkin, Litell 57
Adkins, Alfred 91, 185
  Arinah 176
  Arteminsey 120
  Elisa 12
  Frances Ann 210
  Litle 60
  Little 2, 154
  Lucinda 120
  Lucy C. 215
  Mary 49
  Micky Ann 223
  Paskell 210
  Thomas 120
Ahel, Heinrich 176
Ahle, Robert 177
Aikin, Walter 216
Aimfield, Elizabeth 33
Airs, Leonard 12
  Lydia 12
Aker, Nancy 5
Akers, Charity 68
  Davidson 42
Akin, Walter 61
Albartz, Martha E.
  (Miss) 21
Alberty, Araminta C.
  216
  Frances 204
  Moses 204
  Nathan 117

Alberty, (cont.)
  Polly 134
Aldridge, Delilah 160
  Elizabeth 167, 192
  Joseph, Junr. 3
Alexander, Elizabeth 3
Algood, Henry R. 100
  Letty 100
  Nancy 214
  Obedience 113
Alleman, Norah 49
Allen, Aby 133
  Anna 2
  Catherine 73
  Elizabeth 32
  Elizabeth Jane 66
  Francis 210
  Jemima 220
  Jeremiah 132
  John 3, 65, 87, 111,
    118, 192
  Martha J. 8
  Nancy 152
  Polley 133
  Thomas 185
  William 3, 133, 202
Allgood, Henry R. 9
  R.H. 57
  Royal 4
  Sarah 177
  Susan 57
  Susannah 36
Allin, Nancy 147
  Rachael 13
  Richard 185
Allison, R.M. 132
Allred, H.V. 19, 64,
    97
  Lucinda 178
  Settle T. 86, 194
  Suttle T. 18
Alltiser, Edmonson
    202
  Elizabeth 2
  Mary A. 202
Alltizer, J. 4
Ally, Lucinda 119
Aln---t, Nancy 97
Alred, Lucy 74
  Seth 13
Alspaugh, Emanuel 47
Alston, Polly 79
Altiser, Edmonson 4
Alva, Elizabeth 152
Anders, David 148
Anderson, Caroline
    142
  H.G. 101
  Katharine A. 42
  Lucy A. 98
  Lydia 18

229

Andrew, John 9
  Mary 35
  Sally 193
Andrews, Aggy 167
  Cealy Ann 35
  Joseph 4
Angel, Cornelius 5
  Elizabeth 66
  James 142
  James W. 158
  John J. 196
Angell, John J. 181
Annefield, Sarah 68
Anthony, Amelia 197
  H.G. 146
  J.F. 131
  John 62
  Keziah 162
  S.F. 5
  Sarrah 149
  Serena 5
  T.F. 27
  Thos. F. 32, 144
Anthoy, Elizabeth 144
Apperson, (See also Epperson)
  Alexander 176
  John 161
  Nancy 153
  Thomas 64, 164
Appleton, Susanah 147
Aran, Sarah 188
Archer, Wm. 5
Armfield, Isaac 79
  Mary 79
Armsfield, Nannie A. 79
Armstrong, Elizabeth 173
  F.K. 2, 5, 8, 9, 117, 226
  H.D. 14, 49, 68
  Hugh 5, 173
  Iredel 77
  J. 194
  James 199, 214, 223
  James C. 84
  Jas. 96
  L.M. 5
  Landon 45
  Lendor 127
  Martin 59, 79, 88
  Mary M. 84
  Meredeth 78
  Nancy 78, 173, 184
  Robert (?) 77
  Sally 225
  Wesley 223
  Will 156
  William 5
Arnal, Elizabeth 160
Arner, Lucinda 37
Arney, Polly 166
Arnold, Amelia 105
  Anderson 2
  Benj. 165
  Daniel 32, 52, 85, 110, 156
  David 142, 222
  Elizabeth 156, 213
  Emaline 106
  Jacob 5
  Jane 188
  Jno. 161
  John 106
  Malinda 2
  Margaret 2, 105
  Rhody 113

Arnold, (cont.)
  S.S. 16
  Sally 96, 222
  Sarah 16
  Sheriden S. 54
  Sophia 35
  Thomas 166, 192
Ashbourn, Drucilla 71
Ashbourne, Mary 183
Ashburn, Delphia R. 171
  Denson A. 171
  J.W. 6
  Jefferson 6
  John 6, 145
  Julia Ann 110
  Louisa E. 52
  Lucinda 66
  Martha 174
  Martin 6
  Mary 6
  Mitty 6
  Nancy 217
  Thomas 6
  William 2, 174
Ashby, Choley 196
  Jane 21
  Sarah J. 64
Ashe, ---- (Gov.) 130
Asheby, Polly 4
Ashley, Catharine 12
  Cynthia 188
  Mary 149
  Nancy 147
  Robert 75
  Travis 78
Ashly, James 144
Ashworth, Joel 10
  Lucinda 117
  Thomas D. 185
  Thos. D. 19
Askew, Sarah Jane 83
Astill, Hannah 78
Aten, Margret 119
Atha, Hensen 99
Athan, Betsey 204
Athon, Farfax 122
  Joseph 98
Atken, Cholea 111
Atkerson, Anna P. 6
  E.H. 170
  Elizabeth B. 91
  Johnson 170
  Martha E. 170
Atkins, Alfred 69, 91
  Anderson 9
  Bartlet 7
  Bartlett 65
  Deborah 150
  Elizabeth 211
  Hulda 22
  Martha J. 199
  Mary 29, 213
  Robert 29, 150
  Samuel 199
Atkinson, Elizabeth H. 91
  Johnson 91
Atwood, Betsy 209
  Jesse 184, 209
  Jesse F. 136
  John 7
  Polly 36
  Sally 218
  William F. 163
Auberry, Elijah 94
  Herret 226
  Nancy 188

Auberry, (cont.)
  Wm. 28, 38
Aubery, Wm. 222
Aubury, Susan 2
Aust, Margaret A. 202
Austelle, Lydia 144
Austill, ---- (Major?) 59
  ---- (Major, Jr.?) 209
  Elizabeth 214
  Isaac 33
  Major 59
  Major, Jr. 209
  Moses 51, 192, 197
Austin, (See also Oston)
  ---- (Major?) 160
  Jordan 70
  Major 160
  Nancy 5
  Rodey 160
Austinn, ---- (Majer, Jr.?) 7
  Majer, Jr. 7
Awberry, Elizabeth 187
Axsom, Elizabeth A. 129
  F.A. 36
  Israel P. 151
  Jos. 189
  Joseph 8
  Lizzie M. 189
  Martha E. 115
  Martin 8
  Mary 189
  Mary K. 112
  Nancy Jane 17
  Sarah 196
Axum, Nancy 216
  Susa J. 36
Ayers, Elizabeth 150, 173
  Joshua 148
  Martha 173
  Nancy 121
  Sarah A. 172
Ayres, James J. 8, 41
  John C. 8
  Joshua 8, 81
  Lucinda 3
  Luisa 35
  Mariah J. 81
  Mary 202
  Nancy J. 38
  Robert 65
  Saml. 104
B---, Elizabeth 120
Bacom, Michael 14
Badget, Martha 108
Badgett, Abraham 74, 80, 97, 121
  B.W. 22, 163
  Clarecy J. 22
  Eliza Ann 17
  Elizabeth 8, 32, 39
  James 8, 184
  Lucy 127
  Nancy 104
  Ransom 8, 67
Bagby, John 9
  Margaret 5
  Sally 224
  Thomas 224
Baggerly, Jno. 109
Bagnal, Martha A. 9
Bagnell, Mary 219

Bailey, Lewsy 37
Sarah 216
Baily, Elias H. 219
Martha E/ 219
Baits, George 185
Baity, David 166, 223
David, Jr. 205
Isom 9
Wm., Junr. 9
Baker, Benjamin 224
Catherine 55
David 160
Eastor 16
Elizabeth 39, 136
Elizabeth Reed (?) 134
Esther 134
Jackson 141
James (?) 134
Jane 122
John 9, 66
M.H. 9
Malinda 13
Mary 16, 153
Polly 9
Sarah E. 200
Wm. 16
Bald, J.W. Huchmand (?) 15
Nancy 15
Baldin, Martha 18
Baldwin, Denison B. 59
Eveline 130
Phebe Ann 59
Baler, Rebeccah 22
Bales, Anne 159
Baliss, Eliza. 26
Ball, Elizabeth 175
John 34, 53
Kezasiah 156
Martha M. 184
Mary Catharine 191
Nancy 84
Nicholas 10
Ruth E. 191
Thomas 80
Vincent 10
Vinson 131
Ballard, Alexander 188
Lucinda 134
Sarah 23
Ballinger, Louisa 186
Ballore, Nancy 10
Balwin, Frances 26
Balyjack, Sarah 61
Banister, Polly 13
Banner, C.L. 10, 11, 18, 74, 90
Caroline 206
Cloe 113
E. 11, 14, 48
Elisa 145
Elisha 2, 10, 92, 93, 141, 145, 152, 180, 209
Eliza 184
F.V. 78
Hainer 206
James 10
Jno. 44
Lucinda 10
Mary L. 92, 98
Mary R. 166
R. Ann 146
Rachel E. 145
Sarah Luvina Stone (?) 214

Banner, (cont.)
Sarah R. 97
Wm. 214
Barass, Jonathan 139
Barbour, Sally 122
Barham, B.B. 63
Mary 143
Barker, (See also Parker)
Adaline 110
Eliza (Miss) 73
Esquire 151
Fatima 155
Gideon 11, 186, 226
Greenville 212
Horatio 80, 225
Jesse L. 91
Julina 87
Katharine 16
Levicy 80
Martin V. 219
Mary 34
Nancy E. 187
Sary Ann 11
Squire 11
Thomas 34, 88
Thomas T. 155
Barksdale, Mildred Ann 83
Barnard, Christopher 11
Richard 179
Barnee, Samuel 197
Barnes, Almeda 205
E. 3
Elisha 44
Elizabeth 11
Barnet, Jackson (?) 85
Barnett, Mary 13
William 70
Barr, Isaac 210
J.C. 140
Barron, Newton 205
Barry, Eliza J. 65
Bartlet, Edward 148
Bartlett, Lydia 49
Orvis 57
Owen 226
Robert 91
Bartley, Elija 96
James 144, 211
Nancy 149
Peggy 95
Robert 51
Barton, Ralph 49
Basier, Nancy 7
Bass, Aaron 215
Catharine 147
Charata 213
Elizabeth 73
Hannah 153
Hanner 214
Henry 107
Isaac 12
Mahala 225
Mary 221
Rachel 134
Sally 65
Bates, Anthony 7, 21
Barbara 57
Elizabeth 209
George 12
Mary 185
Polly 103
Batey, Margaret 48
Baugass, Phebe 191

Baugh, Henry 82
Martha 66
Baugus, Susan 225
Bays, Amelia 212
Eliza Ann 66
Francis 184
John 173, 223
Obediah M. 212
Beales, Thomas 200
Beaman, Mary 146
Beamer, Frost 224
Jane 187
Mary E. 190
Reuben 187
Sarah 187, 189
W.H. 12
Bean, Julian 96
Luvisy 54
Susanah 188
Beard, Fanny 97
Bearrod, Rosa 62
Beasley, Elizabeth 76, 88
Hannah 13
Sally 76
Shadrach 85
Beasly, Cathrine 85
Eliza 84
Martha 78
Thomas K. 84
Beason, Jane 13
Beaty, John 135, 202
Beazley, Frances 75
Beck, James 23
Jane 23
Margarett 184
Nancy 15
Sentleger 184
Bedsaul, (See also Redsaul)
Mary 68
Bedson, Martha A. 70
Bedsour, Julina 219
Beeman, Joseph 115
Beeson, Edwd. 93
Isaac 13
Richd. 48, 111
Belejack, Zaml. H. 215
Bell, Alcy 41
Evalina J. 155
Stephen 47
Belletton, Nancy 125
Bells, Daniel, Jun. 13
Gustave 13
Wm. 160
Belton, Adaline M. 106
Ewel 106
Leatha 13
Mary A. 180
Bemer, Elizabeth 34
Benge, Mary 192
Patsey 42
Sally 25
Bengman, Allen 13
Bengum, Susanna 123
Benhan, Belson B. 36
Benhoy, Clayton 18
Bennet, Jesse 159
Bennett, J.A. 222
Mary 122
Bentley, Revel 128
Bently, Isaac 26
Berker, Arminda 91
Bernet, Elizabeth 85
Betton, Eliza J. 4
Bevel, John 61
Bevendor, Elizabeth 125

Beverus, Thomas 197
Bevinder, Lucy 24
Bevins, Joseph 126
Bidsall, Sarah 182
Biggs, Rachael E. 215
Billator, Rachael 78
Billing, Susan R. 10
Billis, Sarah 125
Bills, Alesey 75
  Alsey 114
  Daniel 49
  Daniel, Jr. 140
  Deborah 34
  Gersham 15, 49
  Gershom 64
  John 75
Binge, Samuel 177
Bingham, Anne 218
  E. 26
  Edney 114
  Gemmima 166
  Jane 104
  Stephen 166
  Stephen N. 104
Bingman, J.A. 36, 52, 83, 191
  Keziah 108
  Margaret 127
Bingmon, Elizabeth A. 223
Binkley, Betsey 224
  Daniel 206
  Fridrik 56
  John 182, 194
  Polly 143
  Sarah 125, 161
Binkly, Adam 11
  Friedrich 82
  Mary 210
  Peter 198
Binkney, Catherine 125
Bird, Nancy 176
  Sally 48
  William C. 197
  William L. 181
  William M. 101
Bishop, Elizabeth 30
  Richard 30
Bittaton, Polly 167
Bitticks, Anna 108
Bitting, Mary G. 155
Black, Adam 143
  Catherine 143
  Fredrick 174, 220
  Jacob 166
  John 33, 45
  Sarah 174
Blackborn, Margaret 154
Blackborne, Charlotte 153
Blackburn, Bethursa Covington (?) 15
  Hulch 15
Blackman, Patty 7
Blackwood, C.H. 49
  Eliza 114
  Mary 49
  N.H. 49
  R.H. 115
Blade, Fanny 178
Blair, Frances E. 81
  Geo. 59
  George 134
Blake, Fanny 100
Blakely, Jane 16
  Sempl 16
Blakey, Lucey 205

Blakley, Eliza 187
Blalock, Catharine 211
Blanset, Jane 174
Blaylock, Betsy 5
Bledsoe, Benjamin 148
  Catherine 43
  Charlotta Jackson (?) 212
  Charlotte 106
  Gilley 153
  Gillie 16
  Isaac 140
  Jonathan 117
  Jonathan H. 16
  Lewis 212
  Lucretia 164
  Mary 212
  Sarah 20
Bledsow, Elizabeth 140
Blesing, Nancy 61
Blesoe, Isaac 16
Blizzard, John W. 81
Blume, Sarah 158
Boatright, Catharine 146
Bobbitt, A.J. 223
  Andrew J. 185
Bodenhamer, Jacob B. 17
  Jane E. 189
  Maryann 77
  Salina C. 70
Bohannan, Sarah 126
Bohannon, Neal 209
  Patience 33
  Sarah 9
Bohanon, Margaret Ann 51
Bohmnon, Ann 162
Bolejack, Patsy 148
  Samuel 143
Boleyjack, Saml. H. 17
Bolin, Alexander 213
Boling, Martha 147
  Nancy 142
Bolling, Elizabeth 161
Bolt, C.L. 59
  Warren 156
Boman, (See also Bowman)
  Isham 17
  Melind 17
  Milly 40
  Nancy 159
  Peniny 17
  Peter 17
  Polly 164
Bond, Ellender 23
  Jackson 23
  Keziah 194
  Nathan 51, 172
  Ruth 184
  William 194
Bonds, Salley 80
Bone, James 17
Bonham, James H. 52
Bonn, Jacob 22
Booker, F. 3, 127
  Forrester 61
  G.H. 46
  Granville H. 61
  Henry C. 203
  Nancy 41
Booman, Martha 187
Boomdn, Elizabeth (?) 138
Booze, Mary 47
Bostick, Theney 83

Boswell, Mary 123
Bourne, Wm., Jr. 109
Bovender, Areter 198
  Elizabeth 112
  John 138, 153, 205
  Lidy 55
  Matilda 218
Bowden, Cynthia 220
  Jesse 60
  John 46
  Mary 119
  Sally 48
Bowen, Charity 102
  Mary 46
  Nancy (?) 157
  Sarah 177
  William (?) 54
Bowers, Betsey 120
  David 121
  George 85
  Mary F. 204
  Sarah 95
Bowl, Nancy 14
Bowles, Abraham 135
  Alexander 146
  Amelia 60
  Basheba 120
  Charles 56
  Elizabeth 58, 63
  James 18, 60, 120
  Jno. 64
  John 18, 20, 195
  Louisa 60
  Lucinda Dobson (?) 56
  Lydia J. 163
  Martha 190
  Nancy 46, 208
  Polly 24, 134
  Sally 69
  Theney 217
  William 63, 124, 195
Bowman, (See also Boman)
  Andrew 66
  Celia E. 19
  Cetture 58
  Dolly Ann 47
  Elisha 104
  Jane 147
  Louisa 19
  Mary 18
  Oliver 19
  Susan Ann 155
  William 58
  Wm. 19, 83
Bowmon, Alford P. 144
  Archabel 19
  Clon 19
  Cristina A. 144
Boyce, G.W. 163
Boyd, America 133
  Elizabeth 91, 133
  Irementa 136
  James 91
  Joseph 153
  Leatha 187
  Levina 141
  Mary 84, 91
  Mary M. 46
  William 187
Boyde, Mary 76
Boyer, Adam 194
  John 19
Boyes, John H. 150
Boyles, Alexander 19
  John 14
  John H. 93

Boyles, (cont.)
  Julia Ann 150
  Louvina 14
  Nancy 19
  Wm. 19
Boys, John P. 27
  Levicy 27
  Obed N. 165
  Rachel 165
Boyse, Elmina 26
Boze, Jane Smith (?) 19
Bradner, Thomas J. 180
Brady, Elizabeth 20, 211
  Isaac 20
Braizer, Mary 116
Bramblet, Thodocia 150
Branch, Elizabeth 108
Brandle, Sarah 4
Branick, Joseph 147
  Train 168
Brann, Thomas 181
Brannager, Mary 210
Branner, Metildy 152
Brannock, Lucinda 224
  Margret 224
  Wilson 224
Branoch, Prudence 12
Branscom, Reuben 20
  Rody 147
  Rosey 130
Brassfield, Betsey 224
  Elizabeth 130
  Nancy 120
  Sally 111
  Susan 71
  Wiley 40
Braswell, Jane 102
Bratton, Frances 47
  Franky 178
  Hubberd 211
Bray, Amy 57
  Ann V. 16
  B.F. 21, 131
  Benj. F. 98
  David 21, 155
  David, Jr. 20
  Ellen 77
  H.C. 58, 60, 117, 135
  Hanan 48, 190
  Hanon 21
  Henry C. 131
  James 153
  James L. 3, 130
  Jane 216
  Jemimah 45
  Joel 21, 110
  Joseph 124
  K.H. 26, 39
  King H. 43
  Lebanan 20
  Lewis W. 28, 190
  Mahala 16
  Massy 223
  Matilda Poindexter (?) 16
  Mattilda 11
  Milly 18, 155
  Milton 174
  Moses 45, 155
  Nancy 110, 120
  Rebecca 3
  Reuben H. 33
  Reubin 120
  Ruth 81
  S. Poindexter (?) 16
  Sally 181

Bray, (cont.)
  Sarah 93
  Sarah A. 92
  W.A. 164
  Wm. R. 150, 166
Brazier, William 74, 116
Breeden, Mulvina 22
Breeding, Andrew J. 117
  Sylvester 153
  Wm. W. 70, 162
Breenen, J. 197
Bremmer, Thornton 179
Brendle, George 21
  Mary 21
Brenninger, Joseph 6
Bretton, Sarah 165
Brewbaker, Isaac 7, 193
  Jacob 55
  Patsey 92
Brewer, Elizabeth 111, 138
  Letty 112
  Sarah 111
  William 25
Briant, Beauty 88
  Jackson 85
  Robert 100
Brickell, John 179
  Nicholas 62
Brickhouse, Silpha 68
Bridgefarmer, Martin 73
Bridgefaverall, Martin 181
Bridgeman, Joshua 201
Bridgman, John 192
Briggs, Charity 165
  Charity E. 13
  Elizabeth 92
  Jesse 29
  L.E. 82
Bright, Phebe 177
Brim, Andrew J. 147
  Frances 193
  James 19
  Mary A. 158
Brindle, Ann 30
  Elizabeth 199
  J.F. 96
  John 216
  Rebecca B. 29
  Wm. 30
Brineger, Tallitha 144
Bringar, Joseph 48
Brinigan, Sally 192
Brinkley, Charles 22
  Frances 22
  John 35, 80, 222
  John H. 170
  Lucinda 211
  Martha 90
  Mary 113
  Peter 163
  Rebeca 11
  Robert W. 22
  Robt. R. 58, 113
  Ruthia 91
  Susan 208
Brinkly, Frances 138
  L.W. 124
  Nancy (Miss) 160
Brinnagar, Adam 144
Brint, Nancy J. 16
Brison, Jane 31
Brittain, Delilah 84
  Fanny 176

Brittain, (cont.)
  John 41
  Sallay 74
Britten, Fanny 82
  Josaphene 165
Britton, John 71
Brock, Elizabeth 211
  Sarah 74
Brogdon, Alfred 23
Brooks, Cassa 152
  Harden 152
  Jane 112
  Joel 35
  Matt 101
  Nancy Caroline 152
  Samuel 148
Brookshire, Cynthia 154
Brown, Ann 213
  Anne 98
  Anny 75
  Basheba Jane 191
  Benjamin 54
  Betsey 92, 161
  Betsy 109
  E.C. 25
  Edney 160
  Edny 41
  Elizabeth 89, 113, 128
  George W. 27, 79
  Hannah 112
  Henry 24, 176
  Hetley 135
  Hugh 18, 20, 55, 108, 141
  Isaac 25, 143
  Jacob 23
  James 42, 83, 92
  Jane 113, 219
  Jean 32
  Jefferson 75
  Jesse 54, 80, 135, 164
  Joel 147
  John 70, 80, 115
  Joseph 23, 157
  Joshaway 85, 154
  Joshua 13, 169
  Josiah 82, 83
  Jse. 39
  Lezebeth 54
  Liddy 11
  Lucretia 135
  Lucy 171
  Lydia 23
  Margaret 164
  Martha 70
  Mary 29, 39, 91, 109, 156
  Mary Ann 140
  Mary R. 3
  Maryan 27
  Milly 20
  Moses 23, 209
  Nancy 33, 54, 70, 115, 157, 218
  Nany 176
  Polly 3, 135
  Rachael 2
  Rachel 18
  Rebecca 45, 140
  Rebekah 149
  Riley 66
  Rosanah 124
  Sabrilla 220
  Sally 23

Brown, (cont.)
  Samuel 44
  Sarah 13, 24, 154
  Susana 122
  Thomas 89, 169
  Thos. 54
  William 2, 6, 23, 24, 66
  William N. 23
  Winston 1
  Wm. 91
  Wm., Jun. 104
  Yancy 29
Brubaker, Caroline 116
Bruce, Elizabeth 68
  Jno. 150
  John 25
  John D. 199
  Robert 68
Bruner, Elizabeth 211
Brunnel, William 30
Brunt, Lidia 188
Bryan, Ann 203
  Battaling 14
  Charles 25
  Daniel 214
  Hannah 214
  Isbell 111
  Jesse 26, 54, 67
  John 116
  Jonathan 132
  Letha Ann 192
  Martha 203
  Matilda 4
  Morgan 111
  Pheba Ann (Miss) 160
  Ruth 83
  Saml. 101
  Sarah 18, 99
Bryant, Fanny N. 38
  Frances 223
  Letty 194
  Mary 67, 87
  Nancy 36
  Rebecca W. 36
  Ruthy 87
  Sarah 48
  Thomas 36, 87
Bryson, Betsey 68
  James 225
  John 90, 192
  Nancy 175, 192
  Nathaniel 101
  Ollive 90
Buchanan, David 26
Buckhannan, Elizabeth 209
Buckhannon, David 74, 122
Buckhanon, Mary 90
Buckley, Lucinda E. 77
  Mary 55
Buey, Patsy 199
Bullard, Margaret 65
Bullen, Charles 224
  Edmond 118, 127
  Edward 43
  Elin 12
  Lockey 61
  Margaret 159
  Nancy 103
  Polly 224
  Sally 118, 159
  William 25, 57, 118, 159, 223
Bullin, Ed. 124
  Elizabeth 77

Bullin, (cont.)
  James 52
  Jesse 117
  Milly 210
  Sarah 118
  Wm. 223
Bulty, Courtney 42
Bunagan, Adam (?) 7
Bunker, Caroline 10
  Milly 10
Bunting, Henry 77
Burch, Andrew H. 163
  Benjamin 143
  Charity 114
  George 27
  Isaac 79
  Joel 222
  Joel H. 177
  Julina 223
  Keziah 224
  Lucinda 79
  Malinda E. 79
  Mary 60
  Nansey 224
  Sarah 4
  Sarah A. 99
  Thomas C. 82
  Thos. C. 43, 217
Burcham, Elizabeth 95
  John 207
  Martha 52
  Nancy 45, 188
  Rebeca 56
  Susanna 55
Burchan, Ann R. 32
  G.M. 32
Burd, Ann 43
Burender, Liddia 125
Burge, ---- 10
  Andrew 18, 37, 61, 92, 128
  David 222
  Jane 143
Burgiss, E.T. 123
  William 181
Burk, Nancey 152
Burke, Beaney 193
Burkheart, Frederick 99
  Mary E. 99
Burkins, Elizabeth 147
Burnett, Alviny 172
  Archibald 3
  Henry 172
  Mary A. 172
  Nancy J. 146
Burnham, Bilson B. 226
Burns, Alse 60
  Jeslin 30
  Katharine 186
  Mary F. 197
  Samuel 21
Buron, Patsey 119
Burres, Axes 203
  Callie F. 203
  Georg 76
  John 203
  Matilda J. 40
Burress, Istaney 99
  William 5
Burris, George 145
  Phebe 163
  Polly 7
Burroughs, Judy 207
Burrus, John R. 200, 215
  L.H. 216

Burrus, (cont.)
  Leander H. 39
  Mary A. 33
  Miley 108
  Mily 95
  Sarah 74
  Thos. 28
Burtin, Sarah A. 194
Burton, Mary 6
Busby, Matilda 33
Busey, Mary 99
Butcher, Ayzina 77
Chalwell V: 18
Chatwell 62
Chatwell V. 21, 195
  George 21
  Jas. 221
  Lucy 39
  Nancy 36, 77
  Nicholas 77, 224
  Polly 21
  Sally 62, 195
  Sarah 62
  Suentha 195
  William 220
Buthrell, Joseph F. 116
Butler, Wm. 118
Butterey, Elizabeth 115
Buxton, William 29
Bynum, H.W. 153
  Martha 16
Caims, Nancy 76
Cain, Andrew 29, 41, 127, 166
  D. 26
  David (?) 34
  Elizabeth 166
  Melton 215
  Nancy 34
  Rebecca Ann 166
  Rosy 71
  Ruth 60, 167
  Samuel 88
  Solomon 167
  William 196
Calkeham, Elitha 145
Call, Danl. 73
  Elizabeth 124
  Evea 73
Callahan, Susan 139
  Unity 210
Callaway, Elizabeth (Miss) 105
  Isaac 192
  J. 136
  James 56, 138, 139, 193, 208
  Nancy 20
  Polly 102
  Samuel 27, 29, 221, 224
  Wm. 23
Calliway, Samuel, Jnr. 114
Calloway, Malinda 170
  Samuel, Jr. 114
  Vestal 55
  Wm. H. 47
Caloway, Elizabeth S. 134
  Elizth. 23
Calton, Dicy 105
  Moses 31
  Patsy 129
  Susan 15
  Thursey 222
  Wm. 30

Calvard, Benjamin 101
  Sintha 200
Calvert, Anna 188
  Thomas 40
Campbell, Betsey 16
  Emily W. 141
  Emmett T. 141
  George W. 207
  John 16, 94
  Mary 215
  Nancy 53
  Penlina 33
  Polly 36
  Polly M. 207
  Sally 14
  Sarah 127
Campble, Nacy 213
Canada, (See also Kennedy)
  Midia 160
Canaday, Elizabeth 222
  Jesse 222
Canady, Larcan 173
  Sarah 183
Cane, David 34
  Eliza 155
  John 126
  Rachel 105
Cannon, Lovey 1
  William 126
  Wm. 147, 160
Canny, Jesse M. 37
Canter, Allen 185
  Erasmus 215
  Jas. 220
  Nancy 200
  Robert A. 201
Canting, Martin (?) 2
Captevens, Ann M. 86
Care, Catharine 44
Carey, Elizer 130
Carlan, Daniel 176
Carlile, Rebeckah A. 148
Carling, Elizabeth 61
  Malinda Payne (?) 61
  Wm. 61
Carlos, Don (?) 32, 39
Carlton, Ann 166
  George 31
  Joel 31, 50
  John 31
  Mary 199
  Matilda 136
  Moses 32
  Polly 32
  Rebekah 17
  William 31, 199
Carmical, (See also Cormikel)
  Archibald 31
  Sarah 78
Carmichael, Archibald 126
  Elizabeth 70, 137
  Jane 142
  Richd. 31
  Starling 137
Carnaf, Margarett 31
  Moses 31
Carnaham, Mildred E. 86
Carnahan, Isabela 11
  Margaret 70
Carnder, Edith 163
Carner, Sarah F. 133
Carnston, Rachel 69
Caroll, Charles 72

Carpender, Polly 173
Carpenter, Benjamin 154
  Elizabeth 139
Carr, Lucinda 188
  Mary 164
Carrender, Lydia 163
Carrier, Martin 119
Carrison, Rebeca 87
Carrow, Nancy 205
Carry, Aranna 74
Carson, Jacob 198
  Jesse B. 106
  Robert 51
  Sally 85
  Thomas 31
Cart, Samuel (?) 30
Carter, Abiram 87
  Abram 7
  Benjamin 162
  Caroline Adams (?) 77
  Catharine 60
  Chas. 140
  Christopher 130
  Dinah 102
  Don 39
  E.G. 42, 86
  Edward 32
  Elisabeth 137
  Elizabeth 56
  Hannah 24, 94
  Isaac 102
  J. 113
  Jackson 46
  James 49
  Jane 55
  Joel 129
  John 32
  Joseph 32, 64
  Joshaway 157
  Joshua 32
  Lydia 103
  Madison D. 93
  Margaret 77
  Milton 122
  Pamelia 149
  Peter 77
  Polley 162
  Polly 180, 194
  Racheal 31
  Rhoda 199
  Ruth 84, 224
  Ruthy 163
  Sarah 35, 55, 113, 217
  Sela 49
  Solomon 32
  Thomas 14
  Thomas W. 8
  Vicy 122
  William, Jr. 79
  Wm., Jr. 198
  Wm. H. 119
Cartright, Marium 32
  Thomas D. 151
Cartwright, Eliza 64
  James 17
Carver, George 119, 225
  Polly 98
Cary, Jesse M. 120
  Lillis L. 177
  William 3
Casada, Ann 209
Casady, James 209
  Martha 209
Casey, Henry W. 222
  Jesse M. 7, 217, 222

Cash, Camilla S. 37
  Elizabeth 140
  Leon H. 37, 226
  Lewis 84, 90, 124, 149
Casper, Sarah 124
Cassada, James 34
Cassaday, John 152
  Sarah 17
Cassdas, John 213
Cassleman, Benedick (?) 8
Cassman, Mary 42
Casstevens, John 209
Cast, Elisha 111
  Martha 174
Castephens, Martin 33
Castiphens, Martin 80
Casy, Elizabeth 141
Caudel, Polly 69
  Cintha D. 104
  Elizabeth 215
  Emeline 33
  Jackson 33
  James 33
  Julia A. 45
  Mattilda 104
  Moses 33, 63
  Nancy 63
  Sally 54, 129
Cavaness, Rebecca 12
Cave, Algius 7, 33
  Anna 205
  Charlott 77
  Elias 77
  Franky 143
  Galen 34
  Gius 34
  John 59
  Lucy 26
  Mary 70
  Miley 26
  Reubin 28
  Sarah 100
  Sary 158
  William 33, 96
Cavender, Elizabeth 55
Caviness, Barbary 113
  Joab 12
  Sally 154
Ceasor, Fanney 34
Celly, Ratchal 176
Center, Charles H. 46
Chaffin, Edwin 15, 120
  Judith 101
Chamberlain, Prudence 149
  William 119
Chamberlin, Frances 202
  Franky 106
  Nancy 10
  Wm. 151
Chamblez, (See also groom Joseph Chandlez)
  Campbell 34
  Nancy 34
Chandler, Aggy 212
  Asanett 69
  Clinton 67
  Delila 204
  Elender 168
  Emily 117
  Fanny 22
  George 32
  Isaac 34
  John 121

Chandler, (cont.)
  Lucy 161
  Malissa 126
  Phoebe 11
Chanler, Elezebeth 32
  Nancy E. 7
  William 192
Chapel, Wm. 106
Chapell, Rawsey E. 202
Chapman, Allen 45
  Elizabeth 182
  John 100
  Thomas 78
Chapmon, Elizabeth 206
Chappal, Sherill 199
Chappel, Ambrose 35
  Amos 35, 111, 138
  Elisha 109, 112, 206
  Hester 152
  James 35, 138
  James, Sr. 5
  Jas. 35
  Jas., Jr. 5
  Marinda 110
  Nancy 96
  Polly 204
  Sarah 152
  W.J. 26
  William J. 10
Chappell, Ambrose T. 200
  Elisha 200
  James 96, 204
  Lucinda 183
  Matilda 114
  Polly 96
  Shaerrel 199
Chapple, Sintha 33
Charles, Frances 223
  Joel 222
  Patty 222
Chatham, J.O. 35
Chatman, Thomas 5
Cheek, Amelia 125
  Henry 39
  John 35
Cherkman, Lamy 88
Chesher, Alminda 81
  Julia 56
Cheshur, Saml. 35
Chessure, Elizabeth 220
Childers, Martha 81
  Mathew 65
  Nancy 65
  Patsey 50
Childres, Huldah 151
  Julina 91
  Masse 91
  Robert 91
Childress, Alsey 93
  Catharine 135
  Charity 80
  Eleanor 52
  Elisabeth 80
  Elizabeth 128
  James P. 28, 136
  Jonathan 135
  Letty 134
  Martin 40
  Nancy W. 182
  Sarah 154
  Tempy 153
  Thomas 70
Childris, Amy F. Williams (?) 133
  Mary 133

Chilton, Armstead 36
  Elizabeth J. 159
  Frances J. (Miss) 104
  James A. 186
  S.A. 104
  S.V. 159
  Stephen 159
  Tobitha 36
Chin, Susannah 173
Chinall, Amey 168
  Randol 168
  Richd. 127
Chinalt, Randolph 35
Chinault, Peggy 127
Chinn, Catharine 15
  Jesse 78
  Jesse E. 32
  John H. 116
  Mary 162
Chipman, Thos. 36
Chipwash, Mary Ann 49
Chrisman, Maryann 226
Chrismas, Elizabeth 145
Chrissman, Christina 48
Christian, Sarah 190
Christman, Andrew 76
Christopher, Priscilla 9
Churcher, Eliza 213
Cimmons, (See also Simmons)
  Hanah 43
Clanton, Edward 13, 37, 49, 146
  Fanny 194
  James H. 79
  Jas. 148
  Jos. 9
  Lucy 166
  Mary 194
  Rachel 183
  Saml. 36
  Thomas 36, 49, 219
  Tommus 146
Clark, M.A.F. 204
  Mary 69
  Mary E. 76
  Mary L. 222
  Robt. 4
  Saml. 121
  Sarah 146
  William 101
Clarke, Elizabeth 4
  Lyddia 103
  Robert 103, 114
  Sarah 73
Clary, Nancy 70
Clayton, Britain 125
  Charles 37
  Elizabeth 125
Cleark, Jean 24
  Robert 24
Cleburn, Cora V. 157
Clee, Jennet 132
Clement, Sarah J. 180
Clements, Mary M. 85
Clendinen, Martha J. 9
Cliff, Hannah 149
Cline, Sophia E. 203
Clingham, Francis P. 69
Clingman, Anna M. 37
  Elizabeth 220
  Jno. P. 7, 61, 137
  Jno. S. 158
  Mary 94

Clingman, (cont.)
  Peter 34, 94
  Sarrah 102
Cloud, Emily 144
  Jno. M. 2, 56, 146, 166, 220
  Mary Ann 19
  Reuben 72
Clouse, Mariah 128
Clutton, Penelope 47
Coal, Jane 158
Coale, Mahaley 97
Coalman, Matilda C. 225
Coatney, Columbus 72
  Frederick 211
  Jane 116
Cob, Rebeca 50
Cobb, Chesley 38
Cobble, John 203
Cobler, Leatha R. 101
Cobles, Sallie A. 105
Cocker, Nancy 202
Cockerham, Charity 218, 224
  D.J. 38, 87
  D.R. 62
  Daniel J. 108
  Elizabeth 49
  Frances 102
  H. 161
  Jane 203
  Jesse C. 208
  Joseph 71, 202
  Kezziah (Miss) 116
  Laticy 145
  M.F. 205
  Margaret 138
  Mary 170, 189
  Nancy 161
  Nansey 175
  P.C. 86
  P.L. 38
  Pleasant R. 38, 203
  Polly 71
  S.A. 205
  S.W. 38
  Sally 38
  Sarah 132, 166
  William 38
  William, Jr. 38
  Williams 38
  Wm. 38
Cockerram, Sally 155
Cockerrum, Joseph 155
Cockerum, Hugh 71
Cocklrece, Margaret 184
Cockrum, Mary A. 202
Coddle, Grace 24
Cody, Nancy 79
Coe, A.J. 39, 156
  Adaline 195
  Andrew Jackson 39
  Ann 113
  Catharine 115, 179
  Chamliss 39
  Delila 26
  Elizabeth 64
  Hester 165
  Jemima 122
  Jemmima 197
  Jesse 171, 223, 224
  John, Jr. 137
  Mary H. 156
  Matilda 190
  Nancy 28, 127

Coe, (cont.)
    Obeda 62
    Pantha Merut 223
    Polly 134
    Rachel 39
    Sarah 58
    Thomas 49
    Timothy 49
    William 39, 53
    Wm. 58
Cogshall, Mary 160
Coker, Thomas 24
Cokerham, J.W. 145
Colar, Louiza 178
Colbert, Judith 58
Cole, Robert 32
    Sarah 78
    Winny 178
Coleman, Masse A. 3
    R.S. 28
Colfer, Mary 162
Collans, Levina 74
Collens, Elizabeth 186
    Obadiah 207
Coller, Jacob 124
Collers, Mary 178
    Solomon 178
Colley, Nancy 15
Collier, David 28
    Patty 154
    Shadrach 77
Collings, Elisha 15
    Eviline 211
    Mary 15
Collins, A.R. 43
    Aaron 30
    Anthony 36, 134, 217
    Edney 104
    Elizabeth 23, 224
    Eve 83
    Frances 189
    Francis 59
    Isaac 188
    Jackson 40
    Jacob 57
    James M. 85
    John 140, 161, 221
    Julina 169
    Katharine 15
    Lewezy 11
    Mary 15
    Mary E. 156
    Nancy 134
    Polly 33, 100
    Sarah Ann 199
    Sarah J. 134
    Sidney 90
    W.H. 40
    William 39, 144
Colomer, Rachael 26
Coltrane, Hannah 198
Colvard, A.P. 100
    Benjamin 40
    Demaris 93
    John 40, 101, 144, 147, 166, 205
    Martha 187
    Nancy 205
    Pricilla 172
    Rebecca M. 153
    Rebekah 98
    Thomas 68, 167, 204, 205
Colvert, Cyntha 80
Combs, Byrd 42
    Charles 20
    Churchwell 92

Combs, (cont.)
    E.E. 92
    Elizabeth 202
    Malinder 204
    Mary 81
    Matilda 89
    Matilder 204
    Nancy 198
    Nancy E. 14
    Phebe 202
    Polly 10
    Sarah 132
    Stephen 204
    Thomas 202
    Wm. 10
Comer, Martha J. 88
Compton, Luiza 186
Conley, Lucy 167
Connor, Samuel 196
Conrad, F. Thomas 41
    John 122
Consolvy, John 43
Cook, Alex. 42
    Alfred 184
    Anna 58
    Asslady 30
    Belinda 120
    Betheany 191
    Brison 129
    David 42, 58
    Edith 106
    Edward F. 29
    Eli 17, 51, 106, 141, 184, 192
    Elizabeth 108
    Epsy 217
    Evans 41
    Frances 97
    Grove 39
    Hathy 166
    Henderson 108, 179, 201
    Isaac 106, 129
    James 42
    John 44
    Marthy E. 29
    Mary 32, 42, 129
    Mary A. 191
    Mary Jane 160
    Nancy 4
    Nancy Jane 191
    Peter, Jr. 193
    Pricilla 5
    Priscilla F. 200
    Rurza 84
    Sandy 26, 88
    Sarah L. 160
    Stadge 30
    Susan J. 42
    Susanna 140
    Valentine 4
    William 18, 62
    William E. 155
Cooke, Hannah 143
Cooms, Lydda 46
Cooper, D.M. 20, 46, 88, 171
    Sarah 68
    William 68
Cope, Polly 88
Copeland, Drury H. 146
    Elizabeth 6, 8, 185
    Freeman 134
    Garrott 132
    Irina 211
    Isaac 146
    James L. 43, 140

Copeland, (cont.)
    Jas. L. 89, 133
    Jesse 160, 200
    Lusindy 18
    Mary Adaline 133
    Melren M. 18
    Melvin W. 134
    Nancy 134, 140
    Sarah A. 43
    Sarah Ann 224
    Thirsey (Miss) 134
    William 43
Copland, Isaac 87
Cor, John, Jr. 197
Corchern, America J. 47
Cordal, Nancy 86
    Sally A. 86
Cordel, Betsey 42
    Gracy 17
    John C. 85
Cordell, Eliza Ann 190
    Nancy 85
Corder, Thomas 43
Cordle, Lydia 89
Cormikel, (See also Carmical, Carmichael)
    Richard 70
Cornelius, John W. 115
Cornell, Edward 25, 69
    Elizabeth 130
    John 130
Corrico, Nancy 64
Cory, Ellender 89
Costephens, Martin 175
Cotton, Rebeckah 186
Couch, Elisabeth 61
    Nathan 109
Coudle, Margaret 45
Couper, Martin 129
Cousins, Caroline 101
Cove, Alley 189
    Elizebeth 84
    Mary 130
Covington, Bethursa 15
Cowles, Amos A. 155
    Calvin J. 27, 212
    Eliza Ann 14
    J. 85
    Josiah 40, 44, 53, 124, 197, 217, 220
    Josiah, Jr. 14, 39
Cox, America 59
    Ballwod P. 44
    Br--- 15
    Elisebeth 162
    Elizabeth 19, 203
    Frances 89
    Isham 17
    J.M. 44
    James 210
    Julia Ann 64
    Julyatha 44
    Lucy 15
    Lucy A. 175
    Martin 19
    Nancy 161
    Polly 73
    Rebecca 81
    Richard 159
    Sarah 154, 168
Coyle, Elizabeth 6
Cozort, A.G. 7
    Martha 41
Craft, Vachel 142
    Wiley 192

Crage, Nancy 31
  Sarah J. 31
  William 31
Crager, Julina 8
Crane, E. 162
Cranfield, Andrew 9
  Sarah 205
Cranfill, Lydia 73
  Rebecca 139
Cranor, E. 65
  Josephene 131
Crawford, John H. 15, 50
Creasey, John H. 80
  Melinda 80
Creasy, James D. 124
Creb, Mary 221
Creech, Bennett 15
  Lucretia 11
Creed, Anny 208
  Benet 138
  Bennet 38, 45
  Buri 72
  Elisabeth 11
  Elizabeth 43
  Enoch 45, 58
  Franky 185
  Gemima 91
  J.W. 173
  Jesse 157
  John D. 87
  Justian 125
  Lazes 45
  Mahaly J. 72
  Mary 45
  Nancy 100
  Polly 67, 97
  Rachel 72
  Sarah F. 58
  Tyre 148
Creekmoor, Coartny 4
Creekmore, Caleb 46
  Nicolas 46
  Polly 14
  Thomas 4
Cresom, Celia 40
Creson, Abraham 46, 99
  Catharine 177
  Catherine 157
  Charles 196
  Jane 99
  Mary 157, 196
  Rebekah 116
Cretchfield, Susanah 34
Crisman, George 145
Crissman, A.A. 183
  A.T. 48
  Aaron A. 24
  George 184
Crissmon, Lydia 65
Critchfield, Elizabeth 170
  John 42
  Rhoda 176
Critchlow, Rozeannah 98
Critele, Hannah (?) 43
Critz, Haman 69
  S.D. 22, 136
  Samuel D. 28, 33, 64, 68, 92, 93, 167, 190, 217
Crocket, Elizabeth 163
  Samuel 63, 99
Crofford, Mande 29
Crokit, Ruth 63
Crommel, Sarah 170
Crook, Elizabeth 54

Crouk, Eli 76
Crouse, ---- 156
  Charlotte L. 191
  Frederick 127
  G.C. 73
  Henrietta 47, 191
  Henry 47, 191
  Jacob 92
  James Wm. 116
  John 14, 27, 47, 121
  Mariann 111
  Nancy 47
  Poley 53
  Prudence Lyons (?) 156
  Susanna 110
Crowel, Susan 14
Crumel, Celia 152
Crumpler, Adeline E. 226
  Isbell 4
  T.H. 226
Crumply, Eli 82
Crumpton, Julia Ann 77
Cruse, Nancy 77
Crutchfield, Ira 214, 217
Culbert, Sintha C. 21
Cullar, Benjamin 191
Culler, A.A. 210
  C.E. 12
  H.C. 179
  John W. 19
Culton, Marry 125
Cumings, E.C. 139
Cumming, Polly 82
  Rebekah 82
Cummings, Catharine 47
  Isaac 47
  Keziah 226
  Naomi 47
Cummins, J.W. 200
  Joshua 206
  Moses 48
  Nancy 206
  Polly 215
  Thomas 1
Cundiff, A.B. 28
  Mary F. 28
  Sarah L. 43
Cuningam, Dorcus 94
Cunningham, Abraham 196
  Ann 88
  Christeny 28
  Dorcas 33
  M.A. 145
  Mary 12, 50
  Matilda 95
  Nansey 183
  Rachel 12
  Rebekah 59
  Sarah 145
  William 33
  Wm. 133
Cure, Ruben 27
Currey, Sarah 89
Curry, John 12
  Margaret 182
  Shepard 225
Dagley, Jonathan 147
  Rebekah 203
Dails, Jane 7
Daken, Sarah 174
Dakin, Mary A. 225
Dalton, Christena 44
  Emley 133
Danaly, Martha 111

Daner, Mary 139
Daniel, Dency 81
  Harrison 25
  Joel 112
  Thos. F. 33
Daniely, Mary 35
Danily, Nancy 200
Danley, Sarah 48
  William 48
Danly, Mary Ann 86
Dannad, Fridrich 180
Dannel, Fanney 4
Dannelly, Agnes 122
Danner, Catharine 9
  Christeny 142
  Jane 196
  John 79
Dannor, Fredrick 57
Darnall, Bryson 132, 136
  Elizabeth 226
Darnell, John 155
Davenport, A. 49
  Rebecca 49
Davidson, Hannah 146
  Lewis 146
  Mary 128
  Phebe 146
  Victory 165
Davie, Elizabeth 119
  Sarah 206
Davies, Salley 200
Davis, ---- 93
  Abner 193
  Alf 206
  America 189
  Andrew 149
  Ann 92, 125
  Caroline 128, 131, 198
  Caroline Banner (?) 206
  Catherine 191
  D.K. 34
  Daniel 15, 50
  Deborah 160
  Dinah 91
  Drucinda 158
  Elizabeth 5, 66, 86, 92
  Elizabeth M. 71
  Elizabeth W. 208
  Elizth. 224
  Ellise 77
  Elvina 86
  Emily 93
  Evan 5, 18, 34, 67, 188
  Evelina R.A. 225
  George 50
  George C. 116
  Hainer Banner (?) 206
  Hardin E. 51
  Henry 75, 191
  Hugh 98
  Iredell 47
  J.C. 68, 113
  J. Martain 49
  Jackson 125
  Jacob 49, 50
  James 210
  Jas. 179
  Jemimah 73
  Jesse 74, 153, 173
  Jessee 131
  Jno. 50

Davis, (cont.)
  Joelian 221
  John 51, 58, 68, 77,
    128, 187, 198
  John, Jr. 30
  John C. 153, 158
  Joseph 6
  Julian 221
  Keziah 5
  L. 51
  Laura 76
  Lavina J. 78
  Lemuel J. 5
  Leonard 93, 117, 175
  Louisa 58
  Maleatha 114
  Margret 89
  Martha 27, 65, 87,
    127
  Mary 162, 166, 169,
    171
  Mary E. 6
  Menerva Jane 146
  Nancy 50, 77, 126,
    141, 208, 210
  Nelly 176
  Patcy 77
  Patrick 51
  Patsey 208
  Penelope 51
  Polly 109, 175, 199
  Polly P. 79
  Rebecca 158
  Reece 178
  Rossey 47
  Rutha 32
  S.D. 150
  Sally 130
  Sarah 116, 131, 194
  Stephen 17
  Susan 21, 51
  Thomas 79, 130, 200
  Thomas D. 16, 21, 95
  Thos. C. 213
  Thos. D. 117
  Tolaver 73
  W.H. 41, 103, 150
  William 19
  William H. 25, 92,
    178
  William R. 194
  Wm. 182
Day, Betsey 75
  Caty 205
  Clarisa 36
  David 5, 51, 138
  Elizabeth 27, 160
  James 52, 126
  John 10, 52
  Lorana 139
  Martha 138
  Mary 204
  Nancy 81
  Nelly 59
  Rebecca 23
  Sally 105
  William 99
Deal, John 163
Dean, Abner 17
  Esther 52
  Henry H. 52, 84
  James 77
  James D. 52, 132
  Mary 201
Dearman, Rebeca A. 59
Deatherage, Achillis
  224

Deatherage, (cont.)
  Catey 59
  Christena 201
  John 59
  Polly 58
  William A. 181
Deatherge, Mary 144
Deathrage, Nancy 182
Deathridge, Lucinda 201
Deaver, Patience 25
Deazen, Elijah 67
Deboard, Sarah Ann 216
de Bord, Hannah 182
Debord, Ben 52
  Lydia 52
Deck, Thomas Morrison
  61
Deen, James 121
  James D. 173
  Rachel 101
  Susanah 193
Defrees, David 128
Defreese, Nancy 69
Defrier, Sally 16
Degearn, Elizebeth 168
Dehart, Ida V. 119
  Isaac 119
  Mary 119
Dejarnett, John 150
Dejournett, Martha 62
Delany, Rachel 172
Delph, Elizabeth 186
Demsy, Allen 8
  Wm. 30
Denney, Alsey 145
  Harvey 44, 174
  Lucinda 222
  Sarah 117
  Smith 74
Dennis, Lizy 154
  Sarah A. 57
Denny, (See also Jenny)
  Allen 9, 52, 93, 98,
    102, 106, 209
  Betsy 67
  Candece 134
  Cary 99
  Disa 30
  Edmond 53, 117
  Edmund 64
  Eliza 34
  Ellen E. 117
  G. 13
  Gabriel 53, 93
  George 210
  H. 44
  Joel 53, 118
  John 6, 53
  Jorden 177
  Mary 143
  Mary F. 117
  Nancy 53, 118, 210
  R.B. 118
  Rachael 177
  Rachel 66
Dent, John 123
Denton, Eliza. 42
  Henry 12
  Jeremiah 121
  Lucinda 201
  Mary 85
  Permelia 121
Derrett, Saraah 147
Desern, Charlotty 169
  Elijah 215
  Ephraim 43, 53
Desorn, Nancy 145

Dethrage, Mathew M. 78
  Susan 78
Devenport, Absalom 165
  Agness 149
  Martha J. 35
  Mary 62
  Sarah 99
  Thomas 99
Dewyean, Lucinda (?)
  151
Deyournett, William C.
  62
Dezarn, Sally 173
Dezern, Eliza Jane 162
  Lucy Jane 186
Dial, Jane 89
  Jones 54
  Polly 71, 89
Diam, Betsy 25
Diar, Martha 141
Dick, Kasander 2
  Rebeca 80
Dicken, Ambrose 54
  Malinda 211
  Thos. 158
  William 221
Dickens, B.J. 116, 221
  Elizabeth 19
  Jesse 19
  Julie 19
  Julius 73
  Mary 12
  Nancy 116
  Ransom 54
  Reuben 54
  Wiley 128
  William 61
Dickenson, Jestianer
  225
  Mary 166
Dickerson, Caroline 177
  Fanny 110
  James 69
  John 32
  Polly 163
  William 216
  Wm. 75
Dickings, Julius 72
Dickins, B.J. 117
  Cely 117
  Julius 123
  Wiley 188
Dickinson, Nancy 208
  Wm. 169
Dickson, James 121
  John 196
  Wiley 84
Dilard, Rebecca 19
Dilkin, Wiley 128
Dillard, Mary 98
  Sally 141
Dindino, John 154
Dingler, Rebecca 39
Dinkin, Tildy 17
Dinkins, John 176
  Patssey 24
  Sabird 55
  Sarah 194
  Thomas 107
Dixon, Anna 196
  Mahala 213
  Mary 23
  Sarah 193
  William 23
Dixson, Elizabeth 115
Doak, Margaret H. 53

Dobbins, Abraham 55
  Daniel 193
  John 31
  Nancy 13, 193
  Sarah 27
  Thomas 152
Dobson, A.H. 207
  E.M. 57
  Ed. M. 225
  Edward M. 43, 62, 108, 132, 214
  J.H. 27, 56, 143
  Jn. H. 186
  Jo. 109
  John C. 61, 67
  John H. 36, 190, 191, 221
  Joseph 28
  Leander H. 30
  Lucinda 56
  Mary A. 137
  Sucky 56
  Wm. C. 40
Dodge, Susan T. 132
Dodson, Nancy 65
Dolehide, Sarah 154
Doll, Heinrich 15
Dollarhide, Christina 40
Dolton, Charlotte 84
  Emley 143
  Jane 84
  Mariah 56
Donaldson, Thos. 70
Donathan, Almeda 212
  Arrena 212
  Benjamin 212
  Celia 145
  Elijah 145
  Jacob 48, 54, 219
  Larkin 1
  Martha 220
  Mary 1
  Parthenia 56
  Vincey 1
Donelly, Patsey 92
  Polly 201
Donnar, Sarah 79
Donner, Adam 143
  Catharine 143
  Jacob 152
  Patience 152
Donniley, Thomas 177
  Thos. 177
Dooling, Jenny 162
  Levica 124
Dorne, Huldy 27
Doss, Bennet 18
  Caroline 154
  Isham 2
  James 40
  Jefferson 26
  Martha 53
  Milly 17
  Sally Ann (Miss) 60
  Sarah L. (Miss) 115
  Solomon 86
  Solomon R. 161
  Tho. J. 98
  William 225
  Wm. 182
Dossee, Elizabeth 168
Dosson, J.B. 47
  Lucinda 115
Dotherage, Achilles 118
Doudge, Frances 99
  Peter 225

Doudge, (cont.)
  Polly 38
Douge, Love 225
Dough, Nancy (?) 157
Douglass, Delany 125
  Elizabeth 31, 93
  John S. 135
  Thomas 57
  William 60, 153
  Wm. 23
Doulass, Sally 164
Douling, Jno. 121
  Nancy 219
  Suzanner 25
Doulling, Mary Ann 219
  Sally 219
Douthit, J. Uriah 12
  Jno. P. 52
  Lucinda 110
  Mary 136, 220
  Philip (?) 13
  Uriah J. 12
  William 173
Dove, William 164
Dowden, Zepheniah 37, 142, 203
Dowel, Peter 94, 131
  Polly 69
Dowell, Peter 137, 216
Dowlin, Charity 5
Dowling, Elizabeth 162
  Thornton 193
Downaly, Peter 58
Downey, Mary 147
Dowthit, J.F. 14
  John F. 112
Dozier, Elisebeth 194
  N.B. 33, 131, 162
Dracon, Pheba 22
Draper, Erica 43
  George 58
  Martha P. 45
  Sally 25
Draughn, Frances 215
  Martin 58
  Nancy 48
  Stacy 48
  William 48
Draughon, Elizabeth 174
  John 134
  Lucinda 59
  Mary 21
Dudley, Celia 147
  Charles 105, 144
  Clary 95
  Elizabeth 90, 182
  Lydia 181
  Ransom 68, 92, 185
Dudly, May 19
  Nancy 165
  Ransom 43, 100
Duer, Isabella 101
Dufriest, Hannah 87
Duggans, Rutha 28
Duglass, George 30
  Thomas 41, 58
Duglis, Sarah 124
Dulany, Melvina 4
Dull, Nicholas 15
Dumsigan, Polly 123
Dunagan, A. 103
  Anderson 5
  Lidia 61
  Mary 211
  Reuben 123
  Susannah 135
  Terry 71

Dunagin, Marthy 45
Dunbar, Martha N. 204
  Rebecca W. 148
  Susan 131
Duncan, Rice 17
  Ruth 17
Dunegan, Algias 72
Dunford, Nancy 42
  Thomas R. 5
Dunigan, Henry 114
  Roda 37
  Sally 91
  Sarah 159
Dunkin, Lucindy 4
  Malinda 133
  Molise J. 78
  Rirlina 52
Dunnagan, A. 2, 70, 108, 124, 139
  A.C. 95, 101
  Algias 186
  Allgias 53, 156
  Allgius 76
  Anderson 62, 120, 148, 221
  John 59
  Keziah 135
  Wm. 72
Dunnagen, Allgias 202
Dunnigan, Betsey 72
  Siddy 187
Dunvender, John (?) 64
Durham, Clary 226
  Elizabeth 214
  James 39
  Lizzie F. 150
  Martha A. 45
  Mary J. 165
  Polly 177
  Sarah Ann 45
  Susan 33
  William 59
  Winney 198
  Wm. 59
Durret, Nancy 40
Duvall, A.C. 30
  Alvin J. 123
  Robt. C. 31, 44
  Temperance M. 44
Dyer, Joel 139
  Jonathan 97
Dyerle, Jane 82
Eads, Clary 77
Earley, W.W. 4
Early, Charles S. 152
  Elizabeth 171
  Jeremiah 171
  M.W. 26
  Nancy 69, 99
  Rachael 100
Easley, C.S. 93
  Franky 189
  Miller 190
  Polly 154
  Susanna 33
  Wm. 182
  Woodson 189
East, Agness 154
  Charity 124
  Hughes 6, 124
  John 60, 82
  Morton C. 113
  Nancy 6, 135, 154
  William 60, 62
Easter, Catharine 207
  Daniel 60
  Lewis 207

Easter, (cont.)
  Maria B. 47
Eastham, Miriam 123
Eastrap, Jacob 45
Eastwood, Emily 50
Eatens, Martha Ann 77
Eaton, Albert A. 202
  Ebenezer 18
  Eliza 20
  Elizabeth 68
  Newel 87
  Sarah 197
Eddelman, Celey 83
Eddes, Harrison 171
Eddleman, Jacob 18, 41
  John 163
  Rutha 58
Eddlemon, Reacael 193
  Ruth 193
Edds, Mary 171
Edgington, Elizabeth 53
Edlemon, Jacob 150
  Peter 60
Edmond, Nancy P. 117
  Rachel A. 99
Edmonds, Charlotte 61
  Isham 60, 61
  Jas. T. 18
  Leatha J. 97
  Lucy A. 60
  Sally Ann 212
Edmondson, John B. 56, 148
Edmons, Mary Ann 57
  Nancy 70
  Susan 46
Edwards, Betsey 185
  Edward 182
  Elisha 188
  Elizabeth 19, 61, 89
  Etheldred 62, 186
  Frances 202
  Jane 7, 14, 61
  John M. 16, 28, 214
  Joseph 27, 61
  Katharine 166
  Leanah 130
  Levuna 22
  Lucinda 10
  Mahala 49
  Malinda 11
  Margaret Jane 159
  Margret 119
  Martha 52, 192
  Milley 69
  Patsy 27
  Richard 61
  Sally 111
  Sally Powel 84
  Saml. 129
  Sarah 65
  Sarah Ann 124
  William 61, 89, 110, 202
  William A. 202
  William W. 38
Elcer, Peter (?) 174
Elder, Sarah 53
Eldredge, D.A. 10
Eldridge, Genny 226
  J.B. 22, 75
  Jemima 75
  John B. 62
Elkins, Mary 137
Ellet, Lucy 178
Ellez, Sarrah 68

Elliott, Charlotte 87
  Cloe 96
  Dothe 96
  Mary 67
  Namrod 51
  Nimrod 32
  Wm. 114
Ellis, Elizabeth 115
  Evan, Junr. 29
  Henderson 16, 38
  Isaac 168
  James 3
Ellison, Seluda 46
Ellsberry, Sarah 174
Elmer, Anne 33
Elmore, Abijah 30
  Elizabeth 8, 183
  Mary 35
  Melinda 51
  Sarah 192
  Susanna 40
Elrod, Adam 62
  Solomon 143
  Stephen 100
Elrode, Adam 88
  Alha 56
  Christopher 62
  Elizabeth 66
  Jacob 35
  John 56
  Nancy 35
  Peter 62, 64
  Rachael 60
  Robert 60
  Susannah 168
Elsberry, Benjamin 174
Elsbery, John 5
England, Aaron 85
  Margarett 85
Ennis, Anderson 78
Enyart, Charity 82
Epperson, (See also Apperson)
  Daniel 19
  Thomas 161
  William 127, 187
  William R. 223
Escue, Levina 48
Esteel, Jemimah 135
Ester, Michel 60
Etcherson, Caty 15
Etcheson, Martha E. 107
Evans, Alexander 215
  Andrew 55
  Daniel 222
  Elizabeth 47
  John 63
  Lucinda 5
  Lucinda Jane 24
  Martha 55
  Mary 127
  Nancy 215
  Pleasant 63
  Rebecca 174
  Rebekah 215
  Rosey 98
  Thomas 178
  Unica 45
Evens, Alexander 211
  James 213
  John 63
  Sarah 10
Everage, Polley 68
  Sollomon 63
Everton, James 15
  Nancy 15

Everton, (cont.)
  Polly 156
Faddis, Andrew 31
Fagg, Joseph 93
Fair, Barnabas 13
  Elizabeth 99
  Katharine 217
  Matilda 214
  Polly 193
Faircloth, James 126
  Jane 177
  Polly 104
  William 96
Fare, Mary Ann 13
Fargusson, Dinah 89
Faries, Charles 217
Farington, Phebe 53
Farmer, Catharine 50
  Elcy M. 46
  Elisabeth 168
  Mary 20
  Nancy 55
  Rhoda A. 140
Farr---, James 35
Farrar, Arch 147
Farrel, Nacy 163
Farrington, Wm. 128
Farriss, Polly 217
Faulks, (See also Foulks, Fulk, Fulks)
  Sally C. 74
Fellon, Rachel 23
Felps, Theodore 64
Felts, Archabald 147
  Areny 222
  Beeney 84
  Charlotte 76
  Elisha 217
  Elza 65
  Hiram 65
  Joshua 84
  Mary 197
  Sarah M. 123
Fender, Betsey 194
  Jean 186
  Michael 64, 216
Ferebee, Thomas 107
Ferguson, Robert 22
Ferington, Arabell 18
  William S. 161
Ferrier, Rosannah 164
Ferris, Emezet J. 132
Fesius, Catharine 17
Fets, Jane 76
Fields, James 65
Fillips, (See also Phileps)
  Manda 121
Filmer, James R. 4
Finch, Sally 124
Findley, Nehemiah 149
Finley, Francis 144
Finney, Jos. 84
  Joseph 65
  Robert 64
  Ruth 149
Finniege, Michael 138
Fips, Anne 177
  Littleberry 177
Fisher, Eliza J. 81
  Margarett A. 18
Fister, Elizabeth 148
Fitchgarrel, Suzanner 103
Fitzgerald, A. 35
  J. 145
  James 4, 18, 20, 82,

Fitzgerald, (cont.)
  James (cont.) 83, 87, 109, 120
  James P. 97
  Jane 108
  Jas. 128
  Riney 215
  Sarah Ann 117
  Talitha 22
Flecher, Nancy 181
Fleming, Ailsey 225
  Columbus 144
  Elizabeth 18
  Jane 86
  Jesse 67, 151, 205
  John 1, 2, 65, 99
  Lamuel 66
  Martha A. 49
  Mary 226
  Mordecai 18, 106
  Rachael 4
  Rachel 50
  Ruth 20
  Sampson 150, 174
  Susan M. 175
  Susanna 201
  Uriah 66
  Winston 158
Flemings, Rachael 25
Flemming, Jesse 54
  Ruth 202
Flemmon, Suzana 94
Flemons, Jesse 201
Flenchum, Martha A. 6
Fletcher, Ambrose 152
  Francis 2
  J.M. 66
  James 66
  Jensey 90
  John 213
  Mary 121
  Nancy 213
  Sarah 190, 225
  Susanna 10
Flin, Elizabeth 179
  Thomas 161
Flincham, Lettie M. 64
Flinchin, Mary Jane 6
Flinchum, Manervia 207
Flinn, George 67, 109
  James 57
  Lauflin 66
  Mariann 164
  Mary 109
  Rebecker 164
Flippin, Delia Ann 128
  Leder 94
  Mary 71
  Milton 67
Flipping, Joseph W. 71
Floyd, Vilet 184
Flyn, Betsey 192
  Lusannee 205
  Nancy 155
  Prisilla 138
Flynn, George 67
  Gideon 188
  James 161
  Loughley 24
  Polly 129
  Rebekah 125
  Sarah 205
  Thomas 125
Flynt, Ann 63
  Thomas 63
Foderal, Lucinda 8

Folger, Eunice (Miss) 67
  M.Y. 215
Fomested, Wm. 168
Foot, Elizabeth 169
  John 85
  Milly 86
  Peggy 85
  Rebecker 196
Foote, Catharine 29
  William 67
For, Luan 165
Forcum, Thomas 46
Ford, Katharine 87
  Nancy 85
Forester, Patsey 118
Forker, Susannah 13
Forkner, Elizabeth 43
  Frances 207
  Gabriel H. 73
  James 43
  Jestena 39
  Joseph 189
  Keron 202
  Lewis 47
  Lucy 8, 43, 141
  Malinda 148
  Martha P. 59
  Nancy 131, 225
  Prissey 208
  Sally 34
  Samuel 63, 67, 131, 185
  Sumrel 80
  Susan 93
  Susanah 122
  Thirza 178
  Thomas 165
  Thos. 68
  William 23
Forkum, Hannah 198
  Peggy 96
  Peter, Jr. 198
  Peter, Junr. 82
  Prudence 82
Forrest, James 17, 68
  Mary 17
Forrester, Delpha 87
  Elizabeth 134
  Jane 67
  Lomey 118
  Wm. 154, 164, 166
Fortner, Eliza 144
Fortune, Clementine 213
Foster, Alsey 75
  Anthony 72, 175
  Elizabeth 109
  Henry G. 107
  Hillary M. 68
  Jane 110
  Nancy W. 65
  Peggy 63
  Ruth 35
Foulks, (See also Faulks, Fulk, Fulks)
  Sally Ann (Miss) 108
Fowler, Ezenth 172
  Salena J. (Miss) 2
  Wesley 160
Fowlks, James A. 115
Fraiser, Nancy 22
Fraizer, James 178
  Robert 174
Fraley, Ann 25
France, J.J. 108
Francis, Jeremiah 75
  Mary 64, 85

Franklin, ---- 86
  Ann Susan 36
  Anna 221
  Caroline 44
  Charity 190
  Elisabeth 145
  Elizabeth 48, 127
  H.P. 59
  Harden P. 59
  Hardin 149
  Hardin P. 54, 154, 225
  Jesse D. 69
  Leanna 213
  Lucy 109
  Mahaly J. 80
  Martha E. 69
  Mary 145, 149
  Matilda 146
  Mesheck 149
  Mildred E. 101
  Nancey 186
  Nancy 151
  Rutha 197
  Sally 152
  Sally T. 180
  Sarah 46, 134, 204
  Susan R. 207
  Walter 86
  Walter K. 220
  William 221
  Wm. Lewis 213
Frankling, Sarah 129
Frazer, Sowell 212
Freeman, A.H. 75, 143
  Abbey 51
  Elisha 187
  Elizabeth 96, 159
  Hannah 12
  Henry M. 38, 70, 186, 189
  Hezekiah F. 35
  Iredell 60
  Joshua 70
  Louiza B. 187
  Lucinda 18, 210
  Martha H. 164
  Mary 67, 171, 187, 206
  Mary B. 146
  Nancy 69
  Nicholas 48, 108
  Polley 119
  Robert 129
  S.A. 1, 95, 113
  S.S. 75
  Sarah 129
  Tamer 189
  W.M. 14, 38
  West 12
Freemon, Mary 160
  Robert 36
Freman, Samuel 11
Frick, Fanny 126
  Henry 204
Frost, Jez. Ann 129
Fry, Betsey 24
  Chestiny 23
  Jonathan 117
  Sharlott 70
Fugate, Jesse H. 21
  Leticia 37
  Rebecca 21
Fulford, James R. 57, 165
Fulfred, Elizabeth 221

Fulk, (See also Faulks, Foulks, Fowlks)
---- (Widow) 66
Aaron 66
Adaline 210
Andrew 131
Andrew J. 6
Anny 214
Arilla 66
Belinda 117
C.P. 183
Catharine E. 23
Elizabeth 63, 89, 121
Henry 66
J.L. 20, 71
Jacob 53, 71
Jacob L. 71, 170
James W. 200
John Winley 9
Joseph 47
July F. 60
Nancy 38, 53
Pauline 147
Polly 147
Rachel E. (Miss) 69
Rebecca 53
Rowly 71
Wilson 66
Fulks, James C. 102
Katarine Matilda 184
Leah 102
Martha H. 51
Rebecca Ann 50
Rebecca M. 74
Sally Ann 18
Thomas S. 18, 184
Fuller, Abner 56
Abraham Reece (?) 22
Thomas 98
Fullin, William 41
Fulton, Jane 71
Joel 71
Mary E. 192
Winston 98, 182
Fults, Andrew 29
Creed 165
Polly J. 165
Fultz, Andrew 29
R.C. 197
Furrow, Susan 64
Gadberry, James 55
Lewis 66, 71, 226
Mamcy 226
Gaigean, Herron 54
Gaines, Ambrose 146
Elizabeth 146
Hannah 72
Gaith, Johnsey 156
Galaspie, Elizabeth 72
Ellick 72
Warren 45
Galaspy, Elijah 72
Jesse W. 72
Sally 148
Tirey 72
Galespie, Cely 124
Dianer 130
Rebeca 95
Gallian, Mary 123
Samuel, Jr. 72
Susannah 11
Young 11
Gallimer, Mary 106
Gallimore, Ann 219
Avey 104
Gallion, Betsey 54
Jain 152

Gallion, (cont.)
James 11
Thomas 152
Young 54, 72
Gallyer, Anderson 182
Byram 128
Mahala 182
Galyan, Willy 222
Galyar, William 188
Galyean, Micky 203
Galyear, Ephraim 152
Galyen, Effy 128
Galyer, Andrew 73
Charlottee 173
Rebeccah 128
Gammond, John K. 143
Gardner, B.D. 41, 201, 202
Hannah 49
Isaac A. 166
Garges, (See also Gorges, Gorgiss)
James 208
Gargus, Joel 30, 73, 226
Nancy 30
Garman, Mary 169
Garmer, Catharine 171
Garner, Archibald 169
Benj. P. 194
Elizabeth 117
Ellender 142
Henry A. 169
John 45, 90, 218
Lidey 90
Polly 169
William 141, 142, 179, 188
Garnes, William H. 186
Garret, Isaac 39
Garrett, Beely 196
Lewis 73
Welcom 201
Welcum 52
Garriss, Merinda 23
Garrott, Rachel 132
Gates, A.L. 164
Albert 27, 73
Eatha M. 56
Elizabeth 190
Martha 148
Mary Ann 27
Nancy 190
William 16
Gaton, Eliza. 173
Geiger, Adam 163
Gelaspie, Sally 56
Gennings, (See also Jennings, Jinnings)
William A. 55
Gentrey, (See also Gintry, Jentree, Jentry)
Richard 192
Gentry, Adaline 91
Agnes 65
Alce 180
Alcy (Miss) 62
Betsy 23
Calvin 75, 202, 203
Catharine 119
Claiborn 120
Elisabeth 185
Elizabeth 69, 96, 192
Joseph 69
Lucy 10
Margaret 12
Mary 74

Gentry, (cont.)
Mary Ann 35
Nancy 69, 95
Polly 75
Robert 95
Sally 34
Samuel 23
Sarah 110
Shadrac 91
Shadrach 74
William 217
Wm. 20
George, Jane 44
Reuben W. 224
W.H. 146
Westly 111
Germon, Sarah 135
Gester, Rachal 1
Ghoff, Synthia 37
Gibbens, Catherine 53
Gibbins, James 81
Gibbons, James 150
Mary 169
Sally 98
Winaford 85
Gibbs, Elizabeth 174
Ellina 24
Nancy 143
Olla 20
Thos. D. 123
William B. 24, 75
Gibes, John C. 170
Nancy 170
Gibson, David M. 50
Dizzy 93
Jeremiah 36
John 93
Polly 53
Giddins, Roger 101
Gilbert, Mary 153
Giles, John 98, 220
Gillam, Juliette (Miss) 14
L.M. 181
Louis M. 14
Maryetta C. 181
Gillaspie, Elijah 123
J.L. 22, 39
Jas. L. 173
Lutitia 101
Gillaspy, Mary 159
Pasia 134
Gillespie, Mehaley 95
Phebe 132
Gilley, Elizabeth 12
Gilliam, Elizabeth C. 181
R. 123
William 78
Gillim, Elizabeth C. (Mrs.) 35
Gilmer, J.R. 59
James C. 192
Robt. S. 183
Saml. L. 58, 133, 139
Samuel L. 132, 199
William 76
Gintry, (See also Gentrey, Jentree, Jentry)
Patsy 105
Girdins, Roger 76
Glasby, Ary Ancilvania 150
Glascock, Frances 96
Glass, Elizabeth N. 132

Glassgow, Jackson 69
Glastown, Sally Ann 31
Glazebrooks, Maryan 138
Glen, Elizabeth 100
  Hampson 115
  Hugh 181
  Jesse 101
  Nancy 97
  Patience 129
  Polly 101
  Sarah 100, 162
  Squire 122, 125, 173, 206
  Squire S. 125
  Tempy 226
  Thompson 97, 100
  Tyre 76, 161, 162
Glenn, Tilda 200
Goard, Andrew 133
  Perlina 150
  Sarah 61
  Vinette 199
Godfrey, Sarah 143
  Sucky 194
Goen, Catharine 222
Goin, Polly 62
Going, Mahala 127
  Rebecka 76
  Thomas 76
  William 76
Golden, C.C. 14, 16, 71
  Elizabeth 116
  Jesten 68
  Lucy 59
  Martha 159
  Nancy 114, 186
  Sarah 34, 130
  William 76, 119, 159, 167
  William, Junr. 114
  Wm. 88
Golding, Betsey 51
  Elisabeth 167
  Elizabeth 189
  Frances 190
  Lucy Ann 224
  Mary 12, 189
  Munistree 12
  Nancy 28, 130
  Reubin 28
  William 130
Golwyn, Calaway 12
Goode, Betty 107
  Jno. 46
  Richd. 13, 83, 120
Goodrum, John 219
Gordan, James M. 120
  Joseph 72
  Martha G. 208
Gorden, A.E. 53
  Celia 34
  Charlotte 77
  Colly C. 45
  D.Y. 60
  John M. 145
  Lucy 47
  Lydia 225
  Margaret 11
  Martin 106
  Rebeca 20
  Robert Armstrong (?) 77
  Samuel N. 77
  Samuel P. 77
  Stacy 64
  William 90
Gordin, Celia 106

Gordon, A.J. 143
  Alethea D. 223
  Colby C. 11
  Jos. 27
  Joseph 132, 225
  Joseph S. 174
  Samuel 4
  Thomas 128
Gorges, (See also Garges, Gorgiss)
  John 12
  Peggy (?) 12
Gorgiss, Carney 50
Goss, Kinchin 223
Gossett, John O. 150
Gothard, Mary F. 209
Gouff, Nancy 71
Gough, Catharine 218
  Elezebeth 36
  Hannah 196
  James 12
  Phebe 177
  Polly 80
  Samuel 218
Goughy, Theresa M. 131
Gowen, Patsey 163
Gowin, Rachel 172
  Sally 93
Goyen, James 122
Goyn, Sinthy 89
Grabel, Mary 141
Grace, Abel 206
  George 78
Graham, David E. 168
  Margaret 112
  Nancy 78
  Robt. 112
Grant, Gardner J. 50
  Isaac A. 14
  Martha T. 7
  Nathan T. 176
  R.W. 99
Graves, Peter 71, 134, 150
  Peter, Senr. 78
  Polly 31, 88
Gray, Ann 25
  Annenias 78
  Benjamin 78
  Elizabeth 67, 111, 120, 216
  Emily R. 216
  Isaac 212
  Jeremiah 216
  L.J. 112, 153
  Martha 193
  Mary 181
Grayham, William 45
Grean, Henry 211
Green, Ann 79
  James S. 79
  John S. 96
  Philip W. 175
  Phillip W. 163
  Polly 148
  Stephen 199
  Wm. 122
Greene, Sarry 10
Greenwood, Anner 118
  Bartley 7, 79
  Betsy 141
  Caroline 27, 86
  Caty 7
  Emiline 38
  Frances 57
  James 79, 130
  Joseph S. 46

Greenwood, (cont.)
  Lear 170
  Lidy 79
  Lockey 185
  Maislanna 185
  Mattilda 171
  Meeky 69
  Sally Ann 101
  Sibell 112
  Thomas C. 79
  William R. 27
Greer, Edy 17
Gregg, William A. 208
Greggory, Mary 18
Gregory, Ambers J. 181
  Elizabeth 85, 219
  Gabriel 225
  John 55
  Landsley 23
  Mary Ann 190
  Matilda 73
  Sarah 48
  Sterling 48
Grey, Benjamin 79
Griffey, Liza 80
Griffin, Betsey 126
  Catharine 122
  Mary Ann 145
  Milley 199
  Pleasant 122
  Sarah 188
Griffith, Elender 188
  George 142
  John 204, 211
  Margaret 11
  Martha 88
  Matilda 105
  Melinda E. 181
  Nancy 141
  Sally 107, 141
  William 198
Griffity, Samuel 222
Griffuth, Hannah 204
Griffy, Rosa 146
Grigg, Elizabeth W. 183
Griggory, Matilda 225
Grimes, Ferabee 90
Grissom, Suzanna 99
Groace, Ann 98
  Simon 98
Groad, Mahala 35
Groce, Catherine 89
  Margit 182
  Mary 48
  Nancy 48
  Nancy 48
  Rachael 7
  Rebekah 7
Grogan, Sarah 69
Grooce, Elizabeth 86
Groos, Lizebeth 81
Grose, Levin 6
Gross, Catharine 195
  Delanah 208
  Eliza A. 105
  Elizabeth 81
  George 81
  Rosanna 15
  Sarah 30
  Simon 81
Grouce, Simon (?) 65
Grover, David 171
  Jacob 81
  Melinda 33
Grubb, William 150, 198
Guilpin, Elizabeth 167

Guinn, John 81, 165
  Sarah 83
Gunnel, Elizabeth 36
Gunston, Susanah 70
Gunter, Fanny (?) 206
  Isaac (?) 206
Guyn, Charles 221
Gwyn, Aaron 133
  Caroline M. 193
  Edward J. 89
  Elizabeth 8
  Elmina 105
  Emily 190
  Jane 202
  John 165, 202
  Lemuel 89
  Levy 165
  M.E. 35
  Margarett 212
  Martha 132
  Nancy E. 114
  Sally L. 122
Gwynn, Amelia 200
  Cloe 165
  Edward 119
  Franklin 52
  James 8
  Margaret M. 52
  Martha 52
  Peaga 165
Gymon, Margaret 119
Haback, Nancy Ann 102
Haddocks, Mary 169
Hadley, Elizabeth 192
  Elizebeth 24
  John S. 41
  Patience 172
  Spencer 32
  Unius 46
Hadly, Abigal 23
  Anne 94
  Bidey 94
  Bridgett 49
  Ellenor 49
  Jean (?) 28
  Mary 172
  Peggy 170
  Ruth 169
Hadlye, Mary 222
Haga, Mary 178
Hagan, Eliza 116
Hagans, John 57
Hagard, Sarah 25
Hagins, Frances 95
Hagmon, Blewman 2
Hagy, Jacob 29, 82
  Tazwell 81
Hain, Sintha 76
Haines, Cyntha 75
  Fanny 20
  Jonathan 139, 212
  Jonth. 103, 157, 159
  Jonthn. 82
  Malinda 216
  Peter 159
  Polly 44
  Rachel 69
  Sally 59
Hair, Elizabeth (?) 14
Haixt, Jacob 143
  Margrett 143
Halcomb, (See also
  Haulcomb, Holcomb)
  Cloe 82
Hale, Martha 70
Haley, M.L. 176

Hall, Abby 124
  Alexander 133
  Cyntha 67
  Cynthia 25
  David 104
  Elizabeth 121, 175
  Francis W. 29
  J.A. 31
  Jordan 13
  Joseph 124
  Keziah Ann 89
  Lemesa 211
  Lewis 175
  Mady A. 89
  Mahala Ann 193
  Mariah C. 52
  Martha 79
  Mary 43, 105
  Melinda 110
  Mody A. 103
  Parthania 10
  Patsey 17
  Polly 120
  Robert 77
  Sally 152
  Sophiah 117
  Susanna 110
  Thomas 56
  Wm. M. 189
Halleman, Axum 41
Halley, Thomas 126
Hally, Thomas 126
Haly, James 31
Hambric, William 176
Hamby, E.L. 144
  Eph. L. 144
  Ephraim 144
  Ephraim L. 52, 65
  G.D. 162
  M.C. 38
Hamlin, John 170, 215, 224
  Mary M. 208
  Polly 222
  Precilla 186
  Sally Jane 56
  Sarah 208
  T.V. 2, 8, 16, 21,
    26, 28, 34, 39,
    123, 151, 189, 195
  Thomas 157
  Thomas V. 208
  William 202
  Wm. 164, 222
Hamm, Jane 94
Hammons, Betsey 184
  Elizabeth 222
  Patsey 40
  Rachel 148
  Saml. 196
  Samuel 80
Hampton, F. 7, 8, 9
  Frances 18
  H.C. 2, 3, 6, 8, 12, 13
  H.G. 97
  Harry 77
  Henry 3
  Henry G. 158, 175, 183
  John 27
  John C. 183
  Liney Jane 154
  Nancy 77
  Rosana 175
  Rosannah 216
  Rufus 204

Hampton, (cont.)
  Sarah 3
  T.P. 137
  Tho. F. 215
  Thomas F. 42
  Thos. 216
Hamrick, George 83
  Henry 3
Hancock, Jno. W. 209
Handley, Allmiria C.W. 28
Hanes, Harrison 84
  James S. 121, 169
  Leroy 137
  Litle 84
  Mary 121, 172
  Mary E. 84
  Rebecca 84
  Rosey 137
Hanks, Delila 93
  Edward 84
  Eliza 158
  Enoch 84
  Jane 198
  Julian 158
  Nancy 26
Hannah, James 225
Hansk, Sibana 159
Happas, Mary 216
Harben, M.S. 215
Harbin, Abitha 60
  Reason 125
Harbor, Elizabeth E. 123
  Joyesy 203
  Martha 123
Harbour, Adonijah 84
  M.G. 6
Hardie, Rody 30
Hardin, Greenbury 142
  Jean 183
  Nancy 122
  Rebekah 46
  Sarah 157
Harding, Elizabeth 220
  Keziah 41
  Renny 102, 157, 220
  Thomas 183
  William 40, 57, 221
  Wm. 115
Hardwick, Doshey 212
  Thomas G. 201
Hardy, Andrew J. 85
  Anniss 99
  Elizabeth 195, 208
  Mary 39
Hargrove, James 211
Harison, Dotia 225
  Martha 92
  Matilda 3
Harless, Frances 178
  James 178
  Liona 191
Harman, George 70
Harmon, Malinda 48
Harold, Eliza A. 197
  Eliza A. Stourt (?) 219
  Frances 219
  M.P. 219
Harp, Cinthy 182
  Lewis 85
  Polly 161
  Rossanna 123
  William 224
Harral, Jonathan 171

Harris, Ailsey 81
  Alpheus 95
  C.H. 43
  Chane 86
  Charles 86
  Eli 133
  Elizabeth 1
  Elizabeth (Miss) 42
  Ephraim D. 86
  Giles N. 75
  James 29
  Joshua 224
  Lewis 86
  Lucresy 17
  Lucy 200
  Manervy J. 39
  Martha 13
  Mary 106
  Matilda 124, 185
  Milly 217
  N.J. 114
  Nancy 76, 133
  Newel J. 97
  Polly 81
  Robert J. 154, 181
  Robt. 81
  Robt. J. 7
  Sally 57, 98
  Sarah 221
  Sarah F. 118
  Solomon 97
  Squire 65
  Tempie E. 184
  Turner 85
  William 169
Harrison, Elizabeth 215
  Frankey 22
  Joseph 87
  Lucinda E. 157
  Mahala 142
  Marshall 119
  Maryann 87
  Mesia 184
  Nancy 215
  Pamela 71
  Sarah 53
Harriss, Susanna 5
Harrod, William 3
Harrold, Michel 35
  Thomas E. 87
Harsh, Sarah J. 186
Hartley, Agnus 209
Harvel, Betsey 65
Harvell, James 151
Harvey, John 99, 186, 187
  John, Jr. 99
  Nancy 226
Harvil, Jane 121
  Mary 112
Harvill, Ferryby 185
  Moses 52
  Tennesse 133
Harville, Martha C. 80
Hatcher, Elizabeth 175
  Jeremiah 207
  Lucy P. 12
Hatley, Sally 135
Haulcomb, (See also Halcomb, Holcomb)
  Franky 109
  Sarah 79
Hauser, (See also Hooser)
  F.C. 5
  Jacob 182
  Johannes (?) 30

Hauser, (cont.)
  Joseph M. 211
  L.W. 47
  Mariam 137
  Mary 76
  Sarah 210
  Susan 93
  T.C. 32
  Theopilus 131
  Thomas 162
Havens, July Isabel 209
Hawkins, Lucy Ann 60
  Mary 150
  Matilda 137
  Robt. 188
Hawks, Abraham 211
  Andrew 195
  Elizabeth 72, 88
  Elizabeth E. 211
  Fred 40
  Harden 51
  Henry 41
  Jane 114
  Malviny 88
  Margaret 158
  Mary 152
  Nathan 81
  Richard 193
  Robert 72, 88
  Solomon 152
  Suzanah 195
Hawl, Mary 179
Hawley, Sarah M. 176
Hayes, Salley 128
  Willis 84
Haymore, Blemmon 212
  Blewmon 50, 88
  Bluman 44
  D.B. 82
  Daniel 88, 91, 165, 173, 192
  Elitha 183
  Faitha 44
  James P. 83
  Julia Ann 174
  Mary Jane 173
  Nancy E. 124
  Pleasant 124, 132
  Polly 185
  William H. 83
  Williamson E. 62
  Wm. 46, 90
Haymour, Tempy 200
Haynes, Fempy 198
  James 167
  John 12
  Kittcarn 64
  Margrett 120
  Massy Hariet 19
  Nancy 114, 140
  Sally 62
  Samuel 89
  Sarah 224
  Stephen 10, 62, 86, 114
  Synthia 157
  William G. 196
  Wm. G. 142, 190
Hazelwood, Richd. E. 142
  Sarah 154
Head, Bennet 123
  Hollon 197
  Malinda 3, 123
  Mary 25, 121, 137
  Mildred 182
  Rachel 166

Headly, Ann 17
Healan, Matthew C. 23
Heath, Elizabeth 35
  Mary 41
  Wm. 35
Heckerpeck, Alsey 97
Hector, Elizabeth 141
Hedgeens, Jane 84
Hedspeth, George 105
  Mary 213
Helen, Sarah 189
Helms, Jacob S. 37
Helsabeck, Jacob 93
Helsebeck, Frederick 180
Helsenbeck, Elizabeth 180
Helton, Joseph B. 125
Hemmons, Adaline 124
  James W. 90
Hemrick, Henry 90
Hend----, Michael 46
Henderson, Elizabeth 160
  Emily 129
  Pleasant 137
  Polly 142
  Thomas 90
Hendrick, Belsa 42
  Cinthia 149
  Elizabeth 3
  Sarah 210
Hendricks, Dice 64
  Frederick 90
  Robt. 30
  William 188
Hendrix, A.L. 177
  Sarah 161
Henley, Mary A.M. 75
  Sabey 70
Hensdale, Malitha 122
Henshaw, Mary 197
Herndon, Joseph, Jun. 123
Herold, Minerva Jane 204
Herrin, Charles 52
  Susanah 87
Herring, Clarissa R. 117
  Francis C. 113
  Mary B. 189
Herrold, Mary 196
Hester, Nancy 212
Hewett, Nancy 98
Hexter, Andrew 19
Heymore, Mary Katharine 42
Hiatt, Adaline 41
  Charles W. 70
  Edith 200
  Ephraim 91
  G.W. 11
  Gabriel 14
  Martin 91
  William 133
Hiatte, Adaline 91
Hickerson, Seth 11, 12, 29, 146
  Willis 102
Hickman, Jefferson 135
  John 109
  Keziah 156
  Mary 109
  Mary Ann 103
  Peggy 54
  Rebecca 11

Hickman, (cont.)
  Rebeckah 68
  Sarah 95
  Thomas 14
Hickmon, Jefferson 150
  John 49
  Joseph 40
  Nancy 156
  Polly 156
Hicks, Clement 101
  Elisabeth 121
  Eliza. 192
  Francis 46
  Hettie 152
  Hugh 78
  Jacob 96
  James 14, 92, 185, 225
  Jas. F. 217
  John 4
  John, Jun. 22
  John, Junr. 127
  Matilda 119
  Micajah 19
  Miles 121
  Nancy 4, 208
  Patsey 4
  Polley 154
  Ruth 4
  Samuel 92
  Sarah 91
  Sarah Ann 99
  Sarah M. 202
  Thomas B. 83
  Thos. F. 105
  Will 11
  Wm. H. 91
  Wm. M. 4, 133, 203
  Wm. W. 128
Hiet, Hanah 142
Hiett, Martin 211
  William, Senr. 42
Higgs, Leteford 100
High, Felema 127
Hill, Arbella 51
  Betsey 221
  Betsy 198
  C.D. 64
  C.H. 178
  Caleb D. 89, 91
  Careen 206
  Cintha M. 217
  Elizabeth 55, 64
  Emily 19, 79
  Emily J. 77
  Evaline 79
  Hillika 19
  James M. 101
  James S. 156
  Jane 33, 129
  Jenrel 92
  Joel 19, 79
  John 138
  John H. 93
  Joseph 64
  Lilly 18
  Lucretia 93
  Martha 19
  Mary E. 19
  Mass 180
  Michael 198
  Minerva 96
  Nancy 134, 163
  R. 64
  Richard 45
  Robert 22, 64
  Robt. 113

Hill, (cont.)
  Ruthey 126
  Sally 35, 75, 180, 197
  Sarah 93
  Sarah C. 25
  Susanah 178
  Susannah 174
  Talitha 21
  Thursy 13
  W.E. 114
Hilmsman, Sarenah 206
Hine, Mary 75
Hineman, Mary 27
Hines, Ann E. 183
  John 111
  Richard 165, 198
  Robert 212, 220
  William 90
Hinkle, Elizabeth 26
Hinshaw, Benjamin 12, 94
  Dianna 112
  Edward C. 65
  Elizabeth 46
  Elmida 170
  Huldah Jane 5
  Jacob 209
  Jonathan 31, 93
  Lucy Sabrina 109
  Mary 209
  Rebekah 203, 226
  Thomas 185
  Thomas, Junr. 24
Hiotte, Ann 143
Hite, Francis 22
Hitson, Penelope 23
Hix, Micajah 4
Hixt, Elizabeth 96
Ho----, Stephen 63
Hobson, Anna 108, 153
  David 94, 218
  David, Jr. 94
  George 25
  John 209
  Mary 103, 170, 218
  Samuel 149
  Thomas 172
  Wm. 121
Hodge, Daniel 94
  Elizabeth 175
  Gentry 149
  Mathew 119
  Nancy 74
  Patsy 156
  Rosena 60
  Tabitha 165
  Wm. 13
Hodges, Amy 54
  Andrew 174, 185
  Andy 96
  Carline 139
  Creely 27
  Delala 185
  Dianer D. 187
  Drury 50, 95
  Eliza 150
  Elizabeth 99, 191
  Elizabeth (Miss) 175
  Franky 71
  Gideon 108
  Gideon L. 86
  Giles 116
  Isham 95
  Jiles 95
  John 91
  Joseph 95, 132

Hodges, (cont.)
  Judy (Miss) 153
  Lucy 173
  Lydia 91, 174
  Malissa 91
  Martha 95, 221
  Martha J. 108
  Mary 74, 173
  Matthew 95
  Meredith 112
  Nancy Frances 61
  Phebe 218
  Pleasant 48, 94, 145, 146, 218
  Pleasant C. 112
  Polly 74, 186
  Preston 54, 95
  Rachel 95
  Rebecah 202
  Rebecca 185
  Sally 14, 45, 128
  Sarrah (Miss) 74
  Sophia D. 108
  Susan 54, 74
  Tellitha 73
  Welcome 174
  William 16, 20, 186
  William L. 110
Hoffman, Elizabeth 52
Hogdon, Sally 161
Hoges, James 30
  Rebecker 30
Hoihst, John 56
Holaman, Mary 43
Holcomb, (See also Halcomb, Haulcomb)
  Branch 1, 7
  Cloe 7
  David 44
  Drury 105, 123, 125
  Fanny 82
  G. 112, 152
  G.A. 163
  G.D. 30
  George, Jr. 216
  Grimes 103
  Indiana 197
  James 66
  Jane 139
  John 4, 41, 100
  John S. 40
  Leroy 22, 65, 96
  Leroy E. 210
  Luceanna 220
  Margaret 142
  Mary 103, 163
  Nancy 157
  Nelly 126
  Philip 161
  Philip L. 96
  Phillip 7, 35, 96, 134
  R. 162
  Rachel 174
  Ruth 126
  Sarah 80
  Sarah An 209
  Shadrach 74
  Shadrack 158
  Thomas 10, 96
  Thos. 116, 126
  William 59, 156
Holden, Delila 151
Holder, Baler 97, 157
  David M. 85
  Elizabeth 122
  Frances 85

Holder, (cont.)
  Jesse 72, 122
  Julian 180
  Lutrisa 207
  Mary 45
  Mica 157
  Seney 195
Holderfield, Betsey 170
  Elizabeth 215
  Lucinda 223
  Ralph 97, 131, 176
  Valentine 41
  Watson 208
  Wm. 63
Holebrooks, Sally 32
Holeman, Rebekah 127
  Tilly 132
Holensworth, Elizabeth 189
  Gemima Frances 57
Holiman, Absalom 213
Holleman, William 42
Hollemon, Wm. 97
Holliman, William 198
Hollimon, William, Jr. 97
Hollingsworth, Phillis 75
Hollinsworth, Eliza 106
  Elizabeth 167
  J. 19, 92
  Joseph 184, 191
  Mary 71, 147
  W.R. 10
  William R. 163
  Wm. R. 172
Hollomon, Nancy 116
Holloway, William 71
Hollyfield, Valentine 118
Holmes, Benjamin 17
Holser, Mickey 8
Holsey, Sarah E. 167
Holt, Ann 128
  Martha 44
  Mary 139
  Nathan 211
Holyfield, Cary 223
  E.M. 59
  Eleanor 26
  Eliza M. 91
  Elizabeth 57
  James 160
  Jemimah 120
  John 98
  Letitia 153
  Polly 160
  Rachel 39
  Ralph, Jr. 168
  Sally 26
  Viney 56
  Watson 91, 118, 133, 134, 207, 213, 214
  Wilson 13, 163
  Wm., Jr. 63
Honaker, Cinthia 72
Honey, Meekey 80
Hood, Elizabeth A. 158
Hooker, Robert 74
  Samuel 155
Hooser, (See also Hauser)
  Catharine 182
Hoot---, Sally 9
Hoots, Caty 223
  Henry 222
  Lydia 139

Hoots, (cont.)
  Mary 73
Hopkins, Nancy 138
Hopper, Ann 179
  Elizabeth 157
  Liza 179
  Sallie 109
Hoppers, Edward 51
  Elizabeth 194
  Nancy 210
Hoppes, George 182
Hoppis, Ann 195
  Edward 49
  Sally 49
Hoppos, Nancy 196
Hopson, Rachael 209
  Rachel 161
Horace, Amferd 128
  Sarah A. 128
Horn, Elizabeth 115
  Jessee 197
  John 24, 97
  Judith 21
  Nancy 83
  Sarah 21, 173
  Thos. 115
Horten, Harretta 120
Horton, Henry 99
  Jacob 213
  Jas. 99
  Joseph 170
  Milly 92
  Reachel 179
  Vinson 99
Houchen, Sarah 213
Hough, Catharine 40
  Ephraim 137
  Harriett 57
  Jas. E. 99, 177
  S.A. 83
Houser, Elizabeth 148
  M.A.M. 164
Houston, Amanda M. 183
Houts, Jacob 99
Houzar, Joseph (?) 88
Houzzy, Eliza 151
Howard, Benjamin 129
  Charles 99
  Elener 171
  Elizabeth 26, 82, 181, 200, 214
  India 186
  Jas. 97
  John 112
  Joseph, Junr. 73
  Malsey 214
  Mary 140, 206
  Nancy 97
  Pamala E. 85
  Philip 64, 138
  Phillip 99, 124, 135, 182
  Sally 146
  Samuel 130
  Sarah 97
  Susannah 58, 73
  Wm. 58
Howel, Stephen 196
  Susanna 90
Howell, Alse 37
  Jonathan 87
  Mary 196
  Rebeca 176
  Ruth 87
  Stephen 99
Howlet, Mary Ann 31
Howlit, Rebecca 47

Huchens, John 199
Huchins, Elizabeth 9
Huchmand, J.W. 15
  Nancy Bald(?) 15
  Nancy Kinner Praetor (?) 15
Hudson, Caroline O. 211
  Elizabeth 15
  George 15, 88
  Hampton 198
  Polly 198
  Sally 41
  Summervill 44
  Wm. 161
Hudspeath, Martha 76
Hudspeth, Airs 140
  Carter 98
  Charles 100
  Clarey 144
  George 74, 122, 132, 138
  Giles 178
  Hannah 97
  James 105, 107, 132, 177, 194, 213
  Jas. 100
  John 213
  Jos. 142
  Jourden 182
  M. 55
  Mary 122
  Morgan 177, 200
  Polly 142
  Rhody 125
  Sarah 27
  Thomas 141, 211
Hudspith, Morgan 102
Huett, Franklin 168
Huey, Jane 23
  Thomas 23
Huff, Penelope A. 100
  Susanah 213
Huffhines, Margrett 68
Hugent, Rebecky Emily 51
Hughes, Ann 69
  Mathw. M. 69
  Matthew M. 34, 100
  Mattw. M. 114
  Susan 97, 214
Hughlett, William 85
Hull, James W. 107
  W.G. 113
Humby, Ephraim L. 22
Humphreys, David 200
  Hannah 63
  Isaiah 80
Humphris, Elizabeth 142
Hunt, Amy 180
  B.F. 101
  Barbara 140
  Daniel 7
  Elizabeth J. 164
  Elizabeth M. 81
  Enoch B. 204
  G. 101
  George 58
  J.J. 101
  Judith C. 207
  Matilda 207
  Mildred A. (Miss) 129
  Molley 102
  Nathan D. 101, 175
Hunter, Elizabeth 102, 129
  Elizebeth 40
  John 101

Hunter, (cont.)
　Nancy 103
　Rachel 187
　Sally 100
　William 23, 175, 183
Hurst, Ballard P. 86
　Charles W. 96
　George 102
　Mary 54, 124
　Scena 153
　William R. 71
Hurt, Betsy 224
　Dicy 1
　Elizabeth 170
　Jane 170
　Joel 1, 102
　John H. 70
　Martha Rebecca 1
　Matilda 170
　Sarah 32
　Thusay M. 148
Husbands, Permealia 62
Husk, Malinda J. 166
Hutchans, Sarah 1
　Temperance 141
Hutchens, Alva 80
　Amos S. 141
　Ann 51
　Asa B. 103
　Benjamin 94, 110
　Isaac 220
　Jane 57
　Joel 50
　John 103
　Joseph 195
　Joshua 102
　Josiah 220
　Margarett 195
　Mary 116
　Meriday 102
　Rachel 195
　Rhody 17
　Sarah 1
　Strangeman 81, 108
　Thompson 181
　Vestal 140
　William 66, 82
Hutchins, Aley 194
　Asa B. 103
　Balas 4
　Benjamin J. 49
　Calvin 80
　Elisabeth 103
　Elizabeth 20, 29, 51
　Elizebeth 11
　Elkanah 194
　Enoch 20
　Frederick 79
　Hannah 80
　Icey 163
　Isaac 89
　Isaac W. 218
　James 103
　Joel 141
　John 4, 102, 149
　Joseph 104
　Judy 170
　Mehaly 55
　Nancy 25, 218
　Partrick 75
　Patrick 218
　Pillar 20
　Sarah 32, 220
　Sophrony N. 136
　Strangman 103
　Suzanner 103
　Thomas 157

Hutchins, (cont.)
　Thompson 102
　Vestal 103
Hutson, Ann 2
　Elizabeth (Miss) 117
　Jane 168
　Lucinda 26
　Lucy Ann 39
　Mary Ann 125
　Micky P. 182
　Nancy 198
　Sarah Jane 39
Hyatt, Martin 25
Hyett, Nancy 201
Idell, Michael 57
Ideol, Jacob 171
Idoel, Michael 97
Ilis, William 15
Ingram, Charlot 193
Ingrum, Zilpah 74
Inman, Anna 105
　Elizabeth Jane 89
　Frances 105
　Henry 105
　Morris 105
　Nancy 161
　Rebeca 83
　Sarah 161
　Sarah E. 105
　Thomas 105
Inscore, James 105
　Joshua 105
Iram, Tenea (?) 177
Ireland, Amos 14, 105
　Nancy A. 126
　Nehemiah 105
Irvin, Samuel 218
Isaacks, Ashby 156
　Catharine 156
　Elizabeth 152
　Francis 156
　Godfrey 153
　Jesse G. 95
　Nancy 157
　Nancy P. 218
　Rebeca E. 157
　Samuel 157
　Sarah L. 191
Isaacs, Agga 153
　Godfrey 190
　Rachel 223
　Samuel 153
Isbell, Betsey 91
　Elezebeth 139
　Elizabeth 70, 97
　Hickman 10, 46, 91
　Hickmon 51, 156
　Littleton 14
　Pheby 51
　Richard 91
　Sarah 91
Isley, George M. 167
Ives, Aby 34
Ivins, Elizabeth 144
Jacks, Charity 79
　Elizabeth 32, 41
　Fanny 77, 124
　Larkin 213
　Martin 213
　Nancy 151
　Polly 74, 79
　Rhoda 155
　Richard 176, 204, 205
　Sally 207
　Thomas 14, 186

Jackson, Aleson 185
　Alsa 31
　Andrew H. 42
　Anna 53
　Charlotta 212
　Clary 64
　Edith 167
　Eli 108
　Elizabeth 18, 50, 197
　Iredell 29
　J.W. 13
　James 39
　James W. 39, 181
　Jams 125
　Jason 176
　Jno. H. 136
　John 54
　John H. 85
　Joseph 107
　Lettitia 221
　Lurainey 155
　Mary 19, 108, 157
　Nancy 123
　Nelson 87
　Newel 69, 106, 174, 206
　Newell 158
　Prisila 198
　Rachael 108
　Ruel 127, 202
　Sally 52
　Wm. 106
James, Catharine 218
　Conell 122
　Isaac 100
　Jacob 200
　James 218
　Lucy 92
　Margret 176
　Nancy 48
　Patsy 127
　Polly 15
　S.C. 58, 210
　Samuel 43
　Sarah 171
Jarman, William 119
Jarratt, Isaac (?) 39
Jarrell, Ellis F. 107, 183
　Mariah 206
Jarret, Isaac 164
Jarvis, Bryant 7
　George M. 33, 95
　Hanah 114
　Israel 107
　Jabez, Junr. 4
　James 93
　John 69, 107
　Levi 107
　Lizzey (?) 4
　Lydia 122
　Maryan 143
　Mehetable 172
　Patse 15
　Polly 69
　Sarah 179
　Stephen 69
　William 9
Jater, Nancy (?) 113
Javney, P.C. 100
Jean, Edmond 107
　William 107
Jefferson, Daniel 213
　Elizabeth C. 141
　Sally 90

Jeffery, Mary 183
  William 154
Jemmery, Mary Ann 119
Jems, Ambrose 21
Jenkings, Vallentine 15
Jenkins, Henry H. 99
  Hiram 107
  J.J. 69
  J.M. 135
  John A. 178
  John J. 224
  Lucinda 107
  Lucy An 16
  Mary 9, 189
  Nancy 107, 195
  William A. 115
  Wm. 107
  Wm. A. 109
Jennings, (See also Gennings, Jinnings)
  Jestin 85
  Mary 116
  Matilda 24
  Thomas J. 202
Jenny, (See also Denny)
  Joan 209
Jentree, (See also Gentrey, Gentry, Gintry, Jentry)
  Lear 70
Jentry, Agness 162
  Calvin 74
  Carey 27
  Mahaley 22
Jerrell, Fanny 108
  Fountain 108
Jervis, A.B.C. 71
  D. 36
  Daniel 108
  Elizabeth 50
  Geo. A. 74, 177
  George A. 74, 128
  James 74, 95
  Jehu 18
  Jesse G. 50
  Jesse P. 71
  John 18, 108, 175
  Priscilla 168
Jessop, A. 67
  Anny 34
  Caleb 42
  Calop 179
  Delila 31
  Edith 42
  Eli 130
  Hannah 159
  Jane 5
  Joseph 159
  Lethy 15
  Mahala 67
  Minerva J. 158
  Sally 108
  Samuel 43
  Susanna 212
  Thomas 132
Jessup, Alfred 119
  Bethany E. 108
  Caleb 37
  Elizabeth 108
  Elizey 41
  Jane 119, 174
  M. 43
  Martha A. 36
  Nancy F. 42
  Nancy J. 201
  Prescilla 42

Jessup, (cont.)
  Rebecca 42, 106
  William H. 36
Jester, Betsy 66
  Elizabeth 104
  Isaac 98
  James 109
  John 109
  Mary Ann 75
  Nancy 219
  William 4
Jindkins, Polly 45
Jinia, Hariett A. (Miss) 58
Jinkins, Delight 15
  Elisabeth 139
  Henry 45, 139, 169
  Hugh 212
  Jesse 139
  Nancy 48
Jinnings, (See also Gennings, Jennings)
  Margaret 92
  Mariam 58
Jinnins, Elizebeth 75
Jobe, Thomas 206
Johnson, ---- 224
  Ambrose M. 58
  Anderson 110
  Ann Eliza 110
  Ashley 112, 217
  Baley 110
  Betsey 107, 185
  Bosthenia C. 128
  Calvin 67, 189
  Charles 3, 149, 183
  Charles, Jr. 192
  Clarinda 96
  Clarissa 222
  Creasy 150
  Cristeena 40
  Dealia 136
  Delilah 110
  Elina T. 136
  Eliza 9
  Elizabeth 12, 61, 76, 113, 226
  Elizebeth 13
  Emily 26
  Enoch 18, 118
  Fanny 111
  Frances 67
  Franky 40
  Gideon 103, 217
  Gidion 110
  Gincy 88
  Harriett 112
  Henry 48, 154
  Hiram 20, 150
  Huchins 111
  Hutchens 110
  Jacob 222
  James 111, 145, 157, 208, 226
  James B. 140
  James F. 32
  James H. 111
  Janett 183
  Jas. M. 172
  Jeffery 112
  Jemima 189
  Jesse 27, 82, 104, 107, 110, 112, 118, 147, 202, 214
  Jincy 54
  Jinsey 30

Johnson, (cont.)
  John 9, 98, 110, 111, 139
  John B. 34
  John G. 109
  John T. 83
  Jonas 110
  Jonathan 109
  Jos. 170
  Joseph 33, 138, 139
  Leacy Jane 54
  Lewis 136
  Lidia 150
  Lucinda 41
  Lucy 19
  Lyda 110
  Lydday 102
  Lydia 3, 20
  Mahala 48
  Margaret 89
  Martha 94
  Martha M. 14
  Mary 20, 109, 113, 216
  Mary B. 212
  Maryan 73
  Meddey 138
  Menerva 138
  Milley 68, 111
  Milly 194
  Nancy 56, 89, 115, 118, 152, 202, 211, 218
  Newel 110, 111
  Patience 111
  Patsey 98
  Patsy 61
  Paulina 61
  Phebe 139
  Philip W. 89
  Polly 24, 56, 112
  Preshus 33
  Rachel 107, 112
  Rebecca (Miss) 60
  Reuben 151
  Rosanna 114
  Sallie 150
  Sally 3, 121
  Sally A. 99
  Sammuel 110
  Sarah 13, 53, 204
  Sarah E. 142
  Sarah Mildred 90
  Siller 83
  Squire 56
  Stephen 7, 71
  Susan L. 89
  Susanna 41
  Susannah 99
  Tabitha 8, 55
  Tellunday ? 78
  Temperance 19
  Tennessee 144
  Thompson 12
  Thos. 145
  W.R. 41
  William 8, 61, 76, 112
  William A. 61, 204
  Wm. 94
Johnston, Anne 149
  Betsey 177
  Betsy 122
  Charles 3
  Edy 158
Joiner, Betsy 37
  Dempsy 35

Joiner, (cont.)
 Elizabeth 143
 Holland 205
 Jiles 113
 Margit 97
 Mary 9
 Mills N. 113
 Sarah 68
 Timothy 49
 Willis 113
Jol, Thomas (?) 77
Jones, Adaline 180
 Amelia 145
 Amitintha 111
 Armitta 110
 Bershaba 209
 Charity M. 108
 Daniel S. 43
 David 207
 E.C. 151
 Edward 108, 111
 Elizabeth 39, 43, 54,
   84, 107, 117, 178
 Ellen R. 171
 F.B. 145
 F.H. 226
 Francis 2, 63
 Isaac 113
 J.H. 115
 James 2, 29, 65, 114,
   145
 James, Jr. 46
 James F. 114, 152
 Jane 38, 165
 Jas. 151
 Jesse 115
 John 22, 30, 35, 53,
   117, 171
 John A. 76
 Joshua 194
 Kesiash 207
 Keziah 62
 L.B. 59
 Lemuel 173
 Levi 130
 Lidia 108
 Lucinda J. 200
 Lydia D. 118
 Mahala 6
 Marinda 111
 Martha 163
 Mary 58, 111, 140,
   171, 210
 Mary A. 93
 Maryann 66
 Matilda J. 165
 Nancy 32, 33, 220, 222
 Nancy B. 53
 Nancy M.E. 3
 P.M. 38
 Polly 107, 211
 R.E. 189
 R.W. 190
 Rebeca 76, 109
 Rhoda 152
 Russel R. 113, 117
 Rutha 173
 S.H. 12, 131
 Sally 2, 65
 Saml. H. 114
 Saml. P. 27
 Samuel 1, 54, 128
 Samuel (Min) 49
 Sarah 38, 165
 Sary 2
 Silas 11
 Susannah 207

Jones, (cont.)
 Sytha 11
 Thomas 70
 Wm. 34
 Zachariah 209
Jonson, Polly 180
Jordan, Abigail 155
Joyce, Nancy E. 113
Joyner, Amy 119
 Charles A. 46, 149,
   163
 David 86
 Elizabeth E. 188
 Giles 115
 Jane 116
 Jonathan 162
 Joshua 115
 Martha 55
 Martha C. 55
 Mills 115
 Rachel 55
 Sarah 152
 Thursy 206
 Zachariah A. 152
Kanady, (See also Cana-
   da, Kennedy)
 Larkin 118
Kannedy, Tennessee 38
 Thirsa 38
Kapp, C.H. 115, 194
 Roseltha P. 132
Kare, John 63
Karr, Nancy 82
Katt, Celia M. 57
Kay, Sarah J. 118
Kays, Hannah 197
 Lydia 143
Kearby, Francis 150
 Lucy 121
Keaten, Viney 55
Keath, Eliza 116
Kechely, Christopher
   159
Keen, Eliza. 74
 Keziah 25
 Mary 173
 Samson 21
Kees, Lucinda 132
Keeter, Jesse 116
Keeth, John C. 199
 Rebecca 199
Keister, Mary E. 222
Kell, Polly 24
 William 160
Kellehan, Polly 69
Keller, Emily 65
 Mason W. 3, 44, 165
Kelley, Joseph 166
Kellion, Nancy 30
Kelly, Alexander D. 55
 Benjamin 23
 Cornelia 155
 James 124
 Jemima 140
 Jno. 51
 Juliet 107
 L.D. 17
 Mary 78
 Nancy 51, 100
 Samuel D. 159
 Sarah 169
 Thomas 46, 113
 Thomas D. 6, 68
 Thos. 196
 Thos. D. 46
 Thos. S. 17
 Wm. D. 116, 219

Kemmer, Margaret 226
Kempler, Sarah 64
Kenada, (See also Cana-
   da, Kanady, Kennedy)
 Larkin 151
Kendrick, Ezekiel 82
Kennedy, (See also Cana-
   da, Kanady, Kenada)
 Bettie 83
 Cynthea S. 220
 Phebe 57
 Wilmington 116
Kennida, John 160
Kennidy, Ben Thompson
   (?) 202
 Emily 202
 Nannie Snow (?) 202
Ker, Tobitha 76
Kerby, Anny Hawkins 102
 Francis 102
 Joel 95
 Patsy 134
 Peter 102
 Richd. 117
 Salley 150
 V.M. 87
 Vaney 157
Kerin, William P. 28
Kerkbride, W.E. 197
Kernes, Martha J. 24
Kerney, Sarah 41
Kerr, A.M. 148
 Absalom 117, 121
 Absalum, Junr. 83
 Absolem T. 51
 Archibald M. 65
 Martha W. 137
 Rebekah 83
 Sarah 179
Kerzy, Patience 50
Kesler, John F. 107
 Lettitia 119
Keston, Nancy 217
Ketchum, Polly 15
Kettle, William 179
Key, Achilles 13
 Augustin 71, 114
 Betsy 80
 Cornelia Francis 185
 Delphia A. 215
 Elizabeth 30, 146,
   185, 207
 Emily 71
 Frances 13
 John Anderson 6
 John W. 117
 Lendry 53
 Lewis 132
 Lewis A. 118, 185
 Lindsey 118
 Lydia D. 118
 Mahaly 114
 Marthy 25
 Matilda 30
 Milbourn 118
 Nancy J. 132
 Rue 117
 Saluda 6
 Tennessee 6
 William J. 117
 William S. 118, 185
Keys, Betsy 80
 Elizabeth 186
 Joseph, Jr. 143
 William 118
Keziah, Nancy 12
 Rebecca 147

Kezzel, Elizabeth 156
Kid, Lucy 158
  Robert 158
Kidd, Alen 118
  Allen 210
  Benjamin F. 11
  Elizabeth 195
  Ellin 171
  Jesse 60, 112, 117, 205
  Martha 205
  Martha E. 205
  Nancy 118
  Patsy 118
  Rachel 111
  Robert 158
  Sarah 110
  Serah 110
  Sibby 170, 171
  William S. 171
Kiddle, Jestin 128
Kidner, Elizabeth 97
Killion, Isaac 161
  Nancy 166
Kimbell, John 76
Kimble, Arnette 187
  Mary 76
Kimbrell, John 154
Kimbro, Ormon 206
Kimbrough, Anna 115
  George 206
  George, Jr. 213
  George H. 8
  Goldman 137
  M.D. 85
  Marmaduke 1, 48, 100, 111, 138, 197
  MDuke 99
  Ormon 37, 119
  Polly 99, 213
  Rebekah 22
  Sally 206
Kincanor, Matthew 92
King, Alexander 119
  Amanda J. 96
  Caler 71
  Elizebeth 104
  Hester A. 106
  Jeremiah 16, 69, 83
  Jesse 43
  Jno. Q.A. 124
  John 68
  Julia M. 20
  Keziah 218
  Mary 129, 171
  Mary E. 60
  Pheby 119
  Polly 82, 130
  Richard 119
  Russel 119
  Sarah 107
  Sarah F. 37
  Stephen 171
  William 119
Kingsbury, Sarah J. 41
Kinion, Jemimah 126
Kinley, Thomas J. 166
Kinneck, George 80
  Johanna 11
Kinny, Susanna 25
Kirby, Samuel 95
Kirk, Emmarly 149
Kirkman, Delfina 182
  Eveline 181
Kirkmond, Elisa J. 120
  William 120

Kittle, Martha 12
  Ruth 176
  William 82
Knight, Theany 112
Knighten, Mary Ann 18
Knuckels, Polly 128
Koger, Emily 51
Kreiger, Christina 163
Krouse, Susan E. 202
Kyle, James 83
  Nancy 195
Lacy, Barbary 212
  Burrel 212
Ladd, Amos 120
  Letha 110
  Mary 170
Laffoon, Elizabeth J. 77
  James W. 120
  John C. 77
  Lydia 45
  Martha J. 76
  Mary 33
  Patsy 139
  Rebecca 21, 94
  Sarah 72
  Stephen 120
  Susan 27
  William G. 77
  Wilson 94, 130
Laftice, James D. 120
Lain, Conna 24
  Elizabeth 84, 124
  Suzanner 116
Lakey, Frances 197
  Francis 121
  Frank 160
  Jesse F. 94, 121
  Lydia 116
  Mary 220
  Matilda 94
  Sally 160
Lamb, Christina 21
  Priscilla 82
Lambert, Anney 189
  India 179
  Nancy 213, 223
  Polly 121
  Th. 116
  Thomas 172, 200
Lamkin, M.V. 130
  Thomas H. 87
Lancaster, George 107
  Sarah L. 107
Land, Margaret 219
  William 77
Landreth, Nancy 81
  Sarah 188
Landrum, Mariah 150
  Richard 172
Landy, Isaac 157
Lane, David 149, 175
  Elizabeth 12
  Jane 224
  Lucy 175
  Torler 149
  Vichtler 176
Lang, Ann 96
Langeley, Sary 55
Langley, Elizabeth 107
Langly, James 90
  James W. 26
Lanier, Robt. 29, 42, 125
  Sterling 138
  Thomas 188

Lankester, John 187
  Judith 187
Larrener, Rheda 145
Laseter, Isaac 198
Lash, Margret 73
  Nathl. 48
Lasiter, Mary 221
Laster, James 122
  Mary 122
Latham, Charles 78, 117, 118
Laurence, Richard 10
Lavender, Jane 212
Law, (See also Low)
  Mary 149
Lawder, Lidia 30
Lawless, Polly 212
  Presley 140
Lawrence, Lucy 10
  Lusetty L. 208
Lawson, Claborn 90
  Elizebeth 20
  Equilly 61
  Frances 43
  James W. 60
  Martin 122, 163
  Mary 122, 146
  Nancy 76
  Nesley 10
  Sally 104
  Sinthy 174
  Thomas J. 108
  W.T. 104
  William 17
Layel, Matilda Ann 120
Leagins, Julia 215
Leak, Marthy W. 4
Leath, Dory 150
Leatherage, Alfred 14
  Eliza J. 14
Lee, Eliza 80
Leeke, Wilson 32
Leftwick, James 52
Legins, Tobitha 166
Leibengood, Frany 120
Lemmon, Cattern 145
Lemmons, Susannah 160
Lenard, Eliza Ann 60
Leonard, James M. 70
  Piercy 208
Lester, Ithamer 160
  Jesse 24, 65, 99
  Joshua 136
  Mary 65
  Mary Ann 160
Lewis, Anthony 68
  Asa 49, 182
  Celia 200
  Charles 123
  Dicy B. 190
  Dicy F. 183
  Eleaner 123, 152
  Emely 96
  Jacob A. 106
  Jane 68
  Jno. W. 204
  Katharin 121
  Letty 161
  Martha 138
  Mary 46, 137
  Mehala 123
  Nancy 164
  Nancy (Miss) 22
  Rebecca A. 12
  Rebecca T. 207
  Rhoda 96
  Sally 120

Lewis, (cont.)
  William 61
  Wm. 185
Liggon, James 23
  Susannah G. 48
Lighton, Martha J. 19
Limms, Robert (?) 185
Linch, Anderson 129
Lindley, James M. 111
  Mary Ann 111
  Sally 85
Lindsay, Charlotte 212
  Elizabeth 21
Lindsey, Fany 192
  Judith 54
  Lucinda E. 112
  Pinkney 34
  Susan 217
Lines, Lucretia C. 142
Linkins, Sally 136
Linn, Alexander 122
Linvell, Bracer 50
  Elizabeth 105
  Margret 43
Linvill, Elizabeth 186
  Henry 174
  John 168
  Mahala 168
  Matilda 111
  Samuel 111
  Tabitha 170
Linville, Etha 118
  Jemima 184
  Nancy E. 83
Lion, John 138
  Mary 138
Lions, James 124
Little, Charity 168
  Lewis 124, 125
Loagan, Mary 204
Loagin, Ann 162
  Honner 32
  Lear 113
  Polley 178
Lockett, James W. 100
Lockhart, John 10
  Mary 123
  Thomas 212
Loftess, Ambrose J. 22
Loftice, Jane 53
Loftis, Ambrous J. 2
Loftus, Herod 100
Logan, Catharine 159
  Catherine 54
  Elizabeth 94, 168
  George 166
  Honor 129
  Hugh 113, 125, 166,
    178, 193, 204
  James 129
  John 125, 168, 197
  Katharine 197
  Nancy E. 57
  Polly 166
  Rebeckah 183
  Richard 120
  William 181
London, Amos, Junr. 79
  James 60
  Sarah 198
  Wm. 84
Londy, Isaac 173
Long, Alfred 120
  Anna 163
  Barbara 49
  Cathrain 138
  Elizabeth 96, 208

Long, (cont.)
  Elizabeth M. 62
  Elly D. 186
  Frederick 126
  Fredrick 125, 182
  George 182, 209
  Henry 15
  Isaac 126
  Jed 62
  John, Jr. 126
  John A. 126
  Nancey 31
  Nancy 209
  Nathan 96
  Sally 181
  Wiley 81
Longine, Anne 101
  John Thos. 24, 76,
    126, 163, 208
  John W. 110
  Mary 161, 208
  Thomas 82
Longing, John Thos. 126
Longins, James 5
  Milley 5
Longworth, John 88
Loucks, Susannah 190
Loudon, Elizabeth 136
Love, Anne 121
  Catharin 172
  Daniel 182
  David 127
  Debby 172
  Elizabeth 182
  Elizabeth J. 78
  Gilbert A. 119
  Hannah 7, 172, 189
  Isaiah 172
  J. 116
  James 127
  John 126
  Kerry 76
  Leanah 127
  Lidda A. 131
  Louisa 126
  Mahaly 127
  Malpark 126
  Marget 126
  Marthy 163
  Mary Ann 207
  Nancy 119, 163
  Sarah 172
  Susanah 189
  Thomas 127, 207
  Thomas, Jr. 172
  William 109, 172
Lovell, James 50
  Jane 50
  Margaret M. 214
  Rebecca 22
  Sallie E. 107
  Thos. P. 22
Lovil, Hiram 81
Lovill, E.F. 191
  Edward 168
  Edward, Jr. 180
  Edward F. 47
  Mary 206
  Rebekah 206
  Sarah 39
  Wm. R. 71, 82
Loving, Joseph 18
Lovins, Mary Ann 93
Low, (See also Law)
  Barnet 149
  Cealy 73
  Daniel (?) 121

Low, (cont.)
  Daniel 104
  Edy 116
  Elias 128
  Elizabeth 186
  Isaac 128, 207
  Jackson 54, 127
  Jacob 73
  Kenny 127
  Kerby 73, 129
  Lucinda 20
  Mandy 7
  Mary 73
  Matildia 39
  Nansey 52
  Patsey 186
  Ruth 73
  Sarah 111
  Sealy 188
  Senca 47
  Stephen 127
Lowden, Hannah 86
Lowe, Jane 2
  John C. 2
  John H. 42
  Lucretia E. 41
  Martha 72
  Robert 193
  Sarah 189
Lowell, Elizabeth 164
Lowers, S.W. 6
Lowrey, John 210
  Mary 210
Lowry, Isabella 210
  Thomas 141
Lows, William John 90
Loyd, Joseph 50
Lucado, W.F. 190
Ludd, Elizabeth (?) 98
Lugert, Enos (?) 198
Lumas, Nancy 169
Lunday, John K. 115
Lundy, Churchwell J.
  29
  Jno. E. 212
  Melvina (?) 129
  Rachel 103
  Richard 87
  Sarah 129
  Susannah 8
Lunsford, Elizabeth 25
  Hiram 25
Luper, Margaret (?) 10
Lurle, Arter (?) 143
Lynch, Elizabeth 101
  Frances 162
  Francis 137
  James H. 40
  John 48, 101
  Mary 62, 125
  Sarah C. 180
Lynn, Alexander 194
Lyon, Catharine 75
  Christenia 218
  Elizabeth 223
  Jency 58
  Lucy 128
  Nancy 178
  Polly 218
  Stephen H. 8, 154
  William 113, 129,
    180
  Wm. 73
Lyons, Elizabeth 138
  John 140
  Prudence 156
  Sarah 159

M---, James L. 20
Maab, Emily 40
Mabe, Calvin 156
Maberry, Milly 54
Mabery, Lenina 199
Mabre, Iredell 119
Mabry, William 186
Mabury, Wm. 76
Macalgen, Hew 185
  Rebekah 185
Macey, Lydia 161
Macglean, Elizabeth 226
Macguier, Nansey 207
Macker, Wm. 32
Mackey, Catherine 44
  John 131
  Robert 69
  Ruth 137
MacKie, Gragery 170
Mackie, Catharine 136
  Elizabeth 64
  Jesse 196
  Lyda 184
  Naoma 83
  Rebecca 170
  Robert 44, 162
  Sarah 78
  William 184
Maclain, Willey 130
Macraw, Andrew (?) 130
Macy, Catherine 171
  Mary 13
Madden, Charles 104
Madison, John 53
  Lewis F. 58, 77
  Lucy A. 53
Mager, Pleasant Walton
  (?) 9
  Virginia 9
Mahaffe, Pricilla 99
Mahaffy, Elizabeth 223
Mainard, Caroline 158
Mainline, Elender 101
Maize, Catharine 20
Major, James 124
Malary, Stephen 159
Mallet, Rebecca 46
Manges, Henry T. 13
Mankem, Stephen 21
Mankin, Jesse 134
  Joel 17
  Stephen 133
Mankins, Emeline 144
  Hulda 179
  James 189
  Mary Ann 46
  Nancy 223
Manly, Caroline 107
Manner, Nansey 185
Manom, F.J. (?) 8
Manuel, Matilda 108
March, Sallie 164
Marien, Mary Ann 123
Marion, Anna 134
  Anny 38
  Bartholomew 225
  Eliza 155
  Eveline 63
  Francis J. 47
  Hannah 58
  Isaac 134
  Jeremiah 134
  John M. 30
  Josephine T. 127
  L.N. 126
  Midiam 174

Marion, (cont.)
  Nancy 63
  Patience 174
  Pegy 137
  R.E. 137, 174
  S.V. 137
  Sally E. 126
  Sarah 88
  Thersey 171
  William 13, 174
Markland, Robert 134
Marler, John 3
Marlin, William 136
Marlow, Elijah 61
Marman, Thos. 135
Marmon, Joseph 135
Marris, Rebecca 17
Marsh, (See also Mash)
  Celia 187
  D.H. 159
  Daniel 148
  Elizabeth 63, 80, 187
  Ezekiel 63
  Henry H. 135
  Jeremiah 24
  John, Jr. 135
  John P. 202
  Mary 16
  Mary Ann 117
  Miner 24
  Minor 135
  Nancy 107, 135
  Polly 203
  Samuel 135
  Serena 159
  Susan P. 135
  Thomas 145
  Thos. 135
  William 21, 135, 159, 203
  William M. 135
  Winaford 154
  Wm. 136
Marshal, Rebecah 49
  Richard 136
  Sarah 167
  Simon 55
  Susannah 136
  Tempy 119
Marshall, Ann 136
  Dinah 17
  E.L. 136
  Edward 164
  Eliza Ann 66
  Elizabeth 184
  Elizabeth Ann 68
  Henry 121, 182, 207
  Jane 202
  John 153
  Joseph 136
  Letha 144
  Margaret 47
  Martha A. 178
  Mary 38
  Moses 155
  Parthenia 116
  Rebecca 32
  Richard 214
  Saml. 32
  Sarah 17
  Simon 170, 171
  Susana 22
  Temperance W. 115
  Watson 26, 130, 166
Marshell, Ruthey 186

Marshill, Simon 70, 204
Marsten, Catharine 133
Martain, Crisy 93
  John 81
Martin, Alfred W. 84
  Ann 209
  Benj. H. 125, 136, 193
  Bridgett 218
  Charlotte 161
  Cohull W. 146
  Daniel H. 170
  Drusiller 138
  Elizabeth 10, 137, 139
  Elizabeth M. 212
  Fanney 66
  Frances 201
  G. 219, 220
  George 83, 117
  Henry 137
  Henry P. (?) 148
  Hugh 83, 152
  James 102
  Jane 50, 164
  Jean 115
  Jesse 164
  John 1, 4, 10, 18, 20, 43, 44, 62, 136, 210
  John, Jr. 28
  John, Junr. 94
  John H. 137
  John J. 198
  Leah 174
  Lewis 189
  Lucy 22
  Margaret 58, 172
  Marita 137
  Martha 54, 57
  Mary 136, 179, 192, 213
  Nancy 140, 156
  Nelly 133
  Obadiah 3, 4, 5, 9, 224
  Oby. 30
  P.S. 116
  Patience 33
  Polley 98
  Polly 82, 179
  Presilla 225
  Rachael 100
  Rich. 56
  Richard 137
  Roddy 54
  Sally 106
  Saml. 137
  Samuel 115, 117, 127, 164, 179
  Sarah 90, 117, 170, 193
  Simon H. 93
  Valn. 137
  Vianna 132
  W.R. 37
  William 137
  Winney 141
  Wm. 5, 10, 201, 208
  Wm. C. 5
Masemore, Ruth 3
Maser, Mary B. (?) 8
Mash, (See also Marsh)
  Jeremiah 137
  Peggy 152
  Salley 135
  William 180

Mason, Lurana 223
Thos. 160
Massack, Lovy 24
Massey, Rachel C. 203
Massie, Lucinda 21
Massy, Clarinda 64
William 98
Masters, James 138, 164
John 224
Lizebeth 197
Rebekah 190
Sarah 71, 107
William 40
Masting, Bershaba (?) 39
Matax, Levina 219
Mathas, B.W. 191
Mathess, Benjamin 162
Mathews, Absalom 138, 193
Absolom 191
Bradley 204
Hezekiah, Senr. 138
James 136, 139, 197
Littlebery 138
Louisa 204
Mary 65, 199
Polly 124
Rebeca 138
Susan 182
Wm. 93
Mathias, Martin 76
Mathis, Benjamin 193
Littleberry 138
Luvania 136
Sarah 206
Matrey, Nancy 16
Mattecks, Sarah 115
Matterson, Nancy 115
Matthews, Aaron 110, 111
Absalom 25, 128
Absolam 120
Benjamin 24
Betsey 191
Bradley 205
Hezekiah 139
Jacob 205
James 67, 206, 225
Nancy 115
Raney 206
Ruth Jones 206
Sarah 205, 220
Susanna 201
William 200
Winny 8
Mattison, Elon 70
Matucks, Ann 194
Maxwell, Lydia Eley 226
T.H. 120
William 24
May, Jesse 126
Mark 139
Martin 139
William 8
Mays, Harden 16
Hardin 28
John 98, 105, 139
Nancy 120
Polly 28
Rebecca 190
William 111, 119
Maze, Elizabeth 143, 154
McAnally, Chas. 63
Low 63

McAtee, Thomas 196
McBride, Edward 90, 97
Elisabeth K. 90
Jefferson 19
Jennett 167
John 5, 129, 130
Martha J. 12
Mary 157, 167
Mildred 143
Sarah 88
Wakeman 129
McCallom, James 194
McCammon, Patty 161
McCane, David 50
Sarah 50
McCarter, Philip 198
Sarah 72
McCarthy, Jane 114
McClennon, Neal 210
McClover, Betsey 206
McClure, Ann 125
McCollam, Sally 16
McCollom, Huldah A. 60
Peggy 7
Thomas 198
McCollum, Andrew 73
Elizabeth 104
Jane 198
John 135, 195
Juliann 41
L.A. 46
Mary 37
Nathaniel 37
Rebekah 73
Sarah 61, 198
William 130
M'Colum, Mary 189
McCord, James 226
Margett 226
McCracan, Martha D. 136
Thomas 136
Wilmoth 136
McCracken, Mary F. 107
M'Craw, Matilda 36
McCraw, Andrew 120
Elizabeth 101, 142, 208
Francis 130
Francis M. 130
Gabl. 167
Geo. W. 154, 219
George W. 34
J.W. 130
Jacob 159
Jacob W. 130
James 33, 65, 79, 175
Jas. 50, 175
Mary M. 179
Matilda 213
Nancy 19, 72
Paulina 131
Purlina 169
S.A. 23
Sally 34
Samuel 213
Sarah 219
William 192
Wm. 178
Wm. W. 71
McDade, John 197
McDaniel, Adalade 32
Elizabeth 138
Henry 70
Mary 222
N.C. 142
Sarah 10

McDaniel, (cont.)
Susanna 46
W.T. 32
McDonald, James 106
Janan 87
McDonnel, Emily 88
McGathy, Jane 79
McGee, Albert N. 183
D.M. 42, 85
Daniel 121
Daniel H. 120
Danl. 94
Drury 92
Harmon 131
Iredell A. 11, 34
James Lemuel 182
John 131, 165
Ladoskey 165
Leanna O. 131
Lemuel 89
Mary 217
Mary E. 104
Nancy 165
Nancy J. 89
McGehee, John Amos 22
McGilbary, John 213
McGilvary, John 56, 68
McGlacham, Elizabeth 147
McGlamery, Elizabeth 34
McGlammory, Jeney 221
McGlaughlin, Elizabeth 170
McGlemery, Jane 57
McGrady, Eliza Jane 113
McGraw, Locky 180
McGuffin, Eliza E. 1
Nancy Jane 191
R.F. 1
Sally Ann 226
McGuin, Robert 146
McGuire, Elizabeth 199
John 131, 183
Lucinda 175
Mary 183
Michael W. 171
Polly 21
Susannah 14
McHane, Lew F. 166
McHone, Emsetta 58
McJames, Sally Ann 152
McKenny, Mary 219
McKie, Daniel 102
Elizabeth 193
John 136
McKiney, John 108
Rozannah 205
McKinney, Alexander 108
Eliza Reed (?) 172
Gideon E. 91
Granville 76
James 117, 155, 172
Jesse 188
Louisa 131
Lucinda 172
Mary 51, 77, 82
Nancy 42
Rebeca 40
Sally 37
McKinny, Eliza 170
Emely 178
Francis 165
Mary 35
Olive 35
McKinston, James 24
McLean, J.R. 137
William 203

McLemore, Cary 41
  Wright 41
McLennon, Neil 106
McMicel, Peter 224
McMickel, Permiley 96
McMickle, C--- 94
  Gideon 79
  Gideon J. 79, 120
  Jno. J. 132
  Martha 136
  Maryann 62
  Peter 94, 132
  S.J. 164
  St. Clair 132
  Sarah Jane 217
  Sinclair J. 51, 226
McMikle, Sinclare 224
McMilan, Harmon 133
  P.H. 133
McMilion, Columbia 83
McMillan, Joseph 198
  Letty A.M.J. 8
  Parthenia 188
  Tempy 198
McMillion, E.W. 136
  Elizabeth 113
  James L. 91
  Malinda 155
  Nancy 91
McMillon, James 132
  Sarah 133
  William 190
McMilon, William 91
McNally, Mary 120
McNeff, Sally 196
McPeak, Archibal 15
  Reuben 17
  Ruben 143
  William 206
McPeeack, Wm. R. 133
McPherson, Stephen 133
McRoberts, Bency 133
  Benjamin 104
  John 133, 221
McWiller, Rhoda (?) 135
Mears, James 131
Medkiff, J.J. 22
Meeks, Nathan 53
Megehee, Sarah 30
Mehaffy, Sally 171
  Thomas 171
Melton, Anderson 129
  Elizabeth 28, 138
  Isham 125
  James 67, 125
  Litchey 140
  Lydia 69
  Malinda J. 61
  Polly 125
  Sallie 135
Melvin, Eliza 17
  Mary A. 87
Merchant, Katharine 156
Meredith, Hugh C. 81
  J.F. 176
  Jenny 42
  Nancy 43
  W. 4, 21, 43
  William 90
Merida, Nancy A. 148
Meridith, William 123
Merimon, Elizabeth 166
Merion, Daniel 78
  Sarah 78
Merkle, Julia Ann 31
Merphey, Martha Ann 9
Merrian, Daniel 118

Merrion, Alcy 162
  Amelia 118
  Mildred 150
  William 53
Merrit, James 42
Meskeep, Amanda 50
Messel, William J. 143
Messic, Elisha 140
Messick, Elisha 140
  George 142
  L.J. 140
  Martha 142
  Milinda 74
  Nancy 112
  Wiley 140
Messicks, Elendor 176
  John N. 178
Messir, Linah 111
Meumillion (See also
  Muemillion)
  Elizabeth 173
Miars, George 140
Michael, Harriet J.
  219
Michaels, Elizabeth
  195
Michel, Pouncey 51
Mickey, T.E. 60, 125,
  127
Mickle, A. (?) 26
  Sally 143
  Susanna 103
  William 28
  Wm. 143, 188
Midciff, ---- (Mrs.)
  210
Midkiff, David 90
  John 75, 91, 141
  Mary 39
  Mary E. 210
  Rebecca 67
  Sarah 141
Miers, Elizabeth 150
Mihaffy, Thos. 141
Mikels, Elizabeth 208
  George 141
Mikles, John 124, 141
Miles, Ellender 162
Milgrim, Levi 116
Miller, Adam 73
  Anne 107
  Catherine 144
  Elizabeth 41, 209,
    214, 225
  Frances 55
  Jno. 124
  John 41, 98, 141,
    143, 174
  Josh 98
  Louisa 179
  MaryJane 116
  Nancy 222
  Nicholas 44
  Polly 25
  Sally 209
  Sarah 80
  W.A. 144
  Willeby 61
Mills, John 156
  Luritta 223
  Nancy 185
  Peter 195
  Susan 34
Milraney, Joseph 219
  Mary 219
Milstead, Edward 196
Milton, Isham 129

Mimsk, Louisa Caroline
  90
Minhis, Patsy 128
Minick, Isaac 79
Minish, Isaac 142
  James 142
  Joshua 160
  Judey 75
  Susan 222
  Thomas 33, 92, 148,
    155, 217
Minnish, Mary 105
  Thomas D. 142
Minten, Elizabeth 52
Minter, Flem 143
  Lucy 143
  W.L. 27
Mires, Eliza J. 75
Mirick, Elizabeth (?)
  198
Missie, Mary C. 109
Mitchel, Adaline 34
Mitchell, E--- 78
  Elizabeth 169
  Franky 143
  Reany 56
Mock, Anvell 167
  Henry 143
  Johannes 16
  Lewis 42, 176
  Nancy 85
  Peter 11, 73
  Peter, Jr. 143
  Polly 100
  Sally 15
Mofield, Mary Ann 131
Moles, Elizabeth (?)
  145
Monday, Elizabeth 139
  Lucy 153
  Sarah 193
Money, Elizabeth 3
  Elvira 214
  Hamel 90
  Henry 90
  Henry I. 169
  Henry J. 207
  Howel 144
  Isaac 144
  Jno. 125, 163
  John 59, 126, 144
  Lucinda 27
  Nancy (?) 58
  Prudence 144
  Rachel 126
  Rhoda 35, 40
  Susanah 35
  Tho. H. 144
  William 33, 144
  Zebidee 149
Monfield, Keziah 5
Monkins, Elizabeth 118
Montgomery, Jane 34
  Madison 144
  Milton 2
  Samuel 184
  Sarah 2
  Susan 82
  Zachariah 78
Mony, Isaac 3
  John 3
Moody, Elizabeth 145,
  225
  J.R. 145
  John 154
  John R. 26
  Mary 95

Moody, (cont.)
  Nancy 13, 48
  P.B. 27
  Sally 123
 Mooney, Rachel 100
  Wm. 56
 Moor, Jesse 149
  Priscilla 149
 Moore, ---- 84
  Allis 72
  Amon 185
  Ann 137
  Benjamin 146, 226
  Benjamin, Jr. 118
  Candesia F. 109
  Catharine 92
  Diner 146
  Edward 84, 205
  Elijah 80
  Elizabeth 12
  Ervin 148
  Famey 110
  Galihew 188
  George 63
  Henry 75, 217
  Henry H. 146
  Huldy E. 117
  James 10, 171
  James C. 187
  Jenny 176
  John 13, 53, 66, 99
  Leathy 188
  Lydia 79
  Malinda 146
  Malsey 101
  Margaret 49, 216
  Martha 132
  Martha Jane 194
  Mary 64, 66, 183
  Mary Jane 206
  Matilda 206
  Matilda C. 75
  Matilda J. 71
  Moses 173
  Nancy 13, 145
  Nancy Jane 207
  Nancy L. 217
  Rebecca 45
  Rebeckah 61
  Rebekah 188
  Robert 45
  Rolly 146
  Ruth 63
  S.D. 90
  Samuel 45, 75
  Sarah 37
  Sharlotte 155
  Stephen 145
  Stephen F. 30
  Thomas 162
  Thomas, Jr. 194
  Thomas J. 183
  Thos. 135
  William 145, 183, 195
  Wm. 217
  Wm. A. 146
  Wm. H. 89, 149, 156
  Wm. T. 102
 Moorefield, Phebe 5
 Moores, Hulday 117
 Moorfield, Bedda 6
 More, Rachel 36
 Morefield, John 75, 147
  Letuice 31
  Lydia 187

Morefield, (cont.)
  Mary 78, 106
  Nancy 2
 Moreland, Elizabeth 199
  Jeremiah 58
  Nancy 83
  Polly 58, 88
  Thomas 80, 113
 Morgan, Betsy 156
  Jesse 212
  Margaret 47
  Martha 204
  Mary 29, 98, 213
  Mary Ann 212
  Mary E. 181
  Sarah 222
 Morgenson, Nancy 177
 Moris, Elizabeth (?) 9
 Morison, M. (?) 53
  Nancy 144
 Morlin, Rebecca C. 226
 Morris, David 147
  Edy 75
  Elizabeth 45, 84, 205
  Hannah 25, 193
  Laurence 147
  Mary 17
  Milly 187
  Nancy 176
  Nathaniel 45
  Shadrach 58, 220
  Violetta 38
  William 205
 Morrison, Andrew 147
  James 75, 147
  Jesse 148
  Matilda 147
  Nancy 3, 148
  Nelly 82
  Phebe 83
  Susannah 107
 Morrow, Jeremiah 151
 Morstall, Lucy S. 13
 Morten, Rachel 31
  Sally 62
  Sarah 126
 Mortin, Catharine 142
 Morton, Lucy W. 164
 Mosby, Wm. C. 37
 Moseley, Caroline 190
 Mosely, East 53
  Elizabeth 72
  John R. 175
  Theophilus 72
  West 68
 Moser, Anny 59
  Charity L.C. 52
 Mosier, Sarah 163
 Mosir, Nancy 139
 Mosley, Henry 194
  J.H. 56
  James 204
  Jershia 50
  Keturah 85
  Martha 38, 194
  Rebecca 194
  Samuel, Ju. 22
 Moss, John 87
  Polly 92
  R.D.R. 58
 Mosser, Sarah 11
 Mott, Richbell 1
 Mourning, M.J. 171
 Mouter, Henry 76
 Moyers, Betsey 139

Mozby, Jane R. (Miss) 37
  Joseph 222
 Sabellow 222
 Muckmillion, Agnes 168
 Muemillion, (See also Meumillion)
  Samuel 173
 Mullice, Polly 149
 Mullis, Bashebe 24
  Hannah 46
  Stephen 148
 Muncan, Peter 180
 Muncens, Peter 128
 Munchus, J.K. 186
 Muncus, Henry 48
  Sarah 48
 Mundy, Mary 186
 Muneus, Matilda 128
 Munius, Sandford (?) 12
 Munker, Mary 11
 Munkus, Elizabeth 72
 Mure, Rebecer 30
 Murglorhorn, Sealy 203
 Murphey, Joseph, Jr. 149
  Rhody 160
  Suckey 41
  Valentine 177
 Murphy, Elizabeth 192
  Jane 149
  Jude 94
  Kezia 221
  Margaret 74
  Nancy 213
  Peter 3
  Richard 149
 Musgrove, George 121
 Musick, Elisha 23
 Mustard, Hannah C. 101
  Luvisy 114
 Myers, Barnet C. 4
  John 33, 152
  Sarah 28
  Shadrac 124
  Shadrack 155
  William W. 14
 Myres, John 137
  Lucy 75
  Nancy 217
 Myrs, Betsey 3
  Mary 82
 Nailer, Nancy 217
 Nales, Nancy 109
 Nance, Eliza 129
  Littleton 225
  Nancy 174
  Patsey 66
  Sally 164
  Susannah 171
  Ursula 225
  Wm. M. 62, 64, 163
 Nansey, Susanah (?) 109
 Nation, Caroline 128
  James 108
  Thomas 54
 Nations, Frances A. 123
  Jacob 95
  James 95
  Joseph 145
  Mary V. 95
  Thomas 176
  Thurzy 203
 Nayler, Cynthia 158
 Naylor, John W. 150
  Mildred R. 86
  Polley E. 140

Naylor, (cont.)
  Thomas B. 86, 140, 172
Neal, Elizabeth 126
Needham, James 150
  Jesse M. 217
  Martha 150
  Mary 91
  Sarah 19
Nelson, Ann 204
  Milley 83
  Nancy 155
  Sarah 34
Nesbitt, James L. 29
Nester, James 199
  Jane 199
  John 150
  Joshua 2
Newman, John W. 81
  Sallie 130
Newton, Martha 79
  Prisciler 49
Niblorn, Luista (?) 24
Nicholds, Dudley 216
  Edmond 151
  Sally 216
Nichols, Edmond 200
  Jas. 156
  Jesse W. 28
  John 185
  Lucinda E. 13
  Lucy 128
  Mary Ann Elizabeth 165
  Polly 148
  Rebecca 53
  Sarah 198
  Winny 45
Nicholson, Abigail 115
  E.D. 148
  Elizabeth L. 63
  Ephraim 151
  Jennella 8
  John 215
  John M. 47
  Micajah 224
  Phebe 8
  Prudence 196
  Sarah A. 215
  Setliff 215
Nickals, Martha 185
  Sally 216
Nickolson, Jacob 188
Nicks, Jane 29
  Martha J. 73
  P.M. 41
Nickson, Martha E. 75
Nighin, Jeddida 19
Nix, Joseph 25
Nixon, Elizabeth 151
  F.M. 203
  Francis 151
  Hannah 203
  Jacob 210
  Mary 151
  Thos., Jr. 151
  William P. 202
  Wm. P. 151
  Wm. R. 151
Nixson, Mary A. 20
Noble, Coleman 180
  Leda 220
Noblet, Rebeccah 140
Noblett, Wm. 152
Noblitt, Mary 95
Noland, James 152
  Lewis 141, 162

Noles, Littleton 118, 154
Nolin, Lewis 109
Noling, Delina 56
  Mary 55
Nookester, Michael 168
Nooncastel, Elizabeth 60
Nooncaster, Michael 60
Nooncastle, Michael 60
Noonkerster, Sarah 114
Noonkester, Elizabeth 60
  Michael 203
Noonkestl, Mary 113
Norman, Avery 97
  Caroline 144
  Danel 42
  Elijah 77
  Elizabeth 135
  Elizia 122
  Frances 112
  Henry 131, 152, 153
  Isaac 189
  James C. 188, 219
  John 89, 153
  John, Sr. 102
  L.J. 96, 116, 189, 213
  Lidea 131
  M.C. 88
  Margaret 47
  Mary 139
  Mary Ann 152
  Mary M. 95
  Meridith T. 189
  Nancy 122
  Nathaniel 89, 152
  Peter 76
  Phebery 42
  Polly 72
  Ruth 77, 194
  Sally 70, 199
  Sarah 75, 86
  Sophia A. 205
  Susannah (?) 11
  Thomas 4, 162
  Thos. 123
  Thurman 152
  William 57, 119, 122, 141
  William M. 153
  Wilson 152
  Winny 141
  Wm. H. 158
Normon, Barbara 12
  Elizabeth 179
  Fanny 19
  Martha 141, 177
  Nancy 162
  Susannah 121
Norten, Elisha 77
North, Daniel 1
  John 149
  Jonathan 24, 94, 225
  Larkin 153
  Sarah Ann 115
Norton, Franky 28
  Larken 153
  Nelly 135
Nott, Dortha N. 171
Nuckolls, Lee 155
Null, Elizabeth 183
  Mary 62
Nunly, Mahala F. 182

Nunn, Malinda 7
  William M. 7
Nusum, Emiline 210
Oakly, Mary 105
Oddre, Chesteena 40
Odeal, Ann 127
Odel, Elizabeth 153
Odell, Solomon 81
Odier, Jane 98
Odle, Seania 30
Odur, Marry 196
Ogelsby, Marthy 106
Ogle, Canaan 92
  Isaac 180
Oglesby, C.B. 218
  Elizabeth 182
  Micajah 106
  Shadrach 205
Oley, Loye (?) 5
Oliver, John 176
  Lucinda 16
  Patsey 215
Olliver, Margery 176
Olvy, Jane 176
  Martha 90
Omerer, Martha 117
Oneal, Jas. 139
  Jos. 154
Oneals, Any 181
Ooten, Thomas 140
Osburn, Polly 60
Oston, (See also Austin)
  Beckey 180
  James 180
  Rebecker 180
Owen, David 122, 200, 211
  Elizabeth 143
  J.M. 64, 181
  James 21
  James B. 155
  Jane 65
  John 169
  John H. 155
  Joseph M. 155
  Josiah 101
  Lucinda 200
  Mary 169
  Peyton 179
Owens, Isam 69, 155
  J.M. 38
  Mary 207
  Mary A. 173
Owins, Sarah 133
Pack, John 167, 186
Padget, Polly 142
  Sarah 18
Padgett, Charlotte 213
  Hannah 217
  Jacob C. 44
  Jincey 52
  Judith 142
  Mary 44, 122
  Mary K. 63
  Nancy 185
  Nelly 134
Page, Mary Francis 191
Pain, Lewis 64
  Nelly 117
  Rachael 64
Painer, Rachel 160
Painion, Prudence 211
Pall, Patsey (?) 107
Panther, Christina 226
Pardue, J.M. 203
  Jeremiah 156

Pardue, (cont.)
  Louzena 156
  Mary 203
  Sarah Ann 123
  Thos. 194
  Wm. 156
Pare, Lucinda 195
Parker, (See also Barker)
  Ed 156
  Edmond 197
  Edmund 60
  Eliza 68
  Jestine 151
  John 59
  Joshua 200
  Judith 219
  Luesy 197
  Lydia 1
  Melley Ann 191
  Peggy 120
  Polly 196
  Rebekah 1
  Sally 159
  Sarah 164
  Sarah Ann 123
  Solomon 156
  William 50
  Wyatt 31
Parkes, Meredith 82
Parks, Clarissa B. 151
  Elizabeth J. 47
  Jas. 3, 4, 5, 6, 14
  John P. 81
  Richard H. 47
Parnel, Burrell 66
Parnell, Polley 129
Parris, John L. 59
Parrish, B.F. (Miss) 100
  William 9
Parson, Aaron 105
  Basheba 105
Parsons, Adeny 156
  Allen 156, 157
  E.D. 157
  Elizabeth 144
  Keziah 131
  Rachael 182
  Vinson Ball (?) 131
Partin, Elizabeth 157
Pate, Hardy 109
Paterson, Maryan 104
  Rebecker 84
Paton, Lettitia 168
Patter, Gideon (?) 165
Patterson, Benjamin 157
  Deborah Ann 150
  Harrison 91
  Isaac 23
  James 157, 218
  Jemima ? 26
  Jesse 65, 157
  Jinney 25
  John R. 58
  Joshua 23, 25, 141
  Keziah 158
  Martha Jane 72
  Mary A. 204
  Mary Jane 218
  Nancy 151
  Rebecka 93
  Sally 157
  Saluda 93
  Sarah 212
  Susanna 83
  Thomas 141

Patterson, (cont.)
  Thos. A. 220
  W.E. 178
  William 208
  Winney 124
  Wm., Sr. 158
Patteson, Anna 218
  James B. 218
Pattillo, Henry 63
Paul, Edith 135
  Edmund 148
  Elizabeth 142
  Libby 217
  Mary 43
  Thomas 43
Paune, Sally 156
Payn, An 190
  Matilda 127
Payne, Ann Snow 158
  Asa S. 61
  Barnet 74, 158
  Barnett 159
  Elizabeth 130
  Jackson 88
  John 12
  Levi 159
  Levi, Jr. 158
  Luoiza 180
  Luvinca 159
  Lydiann 127
  Malinda 61
  Martin 124
  Nancy 65
  Polly 197
  Richard 158
  Sary 88
  Stephen 158
  Thomas 197
  Zachariah 65
Paysinger, John (?) 96
Peak, Tabbitha 145
Peake, Drinda 220
Pearce, Rachael 109
  William 108
Pedigo, Jas. S. 190
Pedjo, Jas. J. 157
Peek, Judeth Ann 166
Peel, Crissy 49
  Daniel T. 35, 64
  E---- A. 159
  Elizabeth 159
  George E. 159
  Jesse 159
  Martin 159
  Mehala 69
  Priscilla 93
  Sarah 66
  Thomas 69
  Timothy 69
Pell, Jestin 60
  Mira 28
  Sarah Ann 36
Pellet, Mary 4
Pelley, Nancy 168
Pelmon, Julina 121
Pendleton, Agnes 198
Pendrega, Susannah 144
Pendri, Ann 144
Pendry, Alfred 217
  Jonathan 160
  Marth 94
  Patsey 24
  Peggy 194
Penix, Lawson G. 74
  Mary 85
  Melley 210
Pennington, Martha 31

Pennion, Polly 156
  Susannah 200
Pennix, George 183
Penright, Mary J. 59
  Nancy 59
Perdue, Jemima 123
  Jno. 160
  Lucy 128
  William 4
Perking, Adaline 36
Perkins, Amy 138
  C.W. 130
  Elizabeth B. 121
  Frances 22
  Isaac 22
  John 154
  Lucinda B. 150
  Martha 44
  Mary 66
  Nancy 22
  Paline 73
  Polly 26
  Thos. 160
Perlite, Mary E. Rubery (?) 147
  Rachel 147
  Thomas 147
Perry, Lucy 16
  Nancy 98
Person, Jane 9
Peters, Phebe E. 52
Peterson, Patsey 174
Petit, Cloah 165
  Elizabeth 197
  George 165
Petree, Barbara 19
  Riley F. 9
  Sarah 194
Petted, Zacariah 110
Pettegene, Margaret 133
Petterson, William L. (?) 83
Pettet, Frances 87
  Nancey 87
  William 168
  Zachariah 197
Petticoart, Melchia 148
Pettijohn, Nancy 178
Pettit, Benjamin 66, 164
  Dorotha A. 76
  Francis 127
  George 150
  J.G. 7, 187
  John G. 88, 158, 166
  L.G. 25
  Thomas 166
Pettitt, Benjamin 127, 161
  Charlotte 164
  Elizabeth 193, 196, 209
  Francis 179, 206
  J.G. 214
  John G. 138, 208
  Martha M. 159
  S.G. 97
  William 89
Petty, Betsey 114
  Lucy 133
  Nancy 105
  Rosanna 181
  William 39
  Zachary 105, 123
Pettyjohn, William 14
Pfaff, J.L. 161
Pfoff, Jacob 71

Pharis, Mary Jane 18
Phelps, Hiram 221
  Thos. 154
Phibbs, Anslum 61
Phileps, (See also Fillips)
  Luisa 181
Philips, Abraham G. 138
  Anderson 38, 44
  Elizabeth 125, 179
  Fanny 183
  John 41
  John S. 170
  Joseph 45
  Katharine 8
  Mary 38
  Nancy 44, 48, 121, 150
  Oswell 67
  Paulina 42
  Philip 151
  Preston 161
  Richard S. 55
  Ruth 194
  Sarah 45, 57
  Solomon 161
  Syannah 54
  Tobias 150
Phillips, Abner 161
  Andrew 161
  Betsy 60
  Catharine 175
  Edith 118
  Elizabeth 102, 198
  Hiram 194
  J. 30
  Jo. 11
  John 125, 155, 161
  John S. 9
  Joseph 101
  Lewis 192
  Loueasy 226
  Mary 1, 146
  Mary E. 86
  Matthew 162
  Nancey 126
  Nancy 224
  Phebe A. (Miss) 175
  Philip 66
  Polley 100, 221
  Polly 155
  Preston 168
  Rachel 120
  Richard S. 57, 125
  Salley 115
  Sarah 142
  Sarah A. 135
  William 23, 57, 167, 173, 179
  William, Senior 162
Phipps, George 162
  Martha 135
Pickett, Anne 106
Pierce, Chaffin 219
  Elizabeth 219
Pigg, Anna 24
  Elizabeth 155
  Nathan 198
Pike, Benjamin 163
  Betsy 196
  Elizabeth 2
  Isaac 98
  Lucy 106
Pikes, Sally 90
Pilcher, Alvers 115
  Billsy 212
  Daniel 55, 163

Pilcher, (cont.)
  Febe 176
  Franky 102
  James 163, 194
  Mary 4, 176
Pillar, William H. 88
Pilmon, Polly 139
Pilsher, Daniel 149
Pilson, M. 8
  Martha 8
  Rebecca 8
  W.L. 164
Pinion, Elizabeth 48
Pinix, Polly 62
Pinkley, Cristena 88
  Elizabeth 35
  Peter 88
Pinnix, Overton 163
  William 178
Pinright, Sarah 32
Pipes, Silvanus 123
Pitman, Susan 200
Pitmon, Jane 88
Pledge, Caroline Meteldea 137
Pledger, Stephen 96
Ploughman, Mary 213
  Nancy 12
Plowman, Betsey 183
  Elizabeth ? 82
Poe, Caroline 86
  Elizabeth 138
  Vilenty 123
Poenix, Rhoda 32
Poff, Anna 29
  Michael 191
  Michael S. 62
Poindexter, A.P. 41, 64
  Ametty 138
  Ann C. 137
  David 89, 121, 201
  David H. 212
  Dolly 168
  Elizabeth 63, 78
  Elizabeth C. 88
  Francis 126, 161
  G. 3
  Gabl. 94
  J.G. 164
  J.J. 87
  Jane 37
  Jno. F. 145
  John 70, 116
  John J. 134
  Julia A.E. 151
  Mahala Bray (?) 16
  Margaret 9
  Martha 21, 161
  Martha M. 21
  Mary 173
  Mary B. 226
  Mary W. 134
  Matilda 16
  Milly 163
  Nancy 87, 137
  R.C. 9, 41
  Rebeca 57
  S. 16
  Sarah 9, 127
  Thomas H. 123
  Thomas W. 68
  Thos. H. 63, 164
  Thos. W. 117
  W. Pledger 137
  W.R. 164
  William 63

Poined, Caty 123
Ponsonbay, Mary 217
Pool, James M. 165
Poor, Charles 39, 200
  Faithy 153
  John 165
  Katharine 61
  Nancy 81
  Polly 80
  Robert 80, 211
Poore, Charles 141
  John 165
  Margarett 114
  Nancy 165
  Samuel D. 153
  Thomas 165
  William 165, 212
Pope, Nancy 190
  Sarah 41
Poplin, Alstin 182
Portee, Louisa 171
Porteet, Tho. 160
Porter, Elisa P. 123
  Elizabeth 211
  Ira 112
  Mary 159
  Sarah 159
Porters, Rebeca Jane 141
Portice, Patsey 146
Potter, Benjamin 33
  Fanny 221
  Frances 94
  Mary 95
  Patsy 106
  William 128
Potts, Peggy 192
  Perthenea Ann 191
Powall, Robt. C. 41
Powel, Nancy C. 169
Powell, Phebee 24
Powers, Jane 226
  Rouney Cintha 72
Poyndexter, Rebecca 205
Praetor, J.W. Huchmand (?) 15
  Nancy Bald (?) 15
  Nancy Kinner 15
Prather, Charity R. 10
  Eleanor 66
  Margaret Jane 59
  Ruth A. 5
  Ruthy A. 44
  Sarah Jane 188
  T.F. 118, 191
  T.W. 70
  Thomas F. 26, 138
  W.A. 74
Pratt, Elisha 54
  Elizabeth 34
  Hattie E. 34
  Madison 34
  Margarett 54
Pressley. James H. 163
Prevett, Iredell 175
Prewit, Mahala 107
Price, Duke 166
  Nathan 31, 143
  Rachael 166
  Susannah E. 154
Prichard, Abigal 121
Prim, Enoch 166
  Katherine 66
  Loucetta 29
Primm, Caleb 166
  Frances 72
  James 166

Prior, Sarah Jane 126
Pritchard, Synthey 15
Pritchett, Lucy 190
Privett, Sarah E. 211
Pruet, Milly 101
  Tamsa 37
Pruett, ---- 102
  Jane 127
  Nancy 3
  Sarah 79
Pruit, Abraham 192
  Tempe 192
Pryor, Abner 160
  Dorinda M. 81
  Lucy 160
Pucket, Elizabeth 179, 223
  John 179
  Martha 136, 225
  Read 167
  Sally 167
Puckett, Adaline 24
  Cary 167
  Elisabeth 167
  Isham 225
  Jane 81
  John 167
  Lyddia 106
  Pleasant 167
  Rachel 225
  Shental ? 179
Puckit, Polly 73
Pullen, Nancy 176
Purdan, Polly 56
Purdom, Benjamin 178
  John 98, 161, 167
  Polly 178
  Thomas 98
  William 129
Purdry, Milly 103
Purkins, Nancy 195
Purycoff, Richard (?) 122
Puryear, Richard C. 22, 37
Quesenbury, John 222
Quesinberry, Joseph 167
Quesonberry, Lewis C. 162
Quinn, Pierce 168
Quisinbury, Virginia S. 199
Raasse, Jane 31
Rachels, Nany 182
Rafield, Darkus 119
Railsback, Roseannah 132
Rainey, Joseph 45
  Mary 45
  Matilda 45
Rains, Josaphene 30
  Thomas 120
Rainwater, Alcy 18
Ramey, Elijah 127
  Jane 149
  John 139
  Joseph 168
  Joseph, Junr. 88
Ramsay, Elizabeth 3
Ramsey, Hester 61
Ramsy, Anne 112
  John 73
Ramy, John 128
Ranard, Jane 158
Randleman, M.R. 10
Randolph, William 140
Ranes, Mary J. 31

Raney, Elijah 72
Rannard, James 177
Ransom, Mary 126
  Thomas (?) 148
Ransome, Sarah 132
Rarden, Polly 127
Rarder, Nancy 126
Rash, Mary 46
  Miriam 125
  William 125, 162
Ratliff, Betsy 128
Raughton, Ann 92
Rawley, Darius 169
  J.W. 130
  John W. 166, 180
  Margarett 217
  R.P. 112
  William 77
Rawls, Polly 80
Ray, Braxton 40, 82
  Edward D. 37
  Leonard 135
  Lydia 169
  Richard 169
Raynales, Hanah 78
Raynolds, George 81
Reace, Sarah J. 148
Read, Susanah 54
Reading, William 169
Reaves, Asa 133
  Elizabeth 175
  John 165
  Micajah 99
  Nanceay 165
Reavis, Abigal 40
  Assa 196
  David 8
  Elizabeth 157
  Jesse 169
  Jo. 139
  Joel 169
  John 175
  Joseph 169
  Mary 196
  Polly 169
  Sarah 169
Rece, Jesse 118
Rector, Mahaly 72
  Nancy 72
  Peter 169
  Peter, Jur. 116
  Sarah 116
Redman, Lucyann 88
Redpath, Mary 78
Redsaul, (See also Bedsaul)
  Lucinda 16
Reece, A.Q. 142, 162
  Abraham 22, 46, 55, 170
  Abrm, 171
  Adam M. 182
  Alvis 136, 209
  Ann 48
  Ann D. 170
  Anna 143
  Curlistia 220
  Daniel 170, 186
  Edward 48, 104
  Edward Iredell 4
  Edward J. 184
  Eli 210
  Elizabeth 79
  Elizbeth 94
  Eunice 194
  George W. 152, 179
  Hadly 96

Reece, (cont.)
  James 50
  Jane 50
  Jemima 110
  Jesse 24, 100, 136, 169, 172
  Joel 46, 169, 218
  John 38
  Joshua 22
  Juda 100
  Keziah 94, 210
  Kiziah 191
  Lucinda 38
  Lydia 79
  Malinda 136
  Mary 46, 210
  Sarah 136
  Simon 57, 65
  Thomas H. 55
  William 55
  Wilson 56, 94, 170
  Zechariah 55
Reed, Anny 165
  David 53
  Elender 58
  Elijah (?) 101
  Eliza 172
  Elizabeth 20, 134, 185
  Esther Baker (?) 134
  Isaac 165
  Jacob 170
  James (?) 172
  James 134, 170
  Joseph 145
  Lucinda McKinney (?) 172
  Mary 20
  Nancy 20, 101
  Polly 10
  Sarah 165
  Tabitha 170
Reehtor, Peter 15
Rees, Daniel 170
  Eli 132
  Hadly 186
  Levi 168, 170
  Unus 183
Reese, Daniel 170
  Joel 58
  Martin 9
  Mary 226
  Nancy P. 38
  Sally 209
  Wm. 9
Reeves, J.E. 7, 37, 38, 48, 110, 137, 191, 226
  Jesse 56
  M.C. 171
  Martha 76
  Micajah 59, 80, 104
  Nancy A. 115
  R.E. 187, 197
  Richard E. 107, 171, 226
  Sally 134
Reid, Amos 134
  James 208
  John 139
  Sarah 102
Renagar, John 69
Reney, Hance H. 61
Reng, Elisabeth 63
  Wiley 63
Reniger, Joseph 223
Rennard, Polly 126

Rennegar, Caty 196
Rennigar, Henry 171
Renniger, George 171
  Henry 223
  John 98
  Joseph 223
  Mary 98
Repass, Mariah T. 180
Revell, Lissa 155
Reves, Eliza S. 127
  Richard E. 42
Revil, Fany 213
Reynolds, Abigail 32
  Charles 172
  Cordilla 28
  D.B. 172
  David 172
  Elizabeth 212
  George 172, 193
  J.Y. 34
  Mary 131
  Nancy 172
  Nathaniel 78
  Rosana J. (Miss) 67
  Sally 78
  Thomas 172
Rhoades, Isabella 177
Rhoads, Agnes 162
Rhodes, Polly 104
  William 141, 142
Rich, Moses 25
  William 122
Richards, Elizabeth 142, 156
  Leonard 166, 193, 214
  Letha 68
  Ruth 193
  Sarah 156
Richardson, Ann 188
  Elizabeth 39
  J.M. 52
  John 84
  Joseph 6
  Joseph M. 27, 100, 201
  Mary 130
  Polly 84
  Sarah 59, 210
  Willey 176
  William 86
  Willy 64
  Wm. 130
Richerson, Elizabeth 85
  John 47
  Joseph 129
Richison, Nancy 111
Richtor, Nancy 125
Ricks, Elizabeth (?) 30
Riddle, Ayre 173
  Betsy 173
  Isham 122
  Sarah 62, 80
Ride, Winneford 4
Rideans, Sarah 161
Ridenhour, Nancy 219
Rider, Eli 180
Ridgeway, Eleanor 129
  Osburn 173
Riding, David 15
Ridings, Bechella 51
  Dice 219
  Isaac 36
  Jane 161
  Judith 141

Ridings, (cont.)
  Sarah 36
Ridins, Agness 220
Ried, Lewis 112
  Rachel 165
Riel, Elizabeth 213
Riggans, Polly 28
Riggs, Abagal 152
  Daniel 68, 150
  David 30, 225
  Jane 75
  Jesse 174
  Joel 69
  Lany 94
  Lydia 174
  Polly 72
  Rebekah 150
  Sarah 95, 120
  Silas 30
  Wm. M. 150
  Z. 42
Riggsby, Sarah Ann 139
Rigsby, Lucinda 154
  Polly 148
  Tabitha 80
Riley, Betsy 63
  Edward 178
  Elizabeth 178
  Lucy 33
  Ninian 33
  Thos. J. 4
Rilly, Easter 54
Rinager, Mary 80
Rinchet, John 199
Rinegar, Mary Ann 80
Rinehart, Christian, Jr. 109
  Frederick 28
Riner, Jacob 200
Ring, Adam 174
  Celia 174
  Celia J. 84
  Enoch 8
  Martin 174
  Nancy 6
  Peggey 6
  Rachel 174
  Sarah 2
  Stephen 186
  Susanna 6
  Thomas 6
  William 134
Ritchy, Moses 93
Ritter, Lazarus 168
Roard, Sarah 132
Roberson, Chesley 175
  Liddy 121
  Lucy 112
  Lucy S. 179
  Martha 87
  Matilda 130
  Nathaniel 121
  Nutty 174
  Thomas 175
  William 112
  Robert, Frances 116
  Thompson 19
Roberts, Ben 202
  Celia 217
  Clarice 21
  Elizabeth 56, 108, 117
  G.W. 175
  Hannah Tucker (?) 202
  James 26
  Jane 123

Roberts, (cont.)
  John 27, 156
  John E. 23, 210
  Jonathan 58
  Logan 114
  Logan D. 55, 61, 147
  Lucy 25
  Lucy C. 84
  Malinda 5
  Martha 100
  Martha A. 103
  Mary 136
  Matildy 66
  Nancy 154
  Nancy E. 5
  Patsy 92
  S.W. 5, 175
  Susan 58
  Susanna 192
  Susannah 217
  Thomas 175
  Thomas B. 62
  Thos. 148
  Thos. B. 216
  Woodson 114
Robertson, Emma 153
  James 74, 95
  John 28, 123
  Keedy 16
  Sally 95
Robey, William A. 68
Robinson, Elisabeth 101
  Elizabeth 71
  Henry 24
  Jno. 131
  Keziah 160
  Mary 97
  Sally 143
  Thomas 62
  William 96
Robruth, Ann 212
Roby, M.R. 137
Rodwell, Mary E. 65
Rogers, Ann 177
  Christiana 168
  Ethalindy 125
  Ezekiel 168
  Jas. J. 182
  Levi 176
  Nancy 145
  Samuel 36
Roges, Frances 203
Rollins, Thomas 166
Ronard, Zilpha 126
Roop, (See also Rupe)
  Crockett 2, 57
  Elizebeth 159
  Harmon 28
  Mariah 2
  Samuel J. 20
Roope, Russell 44
Roper, Elizabeth 3
Rose, Abner 107
  Benjamin 107, 176
  J.K. 205
  John 176
  Kezia 176
  Lucy 49
  Sarah 183
  Sterling 183
Roseberry, Jemima 118
  Sally 131
Rosh, Elizabeth 46
Rosingbum, John 178
Ross, Abner 179
  Ann 90
  Jane 207

Ross, (cont.)
  John 123
  Margarett 195
  Martha 144
  Milley 123
Roswell, Betsey 144
Roton, Elizabeth 69
Rottenbury, Eliza 112
  Verinda 210
Rough, Caty Shepperd 167
Roughton, Josiah L. 223
Row, Nancey 185
Rowark, Nancy 59
Royal, Christian 67, 131
  Elizabeth 218
  Patsey 216
  Saly 209
Roynolds, Elizabeth 119
Ruberry, Mary E. (?) 147
  Rachel Perlite (?) 147
  Thomas (?) 147
Runager, Caty 213
Runion, Elliet L. 39
Runnels, Nathaniel 206
Rupe, (See also Roop)
  Russell 144
Russel, Sally 23
Russell, Betsy 55
  Catharine 132
  Charles 78
  Elizabeth 169
  Talbert 55
  Talbot 104
  Tolbert 106
Rutledge, Cathorine R. 195
  Clanpa 57
  E. 8, 9
  Enos 177, 213
  James 67
  Joel 196
  John 114, 196
  Mary 100
  Nathan 177
  Polly 31
  Rachael 31
  Sally 103
  Sarah 213
  W.D. 164
  William W. 57
Rutledges, John 218
Ryans, Milla 200
Sadler, Sarah Ann 175
Saer, Joseph (?) 178
Safley, Disey 214
Safly, Tempy 188
Sailes, Rebecca 44
Sale, M.D. 214
Salmon, Elijah 24
Salmons, Campbell W. 178
  Enoch 85
  Josiah F.P. 217
  Susan 217
Salomon, Elizabeth 142
Sammons, Mary 14
Sams, Sarah 2
  William A. 178
Samuel, Augustin 178
  H. 180
  Henry 4, 105
  Mary J. 83

Samuels, Priscilla B. 214
Sanders, Edy 178
  Elizabeth 164
  James 178
  John 13
  Mary E. 145
  Stephen 159
  Susanna 209
  Thomas 114
Sandifer, Martha 108
  Perm 108
  Susan 108
Sater, Henry 88, 122
  Joseph 143, 167
  Mildred 116
Satterfield, Martha A. 44
Saunders, Susan A. 106
  Syntha M. 13
Savage, Kendal 62
  Sarah 62
  William H. 47
Sawer, Polly 155
Sawyer, John 185
  Sandy 7
Sawyers, Elizabeth 182, 187
  James 187
  Judith 19
  July Ann 179
  Lucinda Ann 185
  Martin 19
  Nancy 59
  Rebecca F. 187
  Rhoda 59
  Zachariah 137
Sayers, Hannah 206
Scaggs, Henry 50
  Rachael 50
Scales, Lina 179
Scantlin, Elender 141
Scokey, Salley 40
Scott, Adam H. 180
  B.F. 132
  Barthilda 95
  Benjamin 45
  Catharine 87
  Daniel 179
  Elizabeth 137, 194
  H.M. 164
  Harriet 179
  Henry 194
  Jarmele 200
  Jesse 223
  Jos. H. 135
  Leonard 155
  Lucinda J. 14
  Manerva 135
  Martha 64, 103, 146
  Martha E. 47
  Mary 122, 162
  Mary S. 108
  Nancy 127, 191
  Permelia 135
  Polly 82, 127
  Robert 179
  S.S. 132
  Sarah 117
  Sarah B. 182
  Shadrack F. 14
  Sicily 86
  Thomas 179
  Virginia 28
  Wm. F. 173
Scritchfield, Elizabeth A. 79

Scruggs, Cynthia 43
Seagraves, Wm. (?) 4
Seagrove, John 124, 200
Seagroves, John 50, 205
Seal, Sarah Q. 184
Seales, Lucey 145
Searcy, Abner 123
Sears, Robert 25
Seasar, Fanny 93
Seaser, Judith 180
  Margaret 93
  Mary 93
  Masrin 180
  Peter 93
Seasor, Mary 217
Sebastine, Daniel 149
Sellevan, Richard 20
Selvey, Edward 68
Semore, Sarah A. 101
Sene, Sarah 222
Senter, Elizabeth 59
  Mildred 5
  Nancy 133
Sentichfield, Hanner 204
Serman, Mary A. 90
Setleff, Polly P. 111
Setliff, Eliza. 117
  John 129, 156
Sexton, Elizabeth 95
Sfarger, Sarough 36
Shadrach, James 159, 209
Shadrick, George A. 114
  George W. 114
Shambling, Mary 82
Sharks, Benjamin 9
Sharmer, John 3
Sharp, Meley 180
  William 180
Shaub, Magdaline 181
Shaver, Suphroney B. 150
Shaw, Ralph 152, 181
  Susan H. 98
  Thomas M. 86
  W.M. 152
  Wm. 220
Sheak, Mary 22
Shealter, Matilda 176
Shearmour, Mary 34
Sheek, James (?) 78, 96, 181
  Jesse E. 160
  Joshua 209
Shell, Floyd 5
Shelton, Anny 89
  Burrel 108
  Burrell 108
  Charles 142, 181
  Cristeny 97
  E.P. 41
  George 183
  Hannah 201
  Henry 147
  James 147
  Jane 181
  Jeremiah 181
  John 182, 201
  Judith 86
  Mark 129
  Mary 56, 105, 197
  Nancy 90, 172, 181
  Nancy E. 119
  Ralegh 221
  Rebecca 104

Shelton, (cont.)
  Sally 166
  Sarah 30, 58, 106
  Stephen 89
  Susan 37
  William 52, 181
  Wm. F. 56
Shenall, Daniel 90
  Richard 182
Sheppard, Charity 16
  Henry T. 117
Shepperd, E.J. 168
  J. 32, 39
  William 96, 100
  Wm. 150
Shepwash, Michael 17
Sherbert, A.H. 56
Shetliff, Ann 161
Shimmel, Elizabeth 174
Shinall, Deborah A. 109
  Reuben 182
Shinalt, Nancy 162
Shinault, Richard 87
  Sally Ann 182
Shinn, Betsy 123
  Nancy 49
  Rebecca 84
Ship, Robt. 168
Shipp, Clawell P. 7
  Colwel P. 50
Shipwash, Michael 18
Shoen, Henry 90
Shore, Adaline C. 163
  Benjamin 174
  Daniel 15
  Eliza 178
  Henry 125, 195
  Isaac 205
  Jacob 182
  John 188
  Lucinda E. 6
  Mary Matildia 174
  Pamelia A. 41
  Philip 144
  Rebecka 174
  Rebeckah 148
  Samuel 58
Shores, Abraham Washington 169
  Catharine 85
  Delpha R. 6
  Elizabeth 4, 144, 146
  Isaac 174
  Jacob 142
  Jalila 215
  John 41, 144, 183
  Jonathan W. 162
  Lydia 101
  Martin 183
  Mary 42, 148
  Mary G. 146
  Nancy 79, 169
  Polley 208
  Sally 100
  Sarah 211
  Susan 105
  William 12, 214
Short, Abraham 37
Shoup, Henrietta 47
Shous, Daniel 183
Shouse, William 106
Shouss, Jacob 81
Showalter, Mary A.E. 144
Shown, John 81

Shugart, Catharine 50
  Cattron 23
  Jinaty 4
  John 38
  Russel 73
Shugert, George 79
Shuts, David 165
Siger, Jacob 148
Sigler, Jno. 210
  Lawrence 184
  Mary 210
Sillevant, Susanna 205
Sillivan, Richard 184
Silvey, Darkus 212
Simkins, Andrew J. 145
  Jane 44
Simmons, (See also Cimmons)
  A. 2, 4, 5, 39, 68
  Ann 206
  E.B. 184
  Elizabeth 68
  Frank 180
  Hannah 179
  John 11
  John A. 184
  Justin 41
  Letha J. 150
  Mahaly 184
  Martha C. 42
  Mary 172, 180
  Mary Jane 51
  Nancy 93
  Newel 105
  Polly 106
  Prudence 44
  Rebeca 41
  Saml. 91
  Samuel 92, 212
  Sarah 29
  Silvany 180
  Tabitha 38
  Vilet Floyd (?) 184
Simms, Mary 41
Simons, Elizabeth 185
  John 185
Simpkins, James 215
Simpson, Amelia 114
  Celia 185
  Eliza F. (Miss) 103
  Elizabeth 185, 187
  Emsly 7
  Frances 187
  Isham 187
  James 110, 185
  Mary 110
  Nancy 151
  Samuel Y. 142
  Tyre 151
  Wm. B. 81
Sims, Ann M. 106
  John 166
  Mary 15
  Parish 137
Sisemore, Sarah Ann 17
Sisk, Allen 42, 44, 185
  Allin 53
  Harison 144
  Hethina 7
  Hosea 111
  Jesse 111, 185
  Mary E. 122
  Patsy 183
  Sally 48
  Temperance 7

Siske, Gilley 109
Sitliff, Sarahann 151
Skidmore, Elizabeth 196
  Henry 78, 186
  John 54, 204
  Mary 54
Slate, Isaac James 68
  Lucy Jane 68
  Margaret 211
  Mary 20
  Sarah 85
Slater, Elizabeth 29, 198
  Jane 204
Slator, Poley 163
  Polly 80
Slaughter, Elizabeth 203
  Jerry 203
Slaydon, Jane 124
  Joseph 113
  Sally 113
  Wilcher 124
Slayton, Joseph 77
  Nancy 77
Slogdon, Sally (?) 161
Slusher, S.J. 186
  Sarah E. 37
Smallwood, Dillaney 40
  Elizabeth 97
Smart, J. 133
Smith, B. 186
  Bartholomew 27, 188
  Bennet 31, 151
  C.C. 109
  Calvin P. 133
  Caroline 45
  Catlet 187
  David 188
  Edna J. 50
  Elender 98
  Elizabeth 28, 62, 73, 109, 114, 187, 207
  Elizabeth M. (Miss) 136
  Elizabeth P. 8
  Ellis 46
  Emboset 31
  Ewel 75
  Ewell 187
  Freeman 187
  George 145, 187
  Hannah 51
  Hezekaih 39, 168, 186
  Huldah 36
  Isabellar N. 141
  J.K. 134
  Jacob 188
  James 186
  Jane 19, 172
  Jemima 195
  Jesse 208
  John 31
  John A. 106
  Joseph 186, 214
  Katharine 109
  Larkin 141
  Lizzie 31
  Lucinda 63
  Lucy 118
  Mahala 27
  Malinda F. 81
  Mallory 60
  Margaret 56

Smith, (cont.)
  Margrett 64
  Mark A. 38
  Martha 21, 159
  Martin 3, 35
  Mary 57, 95, 141, 223
  Massy 187
  Michael 20
  Nancy 108, 142, 151
  Nancy Ann 37
  Prudence 135
  Rebecah 73
  Rebecca 71
  Rebecker 90
  Rebekah 23
  Rhody 121
  Rozena 115
  Rutha 38
  Sally 10, 35, 63, 187, 214
  Samuel 20, 73, 187, 191
  Samuel, Junr. 60
  Santifr 45
  Sarah 11, 58, 60, 151, 171, 187, 199, 200, 208
  Sophia 28
  Sucky 87
  Susan 112
  Susanah 207
  Thomas 175
  Wesley 213
  Westly M. 128
  William 63
  William D. 186
  William H. 207
  Zion 36
Smythers, Stephen 70
  William 188
Smythes, Stephen D. 211
Snap, Elijah 171
Sneed, Anna 110
  Jessefy 102
  Patsey 215
  Polly 22
Snider, Marende 122
Snody, James R. 126
  John 119
  Julia 181
  Martha Ann 181
  William 181
Snow, Adra 200
  Alfred 179
  Ann (?) 158
  Ben Thompson (?) 202
  Benjamin 12
  Byrd 72
  Byrd, Jr. 206
  Calvin 76, 216
  Cary A. 98
  Deep 152, 218
  Elizabeth 158, 208, 221
  Frances 12
  Frost 189
  Frostin 66, 190
  Huldah 38
  Ice 50, 95, 185, 189, 225
  J.S. 23
  James 13, 57
  James M. 51
  James S. 190
  Jane 76
  Jane (Miss) 49
  Jas. S. 77

Snow, (cont.)
  Jincy 97
  Jno. S. 221
  John 59, 97, 128
  Lennard 172
  Lidia 66
  Lucinda 28, 109, 221
  M.W. 203
  Mahaly 130
  Margaret 189, 218
  Martha 26, 167
  Mary 76, 152
  Mary B. 113
  Matilda 167
  Matildah 189
  Matildy 76
  Mitchel 159
  Moore 175
  Nancy 76, 100, 216, 217
  Nancy F. 29
  Nannie 202
  Peggy 203
  Polly 21
  Richard (?) 158
  Richard 29, 40
  Richard, Senr. 130
  S.W. 26, 103
  Sally 95
  Sarah 145, 221
  Simpson 76
  Thomas 189, 190, 221
  Thomas M. 189
  Thos. M. 7
  William C. 190
  Sollomon, Amee 71
  Solomon, Laveter J. 190
  Somers, Emily 52
  James L. 214
  W. 214
  W.D. (?) 1
  Winston 7, 11, 16, 43, 194
  Wm. 12
  Wm. D. 9, 56, 73, 114, 163, 173, 180, 223
Somes, Rebeca 51
Sommers, Wm. D. 29
Song, William (?) 176
Sopshire, Martha A. 39
South, Creed 191
  Samuel 191
Southard, Catharine 27
  Elizabeth 10, 191
  Hannah 155
  Henry 191
  Job 218
  Martin 191
  Martin P. 191
  Nancy 174
  Phebe 214
  Polly 186
  Sally 196
Southerd, William 191
Southerland, Wilie 28
Southers, John 63
Southrin, Nancy 37
Sowers, Doutha 159
Soyars, Jos. 27
  Joseph 211
Soyers, Nancy 197
Sozars, Jane 112
Spague, ---- 106
Spain, Littleberry 201
Spainhour, P.S. 201
Spainhower, John W. 191
  Lidia M. 191

Spainhower, (cont.)
  Mary 179
Spargen, Mary 27
Sparger, Allen J. 45
  Chistena 136
  Easter Joyce 83
  Edith E. 45
  Henry 106, 172
  James 81
  James H. 82
  Jane 201
  Margret F. 158
  Martin 14
  Mary 63
  Mary A. 15
Spargur, Jane 160
Sparkes, William Z. 192
Sparks, Augathee 44
  George 192
  George, Jr. 109
  Jane 173
  Janetty 156
  Margerett 214
  Mathew 35
  Nancy 177, 186, 223
  Sally 147
  Saml. 73
  Sarah 21
  Sarrah 169
  Susan 96
  William 192
  Wm. R. 197
Spear, Barzillia 224
Speas, Mary P. 29
Speer, Aquila 170
  Betsey 166
  Catharine 114
  Daniel 80
  Darkes 138
  Eliza. 187
  Elizabeth 65, 67, 81, 121, 140
  Fanny 89
  Henry 196
  J.H.A.129
  John 101, 193
  Lethey 192
  Margaret 197
  Mary 67
  Nancy 176, 188, 193
  Pricilla 205
  Richard 172
  Richd. 192
  Rody 101
  Samuel 193
  Sarah 55
  Shadrack 197
  Susanna 201
  Syntha 140
  Thomas 193
  William 114
  Wm. H. 51
Speers, Daniel 138
Spence, David 193
  Elizabeth 156
  Hulda 28
  Mary 70
  Nancy Caroline 175
  Rebeckah 115
  Wilie J. 75
Spencer, E.M. 136
  James 132, 159, 193, 198, 201
  Joseph 202
  Leroy 208
  Lucy Ann 158
  Matilda 190

Spencer, (cont.)
  Nancy 130, 180, 202
  Polly 40
  Sally 79
  Sussannah 161
  William, Sr. 193
  Wm. 16, 156
Spenser, Mary 81
Spere, Betsy 157
Sperlin, Catharine 210
Spier, James J. 10
Spiers, Precilla 124
Spikard, Barbara 223
Spillman, William, Jr. 172
  Wm. 66
Spillmon, Rachel 161
Spilman, Osrel M. 140
  Saml. 55
  Samuel 103
Spilmon, Levil 212
  William, Junr. 68
  Wm. 129
Spine, Lusa 82
Spiris, John 194
Sporgur, Eliza 27
Spratlen, James 101, 162
Sprinckle, Michael 36
Sprinkel, G. 154
  Mary 192
  Samuel 194
Sprinkle, Ellis 194
  James 52, 194
  Jonathan 182, 192
  Nancy 194
  Thomas 161
Sprouse, Robert 85
Spurgeon, John 66
Spurlin, Elizabeth 32
Spurling, Susanah 144
Stablefield, Edney 120
Stafford, Sarah 215
Stalmon, Martha 14
Standfield, Mary 92
  Thomas 195
Standley, Jesse 16
  Mary 16
  William 195
Standly, Jesse 69
  Thomas 223
  William 223
Stanfield, James 195
  Rebeckah 29
  Thomas 104, 195
  Thos. 141
Stanley, Delila 107
  Elizabeth 107
  Hallin 180
  Hannah 104
  Hutchins 103
  Jesse 195
  Jno. E. 195
  John 148
  L.J. 107
  Margret 216
  Mary 142
  Nancy 130
  Patsey 98
  Susan 16
  Thomas 55
  William 28
Stanliff, Oliver 42, 180
Stanly, Derinda 85
  E.M. 131
  Garrett 131

Stanly, (cont.)
  H.D. 59
  Jesse 195
  John C. 195
  John E. 195
  Julia 39
  Lemuel J. 195
  Mima 131
  Nancy 131, 223
  Peggy 224
  Sally 18, 195
  Smith 221
  Thomas 187
Stantliff, Lucinda 40
Stantz, Garret 39
  Mima J. 39
  Sarah 39
Starbuck, James 22, 79
  John 31
Starling, J.M. 196
Starr, Adam 129, 165
  Anna 165
  Elizabeth 29
  Mary 22
  Peggy 124
  Rachael 125
  Sarah 129
Static, Anna (?) 143
Stauber, Francis 16
Steagall, Lydia 104
Steal, Perlina 173
Steel, D.T. 153
  Eliza 153
  Thomas 225
Steele, A. 119
  Henry 183
  Thomas 195
Steelman, Becky 54
  Catharine 88
  Charles 49
  Charles, Jr. 177
  George 48, 49
  James 67, 115, 209
  Jo. 36
  John 23
  Joseph 177
  Mary 177
  Mathias 60
  Nancy 23, 103
  Rachel 218
  Ruth 132, 196
  Sarah 172
  William 29
Steelmon, Charles 163, 196
  Elizabeth 192, 218
  George 48, 169, 196
  Jane 169
  John 196
  Joseph 116, 166, 183
  Matthias 192
  Polly 139
  Rachael 78
  Rosanna 126
  Ruth 163
Stenton, Christopher 62
  Margery 62
Stephens, James 186
  Mary E. 102
  Rhoda 113
Stepp, Wm. 189
Sterdant, Jesse 199
Stevens, Spenser 187
Stevenson, Mary Ann 180

Stewart, Abigal 48
  Charlotte 86
  Isaiah 89, 121
  James M. 158
  Jemimah 87
  Jesse 182
  John 64, 192
  Julianny 128
  Mary 168
  Mary Ann 193
  Samuel 43
  Sarah Ann 92
  Shadrack 158
  William 124, 138
  Wm. A. 50
Stinson, Aaron 168
  Joshua 197
  Mary 211
  Moris 149
  Rebecca 67
Stockbuyer, --- 96
Stockern, Elizabeth 114
Stockner, Chestenia 52
  Suffiah 193
Stockton, John 158
Stoe, Abraham 98
  Elizabeth 70
Stokes, Abednigo 183
  Charles 197
  Henry 14
Stolts, Laura 53
Stoltz, Nathaniel 20
Stone, Amanda F. 14, 28
  Augustin 65
  Betsy 52
  Conaway 150
  Conway 59
  Eady 123
  Elijah 87
  Elizabeth 45, 87
  Elliott 81
  Emily 71
  Ephraim 62
  Francis R. 53
  Julia 71
  Mandy M. 185
  Mary 196
  Nancy 62, 118, 121
  Polly 71
  Sally 168
  Sarah C. 53
  Sarah Delphina B. 53
  Sarah Luvina 214
  Stacy 207
  Usley 181
Stoneman, Jestin 49
  Lewis 113, 198
Stonemon, Sarah 159
Stoner, Anna 176
Stonestreet, Benjamin 84
  Elenor 75
  Elisha 10, 75
  John 88
Stonstreet, Nancy 10
Stourt, Eliza A. 219
Stoutz, Nancy 109
Stovall, G.H. 23
  George H. 216
  Sarah J. 167
Stow, Abraham M. 164
  Abraham R. 25
  Amy 23

Stow, (cont.)
  Isaac P. 40
  Joel R. 162
  Nancy 212
  Polly 71
  Sarah 54
Strain, Larkin 106
Strange, John R. 6
  Mary 224
  Mary E.J. 60
Strawn, Betsey 67
Stricklin, Ann Mariah 3
Striclin, Wm. 11
Strong, Larkin 31
Stroope, Katharine 88
Stroud, Berry 222
Stuart, Eliza Ann 180
  Jacob 133
  James M. 180
  John D. 147
  John H. 200
  William 69
Stubelfield, Eliza. 161
Stuls, Chasper 198
Stults, Daniel 53
Stultz, Daniel 100
Stump, Henry T. 143
Sturad, Nancy 18
Sturcly, Polly 27
Sturdivant, Nancy F. 155
Stuthard, Richard 29
Stutman, Rebecca 34
Stutts, C.N. 157
Sufferbarger, Henrietta 119
Sugarts, Elizabeth 211
Suiter, Rebeca E. 118
Suitir, Polly 118
Sullivan, Mary 43
Sumers, Elisabeth 148
  Manning 102
  Waitman 99
Summers, Elizabeth 59
  John 119
  John A. 67
  Mannering 198
  Rachael 135
  Rachel 15
  Sally 176
  Sythia 28
Summons, James 108
  Mary A. 108
Sumner, Absalom 31
  Rachael 224
Sumpter, Minty 4
  Sarah 185
Sumter, Elizabeth 44
Surat, Rebekah 130
Surface, Susan 201
Surratt, Vernon 16, 155
Sutfin, Emeline 133
  Hannah 59
  Irwin 111
  Mary Ann 138
  Raleigh 213
  Thomas 199
Suthard, Mary 140
  Mehala 74
Suthpin, William 199
Sutle, Jinsy 207
Sutlif, Rebekah 176
Sutliff, Jane 17
Sutphin, Elijah 199
Suttle, Isaac A. 118

Swach, Keturah 1
Swaim, Charity 10
  Elizabeth 5, 52
  Franky Ann 1
  Grace M. 40
  Gracy 209
  John 35, 199
  Kessiah C. 35
  Mary 35
  Moses, Jr. 210
  Priscilla 51
  Prudence 131
  Rachael 52
  William 187
  Wm. E. 154
Swaime, Cathorine 192
Swain, Michael 186
  Rachel 192
  Sarah 23
Swann, Esther (Miss) 47
Sweat, William 199
  William, Junr. 100
Sweatt, Edward 125
  Virtue 133
Sweptin, Ruth J. 52
Swiney, Elizabeth 79
Swinney, Elizabeth 154
Swinny, Anderson E. 34
  Haden 215
Tailer, Tabitha 112
Talbert, James 60
  Lamira 77
  Mary 140
  Milly 65
  Nancy 65
Talbott, Jane 33
Taleaferro, Dickerson 193
Taliafero, Betsey 52
Taliaferro, Betsey 49
  Chas. 33, 49, 84
  Chs. 52
  Dickerson 69, 217
  John 33
  Polley 69
Talley, Payton 88
  Tobitha 67
Tally, Isaac 110
  Isaiah 181
  Peyton 210
Talor, Jane 71
  Robert 71
  Sary 71
Tanner, Frederick, Junr. 102
  Fredrick, Junr. 15
  Fredrick, Jr. 183, 213
  John (?) 79
  John 27
  Nancy 207
Tannor, Fredrick (?) 57
Tansy, Sarah 179
Tate, Colly 162
  Jane 127
  M. Jane 51
  Mary 101
  Mary E. 47
  Mitchel B. 193
  Nancy 14
  Rachel 122
Tator, Francis 9
Tayer, Matilda Ann 200

Tayler, Paulina 166
  Pauline Jane 26
  Sarah Ann 156
Taylor, Anderson 167
  Archabald 127
  Archi 189, 201
  Benjamin 10, 30, 167
  Benjamin, Sr. 222
  Daniel 92, 102
  E.F. 201
  Edmon 5
  Edmond 211
  Edmund 106
  Elizabeth 140, 201
  Frances 42, 91, 98
  J. Anderson 201
  James 90, 101, 200
  Jane 50, 87, 89
  Jincy 90
  John 78, 201
  Jonathan 56, 121
  Jones 36
  Julia 92
  Letty 33
  Lewis 42, 154
  Lewis C. 41, 108
  Lucinda 11, 110, 207
  Lucyann 111
  Mahala 91
  Mariah C. 92
  Mark 201
  Martha E. 160
  Martha J. 201
  Mary 29, 31, 62, 92, 164
  Mary Ann 201
  Mary E. 184
  Matthew 89
  Michkey A. 184
  Permelia 131
  Polly 88
  Rebeca 92, 200
  Rebeckah 5
  Richard M. 201
  Sarah 89, 201
  Sary 175
  Starlin 122
  Sterling 49
  Stinlin 176
  Stirlin 201
  Susannah 49
  Veleria 11
  Welthy 57
  William H. 150, 184
Teasley, Mary 100
Tellar, D.D. 67
Terry, Ann 110
  Margaret 114
  Nancy 42
  Wm. 11
Thomas, John 202
Thomason, John 195
  Nancy 193
Thompson, Ben 202
  Ben Roberts (?) 202
  Catharine 149
  Charles 207
  Cilvina 205
  Columbus 87, 89, 184
  Cresy 205
  David H. 208
  E. 203
  Eleth. 65
  Elijah 33, 196, 203
  Elizabeth 199
  Embosset 149

Thompson, (cont.)
  Ezekiel 205
  Hannah Tucker (?) 202
  Harrison 57
  Hugh 36
  Jesse 190
  Jno. 219
  John 29, 143, 151
  John Calven 210
  Jonathan 180
  Julian (Miss) 38
  Luke 35
  M.M. 168
  Martha 92, 151
  Mary 29, 99, 116, 143
  Mary F. 115
  Mary J. 21
  Mary S. 44
  Nancy 26, 153
  Nannie 201
  Nannie Snow (?) 202
  Pheba Ann 173
  Polly 38
  Rachel 30
  Rebekah 102
  Rhody 74
  Rody 72
  Sally 65
  Sarah 137, 190, 203
  Sarah Ann 202
  Sarrah 206
Thomson, Jn. 115
  Rhoda 219
Thore, Francis 203
  N. 203
Thornton, Abraham 112
  Elizabeth 181, 218
  James 203
  James A. 204
  Jas. A. 92
  John 80, 156
  John, Jr. 218
  Lizebeth 1
  Nancy 6
  Pheroby 170, 171
  Rebekah 40
  Sarah 147
  W. 13
  Wiley 12
  Will, Jun. 22, 31
  Wm. 6, 43, 147, 181
Thorp, Anny 105
  Eliza J. 111
  Elizabeth 72
  Martha C. 111
  Mary 141
  Matilda 51
  Metilda 98
  Rachael 68
  Thomas 111
  Thomas M. 68
Thorpe, Lucy 124
Tickle, Eliza 86
  Frances 86
  Henry 86
  Jane 107
Tickles, Henry 86
Tiffney, M.M.T. 197
Tiler, Susan 188
Tiller, D.D. 86
  Drury D. 45
Tilley, Elizabeth 60
  James 86
  Joel F. 204
  John 204
  Lucinda 204

Tilley, (cont.)
  Susan 43
Tilly, Charles 205
  Elizabeth 68
  Jane Hughes 205
  Moses 185
Tipton, Louemma 167
  Lucinda 70
  Patsey 155
  Rhody Ann (Miss) 37
  Rodah 61
  W.L. 101
Toads, Sarah 138
Todd, Margaret 226
  Sally 1
Tolbart, M.C. 149
Tolbert, Jeremiah 203
  Sally 35
  Sarah 65
Tolen, Pereline (?) 124
Tomson, Catron 81
Toys, Polly (?) 108
Trimber, Nancy 29
Triplett, Nancy 52
Tromel, Jackson (?) 67
Truelove, Landon 139
Truit, John 78
  Susannah 78
Truitt, Eli 205
  John 99, 205
Trulove, Aaron 104
  Amy 83
  Charles 139
  Fanny 201
  Landon 139, 164, 206
  Lucindy 147
  Sally 179
Tuburt, J. Calver 116
Tucker, Amelia 90
  Ben Roberts (?) 202
  Benjamin 123
  Benjamin M. 205
  Branch 58
  C.B. 105
  Charles 205
  Elizabeth 203
  Hannah 202
  Henry 185
  Henry B. 214
  James 190
  James F. 26
  Jane 106
  Jas. 10, 18, 154
  Lucy 205
  Margaret 44
  Mary 146, 184
  Matilda 128
  Matilder 205
  Nancy 144
  Nancy Whitworth 29
  Phebe 40
  Salley 190
  Sarah 1, 26, 184
  Tho. 100
  Thomas 205
  W.P. 49
  William 184
  William H. 189
  William P. 191
  Wm. P. 132
Tuggle, Ann 104
  Fanny Gunter 206
  Isaac 206
  Mary Ann 98
Tull, Catherine 139
  Elizabeth 15
  George 167

Tull, (cont.)
  Joanna 66
  Mary 99
  Nicholas 15
  Polly 49
  Rebekah 139
  William 191
Tully, Daniel 123
Turman, Mary 206
Turner, Elias 31, 35, 75, 187, 199
  Elizabeth 117, 126
  Elizebeth 16
  James 213
  John 67, 130
  Mary 59
  Mary E. 50
  Nancy 195
  Rhody 31
  Sarah 78
Turpin, Elizabeth 183
Turrage, Michael 124
Tutteroe, Jesse 112
Tuttle, Elizabeth 86
  Harriet N. 158
  Mary Ann 71
Twiney, Rutha 214
Tyler, Elizabeth 166
Underwood, J.K. 21
  Joel 116
  Narcissa 184
  Nancy 146
  Sarah 107
Unthank, J. 3
  James H. 147
  Jas. H. 2
  Jon. 7
  Jona. 49, 108, 165, 200, 207
  Mary Ann 204
  William 184, 196
  Wm. 167
  Wm. F. 110
Uptegrove, Elizabeth C. 116
  Isaac 206
  Wm. 109
Upthagrove, Sarah 127
Upthegrove, Polly 125
  Rachel 197
Vance, Hannah 128
  Samuel 128
Vancyk, Winney 199
Vandepool, Josiah 52
Vanderpool, E. 53
  Josiah 196, 212
  Milly 66
  Peggy 162
Vandevor, Nancy 161
Vandevur, George 161
Vanhoy, Clayton 40
  Elizabeth 40
  Grace 178
  Liney 160
  Sucky 105
  William 74
Vannoy, William 79
Varnum, Jane 191
Vass, Martha 143
  Nancy 203
Vaughn, Archalous 74
  Gideon Y. 217
  James 207
  Sintha 119
Vaugn, Lucinda 181
Vaun, Fanny 114
Vawter, John 65, 106

Veach, Elizabeth D. 51
Venable, Charlotte 60
  Elizabeth 89
  Iredell 131
  Iredell A. 91
  Isham 43, 208
  Julia 155
  Lucinda 191
  Mary 28, 62, 120
  P. 189, 207
  Pleasant 60, 134, 135, 200, 207
  Rebeca 120
  Rebecca 165
  S. 116
  Sarah 133
  Sealy 185
  Stephen 189
Venables, Jesse 208
  Peggy 97
  Pleasant 117, 120
  Sarah 131
Veneable, Elizabeth 50
Vennable, John W. 122
Vernon, Wiley 208
Vernorn, Lucinda 208
  Nemiah 208
Vernum, James 173
  Mary 173
Vest, Anne 220
  Eliza 41
  F.P. 179
  Frances 17
  Francis 51
  Francis P. 164
  Isaac 220
Vestal, Ann 35
  Asa 25, 177, 209
  Axa 50
  Azeneth 66
  Bethana 126
  David 94, 208
  Elizabeth 48, 125, 209
  Elizebeth 102
  Febe 64
  Hannah 102
  Harriet 67
  Isaac 125, 209
  Jesse 208, 209
  John 153, 170, 209
  Knesel 54
  Leah 22
  Luddy 131
  M.A. 188
  Margaret 20, 102
  Nancy 216
  Niel 93
  Patsy 213
  Phebe 94
  Rachel 153
  Sally 169
  Sarah 93, 150
  Silas 196
  Solomon 64, 126, 213
  Thomas 18, 75, 94, 116, 170, 177, 209
  Thomas, Jr. 157
  William 1, 17, 208
Vestall, Rebecker 93
Vestel, Jams. 209
  Sally 147
Vestell, Mary 83, 199, 209
  Thomas 14
Vhon, James 97
Vhore, Mary 182

Vinzant, Barnebus 107
Vipperman, Lucinda 188
Vissmon, Chrischanica 147
Volentine, Lucy 198
Voling, Lewis 112
Vooten, John 224
Vormon, Elisa J. 126
Wacther, Elizabeth (?) 27
Wadden, Piggy 226
Waddle, Henry 195
  Quintala 162
  Sarah 7
  Susanna 218
Wade, Levina 181
Wadkins, Anna 154
  Olley 19
Waff, Fanny 57
  Nancy S. 90
Waggener, Jacob 33
Waggoner, Elizabeth 24, 64
  Jacob 210
  Jno. 23
  John 177
  Moses 24
  Polly 94
  Sarah 30, 199
Wagner, Adam 160
  Jacob 144
Wagoner, Adam 126
  Daniel 81
Waldridge, Henry 147
Walk, Mary 52
  Rosy 121
Walker, Anne 11
  Barbary 146
  Betsey 99
  Caroline 169
  D. 139
  Elizabeth 99, 134
  F.M. 103
  Hannah 29, 225
  Huldah F. 58
  Jane 142
  John 21, 151
  Lucrecy 19
  Lydia C. 224
  Mary 122
  Nancy 21, 222
  Nancy J. 58
  Nelly 182
  Polly 189
  Robert 29, 210, 225
  Samuel 15
  Sarah 130, 155
  Seba 158
  Talitha 175
Wall, B.T. 86
  Crawford 70
  Evalina H. 56
  Fanny 222
  Henry J. 211
  James A. 2
  Jerusha A.C. 154
  Lucy Ann 125
  Mary 14, 211
  Milly 111
  Newel 160
  O.H.P. 210
  Russel F. 210
  Samuel 187
  Sarah (Miss) 2
Wallace, Polly 191
Wallander, Lucy 131

Waller, John 20
  Rachel 75
Wallis, Polley 9
Walls, Crofford 154
  Sarah A. 159
Walsh, E.B. 142
  Elza 86
Walters, Martha A. 26
Walton, Francis M. (?) 67
  Hannah A. 178
  Louisa A. 91
  Missouri A. 157
  Pleasant 9
  Virginia Mager (?) 9
Waram, William (?) 85
Ward, Amey 95
  James M. 173
  Jeremiah 74
  Lydia 68
  Mary 88
Warden, Cary 55
  Elizabeth 167
  Elvina 188
  Isaiah 212
  Izaah 212
  Johnston 178
  Malinda 41
  Michael 128
  Nancy 168
  Paulina 212
  Perlina 212
  Riley 34, 81, 188
  Robert 211
  Sinthy M. 178
Ware, Elizabeth 14
Warf, Rebeca 119
Warner, Joseph W. 116
  Mary Ann 168
  Sally 70
Warren, Rebecah 85
Warters, Barbary Lacy (?) 212
  Burrel (?) 212
Waters, Nancy 25
Watkins, Alse 195
  Keziah 196
  Mary 19
  Sarah 78
  Thomas 129, 195, 196, 212
Watson, Alexander 168
  Claborn 148
  Cynthia June (Miss) 154
  David 212
  Elizabeth 91
  Ezekiel 134
  Susanah 148
  William 97
Watters, George 69
Watton, Francis M. 67
Waugh, H.M. 61, 169
  J.R. 103, 146
  Jessa A. 106, 137
  Jesse A. 85, 165, 180
  L.G. 132
  S.A. 38
  Susan E. 70
  Wm. 179
Wealch, Nancey 103
Weatherman, Chrestin 82
  Christian 105
  Christopher 20, 82, 163, 209

Weatherman, (cont.)
  Cornelous 105
  John 21
  Pegy 216
  Polly 105
  Saml. 17
  Sarah 100
  Susannah 74
  Wm. 73
Weathermon, Sally 177
Weatherpond, Mary Ann 178
Weaver, Elizabeth 31
  Waller 113
Webb, Catherine 167
  Chroet 167
  Greenville 99
  Isaac 213
  Jemima 65
Webster, Andrew 146
  Anne 90
  Ruth 25
Weeks, Chapman D. 213
Welborn, John 217
  Richd. 175
Welbourn, Temperance 220
Welch, Charles 174
  David 54, 226
  Elizabeth 6, 176
  Harriet N. 156
  Isam 202
  Polly 126
  Sarah 177
Welding, Elizabeth 8
Wellborn, Sarah 27
Wells, Elizabeth 53
  John 104, 149
  Marilda 149
  Martha 119
  Mary 13
  Nancy Emeline 140
  Stephen 222
Welmoth, Lettice 202
  M--- 7
Welmouth, Margaret 82
Wels, Rachel 104
Welsh, David 214
West, Elizabeth 186, 187
  F.P. (?) 59
  James 177, 196
  Jeremiah 1
  Lucy 77
  Marsy C. 205
  Mary Ann 151
  Mathew 129
  Nancy 136, 147
  Polly 90
  Ruthy 129
  Sarah 176
  Wm. 161, 192
Weyniss, John 19
Whalen, A.J. 206
  J. 105
Whaling, John 207
Wharton, Andy 214
  Sarah 214
Whealoss, Nelly 20
Wheaton, Calvin 176
Wheeler, Eliza 225
Wheler, Seany 46
Wheliss, Lewis 125
Whelus, Sarah 39
Whitacre, Nelly 160
  Tildalita 28

Whitaker, A. 134
  A.L. 119
  Abraham 8
  Achsoh 28
  Anderson 146, 215
  Anna 134
  Betsey 111
  Dasha 93
  Dicy 118
  Edmond 215
  Edmund 214
  Elizabeth J. 63
  Ellin 117
  Elmina 187
  Elviria 209
  Emsey 117
  Green 215
  H.M. 211
  Hannah 187
  Isaac 63, 111, 145, 216
  Isaac, Jr. 63
  Isaac, Sr. 214, 215
  Isaiah 136, 187
  John 146
  Johnson 79, 149
  Jonathan 214
  Jordan 215
  Jorden 221
  Jourden 214
  Levicy 17
  Liddy 135
  Lucinda 221
  Lydia 214
  Lydia R. 215
  Mahala 216
  Martha 101
  Mary 20, 215, 221
  Matilda J. 16
  Nancy 25, 146, 174, 181, 215
  Nancy Ann 17
  Nicy 119
  Patcy 8
  Permelia (Miss) 134
  Sally 8
  Sally Ann 171
  Sarah E. 157
  Thomas 215
  Vergarina 214
  Vicy 211
  William 87, 146, 215
  Wm. 215
  Wm. A. 42
White, Albert 8, 216
  Cleo 124
  Eathy 34
  Elizabeth 167, 216, 219
  Etta M. 73
  Francis 195
  Henrietta 124
  James 216
  James P. 219
  Jane 101
  Joel 216
  John 73, 155, 216
  John, Jr. 216
  Joseph 216
  Lucinda 3
  Mary 7, 216
  Meriah 135
  Milley 45
  Nancy 145
  Nancy (Miss) 118, 164
  Nancy B. 212

White, (cont.)
  Ruth 153
  Sallie 164
  Sarah 36, 216
  Shaba 164
  Thomas 223
  Wm. 36, 214
Whiteackers, Litle 117
Whitecer, Wm. 139
Whitehead, Anna 209
  Archibald 163
  Elizabeth 104
  Francis 216
  Joel 209
  John 160
  Sarah 209
  William 216
Whiteker, Nancy 171
Whiticeker, Elizabeth 194
Whiticher, William 32
Whiticker, William 194
Whitiker, Robert C. 157
Whitlock, Agness 56
  Betsy 223
  Caroline 34
  Charles 18
  Elizabeth 106
  Elizabeth A. 29
  Jacob 178
  James 140
  John 142, 207
  Mary 5
  Mildred 102
  Nancy 115, 116
  Polly 152
  Ruth 66
  Samuel 171
  Susan 106
  Thomas 69, 128
Whittaker, Elmirah 18
Whitteker, Jane 17
Whitticor, Jesse 157
  Johnson 112
Whittimer, Lucinda 9
Whittington, J.A. 76
  Nancy A. 93
  Sally 14
  Smiley 204
  Smily 131
Whittrek, Jane 200
Whitworth, Thos. 29
Whotan, Amia 42
Whoton, Sally 97
Wials, Agnus 184
Widdle, Eliza J. 37
Wigfield, Mary 202
Wilbourn, Lucindy 74
  Richd. 4, 136
  Robert 74
Wilburn, James H. 82
Wiles, Catherine 154
  Elizabeth 157
  Gilliam 177
  James 153
  Janes 153
  John 218
  Lewis 174, 218
  Lucy 174
  Luke 36
  Mary 36, 209
  Pinson 169
  Polly 160
  Thomas 160, 209
  Thomas, Sr. 218
  William 218
Wiley, Cerepta 189

Wilkerson, Henry 2
  Judy 129
  Peggy 53
Wilkes, Pinkney 2
  Polly 118
Wilkins, George 127
  Isaac 112
  Nancy 169
  Polly 81
  Will 218
Wilkinson, William 223
Wilks, Nancy 149
Willard, Allen 103, 154
  Augustine 218
  Cintha 24
  Fanny 123
  Fanny D. 14
  Phebe 139
  Sarah 199
Willey, Ferebee 105
  Nancy E. 38
  Sophia 153
  Wiley 10
  Wilie 218
Williams, Amy F. 133
  Anne 26
  Azel 59
  Benjamin 214
  Biddy 209
  C.W. 102, 143
  Charrity 104
  Cicero 47, 86, 202, 225
  D.L. 177
  Darkas 21
  E. 181
  Elizabeth 13
  Elizabeth Jane 55
  Ely 44
  Enoch 159, 219
  Ephraim 133
  Fanny S. 63
  Gemima L. 32
  Gene 181
  George D. 121, 180
  Hiram 219
  Isaac 32, 103
  J. 1
  J., Jun. 8
  J., Junr. 7
  James 219
  Jane 128
  Jason 36
  Jean 125
  Jesse 153, 209
  Jessee 94
  Jno. 1
  Jo. 46, 129
  John 17, 21, 84, 162, 219, 220
  Jonathan 220
  Joseph 88
  Joshua 220
  Keziah 162
  Labourn 220
  Letitia 153
  Levina 87
  Lewis 24, 30, 63, 115
  Lidia 18
  Lourena F. 159
  Margaret Matilda 103
  Margit 220
  Mary 13, 103, 214
  Mary Childris (?) 133
  Matilda 177
  N.L. 4, 5, 9
  Nancy 32

Williams, (cont.)
  Nancy S. 197
  Nicholas 219
  Peggy 205
  Polly 158
  Rachael 78
  Rachel 148, 219
  Rachell 159
  Rebecah 94
  Rebekah 67
  Rebekah L. 222
  Rhodey 172
  Robert 62
  Robt. 3, 5, 21, 23, 35, 48, 56, 67
  Sally 36
  Silva 44, 184
  Sophena 46
  Suffina 88
  Susan 56
  Susanna 8
  Susanna M. 6, 15, 23, 24, 26, 32, 36
  Temperance 136
  Thomas, Junr. 103
  Thomas L. 222
  Thos. 157
  Toms. 219
  Wm. 220
  Zachariah 100
  Zael 122
  Zilpha J. 94
Williamson, Ann B. 196
  Catharine 128
  Charlott 121
  Elizabeth 2
  Lettie 135
  Louisa E. 47
  Lucinda 82, 210
  Mary 135
  Nancy 214
  Park 135
  Peggy 27
  Ruth 47
  Sarah E. 188
  William 47
Williard, William 177
Williason, Cristena 152
Willis, Celia 136
  Charlotte 136
  Delila 37
  Greensvill 37
  Greensville 18, 203
  Greenville 136, 187, 203
  John 167
Willmorth, Cloah 190
Wills, Hamilton 82
  Rhoda 128
Willson, Katharine 59
Willy, Christopher 204
  Sarah 204
Wilmoath, Sallie 86
Wilmon, Jeremiah 135
Wilmoth, Betsey 190
  Lot (?) 69
  Lot 189
  Lucy 195
  Matilda 151
  Richard 190
  Sally 195
  Tyson S. 109, 190
  Wm. R. 223
Wilmouth, Elizabeth 223
  Polly 216
  Rebecca 200

Wilson, Amanda J. 184
  Carroline 81
  Dorathy B. 94
  Eliza 200
  Elizabeth 83, 172
  Joshua 104
  Luemma 145
  Mary 97, 152, 217
  Matilda 221
  Peyton 165
  Polly 1
  Thomas 113
  Willes 222
  Willis 83
Wily, Michael 15
  Nancy 133
Wincter, Spragg 73
Windel, William 82
Windsor, Aquilla 53, 222
  Bennet 222
  Caroline 52
  Elizabeth 53, 143, 151
  Enos 114
  James A. 143, 174
  Lucy 51
  Margaret 32
  Melinda 140
  Nancy P. 27
  R.R. 27
  Riley 32
  William H. 52
  William W. 51
Winesit, Polly A. 82
Winford, Margret 169
Winfree, Jobe 97
  John 96
Winfrey, Elizabeth 43
  Isaac 107
  Mary 96
  Nancy 51
Winfry, Caroline 163
Winfrys, Nancy 175
Winningham, Sarah 61
Winscott, Abraham 9
  Catharine 9
  John 62
Winsor, Amelia 41
Winston, Jo. 44
  John 63
Wirick, Elizabeth 198
Wishan, Charlotte 166
Wishon, Catron 180
  Clary 23
  Honor 7
  Leonard, Jr. 222
  Philip 37
  Susan 53
Witch, William 106
Witcher, Elizabeth 175
  Sarah M. 192
Wohlford, Sarah 149
Wolf, Ann 152
  Lewis 152
  Mary 221
Wolfe, Annette A. 84
  H.N. 84
  Rachal 84
Wolff, D.C. 12, 17, 27, 76, 120
  Daniel C. 179
  Frederick 221
  N.A. 211
  W.H. 86
  W.W. 6, 17, 34, 177
  William W. 223

Wolffe, Mary Ann 29
Womack, Allen M. 148
  Ceasor 2
  Pauline J. 148
Wood, Amey 158
  Andrew 61
  Arritter 181
  B.F. 6
  Bird 26
  Bonnet 217
  Burgess 98
  Charlotte J. 92
  David 40
  Francis 153, 192
  Henry B. 224
  James 223
  Jane 22
  Lucinda 61
  Martha 61
  Martha F. 104
  Mary 158, 224
  Michael 158
  Polly 118
  Rebecca 36
  S. 33
  Sabra 57
  Stephen 223
  Stephen, Jr. 154
  Stephen, Jun. 53
  Susan Green 132
  Thomas 47, 223
Woodde, William 224
Woodfork, Hennadel 122
Woodhouse, Anthony 110, 170
Woodroof, Betsy 151
  John J. 194
Woodruff, Charlotte 26
  David 224
  J.W. 74
  Jennett 7
  John J. 170
  Lucinda 183
  Micajah 7
  Phebe E. 51
  Polly 132, 225
  Prudence 151
  Rebecca 7
  Sarah 9
  William 224
Woods, Andrew 61
  Will 104
Woodson, Ailsey 75
Woolff, Charity 133
Woolford, Roxanna 63
Wooten, Amey 42
  B. 87
  Edmund 111
  Elizabeth 31, 53
  George 140
  John 171
  Leah 224
  Mary 148
  Mosses 199
  Rosanna 224
  Sally 171
Wooton, Edmund 49
  Isaac 58
  Malinda 12
  Rebekah 63
Woottan, R. 220
  Rebekah 220
Word, Caroline 64
  Mantur D. 204
  Martha 101
  Martin D. 20, 117
  Tho. A. 7, 44

Word, (cont.)
  Thomas A. 64, 65, 225
  Thomas J. 37
  Thos. A. 11, 101, 224
  Thos. J. 72
Worden, Lucy Jane 80
  Mary P. 25
Wordline, Betsy 149
Worth, Eliza 49
  Jno. L. 178
  Job 83
  Lettuce 39
  Zeno 161
Woten, Martha 48
Wright, Amelia 137
  Dan. 97
  Deborah 76
  Elizabeth 67
  Isaac D. 138
  J. 3, 5, 7
  James 196
  John 1, 2, 3, 7, 9, 10, 14, 20, 27, 137, 147
  John, Jr. 137
  Lorrenzor 169
  Lydia 155
  M.Z. 145
  Marry 67
  Peggy 135
  Phebe 177
  Polly 4, 8, 13, 46, 51
  R.E. 195
  R.M. 26
  R.W. 43
  Rebecca 47
  Richard 105, 190
  Serren 24
  Tho. B. 191
  Thomas 30, 83, 92, 100, 135
  Thomas B. 27, 123, 142
  Thos. B. 169, 175
  Welborn 225
  William 22, 73
  Wm. 222
Wuesenberry, W.J. 204
Yale, Vollet 130
Yarborro, Catherine 103
Yarbrough, Mary 33
Yeats, Elizabeth 129
Yerbs, Nancy (?) 87
Yerrell, Solomon S. 93
York, Adam 21
  Ann A. 96
  Betsey 27
  Daniel 226
  Deborah 97
  E.H. 167
  Eliza (Miss) 198
  Ham 148
  James 71, 170, 225, 226
  Jane 170
  Joel 226
  John 174
  John W. 226
  Jonathan 26, 102, 171
  Keziah 193
  Laura F. 139
  Lucinda 21
  M.A. 8, 26, 100
  Mark 226
  Mark, Junr. 109

York, (cont.)
  Mary 14, 21, 23, 148
  Mary A. 156, 167
  N. 175
  Nancy 173
  Nimrod 170, 171
  Rebecka 70
  Richard 226
  Ruth (Miss) 20
  Sally 58
  Sarah 171
  Susan 72
  Susan T. 148
  Thomas 104
  Thos. 47, 225
Young, Catharine. 118
  Eda 36
  Elizabeth 47
  Henry 81
  Isham 133, 187
  Jane 86
  Laura 36
  Mary 46
  Nancy 129
  Patsey 119
  Polly 113
  Solomon 36
  Solomon W. 122
Yourk, Jean 149
  Nancey 220
Youse, Fanny 100
Zachary, Alford 11, 51
  David 73, 204
  Elizabeth 73
  Jnon. 218
  John 1
  Polly 204
  Wm. 110
Zackery, Mildred O. 92
Zeglar, George 98

ADDENDA

Eads, Elizabeth 87
Earhart, Margaret P. 100

www.ingramcontent.com/pod-product-compliance
Lightning Source LLC
Chambersburg PA
CBHW071245230426
43668CB00011B/1591